Wendell Phillips

Wendell Phillips

Brahmin Radical

By Irving H. Bartlett

GREENWOOD PRESS, PUBLISHERS
WESTPORT, CONNECTICUT

Library of Congress Cataloging in Publication Data

Bartlett, Irving H
   Wendell Phillips, Brahmin radical.

   Reprint of the ed. published by Beacon Press, Boston.
   Bibliography: p.
   1. Phillips, Wendell, 1811–1884.
[E449.P56B37 1973]   973.7'114'0924 [B]
ISBN 0-8371-7071-0   73-11849

Originally published in 1961 by Beacon Press, Boston

Published by arrangement with Beacon Press

Reprinted in 1973 by Greenwood Press,
a division of Williamhouse-Regency Inc.

Library of Congress Catalogue Card Number 73-11849

ISBN 0-8371-7071-0

Printed in the United States of America

This book is dedicated to Adam *and* Idabelle Kostulski

Acknowledgments

It is impossible for anyone who has written a book on the basis of several years' research into historical sources to ever "acknowledge" his debt to all those who have helped him. The chance remark of a lecturer, the bibliographical hints in the back of another book, the insight of other writers one has read but never met, the casual but illuminating remark in private conversation—such influences are easily overlooked. In this sense every book is partly derivative, and the author does an injustice to some whenever he tries to specify his debt to others. Nevertheless, I would express my gratitude to librarians as a profession and to the librarians in the Rare Book Room of the Boston Public Library, the Houghton Library and the Massachusetts Historical Society in particular.

This volume grows out of an interest in the American past which was stimulated by Professors Benjamin Spencer and Henry Clyde Hubbart at Ohio Wesleyan University and nurtured under the direction of Professor Edmund Morgan in graduate school at Brown. In writing this biography I have profited greatly from the generosity of Mr. John Lawlor, who gave me free use of the Phillips manuscripts collected earlier by Oswald Garrison Villard. Mr. William C. Phillips was kind enough to let me examine his Phillips papers, and Professor Walter Merrill, working in a similar field of research, willingly shared his information about Wendell Phillips with me. Professor Donald Fleming read the early chapters of the book with a sharp and critical eye.

I am grateful for financial help from the Humanities Department in procuring microfilm, for the moral encouragement of my colleague Carvel Collins, and for the efforts of Alfred Chandler, Roy Lamson and Andrew Turnbull, each of whom read parts of the manuscript. Thanks also are due Mrs. Ruth Dubois and Mrs.

Bettie Hurst for their invaluable help in preparing the manuscript. If some chapters of this work are better written than others, I am sure that it is because I benefited by the discriminating criticism of my wife, Virginia.

Contents

Prologue   *1*
1 The Beacon Street Background 1804–1827   *3*
2 A Brahmin at Harvard 1827–1832   *17*
3 Law Career and Marriage 1833–1836   *26*
4 Phillips Makes a Speech in Faneuil Hall 1836–1839   *41*
5 Europe 1839–1841   *59*
6 The Church, the Negro and the Irishman 1841–1850   *75*
7 Phillips and the Cranks 1841–1850   *99*
8 No Union with Slaveholders 1841–1850   *114*
9 The Fugitive Slave Law and Thomas Sims 1850–1851   *138*
10 Kossuth, Horace Mann and Anthony Burns 1851–1854   *158*
11 The Eloquence of Abuse 1854–1856   *188*
12 "A Lord High Admiral of the Almighty": Phillips and
   John Brown 1856–1859   *208*
13 Under the Flag 1860–1861   *219*
14 Phillips and Lincoln: Early War Years 1860–1863   *240*
15 Phillips and Lincoln: Later War Years 1863–1865   *256*
16 The Split with Garrison 1865–1867   *276*
17 Phillips and the Radicals 1865–1870   *293*
18 The Moral Legacy of the War 1870–1880   *316*
19 Labor Reform 1870–1880   *336*
20 The Universal Reformer 1870–1880   *367*
21 Conclusion 1880–1884   *386*

Notes   *402*
Index   *433*

Whether in chains or in laurels, liberty knows nothing but victories.

—WENDELL PHILLIPS

Prologue

Two months after Wendell Phillips was born in 1811, Thomas Jefferson wrote to John Adams that only seven signers of the Declaration of Independence were still alive. Two days after Phillips died in 1884, New York State Assemblyman Theodore Roosevelt notified his wife that he was launching a campaign to weaken Tammany Hall. Born in the afterglow of the Revolution, Phillips lived long enough to influence the generation that would lead America into the twentieth century. Although he never wore a uniform or held public office, he did as much as any other one man to keep the ideals of the Declaration of Independence alive during this period.

The story of Wendell Phillips is significant for many reasons. There is, first of all, the drama of a man born to wealth and family distinction, who married a neurotic invalid, broke with his class and family to take up subversive causes and lived his entire life in two worlds—the Brahmin world he could never completely forsake and a bizarre world of crackpots, fanatics, cranks and saints, who wanted to remake America according to their separate visions.

There is Phillips the most eloquent man of his time, the golden-voiced orator who made the abuse of popular heroes his stock in trade and got away with it. He could publicly label Lincoln a "slave-hound," Edward Everett a "whining spaniel" and Senator Robert C. Winthrop a "bastard," with the matter-of-fact finality of a man reading from the Scriptures or calling out the time. Infuriated crowds bombarded him with rotten eggs and tried to lynch him, but Phillips never met an audience he couldn't tame. His secret, wrote the hostile Boston *Courier,* was that, although he thought "like a Billingsgate fishwoman, or a low pothouse bully," he spoke like Cicero.

There is Phillips the intellectual leader of the radical abolitionists. In the face of overwhelming disapproval from almost everyone, including most of the other abolitionists, he made a rational case for the propositions that the Constitution was an agreement with hell, that the North should secede from the Union, that righteous men could not vote or hold office in a land which tolerated slavery.

There is Phillips the unrelenting reformer. When most of his friends were content to tie their kite to the Republican party, he insisted that the aftermath of the war be accepted purely as a moral inheritance. He had been for the immediate abolition of slavery; now he was for the immediate enfranchisement of the freedmen. And in the frenzied decade of the seventies, the age of skillful confidence men like Jay Gould and Jim Fisk, when plunder seemed more important than justice, Phillips became the great anachronism of his day by continuing to fight for the rights of Negroes, Irishmen, Indians, women in bloomers, mill workers and condemned murderers.

There is Phillips the practicing radical, whose most explosive pronouncements were always based on a carefully articulated theory of American institution. When he praised the Russian terrorists, denounced every politician as immoral, and contended that the best way to keep the railroad tycoons in line would be to pick out any twenty and send them to prison for life, men called him a fanatic. But he spoke without passion, convinced that the kind of radical criticism he supplied was essential to the success of American democracy.

This is the story of his life.

I

The Beacon Street Background
1804–1827

It was only a short walk to Faneuil Hall where the body of Wendell Phillips was laid out, but most of the mansion dwellers on Beacon Hill preferred to stay home. Although they would not go to the funeral, they let it be known that they approved of it. Phillips would not have minded the snub, especially since the others did come – longshoremen straight from the docks, butchers still in their aprons, Irish teamsters and Negro porters, factory hands and Yankee farmers. All afternoon they filed into Faneuil Hall to get a last glimpse of the man who fifty years before had turned his back on fashionable society to throw in his lot with them.

Wendell Phillips was born on Beacon Street. The house in which he was born had been built by his father's order six years before, when the fashionable place to live was in one of the mansions on Summer Street, only a few steps from the counting houses, the shops and Boston Harbor. At this time Beacon Street showed little of its future glory. There were a number of shops lining the street as it ran from Tremont to Park Street, but the long stretch which flanked Boston Common from the State House at the top of Beacon Hill down to the waters of Back Bay looked more like a rutted country lane than the site for some of America's most stately residences. The Phillips place, which went up on the corner of Walnut Street, was the first brick house to be built on Beacon

Street, and in this house Wendell Phillips was born on November 29, 1811.

It was a good place for a boy to live, blending as it did the better parts of both town and country. Boston was growing rapidly. The population had increased from twenty-four thousand to thirty-four thousand in ten years, and Wendell needed only to cut across the Common to find himself in the middle of all the bustling excitements of the city. New buildings were going up everywhere, but the most spectacular exhibit, the symbol which marked Boston's transition from town to city, was Charles Bullfinch's latest triumph, the Exchange Coffee House on Congress Street. Wendell's father must have taken him to see this mountain of a building. Seven stories of marble, stone and brick, surmounted by a dome which towered dizzily eighty feet above the open lobby within, it was said to be the tallest building of its kind in the country.[1]

Nevertheless, the enduring impression on Wendell as a boy came not from the new Boston but from the old. On summer nights he lay in bed and was lulled to sleep by the singing of the frogs on the Common. The rustic atmosphere of the eighteenth century still lingered in parts of Boston, especially near Beacon Street, and the boy once saw his neighbor Dr. Joy harvest load after load of hay on his land in the very shadow of the State House.[2]

Almost as soon as he outgrew the nursery, Wendell began to play on the Common. It was but a step across the street and through the rail fence surrounding it before he and his friends could share the grassy playground with the Boston cows. The Common was largely treeless then except for a line of poplars along the Beacon Street side and near the pond a few willows which supplied the boys with whistles every spring when the sap began to run. On a typical summer day the boys might begin their adventure with a meticulous examination of the frog pond and then bound off like Indians to stalk the cows with homemade bow and arrow. In the winter they skated on the pond and ran coasting races on the hill near the State House. Coming from a prosperous family, Wendell probably enjoyed the prestige of owning a "Nimble Dick," one of the wooden-runnered sleds made by a local Negro crafts-man, with rings along the sides that rattled as he hurtled down the slope.

Wendell might use a sled the Negro had made, but he was not expected to enjoy the coasting with the Negro's son. There were about fifteen hundred Negroes in Boston when he was born, and most of them lived on Nigger Hill, "a place of vague horror" on the reverse side of Beacon Hill down near the Charles River. Whenever a group of Negro boys made an appearance on the Common, the white boys would make common cause to drive them away. There were two ways to get rid of arrogant young Negroes so far as Wendell and the other white boys were concerned. You stoned them, or, if that failed and you were reduced to hand-to-hand combat, you simply kicked the Negro in the shin and waited for his nose to bleed.

In such inglorious manner the revolutionary tradition of Boston Common as a battleground was sustained. Not that these youthful racial conflicts were particularly fre-quent or conducted on a grand scale; they were not. What they did demonstrate was the halting progress which the ideal of equality had made in Boston by the early nine-teenth century. A more democratic rivalry in which Wendell participated was that between the "West Enders" and "South Enders" to see which group would dominate the Common. As a West Ender, Wendell participated in the kind of high strategy which on several occasions was able to lure the South Enders up the hill near the State House, where they were ambushed by a group of fierce young Yankees concealed in John Hancock's barn.[3]

The waters of Back Bay in those days lapped at the foot of the Common not more than two hundred yards from Phillips' house. Here he learned to swim and to prowl among the pilings along the shore, scooping up glittering small fish and eels with his straw hat. He explored the mysterious buildings along the shore too, places far more exciting than the stodgy Exchange Coffee House.[4] The rope walks extending out over the water fascinated him with their long, shadowy interiors, and when this interest flagged there was always "The Laboratory," a large three-story building surrounded by a high brick wall with heavy gates. This was the nickname for the state arsenal just beyond the lower end of the Common in Park Square—a challenging place for a boy whose imagination had been spiced by parental warnings that it was filled with enough gunpowder to blow him sky high if he ever ventured close to it.[5]

Living practically on the Common meant that Wendell rarely missed any of the celebrations which took place there. Whenever the circus came to town, the camel and the lion would be caged almost next door in the Hancock barn, "and the roar of the lion would strike a terror to the children up and down the street." [6] The happiest holiday of the year and the most exciting was Election Day, when the Common was transformed into a carnival almost in Wendell's own front yard. The various military companies would be out in full regalia, from the "Sea Fencibles," a club of grizzled retired sea captains, to the elite Boston Hussars, led by Josiah Quincy and handsomely mounted in scarlet and green. How it must have appealed to a boy —the crowds surging around booths offering gingerbread and egg pop, the clamorous bells of the ginger-beer carts, the fiddlers playing "Money Musk" while sailors danced the double shuffle, gentlemen with their ladies dancing strenuous jigs and everyone happily flushed from the free-flowing rum. This was Boston at her most relaxed, democratic best.[7]

All of this was the normal experience of a boy growing up in Boston in the first quarter of the century. Wendell Phillips, however, was no ordinary boy. Indeed, it would be difficult to find a boy more wellborn, in the Boston sense, than he. The Reverend George Phillips had been a fellow passenger in the *Arbella* with Winthrops and

Saltonstalls, and the Phillips family had had a large share
in forming the institutions of New England since 1630.
Wendell's father, John Phillips, was squarely in the family
tradition. His public career was exemplary in every
respect. The son of a successful Boston merchant, he
graduated from Harvard as the valedictorian of his class
in 1784, and quickly established himself in a successful
law practice. In 1794 he gave the Fourth of July oration
in Boston. In 1803 he was elected to the General Court,
and in 1804 he entered the state senate, where he held
office for eighteen successive years, ten of them as presiding
officer. Judge of the Court of Common Peers, member of
the Corporation of Harvard College, a good Federalist who
loved stability and loathed Thomas Jefferson, John
Phillips was universally admired as one of the "safest,"
most capable men in the state. People remembered years
afterward his conservative influence at the state constitutional convention in 1820, when he cautioned his fellow
delegates against rash action by reminding them of the
tombstone epitaph: "I was healthy; I wanted to be better;
I took medicine; and here I am." [8] In 1822, when Boston
was electing her first city government and the two leading
candidates, Harrison Gray Otis and Josiah Quincy, were
deadlocked, it was natural that John Phillips should have
been selected by all parties as the ideal compromise. In
this way, Wendell Phillips' father, "a man of rather pliable
disposition, but of strict integrity and general good
judgment," became the first mayor of Boston.[9]

Bostonians liked to describe their community as the
"Cradle of Democracy," but most of them were careful to
respect the rights of the local aristocracy. True, there was
no special privilege; rich boy and poor boy rubbed elbows
in the public school, "West Ender" and "South Ender"
played together and sometimes bloodied each other's nose
on Boston Common. Still, there existed in the town "a
decided first circle," to which the only sure access was
gained by birth. Wendell Phillips was a child of this
aristocracy. By the time of his birth in 1811, his father's

friends no longer wondered why he had moved to the country, for Beacon Street was now coming into its own. The handsome Phillips mansion, three floors of solid brick, elegantly simple in the Georgian manner, with its magnificent view of the Common and the bay, and the deep, lush gardens behind, now stood proudly among the finest residences in town. A few steps closer to the bay on Beacon Street was the Harrison Gray Otis mansion. Expansive enough to house four families and still devote an entire floor to entertaining, it was one of the nation's showplaces. Otis, a political associate and friend of John Phillips, was famous for his hospitality. John Quincy Adams once called him the most skillful host he had ever met. He could put up the President of the United States or stage a party for two hundred or more friends with equal ease, and he was careful always to keep a ten-gallon punch bowl filled outside his drawing room for the benefit of thirsty visitors.[10]

Between the Phillips' house and the famous Hancock house lived young Tom Appleton, whose father was accumulating a vast fortune in textile manufactures. While up the hill on Walnut Street not far from the Jonathan Mason place, renowned for its imported crystal chandeliers and Italian marble mantles, lived Lothrop Motley. As young boys, Motley and Appleton were Wendell's best friends. The three young aristocrats used to play together on the Common, or sometimes up in Motley's attic where they would masquerade as bandits in "cloaks, doublets and plumed hats."[11] It was an association of equals which they would be expected to continue when they grew older, at private balls and cotillion parties and elaborate suppers. John Phillips held his share of these affairs, and, although Wendell ultimately became a noted advocate for the temperance movement, he did not inherit the prejudice from his father, who was in the habit of ordering his Madeira "a double hogshead" (126 gallons) at a time.[12]

The details of Wendell's early life at home are

meager. His mother, Sarah Walley Phillips, daughter of a distinguished Boston merchant, was a vigorous-minded, strong-bodied woman who had brought seven children safely into the world before Wendell. Of his relationship with his brothers and sisters, either now or in later life, we know little except that Wendell was the favorite son. John Phillips was a wealthy man who kept an elegant house and cared something for society, but, like most parents reared in the Puritan tradition, he and Sarah were anxious lest their children be seduced by the prospect of inherited wealth. One of the rules of the household early dinned into Wendell's ear was "Never ask another to do for you what you can do for yourself; and never ask another to do for you what you would not do for yourself if you could." Accordingly, young Wendell learned how to use carpenters' tools and was expected to help with the handyman work around the house.[13]

Mastering a useful trade, even though his parents could have afforded to buy the services of a dozen carpenters, was a part of the boy's moral education. Idleness, he learned, was a sin; to pursue one's calling with diligence and integrity was a virtue. Even though several generations of merchants separated Wendell from the Reverend George Phillips, first pastor to the congregation at Watertown, the spirit of that Puritan stalwart still permeated his family. When Wendell's grandmother, Margaret Wendell Phillips, a hardy woman who had outlived her husband by half a century, lay on her deathbed, she summoned Wendell's father, who was then mayor. Raising herself and "addressing him in a manner of the most emphatic solemnity, she charged him to remember the many official oaths he had taken." [14] John and Sarah were simply continuing the tradition when they undertook to raise their own children "in the nurture and admonition of the Lord." Wendell received most of his religious instruction from his mother. As soon as he was old enough to read, she gave him a Bible. She taught him his prayers and the importance of making his life obedient to the purposes of God, and every Sunday she took him to the family pew in the Old South Meeting House. These years of Wendell's boyhood were momentous years in Boston's religious history. Although the eloquence of William Ellery Channing was turning many of Boston's prosperous families away from the Calvinist doctrines of original sin and predestination, the Phillips household stood firm in the old faith. This meant that, until each of their children had been converted, neither John nor Sarah Phillips could rest peacefully. Their anxiety and the atmosphere of religious intensity in which Wendell was reared is suggested by the following letter from John Phillips to one of Wendell's older brothers at Harvard:

> Now my dear son, you have not received the benefit which, I trust, the actual view of your expiring grandparent would have produced, yet you may recollect all the admonitions and advice she has given you. . . . Pray therefore daily to God. . . . Read your Bible, also, every day, and frequently repeat those hymns which you have committed to memory. . . . You may be called in a short time—if prepared, it cannot be too soon. In the meantime Providence has directed us, while on earth, to be active and diligent in the discharge of duty . . . the most important hours are now passing both as it respects the present and the future life. Be studious, be virtuous and God will bless you.[15]

Unlike many sensitive young men and women growing up in New England at this time, Wendell was not revolted by the harsh terms of Calvinism. There is a story, perhaps apocryphal, that as a tiny boy he used to arrange the parlor chairs in the form of pews and preach to them.[16] If it is true, the story suggests a youthful inclination for oratory. Whether true or not (the same story is told of many famous New Englanders at this time), it indicates the importance that religion was supposed to play in the child's life. He was expected to be concerned above all with the state of his soul, because such concern ordinarily preceded the act of conversion. In Wendell's case the

long-awaited day came sometime in his fourteenth year.
He heard that an impressive new preacher was visiting
Boston, and he went out to an old church at the north
end of town to listen. As he sat in the congregation,
transfixed under the spell of Lyman Beecher's great voice,
the sense of the words "you belong to God" washed over
him for the first time with a sure, awful conviction. After
the sermon he went home, locked the door to his room,
fell on the floor and made his commitment.[17]

Although John Phillips had attended Phillips
Academy, Andover (founded by another branch of the
Phillips family), he chose to send his boys to the Boston
Public Latin School. After absorbing all the learning his
parents could give him at home, Wendell was enrolled in
this school, which he attended for five years, beginning in
1822.

Everyone in Boston was proud of the Latin School.
It enjoyed the longest continuous history of any school
in America, and the impressive new three-story granite
building which now housed it stood on School Street opposite King's Chapel, behind which the first Latin School
had been erected in 1635.

Motley had gone to Northampton to school, but Tom
Appleton and Phillips attended the Latin School together.
Among the new students who entered with him, Wendell
noticed a tall, awkward-looking boy who always seemed
to hold himself apart from the games and enjoyments of
his classmates. The boy was Charles Sumner. Phillips
and Sumner would meet again at Harvard, but here they
knew each other only slightly, for Sumner, who came
from a family of modest means, was not a member of the
exclusive social circle so familiar to Phillips.

There was a lot to be learned at the school. Latin
school it was, and the first-year boys were expected to
learn their Latin grammar by heart. The inattentive
scholar who sought to immortalize himself with his
jackknife on the notched and battered desk was quickly
jolted back to the business at hand. Master Gould was

noted not only for his scholarship but for the "singular dignity and grace" with which he wielded the rod.[18]

Sometime during his first year at the Latin School, Wendell turned in what was probably his first written exercise. Written in the form of a letter to Master Gould, it is the earliest writing we have from Phillips' hand.

DEAR SIR

You requested me in your last letter to give you some account of the short excursions which, you say, I frequently make. In compliance with your request, therefore, I will give you an account of a little journey I made to Andover and Tewksbury a few days ago.

I started from Boston on Wednesday last at about ten oclock accompanied by T—— and A——. It was one of those delightful days that render the prospects of travellers doubly beautiful. We passed through Charlestown and beheld 'Bunker's awful mount' with admiration. We next passed through Medford and very near the residence of the venerable Gov. Brooks. But as you must be very well acquainted with these towns lying so near Boston, I shall not give any account of them. After leaving Medford we arrived at Stoneham where you may recollect there occured a horrid murder some time since. In this town there is a very pretty pond called the Spy Pond. We dined at Reading and proceeded on our journey at about three oclock. The road which we travelled on passed by the romantic seat of Mr. Forester which is beautifully situated on an eminence and commanding a view of the Reading Pond. This pond is surrounded by a row of willows, and the whole scene was very picturesque and beautiful. I believe we missed the direct road owing to the different information the laborers gave us. For suspecting we were not right, we inquired of the persons we met in the way or saw in the fields. Let that be as it may, we did not enter Andover in the quarter we meant to. It was the day of the exhibition of the Andover Academy but as it was late and the exhibition almost over we did not visit it.

After having supped and rested ourselves we proceeded to Tewksbury just at dusk. On this road there lies a beautiful wood through which we passed. The silence of this little wilderness seemed to be disturbed only by our own untimely interruption. We reached Tewksbury at about half past seven oclock and passed the night there.

Of my return I will inform you in an other letter, meanwhile

I remain your affectionate friend

WENDELL PHILLIPS[19]

To —— —— Esq.

Later in the year Wendell participated in his first formal debate on the question "Whether Wealth in Families Is a Blessing." His speech, well written certainly for an eleven-year-old boy and a masterpiece of the kind of circumspection that made his father mayor, concluded that "Moderate circumstances seem to be the best for the gaining of wisdom since poverty turns our thoughts too much upon supplying our wants and wealth upon enjoying our superfluities." [20]

In all of his written work at the Latin School, a full record of which has been preserved, Wendell showed the moral earnestness, the grave outlook on life that was typical of a Calvinist upbringing. In an essay on a career in public life he warned: "There will be dangerous rivals to excell, implacable enemies to overpower and a fickle mob to conciliate. . . . The youth, who would possess himself of accurate or uncommon attainments, and maintain the first rank among his school fellows or become a second Cicero among his associates, must remember that attention is the key to knowledge and that persevering industry and steady application lead to eminence." [21] On another occasion, perhaps near the time of his religious experience, he wrote: "It is not meant that man should suffer merely for the sake of suffering: but that in a future period of his life, he might recall these lessons to his mind and learn from them how to conduct himself in the perilous path of duty. . . . Let us then remember that man has been blessed by the creator with the most noble grand and invaluable faculties. Let us all be careful that we neither benumb them by idleness and disuse or degrade them by applying them to improper or unworthy objects." [22]

Despite this highly moralistic, almost melancholy, attitude, Wendell continued to enjoy life as he moved from his eleventh to his sixteenth year. He was already fascinated by declamation and was eagerly memorizing the classic orations. Moreover, he had developed a zest for athletics and was recognized by his classmates for his excellence in boxing, fencing, riding and shooting.[23] Still, he was on occasion a condescending, haughty boy from Beacon Hill. The condescension showed through when he wrote a theme on Benjamin Franklin (whose father had been a Boston candle maker). "His knowledge and virtues were of an order not often found in the class with whom he associated in the first part of his life and his faults, those few which even Franklin had, were those peculiar to and always attendant upon the circumstances through which he had passed." The haughtiness was revealed when he graduated in August 1827. On the back of the Salutatory Address, which he delivered in Latin, Wendell wrote: "I can hardly call this oration my own it having been twice corrected by the Masters: i.e. 2 masters corrected it; and it has undergone many changes in their hands so that not more than *half* of it remains as I originally wrote." [24]

The purpose of the Latin School was to provide the student with a solid grounding in the classics and prepare him for Harvard University, but there was another kind of education which every Boston boy at this time received both in and out of the classroom—an education in the traditions of a people which had newly won its freedom. Phillips' father had been born in 1770 and could remember the Revolutionary War himself. Even when stories failed, the symbols of recent glory were everywhere in Boston. From his doorstep the boy could see Bunker Hill. A hundred yards up the street was the house in which the proud John Hancock had lived, the house which had

sheltered the wounded from Bunker Hill, had been
pillaged by British soldiers, had provided the headquarters
for General Clinton and had still survived to tender
hospitality to Lafayette and Washington after independence was won. In ten minutes he could cross the spot of
the Boston Massacre, pass by the Old South Meeting
House and go on to Faneuil Hall. No tablets were needed
then, no inscriptions, no guide books, for, as Phillips
himself later said, the Boston air still trembled and
burned "with Otis and Sam Adams."

On August 24, 1824, the citizens of Boston and the
thousands who had poured into the city from the country
were feverishly crowding into the streets. The air
resounded with ringing bells, trumpeting and the roar of
cannon; city officials and officers of the militia galloped
furiously on last-minute missions, and Margaret Quincy,
the mayor's daughter, fainted twice in the same morning
—Lafayette was coming to Boston.[25]

By the time the procession reached Tremont Street,
the great crowds had begun to chant his name; as he passed
by, "Lafayette! Lafayette! LAFAYETTE!" rolled on like
an ocean wave. Old men who had fought in the Revolution stood with heads bared and wept unashamedly.[26]
Wendell, along with the other Latin School students, stood
with a portrait of Lafayette pinned to his jacket and waited
for hours to catch a glimpse of "the grand old man." He
never forgot that day. When he returned to address the
Latin scholars forty years later he recounted the incident
with all its vividness, boasting that "these eyes have beheld
the hero of three revolutions; this hand has touched the
right hand that held up Hancock and Washington." [27]

Two years later, while he was poring over his lessons
at the schoolhouse, the sound of tolling bells came through
the open windows, announcing the solemn news that
Thomas Jefferson and John Adams had died on the same
day.[28]

If Wendell Phillips was ever tempted to think of all
this as history and somehow not a part of his own life,

there was always a special reminder. On May 28, 1823, his father presided as usual over the proceedings in the Massachusetts senate. After attending church to hear the election sermon, John Phillips returned home, where during the night he was stricken with a heart attack. The next morning he died. The senators passed a resolution expressing their sense of loss "for the *urbanity, integrity and wisdom* of their deceased colleague," and every senator wore crepe on his left arm for the duration of the session. The former mayor was buried in the Granary burial ground across from Kings Chapel. Every day on his way to school Wendell passed the spot where his father lay— between the graves of James Otis and Samuel Adams.

2

A Brahmin at Harvard
1827–1832

On the bleak, drizzly morning of August 28, 1827, Wendell Phillips assembled with a group of about eighty shivering young men on the steps of University Hall to offer himself for admission to Harvard. The candidates represented a cross-section of the country. Some of them had already taught school to raise money for tuition and were self-consciously dressed in long, black coats like professors of Greek. Others were clad in homespun or the bobtailed coats of the militia.[1] Wendell, who had probably been driven to Cambridge that morning in the Phillips carriage, undoubtedly wore, in addition to his expensively cut suit, the quiet air of assurance typical of the wellborn Bostonian brought up to think of Harvard as a kind of family institution.

The entrance examination (which lasted all day and was mostly oral) in Greek and Latin grammar, Virgil, Cicero, the *Iliad*, geography and mathematics, eliminated more than a fourth of the group but was no trouble for a graduate of the Boston Latin School. Academic preparation, however, was only part of the business of getting ready for college. Wendell had to purchase the Harvard uniform—coat and pantaloons of all black or "with a mixture of not more than one twentieth nor less than one twenty-fifth part white."[2] He was expected to furnish his first-floor dormitory room (freshmen studied at the bottom), a requirement satisfied with about ten dollars worth of battered pine furniture. Finally, he had to arrange, for $1.75 a week, to board in the Commons on the first floor of University Hall, where he would take his meals with two hundred or more chronically dissatisfied students, convinced that the food was only fit for the pigs penned behind the building.

Unfortunately, Phillips never wrote down the recollections of his student days at Harvard, and we are forced to recreate the picture from the reminiscences of his classmates. Being the son of Boston's first mayor, it is possible that he was treated more gingerly by the sophomores than were other freshmen. Nevertheless, the diaries of several of his classmates testify that September and October were harrowing months for the class of 1831. In addition to regular harassments like ducking and "scotched" beds, the freshmen endured special torments at night. "We were obliged to sleep very close," wrote Frederick Holland on September 2, "for the fear of punkins, squashes, brick bats and squibs [improvised bombs], obliged us to shut every entrance— Toward evening we heard a great noise in the entry and out of doors. We went out and saw a great many sophs. They sent and procured some tobacco and pipes, and whilst we were yet out, marched in our room to the number of 18 or 20 and commenced smoking with segars, white pipes and (most terrible of all) with a large black Turkish pipe: from the last mentioned article, the performer blew out wonderful columns of smoke intermixed with sparks; the sight was all sufficient, but the smell was unutterable." [3]

Despite such torments, the new class soon grew accustomed to the routine and folkways of the college. The day for Phillips began at six o'clock with prayers in a chapel noted for its arctic temperatures. He followed this with recitations, a breakfast of coffee and rolls, more recitations, dinner, more recitations, evening prayers and supper. The study bell ordering complete silence rang at eight o'clock. This was the schedule five days a week. Sunday was one long religious service with everyone required in residence.

Saturday was the happy exception and invariably saw a general exodus of students from Cambridge to Boston, where the chief diversion was to parade on Cornhill Street and "be admired by all the blooming ladies," or perhaps to have supper at the Exchange Coffee House, thereby avoiding the dismal menu of salt fish offered back at Commons.

Except that he was in closer touch with his mother than were students from out of town, Wendell's experience at Harvard must have been typical in most respects. In the winter he spent the frigid evenings huddled over his books, warmed by a small wood fire or by a heated cannon ball with a skillet serving as reflector. In the summer he arrayed himself like a proper Oxonian in the approved campus costume, "a full calico printed gown and reaching to the ankles." When a sophomore he rejoiced to have sewn on his jacket sleeve the "crow foot" that told the world he was an upperclassman. Like his friends he soon picked up the campus jargon and realized that the essential thing in recitations was to strike the proper balance between "squirt" and "tick" (a squirt was a correct recitation; to go to class "in tick" was to go unprepared).[4]

Since he was generally popular and ultimately became a leader among his classmates, Phillips could not have been intimate with any of the faculty. According to the student code, fraternizing between professors and students was strictly forbidden. "The students considered the faculty as their natural enemies. . . . If a student went to a teacher's room it was almost always by night. It was regarded as a high crime by his class for a student to enter a recitation room before the ringing of the bell, or to remain to ask a question of the instructor." [5] In keeping with the code, Phillips probably applauded when a boisterous soul jammed the lock of Professor Palfrey's recitation room so that he had to smash his way into class with an axe. He must have laughed when "Old Pop" (Professor Popkin in classics) was hanged in effigy, and shed no tears

for the meddlesome tutor who tried to interfere in a
student initiation and was thrown downstairs and hit with
a piece of firewood for his trouble.[6]

Everyone who knew him at this time testified that
Wendell was a handsome young man. About average
height, he had sandy hair, a high forehead and a refined,
aquiline profile which exploded suddenly into a stubborn
jaw. He was built like an athlete and was undoubtedly a
regular visitor to the new gymnasium which Dr. Follen,
recently returned from Germany, had fitted up with hori-
zontal bars and ladders after the Continental manner. A
good fencer at the Latin School, he probably improved
under the tutelage of the honorably scarred Monsieur
Vailly, the Harvard fencing master who had learned his
craft in the Napoleonic Wars. In any event, we know that
Phillips' physical prowess had become so famous that on
one occasion a group of students invaded his room to take
his measurements and compare them with those of Apollo.[7]

His circle of intimate friends was probably small and
exclusive. Tom Appleton was there, relaxed and jovial as
ever, already developing his famous talent for conversation,
also Lothrop Motley, too haughty and aloof to make new
friends and too absorbed in his own writing to pay attention to his studies. History would soon become the passion
of his life, but now it was poetry and fiction—novels which
opened, Phillips later recalled, "not with one solitary
horseman but with two, riding up to an inn." [8] Then
there was his cigar-smoking Cambridge kinsman, a young
man short in stature but long on wit and noted for his
verses in the Harvard *Collegian*—Oliver Wendell Holmes.

What these four young men had in common was a
privileged social background. Because Beacon Hill exclu-
siveness did not stop at the banks of the Charles, social
distinctions were important at Harvard. Thomas Hopkinson, a raw-boned, self-taught country boy who in 1826 left
his father's farm in the Maine backwoods to try his luck
at Harvard, tells the following story about his introduction
to student "society."

I took the stage at Boston and in it I found a man very neatly dressed, in the College Uniform, and expecting to find sympathy I made conversation with him and let him know I was going to enter college. He looked with great scorn on my country dress and green country manners, drew himself up with much dignity and said no more. This was Robt. C. Winthrop of Boston. . . .[9]

This was Hopkinson's first acquaintance with a Boston "Brahmin," and the incident clearly indicates the importance of social status at Harvard. If Wendell Phillips had been in the coach rather than Winthrop, the story would probably have been no different, for Phillips became the acknowledged leader of the student aristocracy. The reasons for this are obvious enough. His family was socially prominent and wealthy. A classmate later recalled that he was the only student regularly called for on Saturday by a private carriage. Moreover, he had all of the personal qualifications for leadership. He was handsome, athletic, probably the best in his class in the prestige arts of oratory and debate, meticulous in observing university regulations and, ever since that day in Lyman Beecher's congregation, markedly more serious-minded than the average student. He was taken quickly into the two most exclusive clubs, Porcellian and Hasty Pudding, and soon became an important figure in campus politics. Nevertheless, because he was known as "the pet of the aristocracy," the antiaristocratic clique among the students conspired to defeat him in the election for captain of the Washington Corps, the celebrated student military order. He apparently took the defeat gracefully but was too proud to accept the office of adjutant. The story has to be pieced together from fragments, but it is apparent that, while his friends admired his patrician manners, a substantial number of students thought that Wendell Phillips was a snob.[10]

The classroom was not a very exciting place at Harvard in the 1820s. Most of the recitations were handled in a methodical way, and Phillips usually knew in advance

when he would be called on. The professors by and large
confined themselves to maintaining discipline and noting
the satisfactory or unsatisfactory recitation performance of
the student. Very little attempt was made to elucidate the
text or to stimulate the student.[11] For this reason, the most
important part of Wendell's education came from his conversation with other students and from his own reading.
His classmates recalled that his chief excellence lay in
oratory and debate and that he displayed a passionate interest in history. The record of his withdrawals from the
college library bears this out. During his freshman year
he withdrew the works of Milton, Machiavelli, Locke,
Cicero and Pascal. Over the four years, however, his reading seems to have been most prolific in history (eight
volumes of Gibbon's *Rome* and eight of Hume's *England*)
and biography. He was particularly interested in the Puritan revolution of 1640 and the American Revolution.[12]

Phillips wrote about fifty essays at Harvard, and he
preserved approximately half of them. Many of them, like
his first college theme on "A Knight Errant of the Middle Ages, compared with Achilles, Theseus, or Hercules,
and with a modern soldier," are innocuous and not worth
mentioning. Others are more revealing. At the end of a
long, flowery discussion, for example, he wrote that Joshua
Reynolds "has produced a work no less interesting to the
general scholar than to the artist." Beneath this paragraph
he penciled some years later: "I never read the book W.P.
1832!!!" [13]

He must have been conscious of his special gift for
oratory, and he discussed the subject in two papers. On
extemporaneous speaking he wrote, "Few men find any
difficulty in expressing their thoughts who have a proper
confidence in themselves." [14] (Not even Phillips' harshest
critic would ever pretend that he lacked self-confidence.)
On another occasion he distinguished poetry from eloquence. "Poetry then is based on the common feelings of
our nature, the same in all circumstances, and easily ex-

cited in every individual— Eloquence is addressed to men, in whom their feelings are centered with burning interest upon one object." [15] (Whether the subject was free speech, chattel slavery or wage slavery, Phillips would never take his eyes off that *one object*.) One paper, written on European criticism of American culture, fairly rings with national pride, and anticipates Emerson's famous *American Scholar* address of several years later. "A community as generally well informed, perhaps better than they, we are equally competent to judge of literary or any other merit," Phillips wrote. "Had we but a proper confidence in our own judgment, and a proper respect for ourselves we should disregard the petty slanders of hireling authors and scribbling clerks, slanders, of which, as Irving has well said, every step of our progress is a volume of refutation." [16]

The political bent of Phillips' mind when he was at college, in keeping with his aristocratic position, was decidedly conservative. The influences of his home were obviously at work here. John Phillips had been a staunch Federalist, and Wendell had grown up in a society which knew few epithets stronger than the word "Jacobin." Boston society was supposed to be a proper breeding ground for gentlemen, not reformers, and that Wendell Phillips was well bred by these standards can be seen in his youthful orations at Harvard. Among the major events of the year in Cambridge were the college exhibitions, the purpose of which was to display the talents and learning of promising Harvard students to the public. On July 12, 1830, Wendell Phillips participated in an exhibition by debating the question: "Whether attachment to ancient usages be a greater evil than fondness for innovations."

In this speech the innovator, with his "untried theories and mad schemes," is clearly the villain, akin to "the mad enthusiasts who conducted the French Revolution," surrendered France to "the licentiousness of an ungovernable populace," polluted "the altars of their fathers"

and sealed every day with blood. The echoes of Edmund
Burke, the greatest conservative of them all, are clearly dis-
tinguishable in Phillips' peroration:

> Substituting for the worship of religion, the mockery of reason,
> urging their often repeated and as often refuted objections against
> institutions which have triumphed over every opposition, and come
> down to us with the concurring approbation of succeeding centuries,
> these advocates of reform attempt to put the 'wisdom of yesterday
> in competition with the wisdom of ages,' compare the facts of ex-
> perience with the suppositions of hypothesis, balance the suggestions
> of a single mind against the testimony of trial, the approbation of
> humanity, the sanctity of heaven.[17]

Good Beacon Street doctrine, this. The old Federalist
John Phillips would have been the first to applaud. And
it is not too much to presume that if Sarah Walley Phillips
sat in the audience that summer afternoon, listening to her
son's sensible eloquence, she felt confident of his and the
family's future.

In the spring of 1831 the seniors prepared for Class
Day. The records of their meetings indicate a desire for
unconventionality. The cost of renting academic robes was
prohibitive; they would march without robes. In four
years they had heard enough of Henry Ware's long-winded
sermons; they petitioned President Quincy to "forbid any
person from entering the pulpit upon Class Day." But in
the end, properly robed, they marched meekly to the
chapel where "Sykes" prayed over them once again. From
the chapel, with Marshall Wendell Phillips leading the
way, the class went into the president's house for wine, cake
and congratulations. The light heart ruled the day . . .
"and even the iron visage of Dr. Ware, by some fatality, did
absolutely smile." [18]

After these formalities the class adjourned to the
famous Liberty Tree

> where after showing a sovereign contempt for hatters and tailors by
> divesting ourselves of their sometimes useful hats and coats, we took

hold of hands, formed a ring around the tree . . . and, from some unaccountable impulse, fell to running and capering and dancing round and round and round, as if a streak of lightning had been following close at our heels, and trying with all its might to catch us. We then laid ourselves very quickly down upon the grass, and commenced bawling and singing, each on his own tune . . . at this time, the weather being very hot and sultry, Br. Simonds struck up the well known song:

> I wish I had a quart of punch
> Of ice and half a pound
> Into the punch I'd put the ice
> And stir it round and round.

The punch was procured, and, after several gallons were downed, the hymn to Harvard was sung, and Wendell and the others, classmates about to become men, drifted back to their rooms.[19]

A few weeks later, on August 31, commencement exercises were held. Wendell Phillips, graduating seventh in his class, spoke on Parliamentary reform and the British aristocracy. He had worked on the oration while vacationing at his mother's summer home in Nahant, a narrow neck of land thrusting out into the Atlantic near Lynn, Massachusetts, and the most fashionable watering place for Bostonians. In these sunny surroundings he wrote a good Tory speech defending the upper classes in England. "Her peers are the noble spirits of each successive generation," he maintained. "So much wealth the evidence of personal industry and skill—and the first aspiring of the man of talents is to gain for himself a family and a name." [20] These were the parting words of Wendell Phillips, a young man who, as one of his student friends later recalled, might well have been selected by his classmates "as *least likely* to give the enthusiasm and labor of [his life] to the defense of popular rights." [21]

3

Law Career and Marriage
1833–1836

Wendell Phillips' choice of law as a career was probably a result of circumstances. There were really only two choices open to a young man of his background: law and the ministry. When Wendell graduated from college in 1831 his three older brothers were already embarked on their careers. Thomas, the oldest, had been practicing law in Boston more than ten years and was already prominent in local politics. John Charles, closest to Wendell of all his brothers and sisters, was preparing for the ministry at Andover, and George William, just a year older than Wendell, was studying law at Litchfield, Connecticut. Wendell apparently never seriously considered a career in the ministry. In September 1831 he enrolled in the Harvard Law School, more as a matter of course than out of any deep sense that he had found his calling.

A few years earlier the law school had been in rather feeble condition. Under the energetic leadership of Supreme Court Justice Joseph Story, however, it was quickly coming back to health. The Judge was one of the real ornaments in Cambridge, and Wendell must have appreciated the opportunity to learn the law from a man who sat by John Marshall's side. Whenever Story would return from Washington his first stop would be Dane Hall, the small Greek temple which housed the law school. There the students would crowd about him waiting for the latest news about the Court.[1] Sometimes it would be about a weighty point of law, but Story was a sophisticated, good-

humored man with a weakness for fine wine and bad
poetry (to fight off boredom on the bench he sometimes
took his notes in verse), so that the anecdote would often
turn on lighter matters. Peering through his steel spectacles at one of the impressionable young men, the Judge
would say soberly that in Washington the Justices take
their meals together and discuss cases over dinner. "We
are great ascetics, and even deny ourselves wine, except in
wet weather." Then, after an impressive pause, "What I
say about wine sir, gives you our rule; but it does sometimes happen that the Chief Justice will say to me when
the cloth is removed; 'Brother Story, step to the window
and see if it does not look like rain.' And if I tell him that
the sun is shining brightly, Judge Marshall will sometimes
reply 'All the better, for our jursidiction extends over so
large a territory that the doctrine of chances makes it certain that it must be raining somewhere.' " [2]

After Story, the most interesting person at the law
school was Charles Sumner. He and Phillips had been at
the Latin School together and at Harvard, but it was only
now that they became close friends. There was nothing
ordinary about Sumner's appearance. He was a tall,
gangling young man, and the inflamed eyes in his gaunt
face testified to the almost constant attention he gave his
law books. Law was a passion with him, almost an obses-
sion, and, when he set out for a pleasant jaunt to Boston
with Phillips or another friend and quickly outdistanced
them with his great strides, they knew that his mind was
still roaming the stacks of the law library.[3]

Phillips was more casual about the law. He read his
cases with reasonable diligence and argued his points in
the mock trials, which Story had instituted, with more than
customary eloquence. All of this, however, like his studies
as an undergraduate, was taken in stride with little expenditure of real enthusiasm. Indeed, enthusiasm of any
kind does not appear to have been characteristic of him at
this time. One Sunday afternoon in June 1833 the belle
of Cambridge, Anna Quincy, descended to the parlor,

where the usual complement of college visitors was waiting. In her diary that evening she recorded her surprise at
finding Wendell Phillips in the group. "Mr. Phillips was
very agreeable," she wrote, "tho it is a mystery how he
came to favor us this evening as in general man delights
him not, nor woman either, but he was gentlemanly and
agreeable this evening." [4]

For Phillips the most memorable event in his whole
law school experience was Fanny Kemble. As an old man
he recalled what it was like to be a student when the
famous actress played in Boston. "We saved all our money
to buy tickets . . . some of my friends literally sold whatever they could lay hands on, books, clothing, or what not,
to raise funds. Then we walked in from Cambridge; we
could not afford to ride when tickets to see Fanny Kemble
were to be bought." After the play they would wait at the
rear entrance of the old Tremont Theatre, and when the
great woman appeared, "we would give three student
cheers for her, and walk out to Cambridge to bed." [5]

Phillips remembered that he went nineteen nights in
a row to see Fanny Kemble. Here, certainly, was the enthusiasm that Anna Quincy missed. Perhaps it is stretch-
ing the facts to read any particular significance into this
youthful infatuation with a queen of the stage. Fanny
Kemble was a very beautiful and exciting woman, and
Wendell Phillips was a very young and rather bored young
man, but he may have seen in her life a kind of success
which he would never be able to taste. Wherever Fanny
Kemble appeared on a stage, thousands of people came
thronging to see her, to hang breathlessly on her every
word and gesture—while he prepared for a career to be
spent in cramped courtrooms arguing over dusty briefs
before dour judges and indifferent juries. Those nineteen
successive performances must have broken the monotony
of law school and may have stimulated Phillips' doubts
about his chosen career; they may also have stirred within
him the dramatic instincts which would one day make him

as celebrated as Fanny Kemble on lecture platforms
throughout the country.

In any event, the fact that he could abandon himself
to such a seemingly unprofitable activity suggests that on
occasion, at least, he permitted a natural exuberance to
overwhelm his Puritan inhibitions. This suspicion is
strengthened by a reading of the following poem, which he
wrote sometime during his second year in law school:

Away Away over the deep deep Sea
To the islands of Devils they're waiting for me
I hear the loud shout of their mirth from afar
That rocks with its thunder the din of war

And a skeleton form with his boat on the strand
Is waiting to waft me away from the land
His boat is a coffin, the sail is a shroud
His fee but a farthing, yet fears not the crowd

For they shrink from the glance of what once was his eye
And the proud and the brave swing fearfully by
And the bright eye of beauty grows dim in its dread
As her glance is withdrawn from the boat of the dead

Then away, away, over the deep deep sea
To the islands of Devils, they're waiting for me
I catch the bright glance of their eyes from afar
Through the bones of my helmsman it gleams like a star

Our boat cleaves but slowly the motionless deep
From eternity waveless in unbroken sleep.
But the steersman is nervy the sail is widespread
And the ocean is teeming with sepulchred dead

Hurra Hurra our keel cuts the strand
Then bear away cheerily, quick let us land
How much separation of interest lends
To the parting and meeting of long beloved friends

They point to the ocean, I turn my glad eyes
But up to the heavens its billows arise

The island is sinking—above roars the deep
T'was the thunder of Cannon—I woke from my sleep

Whatever his destiny, Wendell must have known that the
touch of the poet was not in him. He apparently created
the lines as a drinking song, and at the bottom of the
manuscript he wrote, "Durante headache posce versiculos
feci" ("I have composed these little verses while enduring
a headache").[6]

After taking his law degree in September, 1834,
Phillips took a trip to Philadelphia. En route home he
spent some time in New York, where he met a young lady,
Mary Elwell, who was impressive enough to elicit another
poem, the first and last four lines of which are:

There was a Yankee lass I knew
She rivalled all the poets drew
But she, alas! would ne'er confess
Her northern birth and Yankee-ness

. . . .

I hate her—for the land I prize
Far, far beyond Point Judith lies
I hate her, may her only aim
Be soon to get some hard Dutch name.

The "hard Dutch name" probably refers to "Wendell,"
since Phillips' grandmother, Margaret Wendell, was
Dutch. This romantic interest must have been fleeting,
because beneath the poem in his notebook he wrote:

New York 1834
To Mary Adeline Elwell
Eheu! [7]

Returning to Boston, Phillips spent some months during the winter of 1834–1835 in the law office of Thomas
Hopkinson at Lowell. Hopkinson, only an acquaintance at

college, was a friend of Charles Sumner. He and Phillips had little else in common except a law degree and similar political prejudices. There is no evidence prior to this to indicate that Phillips had any interest in politics. The liberalism of Jacksonian democracy which was sweeping the country, and had even made a determined assault on the bulwarked conservatism of Massachusetts, seems to have passed him by completely. If he had any qualms about the exploitation of factory workers or the tyranny of monopolistic wealth, he kept them to himself. He would have had two good reasons for shunning the Jacksonian Democrats. In the first place, they were for changing the established order, and Phillips had already expressed himself eloquently on the danger of "innovation." In the second place, the Jacksonians were not the right people socially. The only proper course for a Beacon Hill man was to follow the lead of Daniel Webster into the new Whig party in 1832. Phillips took the proper course, probably as much out of a personal admiration for Webster's genius in oratory as for any other reason. He had first heard the great Daniel in 1828 in Faneuil Hall, and since then he had listened to him at every opportunity, both in public meetings and in court. That Webster became one of his idols in college is shown by what he wrote in the class book when he graduated: "Wendell Phillips born Nov 29 in 1811. I love the Puritans, honor Cromwell, idolize Chatham & Hurray for Webster." [8] Thomas Hopkinson shared this admiration for Webster. "How every year and every occasion developes [sic] Mr. Webster's transcendent worth," he wrote to a friend. "Mr. Phillips and myself have just been saying we wd go heart and soul for him as President, tho' we were perfectly certain of defeat." [9]

Phillips' association with Hopkinson was brief. The former returned to Boston to open his own office, while the latter remained in Lowell and soon launched a modest career in politics by leading a mob against an abolitionist meeting.[10] In a few years Wendell Phillips would find it difficult even to recognize a man like Hopkinson on the street. That they could work together so closely in 1834 is one more evidence of his indifference to the great reform issues of the time.

Sometime in the spring of 1835, Phillips rented an office on Court Street and sat back to wait for clients. A year later he was still waiting and had enough spare time to do research on a history of the Phillips family for a genealogist in New Hampshire. He discovered, among other things, that Samuel Phillips of Rowley graduated from Harvard in 1650 and not 1651, and he assured his correspondent that, as "a young attorney not much employed *professionally*," he was happy to do whatever he could to help.[11]

By this time Wendell and his younger brother, Grenville, who was still at Harvard, were the only members of the family who were not yet married or betrothed. Wendell already had a raft of nephews and nieces, who kept him busy scribbling in their "totty albums"

> By and by you'll find out there are but a few
> Who care half a cent for yr album or you
> So to make sure of some, yr best way will be
> To love all your uncles—specially me.[12]

In most eyes Phillips must have appeared as a very lucky man at this time. He was young, handsome, talented, healthy, heir to a family fortune and a member in good standing of the most exclusive society in America. But there was something lacking. Perhaps life had been too easy. Perhaps he chafed under the responsibility of emulating the career of an extremely influential father. It must have been obvious by now both to Wendell and to Sarah Walley Phillips that if any of the children had special gifts it was he. What he lacked most was a sense of personal involvement. He had played his part well enough so far, going to the right places, doing and saying the right things, but he was not committed to this kind of life. In fact, he was not committed to anything. He had no wife, no children and no calling. Religion was no comfort, for a fundamental article in his belief was that a man must make his life count for something. Perhaps it was his brooding about this problem that gave Phillips the melancholy air which Anna Quincy had noticed. However this may be, we know for a fact that Phillips at this time was searching for something. He would hang on to his law practice a few months longer, he told a friend, and, if it did not improve, he would forget the law and devote himself to some more meaningful profession.[13]

Sometime in November or December 1835, Wendell was sitting in his law office, chatting with Charles Sumner. Their offices were closely located on Court Street, and as brand-new lawyers they had plenty of time to talk. Suddenly James Alford, a friend of Sumner's, came in with an urgent plea for help. The next morning he was to take the stage to Greenfield with his fiancée and her cousin, Miss Greene. The cousin was a lovely girl, and Phillips and Sumner would be most obliging if they would escort her and allow Alford to focus his attention on his future bride. The two young lawyers, who had no other clients to attend, readily agreed.[14]

The next morning, however, was stormy, and Sumner reneged. Phillips attended Ann Greene by himself, and the chore turned out to be a delight. Alford had warned him that the girl was pretty, vivacious, clever in conversation, but—beware—a convinced abolitionist. As the stage lumbered over the rutty Massachusetts roads that day, Wendell Phillips learned much about the two things to which he would soon devote his life—Ann Terry Greene and the antislavery cause.

It was true what Alford had said about Ann's convictions. After her parents' death (Benjamin Greene had been a prosperous Boston merchant), she had gone to live with her cousins, Maria and Henry Chapman. Maria was a tower of strength in the Boston Female Anti-Slavery Society, and she and her husband were lavish in their support of William Lloyd Garrison and his abolitionist paper, the *Liberator*. All this was interesting to Wendell, but we can imagine that what fascinated him most was her first-hand account of the Garrison mob in Boston a few weeks previous.

The middle weeks in October 1835, had been a tumultuous time in Boston. When an obscure young man by the name of Garrison had launched the *Liberator* four years before, nobody in Boston paid much attention. New papers, like spring insects, were always rising out of no-where to fill the air with a few weeks or months of angry noise before vanishing as quickly as they came. Garrison's sheet, however, refused to die, and, when the Southern editors learned of the epithets with which he attacked slavery and the slaveholder and how he planned to agitate for the immediate destruction of that institution, they soon roared back their protests. The bloody Nat Turner slave uprising in August 1831, helped to inflame the controversy. Some actually believed that Garrison was responsible; others feared that the real purpose of the *Liberator* was to raise up new Nat Turners in the future. Senator Hayne of South Carolina wrote to Harrison G. Otis, mayor of Boston, demanding that the editor be silenced. The mayor didn't even know who Garrison was, but he found out. So did the rest of Boston. The merchants, the editors of the respectable press, even the preachers, began to grumble about the aggressive interloper. His paper was a trouble-maker—enraged Southerners were not good customers; violent language which might incite slaves to rise up and drench the entire South in blood was not in the Christian spirit, and, God knew, the slavery issue was a profound em-barrassment to politicians of all stripes.

By October 1835, the grumbling in Boston had be-come ominous and widespread. Garrison was advertising the arrival of George Thompson, a British agitator who was to address the Boston Female Anti-Slavery Society. The meeting was scheduled for October 21. Several local papers warned that the state of public opinion would not allow such a meeting to take place; no wild-eyed foreigner would be allowed to seduce "a parcel of deluded women in Boston." The agitation was so intense that Garrison finally sent Thompson out of town to lecture in other parts of the state before audiences promising a more congenial reception, but the meeting on October 21 was to be held in any event; Garrison planned to address the ladies himself.

About twenty colored and white ladies assembled in the antislavery rooms that afternoon, and Ann Greene was among them. There was no speech. A mob had gathered in the street outside, hooting and yelling for George Thompson. When it was discovered that Thompson was not there, the mob began to yell for Garrison. At this point, Mayor Lyman fought his way through the crowds and up the stairs leading to the room where the meeting was held. He implored the ladies for their own safety and for the good of Boston to abandon the meeting. At first there was some resistance to this suggestion. A few heroic souls led by Maria Chapman wanted to lay down their lives on the spot. They followed the mayor's advice, however, and filed down the stairs and out into the street, proceeding in pairs, a group of half-frightened, half-resolute women, down a narrow lane cleared through the mob, which now numbered close to five thousand jeering men.[15]

Phillips, who always insisted that his wife converted him to abolition, must have heard this story from Ann's lips. He had heard most of it before, and he knew what had happened later that afternoon. The mob had found Garrison in a neighboring carpenter shop, hiding under a workbench. Phillips had been in his office at the time and, hearing the uproar, had hurried down Court Street in time to see the crowds press triumphantly by with their loot— a bland-looking, bare-headed man in ripped clothing with a rope around his body, blinking blankly at the mob which he could barely see without his spectacles.[16]

The mob swept down State Street out of sight, and

Phillips learned later that Garrison had finally been rescued by the mayor and deposited in the jail overnight for safekeeping.

All of this must have come back to him in the stage with Ann Greene. It had happened in Boston—a meeting forcibly broken up, an editor lynched, for daring to attack slavery. He was proud of the girl, so pretty, so earnest and so involved with what she called "the cause," and he was proud of Garrison, a man he had never met, but he was ashamed for himself and for Boston.

Phillips saw a great deal of Ann Greene in the following months. Henry Chapman's house in Chauncy Place, where Ann lived, was almost an antislavery headquarters for Boston. Henry was a highly successful merchant in Boston and devoted a considerable amount of his fortune to support Garrison's cause. His wife, Maria Weston Chapman, a golden-haired beauty whom Harriet Martineau described as the handsomest woman in Boston, had been one of Garrison's earliest converts.[17] She was a woman of many qualities, all of them heroic. When Mayor Lyman had tried to disperse the ladies on the day of Garrison's mobbing, it was Maria who, scornfully reminding him that the instigators of the mob had been his personal friends, said "If this is the last bulwark of freedom, we may as well die here as anywhere."[18] When the antislavery ladies were taunted for meddling in affairs that were not proper for them, she called up a vision of "the mothers of Concord" who said to their patriot sons and husbands "never heed *us*. We can bring your bread and water, and serve out ammunition and fill the places of the fallen." Maria ignored the nonsense that men spoke about the weaker sex; she was a woman with a heritage and a mission, who liked to quote the lines:

> I grant I am a woman; but withal
> A woman that Lord Brutus took to wife.
> I grant I am a woman; but withal
> A woman well-reputed, Cato's daughter

Think you I am no stronger than my sex,
Being so father'd and so husbanded? [19]

It was at the Chapman house that Phillips first met
Garrison. There is no record of what happened at their
first meeting. Phillips implied many times later in his
career that it was a turning point in his life; Garrison, for
his part, must surely have been excited by the possibility
of recruiting such a competent and wellborn Bostonian as
Phillips for "the cause."

Except for abolition, the two would probably never
have met, for Garrison's background had almost nothing
in common with that of Phillips. Six years older than
Wendell, he was born in Newburyport in 1805. When he
was very young his father deserted his mother, leaving the
family almost destitute. As a boy, he was forced to collect
leftovers from the tables of wealthy High Street homes
to find food for the family. He received little formal education and was apprenticed to a shoemaker at the age of
thirteen. After several unhappy apprenticeship trials the
boy finally settled on printing. In 1826, when Phillips was
preparing to enter Harvard, Garrison began his first publishing venture in Newburyport.

During the following five years he labored in obscurity as either printer or editor in Newburyport, Benning-
ton, Boston and Baltimore. After meeting Benjamin
Lundy, an itinerant Quaker journalist, Garrison began to
take up the antislavery cause. By 1829 he was co-editor,
with Lundy, of an antislavery paper in Baltimore. In the
spring of 1830, when Phillips was finishing his third year
at Harvard, Garrison spent six weeks in the Baltimore jail
for libeling a sea captain engaged in the transport of slaves.

In January of the following year he returned to Boston and, settling in a dingy office in the old Merchants
Building, brought out the first issue of the *Liberator*. He
knew what he wanted now—"to lift up the standard of
emancipation in the eyes of the nation, *within sight of*

Bunker Hill and in the birthplace of liberty." And he knew how he would go about it. "I *will* be as harsh as truth and as uncompromising as justice. . . . Tell a man whose house is on fire to give a moderate alarm, tell him to moderately rescue his wife from the hands of the ravisher . . . but urge me not to use moderation in a cause like the present. I am in earnest—I will not equivocate—I will not excuse—I will not retreat a single inch—AND I WILL BE HEARD." [20]

It was a brash manifesto, but subsequent issues of the paper proved it to be prophetic. When Phillips met him for the first time, Garrison was already a celebrated (many of Phillips' friends would have said notorious) personality in Boston.

In the absence of contrary evidence we can assume that Phillips listened with interest to what Garrison had to say. He did not, however, leap into the abolitionist ranks immediately. Having been brought up, as he later admitted, in an "unqualified admiration and acceptance of the great Republic, and a believer in the eulogistic tone in which our institutions were both criticized and admired," he could not immediately sympathize with a man who insisted that with slavery the very words "American democracy" were a lie.[21]

The big thing in his life at this time was Ann Greene and after that his law practice and a gradually increasing number of lecturing engagements. He had already begun to develop a modest local reputation as a speaker, and he frequently appeared before lyceum audiences to lecture on patriotic or scientific topics. When he lectured at the New Bedford lyceum in January 1836, he stayed at the same house where Ann's cousin Deborah Weston lived. The Westons were strong abolitionists, and Deborah must have looked the young man over very carefully. "Wendell I like," she reported to her sister. "There seems to be a great deal of straight forwardness and simplicity about him. . . . Intercourse with the abolitionists will I think do him good. His lecture before the Lyceum this evening was considered

very fine, slightly whiggy and rather conservative. . . .
He did better than I expected. . . . I think Ann Terry
has done very well." [22]

In the late summer of 1836 his courtship was brought
to a crisis when Ann became ill. Whatever the sickness
was, apparently it was serious. By the middle of September
she seemed to be recovering but could eat nothing but
peaches. The next month there was a relapse, and by
November 19 it seemed she could not survive. "They have
given up all hope of poor Ann Terry's recovery," one of
the Weston girls wrote. "Ann Chapman does not expect
her to live more than a few weeks longer. She seems entirely debilitated, no constitution, nothing to build on." [23]

On several occasions Ann was too ill to see Wendell
when he called at the Chapman house. He was apparently
not advised of her real condition until sometime in December. How this news affected him is revealed in a letter
from Anne Weston to her sister. "Learning how ill Ann
was he fell into great distress and came strait [sic] to Mr.
C's and insisted upon seeing her. Ann at this time was at
the worst and at first thought she could not see him, but
finally she consented. To use Maria's language, 'He went
upstairs, saw her alone 20 minutes and came down à
Fiancé!' Ever since this time he has been with her two
hours each day and she is getting much better." [24]

A few days later the exultant young man attended an
antislavery bazaar and dazzled the ladies there by purchas-
ing a cameo ring for several times its original cost.[25]

The news traveled fast. Amos Lawrence heard about
it that same month in St. Louis. In a gossipy letter from
home, he learned that Boston society was buzzing over two
events. The first was the marriage of Daniel Webster's
son, Fletcher, at which all the men wore "white *tights*,"
and the second was the news that "Wendell Phillips is
engaged to a Miss Ann Greene who lives at Mrs. Henry
Chapman's in Chauncy Place, and she is reputed, of course,
to be a young abolitionist." [26]

What did Sarah Walley Phillips think when she heard

that her son was engaged to Ann Greene? Surely she did not rejoice. Ann was a charming, clever girl—everyone attested to that—and as Benjamin Greene's daughter she inherited station as well as fortune, but what would the mayor have thought of her abolitionist friends? "Christian reformers," indeed! Sarah knew that Garrison was called the most abusive, foul-mouthed editor Boston had ever seen. He had already turned the city upside down with one riot, and there would probably be others. His friends were not welcome on Beacon Street, as Maria Chapman and her husband well knew. Wendell was no abolitionist yet—just an interested spectator—but who could tell what would happen after the marriage? Would he be so foolish as to throw away a career filled with social and political promise?

It was an October wedding, a small ceremony with only the Chapmans and Wendell's immediate family. Wendell's brother John performed the service, and Ann, the picture of health for at least one day, was radiant "in embroidered muslin with pink scarf and belt." In a letter to her sister Deborah, Anne Weston concluded her description of the occasion by remarking "The old lady Phillips . . . behaved like a perfect dragon." [27]

4

Phillips Makes a Speech at Faneuil Hall 1836–1839

During 1836, Wendell's interest in Ann and the antislavery cause had grown apace. Despite her enthusiasm, however, he found it impossible to swallow abolitionism at one gulp. Although he makes no mention anywhere of the social sacrifices involved, these were probably one consideration.[1] He must have given some thought also to his law practice. Boston merchants would be unlikely to take their fees to a young abolitionist lawyer. Even more important was the prospect of a breach with his family. His brothers were all well on their way toward becoming pillars of the community, and his sisters had taken their places as wives of other pillars. Wendell was the only one who threatened to rock the foundations. What arguments his mother and the other members of the tribe used to persuade him, we can easily surmise—the untarnished family name, the memory of his father, and, not least certainly, since this had always been a strong churchgoing family, the argument that slavery was compatible with Christianity.

Always intensely in earnest about his religious faith, Wendell could not take this last point lightly. During the months of his courtship in 1836 he studied his Bible to determine if the Scriptures sanctioned slavery. He and Ann probably talked the problem over together. In any event, it was not until the end of the year that he saw the light. On December 21, 1836, very close to the date of his engagement, he entered some thoughts on the subject in his notebook. Admitting that the Bible nowhere condemns slavery, he believed it possible to hold that slavery, like despotism of any kind, was "against the spirit of Christianity." Confronted with the fact that the early Christians frequently held slaves, Phillips concluded that this had been permitted "in the inevitable wisdom of providence." The same inscrutable force, he decided, now enjoined men to "waken to duty" and abolish slavery.[2]

Having awakened to duty himself, Wendell began to see more and more of the abolitionists in the months following his engagement. Between January 25 and January 28, 1837, he spent most of his time in the loft of a Boston stable, where the fifth annual meeting of the Massachusetts Anti-Slavery Society was held. The fact that they were forced to meet in a stable, because the proprietors of more suitable halls turned them away, did not really bother the members.[3] Their mission, after all, was to redeem a sinful society, and they could hardly have overlooked the symbolism implicit in this occasion. To Phillips, however, it was one more example of an arrogant, supposedly free, society trying to muzzle its critics.

One of the big attractions of this meeting was the personal appearance of Amos Dresser. Dresser was a celebrated figure in the antislavery cause—one of the early martyrs along with Garrison and Prudence Crandall, the intrepid Canterbury, Connecticut, schoolmistress who had been jailed in 1833 for daring to operate a private school for Negro girls. Dresser had been a theological student on a Bible-selling mission in the South. In July 1835 he was apprehended by a vigilance committee in Nashville, Tennessee. After searching his luggage and discovering some antislavery papers and antislavery opinions in his diary, the vigilantes dragged Dresser to the market place in Nashville, gave him twenty lashes on the bare back and threw him out of town.

Phillips attended the meeting at which Dresser told the story of this experience and how, on the Sunday preceding it, "he had received the bread and wine of the communion from the hands of one of the members of that Vigilance Committee." [4]

Also on the program at this January meeting was a Mr. Johnson, originally from the banks of the Gambia River in Africa. Johnson was a former slave now living as a freedman in Providence. It is difficult from this distance to visualize the effect which he must have had on such a group. He was obviously not a Negro of exceptional intellect like Frederick Douglass. The audience often laughed at his ignorance, as, for example, when speaking of Africa he said "Fine country dat, but we are called heathen in dis Christian—I don't know what to call it—in dis—*enlightened heathen country*." Moreover, he himself had apparently known no physical cruelty as a slave and called his former owner "more father than master." Still, when he announced "I WAS IN SLAVERY," the *Liberator* reported, "a deep emotion was produced in the audience by this simple narrative."

The man who had known slavery went on to describe it: "I have seen a Christian professor, after the communion, have four slaves whipped together and whipped raw, and then washed with beef brine. I knew one Tom Buckine, he was whipped 150 lashes every Monday, and washed with brine, for going to meeting, but that did not stop him. Directly he was whipped, he would jump over fence and pray for his master." The stories he told were like the stories that fifteen years later inspired Harriet Beecher Stowe to write her momentous novel, *Uncle Tom's Cabin.* "If child cries, and mother has to stop to nurse it, and so the row gets behind, the husband helps it along to keep whip off wife's back, and frequently gets it on his own, for who could see a woman whipped for taking care of his own chile?" [5]

Mr. Johnson's account of slavery appears to have been the product of a hazy memory, a lurid imagination and a shrewd understanding of what his audience wanted to hear. Still, it is idle to ask why a highly educated man like Phillips made no attempt to distinguish fact from fancy.

He knew nothing of slavery at firsthand, and Amos
Dresser's experience told him what he might expect if he
ever did try to study it on the site.

There were other ways of verifying Mr. Johnson's
story. Phillips may have already met the Grimké sisters,
but, even if he had not, he must have been familiar with
their grisly reminiscences. Before they were caught up in
the antislavery cause, Sarah and Angelina Grimké had
been reared on a South Carolina plantation. They
remembered having seen a Negro head stuck on a high
pole by the side of the road to discourage runaways, and
recalled how a handsome mulatto woman was once
whipped so badly "a finger could not be laid between the
cuts." They remembered the fashionable lady who had
her house servants whipped so severely that they would be
kept out of the house because of the smell of the putrefying
flesh on their backs. If these stories were not convincing,
there was always the testimony of the slaveowners
themselves. Many of the abolitionists collected Southern
newspapers and made a record of advertisements for
escaped slaves. It was common for the master to identify
his property in such ways as the following: "a yellow boy
named Jim—had on a *large lock chain round his neck*";
"the neger wench Myra—has several marks of *lashing* and
has *irons on her feet*"; "a Negro girl named Mary, has a
small scar over her eye, a *good many teeth* missing, the
letter A is *branded on her cheek and forehead*." [6] All of
the evidence seemed to fit together. Mr. Johnson's story
may not have been extravagant after all. Moreover—and
this was a decisive consideration for a man like Phillips—
if free white citizens like Garrison, Prudence Crandall and
Amos Dresser could be so barbarously treated for merely
criticizing slavery, what savagery might not be meted out
to the slaves themselves?

When Ellis Gray Loring rose to address the meeting,
Phillips perhaps thought he was speaking directly to him.
Loring came from one of the fine Boston families, and
Phillips knew what he had to show for openly espousing

the cause of abolition some years before—cold hospitality on Beacon Street and a vanishing law practice. The resolution which Loring proposed was simple and pointed: "True allegiance to his country, to liberty, and to God, requires that every man should be an Abolitionist, and openly espouse the antislavery cause." [7]

The impact of these meetings on Phillips was noticed by some of Ann's friends more advanced in the cause, who attended with him. Afterwards Maria Chapman reported hopefully to her friends that Wendell had subscribed to the *Liberator* and was "beginning to be quite an abolitionist." [8]

In March 1837, Phillips made his first antislavery speech. The occasion was a meeting of the state antislavery society at Lynn. At this time, abolitionist societies throughout the North were engaged in a campaign to inundate Congress with petitions urging the abolition of slavery in the District of Columbia. Southern senators and representatives reacted violently by trying to prevent Congress from hearing them. With Southern support, a "gag rule" was passed in May 1836, and renewed in January 1837, for the purpose of tabling all such petitions. In the ensuing debate, John Quincy Adams, former president of the United States and now representative from the Plymouth District in Massachusetts, emerged as the champion of the right of petition. Day after day Adams, dubbed "Old Man Eloquent" by his supporters, battled for the right of the petitioners to be heard. On February 6 he threw the House into an uproar by introducing a petition from twenty slaves. In the bitter debate that followed, Adams maneuvered his Southern colleagues into a position whereby they denied slaves the right even to petition God and anyone of "poor moral character" the right to petition Congress. When it was all over and Adams revealed that the petition had been for the purpose of supporting slavery, the Southerners were even more enraged and tried unsuccessfully to pass a resolution of censure.

So far as Wendell Phillips was concerned, the struggle in Washington was part of a general pattern. The mobbing of Garrison, the whipping of Amos Dresser and the gagging of John Quincy Adams were all manifestations of a national conspiracy to keep Americans from criticizing slavery. This was the logical time for a man like Phillips to raise his voice. He did not have to make a real antislavery speech or to identify himself as a Garrisonian. He had only to reaffirm the ancient American right to free discussion. This is precisely what he did at the Lynn meeting when he introduced a resolution commending Adams. The speech accompanying the resolution was devoted exclusively to the petition issue. The point of the speech, a point which Phillips would make time and time again throughout his career, was that slavery was not only a violation of the slave's rights as a man—it threatened the rights of every free American. In language remarkably like that which Lincoln would later make famous, he insisted, "Our fate is bound up with that of the South, so that they cannot be corrupt and we sound; they cannot fall and we stand. Disunion is coming *unless* we discuss this subject; for the spirit of freedom and the spirit of slavery are contending for mastery. They cannot live together. . . ." [9]

Up to this time, Phillips' introduction to "the cause" had been through a gradual series of experiences—the mobbing of Garrison, his romance with Ann Greene, the beginning of associations with antislavery leaders and a growing awareness of their struggles and sacrifices. In December 1837, not quite two months after his marriage, a series of events combined to thrust him suddenly into a position of leadership in the movement.

It happened more than a thousand miles away—in Alton, Illinois—and it involved a man Phillips never knew. Elijah Lovejoy came from a rural background in Maine. As a graduate of Princeton Theological Seminary, he settled in St. Louis in the early 1830s to publish a religious paper. Although not a member of any aboli-

tionist organization, Lovejoy turned public opinion
against himself by discussing the slavery issue in the
columns of his paper. In 1836 he was forced to leave St.
Louis because of his editorial attack on a mob that had
lynched and burned a Negro.

Moving to Alton, in the free state of Illinois, Lovejoy
undertook to publish an abolitionist paper. Public
opinion in Alton and the surrounding country at this
time was decidedly hostile to antislavery agitation of any
kind, and Lovejoy's press was destroyed by a mob almost
as soon as it arrived. In August and September of 1837
his offices were pillaged again and two more presses
destroyed. On November 7, Lovejoy and a small band of
armed supporters barricaded themselves inside the
warehouse. A mob gathered outside and attacked the
building. In the rioting and shooting that resulted, Elijah
Lovejoy was shot dead.[10]

The story spread through the North. The first
martyr for the cause of free speech in America had been
an abolitionist. People who had hitherto ignored the
issue began to reconsider. "Right-minded men have
recently been called to decide for abolitionism," wrote
Emerson in his journal. "The brave Lovejoy has given
his breast to the bullet for his part and has died when it
was better not to live. He is absolved." [11]

The men who killed him were not absolved, and
abolitionists throughout the North held meetings to denounce the crime. In Boston a group led by William
Ellery Channing asked the city authorities for permission
to use Faneuil Hall for such a purpose. Permission was
granted but only after Channing, Boston's most influential
minister, had addressed a public letter to the mayor and
aldermen. The meeting was held in the forenoon of
December 8. A riot was generally expected, and the
Boston *Courier,* a neutral observer, cautioned those who
opposed the meeting to stay away, because many of the
abolitionists "not only anticipate but hope for a riot" to
make their case against mob law more convincing.[12]

Nothing could have kept Phillips from that meeting. The news of Lovejoy's death had left him with a profound sense of shock. It had been difficult for him to understand how abolitionists could be mobbed in a nation dedicated to freedom; that an American citizen could be lynched and murdered for daring to speak his mind against slavery he would never have believed possible. The only interpretation he could put on the matter was that Garrison had been right all along: The slave power did control the nation and would stop at nothing to retain this control.

At first glance, the great crowd which pressed into Faneuil Hall that afternoon seemed to indicate the unanimity with which Bostonians were prepared to denounce the outrage at Alton. Looking around more closely, Wendell saw that this was not true. There appeared to be a heavy sprinkling of abolitionists there, including a little group of ladies in the gallery, captained, as usual, by Maria Chapman. Most of the men in the audience, however, had never been friendly to the abolitionists, and Wendell guessed that a substantial number of them were out for mischief.

When the gavel sounded, the chairman, Jonathan Phillips (a distant cousin of Wendell's), explained the purpose of the meeting and introduced Benjamin Hallet, who read a list of resolutions prepared by Dr. Channing and directed against "the fearful progress of lawless force in the country." The crowd listened to these remarks and those of the following speaker with obvious impatience. At this point a voice was heard from the gallery. Wendell looked up and recognized James Austin, the attorney-general of Massachusetts, who was asking permission to speak. The request was granted, and, to Phillips' horror, this high official of the Commonwealth proceeded to throw the whole weight of his prestige and argument against the memory of Elijah Lovejoy.[13]

The point which Austin made was that the Alton mob had been within its rights in putting down Lovejoy. By publishing the incendiary doctrines of abolition in

Illinois, only a few miles from the slave state of Missouri,
Lovejoy had threatened the safety of his community.
Austin compared the situation there to the situation in
Boston if a huge menagerie of wild beasts were installed
in the midst of the city. "Suppose now some new cos-
mopolite, some man of philanthropic feelings . . . who
believes that all are entitled to freedom as an unalienable
right should engage in the humane task of giving freedom
to these wild beasts of the forest . . . should try to induce
them *to break their cages and be free?*" [14] The people in
Alton, Austin insisted, had as much right to protect themselves as Boston would have in such a situation.

Moreover, declared Austin, the mob in Alton was
acting squarely in accord with our revolutionary tradition.
Men say that Lovejoy had "a right" to print his paper.
But surely the British had possessed as good a right to tax
the colonies, yet our ancestors had finally been forced to
"take their protection under the security of their own
arm, and marching down from this Hall—*an orderly mob*
—pour the disgusting instruments of their degradation
into the sea." And, he warned, the people of Massachusetts will act in a like manner when "their lives are
threatened by these abolitionist conspirators." Lovejoy was
a fool who worked in league with these conspirators, and
he died a fool's death.[15]

The speech was harsh and the language violent, and
the meeting was almost broken up by the applause and
hooting which accompanied it. The abolitionists in the
audience were outraged. Their opponents were ecstatic,
and it appeared to many that the resolutions condemning
the Alton mob could never pass. On no one, however, was
the impact of the speech more profound than on Wendell
Phillips.

Although Phillips was not certain that he would be
called on to speak, he had pondered the subject at length.
Without waiting for an invitation, he got the attention of
the chairman and with some difficulty made his way to
the platform. Everyone had known Austin, as a public

figure, but most of the audience failed to recognize
Wendell Phillips, and they wondered who the sandy-
haired young man was who stood there, well groomed and
impassive, waiting for a chance to speak. More out of
curiosity than for any other reason, the crowd grew quiet,
and Phillips began to talk. In contrast to the ranting
oratory of Austin, he stood quietly and spoke with
compressed passion. The meeting had been called in the
interest of free discussion, he said, and he wished to
comment on the preceding speech and to express his
surprise "not only at such sentiments from such a man,
but at the applause they have received within these walls."
As the audience soon discovered, this was a polite way of
saying that the attorney-general of Massachusetts had just
desecrated the reputation of Faneuil Hall. Austin had
equated "the drunken murderers of Lovejoy" with the
patriotic followers of Samuel Adams; he had suggested
that a rabble action taken to destroy a citizen's rights
could be compared to the actions of people struggling to
secure their traditional liberties. The words came out
effortlessly, but the scornful, icy edge in Phillips voice
seemed to say that Austin's distortion of American history
showed him up as a common barroom demagogue. The
walls of Faneuil Hall were hung with portraits of the men
who had played an illustrious role in the Revolution.
Phillips, who had stood quietly on the platform this far,
now pointed to the portraits and said, "Sir, when I heard
the gentleman lay down principles which place the
murderers of Alton side by side with Otis and Hancock,
with Quincy Adams, I thought those pictured lips would
have broken into voice to rebuke the recreant American,
—The slanderer of the dead. . . .   In the sentiments he
has uttered, on soil consecrated by the prayers of Puritans
and the blood of patriots, the earth should have yawned
and swallowed him up." [16]

At this the audience broke into a roar in which the
abolitionists' cheers were drowned out by furious demands
that he take back his words. As the supporters of Austin

became more vociferous and abusive, Phillips remained
on the platform, apparently at ease and contemptuously
aloof to the boisterous, hooting crowd boiling up in front
of him. Finally he was allowed to proceed, and, although
he was interrupted again before the finish, the hecklers
gradually grew less vocal and it became obvious that they
were willing to hear him out. Not once did he mention
slavery or abolition. His whole appeal was to the patriotic
sentiments of his audience, sentiments which united
abolitionists with their critics. Lovejoy died because he
dared put his convictions into print—that was all—and
no American could call him foolish for that. "James Otis
thundered in this Hall when the King did but touch his
pocket. Imagine, if you can, his indignant eloquence, had
England offered to put a gag upon his lips." [17] The
residents of Alton, Phillips reminded his listeners, had
come originally from the older states, but they had
"forgotten the blood-tried principles of their fathers the
moment they lost sight of our New England hills." Elijah
Lovejoy was a New Englander who had not forgotten, and
his great achievement was to show all America "the
priceless value of the freedom of the press." [18]

The resolutions were passed, and the meeting was
adjourned successfully, but as the crowd left the hall more
people were talking about Phillips than about Lovejoy.
It was his first great success as an orator. Many of those
who heard him remembered the performance as one of
the thrilling experiences in their lives, and even those he
did not convince must have realized that on that day the
forces of William Lloyd Garrison had been mightily
reinforced.

Garrison was transported by what had happened.
Austin's speech he described as "fraught with moral
stupidity and sulkiness, and all that is malicious, defam-
atory, mobocratic and murderous," and "the reply of the
youthful, accomplished and gifted Wendell Phillips
electrified the mighty assembly. It was sublime, irresist-
ible, annihilating." [19]

Looking back on the event thirty years later, Phillips saw how decisive the killing of Lovejoy had been in shaping his own life. His first associations with the abolitionists had been in a large measure an expression of youthful exuberance. "I pronounced the shibboleth of the society with the buoyant enthusiasm which young men usually entertain towards such questions—confident of a large reserve of strength and a lavish opportunity so that we can throw away any quantity upon any movements we chance to fancy." The tragedy in Alton educated him by revealing the demonic possibilities of a slave power supported by public opinion in America. "A lawyer bred in all the technical reliance on the safe-guards of Saxon liberty, I was puzzled, rather than astounded, by the fact that, outside of the law and wholly unrecognized in the theory of our institutions, was a mob power—an abnormal element which nobody had counted in, in the analysis of the system, and for whose irregular actions no check, no balance, had been provided. The gun which was aimed at the breast of Lovejoy on the banks of the Mississippi brought me to my feet, conscious that I stood in the presence of a power whose motto was victory or death." [20] The law could not prevent Garrison from being mobbed, Dresser from being whipped or Lovejoy from being lynched so long as these things represented the will of the community.

What was needed, Phillips saw, was a man or an organization invested with the patriotism of the Revolutionary fathers and devoted to the task of replacing a corrupt public opinion with a public opinion that would not only defend traditional American liberties but ultimately destroy slavery. A lawyer called to this task would have to forget the dry precision and technicalities of the law. He would have to persuade, to cajole, to enchant, to castigate a jury of millions of his countrymen until they brought in the verdict for justice. Wendell Phillips was beginning to see his calling.

From December 1837 until June 1839, Phillips took

an increasingly important role in the New England antislavery movement. Reports of the Lovejoy speech spread rapidly, and he was in such demand as a speaker that he was forced to turn away more requests than he could fill.[21] He took an active role in the abolitionist organizations and was soon made president of the Boston Anti-Slavery Society.

By the end of 1838, Phillips had become deeply committed to the abolitionist cause.and was willing to stand with its most extreme advocates. A good opportunity to put his militant convictions into practice came in February 1839, when a group of ladies in Lynn submitted a petition to the legislature urging the repeal of all Massachusetts laws which discriminated against people on account of color. Because the obvious target of the petition was a law preventing intermarriage between Negroes and whites, a controversy immediately ensued. The Boston *Post* accused the white ladies who signed the petition of praying for "the privilege of being married to black husbands." Every attempt was made to make the petitioners look ridiculous. One legislator introduced a second petition from Lynn, which asked mockingly that the ladies of the town be permitted "to marry, intermarry, or associate with any Negro, Indian, Hottentot or any other being in human shape at their will and pleasure. . . ." [22]

The upshot was that the lawmakers chuckled and let the affair go at that. The abolitionists held a meeting of protest in Boston's Marlboro Chapel, and Wendell Phillips led the attack. His speech was not recorded, but, according to Anne Weston, it was a strong performance. "He tore the Legislature all to pieces, then ground them to atoms, then strewed them on the waters . . . and condemned Lincoln [the governor] as only fit for the representative of scurrilous and licentious profligates. . . . Mary Robbins, who called here this morning says that the town is convulsed with rage . . . the Legislators are ready to lynch Wendell." [23]

A good many of Phillips' former friends, especially those who had known him at Harvard, must have rubbed their eyes in wonder, remembering the darling of the young aristocrats in college. Wendell himself, a few years earlier, could never have conceived of making a personal assault on the state legislature. He had been brought up to respect the political institutions of the country, and in his family there had always been a special regard for the legislature, over which John Phillips had presided for so many years. Mere political ambition would never have caused him to reject this part of his inheritance, and what friends and family alike failed to understand was that his primary motivation had not been political but religious.

As he grew more intimate with the leaders of the antislavery movement, Phillips had gradually come to appreciate the profound religious significance which they attached to it. He himself had been drawn into the ranks by the influence of his wife and by his conviction that the abolitionists were being denied their American right to free discussion. During the early 1830s, however, when the antislavery movement was being organized, other men and women throughout the North had given themselves to the cause with the fervency which the new convert reserves for his church. The early followers of Garrison had been convinced not only of the justice but of the sacredness of their cause, convinced that their little holy band had been sent to redeem a sinful nation. There had been twelve founders of the New England Anti-Slavery Society in 1832. On a slushy January night they had come together in the African Baptist church on Nigger Hill and pledged themselves to the slave. The analogy with the early Christian church was not overlooked, and during the early years when the founders met they would kiss each other on the cheek in the manner of the twelve disciples. Like the disciples, they.too believed that sin was enshrined in God's holy temple, that the day of judgment was at hand and they appointed to bear testimony to it. Oliver Johnson, who lived through these days himself, has captured the mood and conviction of these men, their attitude toward the sinning nation and Garrison the redeemer.

Commerce, greedy of grain, piled her hoards by the unpaid toil of the bondman. Judgment was turned away backward; Justice stood afar off; Truth was fallen in the street and Equity could not enter. The hands of the people were defiled with blood, their fingers with iniquity; their lips spoke lies, their tongues muttered perverseness. Men talked of slavery in that day (when they talked it at all) with an incoherency like that of Bedlam, with a moral blindness and perverseness like that of Sodom and Gomorrah. That in this hour of thick darkness a voice was heard pleading, trumpet-tongued, for immediate emancipation . . . seems to us now one of the most signal illustrations of the immanence of God in human affairs. I must believe that that voice, crying in the wilderness and calling the people to repentance, was divinely inspired—not indeed, in a miraculous, but certainly in a providential sense.[24]

The appeal for immediate abolition of slavery was in itself a religious appeal. Just as the great revival preachers, such as Lyman Beecher and Charles Finney, were thundering before their congregations the duty of the sinner to repent now, so was Garrison insisting that the slaveholder repent now by freeing his slaves and the nonslaveholder by rebuking the slaveholder. Just as the early Christian church owed much of its success to its martyrs, so did the martyrdom of abolitionists bring new converts into the fold and strengthen the hearts of the faithful. These reformers knew the value of tactics and welcomed abuse for the good it would do them. Therefore, the exasperated Whig who aimed a brick at Garrison at an antislavery meeting might hear the next day that the abolitionists had hung it in a place of honor on the wall of their office. When Prudence Crandall was jailed, the abolitionist minister Samuel May arranged to have her spend her night in jail in the cell recently occupied by a convicted murderer. She slept in a bed moved in from

May's own house, but this did not impair the publicity
value of her "humiliation." [25]

Such examples illustrate their shrewdness as men, but
do not reflect unfavorably on their sincerity as abolitionists. What May said of Francis Jackson, one of the
few Boston merchants to share his fortune and energy with
Garrison's cause, could have been said of most of the
leaders of the movement. "More than twenty-five years of
his life had been spent in endeavoring to make 'atonement,' as he himself said, for his own sins and for his
father's sins" against the Negro.[26] It was this intense
awareness of the sin of slavery that set the abolitionist
apart from the average citizen and made him appear
fanatical. After five years in Europe, while the ship in
which he travelled was still outside Boston Harbor, Henry
Wright was moved to write in his journal: "A strange
feeling comes over me. I feel that I am once more breathing the pestiferous atmosphere of chattel slavery." [27] The
only way to live in such an atmosphere was to consecrate
one's life against it. Thus, the epithets and stones and
rotten eggs, the near lynchings and the broken bones that
antislavery lectures encountered in their ministry were
not only welcomed but invited. It was blessed to be persecuted for righteousness' sake, and the abolitionists
constantly saw themselves in the martyr's role. "Blessed
are they who die in the harness," wrote the crusading
Theodore Dwight Weld, "and are buried on the field or
bleach there." And the woman he married, Angelina
Grimké, once said "A *hope* gleams across my mind, that
our blood will be spilt, instead of the slaveholders'; *our*
lives will be taken, and theirs spared." [28]

This is the language of enthusiasts. Those who
launched the antislavery movement, and most of the
faithful among the rank and file, were enthusiasts. They
embodied the same piety which had kindled in the hearts
of William Bradford and his company the desire to plant
a new Canaan on the rocky Massachusetts coast, the piety
which, fanned by the preaching of Whitfield and Edwards

in 1740, had roared like wildfire through the colonies during the Great Awakening and had invaded the great camp meetings on the frontier at the turn of the nineteenth century. It was this piety, which no church had ever been able to contain, which sustained the reform movements of the 1830s and showed Wendell Phillips what to do with his life.

As an agent for the Massachusetts Anti-Slavery Society in the spring of 1839, Phillips was not only a lecturer but a fund raiser, and this experience went far to show him how closely related were his religion and his abolitionism. Previously, he had had almost no contact with people outside his own social sphere. Now he solicited door to door. In Taunton, Massachusetts, he raised $42.80. The sum is not impressive but the manner of its collection was—twelve cents from one household, twenty-five cents from another, "a widow's mite" of two dollars.[29] These were the people who made up the bulk of Garrison's support in New England. Poor and uneducated, by the standards of Beacon Street, these simple, faithful folk made Phillips wince when he thought of his own life of careless luxury. Remarking this experience at an antislavery meeting he said, "Who are we that we should presume to rank ourselves with those that are marshalled in such a host? What have *we* done? Where is the sacrifice *we* have made? Where the luxury *we* have surrendered? . . . He dared hardly stand by the side of those, who, by drudgery and daily toil, and by the sweat of their brows gained a living, and who yet . . . poured their all into the treasury of the common cause, while others were pampered with luxury and never felt for their brethren in bonds as bound with them." His association with such people showed Phillips where true religion dwelt—not in the pulpit but in the antislavery convention. "There lived the religion of the present, while the pulpit was busying itself with the Pharisee and the Sadducee—with forms of sin that had lain buried in the graves of 1800 years." [30]

It is important to understand that for Phillips moral reform became not a substitute for, but the natural expression of, religious faith. In other words, Phillips did not cease to be a Calvinist when he became an abolitionist; he became an abolitionist because he was a Calvinist. In the speech quoted above, while denouncing the moral blindness of the nation, he is reported to have said: "But there was an eye which never slept—there was an ear which had never been closed to the prayer of the oppressed; and even now the red right arm of the avenger might be stretched over the land." The abolitionists were offering the only atonement for the nation, and their duty was clear: emancipation here and now. "No matter if the charter of emancipation was written in blood . . . and if when the slave was emancipated, ruin should succeed improvement, and anarchy stalk abroad with giant strides —if God commanded, it was right—they must trust in him that out of evil he would bring good." [31] Phillips' Calvinism, his belief in the "red right arm of the avenger," reinforced his radicalism. When in a few more years he was forced to the ultimate position, when his every effort was to pour contempt on the Constitution and urge the destruction of the Federal Union, he did not have to worry about the possible results if such agitation were successful. A man could only do his duty and let God do the rest.

5

Europe   1839–1841

Ann Phillips never allowed herself to be photographed or painted. The only likeness that we have of her is a silhouette taken a few years after her marriage. She wore her hair coiled in a bun at the back of her head, and her slightly upturned nose and firm mouth suggest a pert and determined young lady. She was as proud of Wendell's abolitionist activities as his mother was disappointed. What other people thought apparently bothered her not at all, for shortly after her marriage she was boasting to her cousin of "frightening the ministers' wives about the country with her views of the woman question." [1] Unhappily, however, Ann did not possess the physical resources to sustain this kind of intellectual and spiritual vigor for more than brief periods at a time. Her marriage was hardly into its second year when her health began to fail again. The doctors, unable to make any definite diagnosis, fell back on what was then an almost universal prescription for ailing Americans who could afford it—a trip abroad.

Even though this meant that Wendell would have to interrupt his infant law practice and surrender his office as general agent for the Massachusetts Anti-Slavery Society, he and Ann looked forward to the experience as both a quest for health and a kind of extended honeymoon. Sarah Walley Phillips, for her part, was positively delighted and hoped that the old world's fascinations would bring not only Ann back to health but the hot-headed Wendell back to sanity.

They sailed from New York on June 10, 1839. Before

59

their departure the Massachusetts society had tendered
Wendell a formal vote of appreciation for his services, and
Garrison, always mildly intoxicated with a pen in his hand,
wrote: "In the springtime of manhood, when the love of
popular applause rather than of doing good generally
inflames the youthful mind, you turned your back upon
the blandishments of a seductive world . . . made yourself of no reputation for the benefit of the perishing bonds-
man, and became the associate of those who are up to this
hour subject to popular odium, to violent treatment, to
personal insult." [2]

The plan was for Wendell and Ann to spend a short
time in London and then set off for the arduous stage journey across the continent to Rome, where they would spend
the winter. The high spot of this first, brief visit to London was their introduction to Elizabeth Pease and George
Thompson.

The sprightly Elizabeth Pease belonged to a prominent English Quaker family which was immersed in the
principal reform movements of the day. She had organized
a Woman's Abolition Society in Darlington in 1836 and
was a regular correspondent of Maria Chapman and other
abolitionists in America. She took to Ann and Wendell
at once, and they to her, and through Elizabeth Pease the
young Americans were introduced to George Thompson.

Thompson, who for a while had been as infamous in
America as he was famous in England, had risen to international prominence as a lecturer for the London Anti-
Slavery Society. A rugged-looking man with a bulldog
jaw and a powerful voice, Thompson was considered one
of the great British orators of the day, and his efforts had
been instrumental in getting Parliament to abolish slavery
throughout the empire in 1833. Garrison had met Thompson during a fund-raising visit to England in that year.
The two had had much in common, both having come
from humble beginnings to build substantial reputations
in the antislavery movement, and they had become good
friends. They had made a pilgrimage to the home of the

aging Lord Wilberforce, who had initiated the great work
against slavery a half-century earlier, and before Garrison
left England he had proposed to Thompson the possibility
of his undertaking a lecture tour in the United States.

Thompson had arrived in New York on September 20,
1834. Although Garrison had been extravagant in his welcome, likening the British reformer's visit to that of Lafayette, Thompson's reception in other quarters had not
been so happy. The American press, unable to see the
resemblance to Lafayette, had denounced him as a foreign
fanatic hired by the abolitionists "to come among us and
disseminate those precious doctrines of social equality and
physical amalgamation." [3] The lion's tail had been pinned
to the abolitionists, and healthy twisting by American editors had compounded the customary results. Almost immediately after their arrival, Thompson and his family
had been turned out of their New York hotel. During a
tour through New England his meetings had repeatedly
been broken up by mobs. While lecturing in a church in
Abington, Massachusetts, a heavy lamp had come crashing
through the window behind the pulpit. Later, in Concord,
New Hampshire, he had barely escaped a furious mob,
which then found some solace in pelting one of his companions, John Greenleaf Whittier, with rocks.[4] Thompson
had been quoted by his critics as saying that the slaves
should rise up and cut their masters' throats, but by
October 1835, it was his own throat that was in danger.
When Garrison was mobbed, it was Thompson the crowd
had been after, and so ugly was its mood that Louisa May
Alcott later recalled hiding his portrait under the bed in
her house during the rioting.[5]

George Thompson had brought the slavery issue into
national view—so much so that President Jackson had
publicly denounced him in his message to Congress in
December 1835. When Thompson left for England a few
weeks later, he was covered with glory so far as Boston
abolitionists were concerned. He received a martyr's welcome in Edinburgh, and in 1839 he was leading the fight

against the apprenticeship system in the English colonies.

"We are in London and have seen Thompson," Ann wrote to Maria Chapman shortly after their visit. Elizabeth Pease had taken them to his lodgings in Tisbury Square. Ann was ecstatic over the experience and very feminine in her observations. "For your particular edification I will begin with the room. About the size of your small parlour, Maria,—sofa, centre table, books on shelves, beautiful portfolios for papers, lovely inkstand . . . I looked around à la Yankee." Wendell had earlier written Thompson a long letter explaining the philosophy and progress of the antislavery movement in America, and their discussion was undoubtedly in this vein,[6] but Ann, for all her zeal about women's rights and other serious questions, could remember to write only about the things that Thompson had picked out to contribute to the antislavery fair which the Boston ladies were about to hold. "His hands unfold the papers, think of that Caroline, and he says there that blue basket is my taste, that green pincushion with the white fringe is my choice, this little Scotch thistle also. Think, you will see the things he has handled!" [7]

In September, Wendell and his young bride were in Paris en route to Rome, where they arrived before winter. There they lingered several months, fascinated as their countrymen have ever been by the antique glories of that city. They spent hours in the Pantheon, climbed up Trajan's pillar, "rode over the pavement on which Constantine entered in triumph," saw the Colosseum by moonlight and lost themselves in the Vatican, "that little world of dazzling, bewildering beauty . . . where the Laocoön breathes in never ending agony." [8]

While they were so happily engrossed, the antislavery movement at home was falling on unfortunate days. Garrison, the man whom Oliver Johnson likened to Moses "raised up by Divine Providence to deliver this republic from the sin and crime of slavery," had never really been the national leader of American abolitionism. During

1831 and 1832, when he was engaged in launching the *Liberator* and organizing the New England Anti-Slavery Society, a group of men in New York led by the famous philanthropist brothers, Arthur and Lewis Tappan, were independently laying plans for a national antislavery organization. New York at this time was the center of the reform impulse in America, and at the center of reform in New York were the Tappans. Originally from Massachusetts, they combined the two qualities so often associated with the descendants of the Puritans, a sharp sense for business and intense religious convictions. The former resulted in a fortune amassed in merchandising, the latter in lavish expenditures to support religious causes. In 1831 the Tappans, strongly influenced by the example of the British abolitionists, had gathered a group together to discuss ways of fighting slavery in America. When the American Anti-Slavery Society was organized in New York in 1833, it was as much the work of the Tappan group as of Garrison and the Boston abolitionists.

The spiritual father of this movement was Charles Grandison Finney, one of the greatest evangelists of the nineteenth century. In the mid-1820s the surpassing power of Finney's preaching had set the fires of religious enthusiasm blazing throughout Ohio and New York. In his path he left thousands of eminent men and women burning with the knowledge that a Christian's duty is to cleanse himself and reform mankind.

Finney's most influential disciple, Theodore Dwight Weld, became the principal antislavery agent for the Tappan brothers. In 1833, Weld—a shambling, raw-boned New Englander whose fierce pulpit eloquence belied an almost psychopathic desire for obscurity—promoted a series of debates on abolitionism among the students of Lane Seminary, a Tappan-sponsored institution in Cincinnati. Under Weld's influence the students voted to support immediate emancipation. As a result of these debates, widely reported in the press, and of the controversy which followed, the students withdrew from Lane and entered

Oberlin College. By 1835, the year that Garrison was mobbed in Boston, Oberlin had become the center of antislavery activity in the West, and Weld and the other "Lane rebels" had launched a mighty evangelical effort to spread the gospel throughout New York, Ohio, Pennsylvania and parts of New England. In the following year hundreds of local antislavery societies were founded as a result of their work.[9]

Almost from the beginning there was a distinct coolness between Garrison and the Weld-Tappan group. The latter thought that Garrison took too much credit upon himself as the personal embodiment of abolitionism. They were unhappy with the rancorous, abusive tone of the *Liberator,* which they suspected of alienating many prospective friends. They accused Garrison of identifying the antislavery cause with a variety of his own personal hobbies, such as pacifism, vegetarianism, no-governmentism and temperance.[10]

Even among New England abolitionists, Garrison made enemies. Early in 1835 a group of ministers tried unsuccessfully to seize the leadership of the movement in New England and place it in more moderate hands. This attempt only made the editor of the *Liberator* all the more vehement in his denunciation of the "black-hearted clergy" who temporized with slavery and turned the church of God into "a cage of unclean birds and a synagogue of Satan." [11]

By 1837 antislavery leaders in America were almost as divided in their opinions of Garrison as they were united in their hatred of slavery. Two major issues developed which ultimately forced all abolitionists to line up with one side or the other.

The first involved the position of the abolitionist in politics. The Weld-Tappan group believed that every abolitionist had a duty to use his political influence to attack slavery. Garrison, however, argued that the antislavery cause was purely moral in its purpose and that abolitionists should content themselves with stirring the conscience of the nation against slavery. Moreover, Garri-

son himself and many of his followers considered it a sin
to vote and thus acknowledge the authority of a government which sanctioned slavery.

The second issue was "the woman question." Women
had been active in the abolition movement from the beginning, but they were expected to confine their activities
to their own female antislavery societies. In 1836, however,
the American Anti-Slavery Society appointed Angelina and
Sarah Grimké lecturers. As these courageous South Carolina Quaker ladies toured the North, frequently addressing
mixed or predominantly male groups, many abolitionists
grew restive. Those who sincerely hated slavery often just
as sincerely opposed any attempt to remove woman from
her "rightful sphere." Garrison, however, campaigning
for women's rights as eagerly as he campaigned against
slavery, sought to include women in the antislavery organization on an equal basis with men.

At the national antislavery convention in 1839, the
Garrisonians and anti-Garrisonians fought bitterly but to
no decisive conclusion over the rights of women delegates.
At the New England convention the same year, however,
the same issue prompted the anti-Garrisonians to withdraw
from the New England Anti-Slavery Society and establish a
Massachusetts society of their own.

The stage was thus set for a showdown at the national
convention in 1840. Anticipating a fight, Garrison char-
tered a steamboat in Providence for the purpose of trans-
porting some 450 "friendly" delegates to the convention in
New York. When the convention met on May 12 and the
Garrisonians mustered enough votes to put a woman delegate, Abby Kelly, onto the business committee, the breaking point was reached. Such an action was a violation of
the society's constitution, protested Lewis Tappan, and
"contrary to the usages of civilized society." [12] The fact
was, however, that the "uncivilized" forces had the votes,
and the result was that the Tappan group withdrew from
the convention and established a new national organization.

Because he was in Europe at the time, Phillips was not involved in the split. Although definitely a Garrison man, Wendell had never been partisan to all of his friend's causes. In October 1838, for example, he had attended a peace convention in Boston. Under Garrison's leadership, a great majority of the hundred or more delegates had agreed that "Our country is the world, our countrymen are all mankind. . . . Hence we can allow no appeal to patriotism to revenge any national insult or injury." Phillips had argued against the resolution. He was too much a child of the American Revolution to take up the doctrines of pacifism, especially when they were carried so far as to make their believers oppose the raising of a monument on Bunker Hill because it would "hold up for admiration the bloody achievements of military heroes." [13]

Phillips had refused, however, to let his disagreement with Garrison at this point obscure their essential agreement over slavery. He believed that Garrison's harsh radicalism and his violent rhetoric in the columns of the *Liberator* were justified, and, before leaving for Europe, Phillips had congratulated that paper for basing its policy on the realization "that rights are more valuable than forms . . . that all forms of human device are worse than useless when they stand in truth's way." [14]

Garrison's critics had argued that his radicalism alienated the Southern states and thus threatened the strength of federal union. To this Phillips had retorted, "If lawful and peaceful efforts for the abolition of slavery in our land will dissolve it, let the Union go . . . perish the Union, when its cement must be the blood of the slave." [15]

So far as the relationship among abolitionism, politics and feminism were concerned, Phillips had made it clear before he left for Europe that he would refuse to make political activity a requirement for abolitionists.[16] His position on the second issue had been settled when he was married; no husband of Ann Greene could be anything but a convinced feminist.

After wintering in Italy, Wendell and Ann returned

to England in the spring of 1840 as delegates to the first world antislavery convention. On June 12, 1840, when they entered Freemason's Hall in London, the great auditorium was teeming with delegates from all over the world, and the question being hotly discussed among them before the meeting involved that bugaboo of American abolitionists, the "woman question." The Garrisonians had sent a number of women delegates, including Ann, to the convention, but the delegates from the other wing of the American movement, led by James G. Birney, were determined to keep the women from being seated. The British sympathized with the latter; consequently, Ann was forced to join the other American ladies in a space at the end of the hall marked off by a rail and a curtain. Before Wendell left her to take his place with the rest of the delegates, she made him promise to carry the fight to the convention floor. "No shilly-shallying, Wendell," she cautioned. "Be brave as a lion." [17]

As it turned out, the company inside the rail was fully as distinguished as that outside, for Ann found herself sitting beside Elizabeth Cady Stanton and Lucretia Mott. The younger lady, Elizabeth Stanton, wore her stylishly cut silk in a way that belied her unfashionable ideas. Only a few weeks earlier she had married fiery abolitionist orator Henry Stanton over the violent objections of her family. During their trip across the Atlantic she had constantly embarrassed their conventional-minded traveling companion, James Birney, by exploring every inch of the ship in a most unladylike manner.[18] A woman who insisted on being hoisted to the masthead in a chair was not likely to keep her ideas to herself, and Elizabeth had a great many ideas, especially about the rights of women. She still remembered with indignation when she had first learned from her lawyer father that a woman lost all property rights after marriage. Determined to hold on to her own rights, Elizabeth had astounded the minister before her marriage by refusing to proceed until he agreed to omit the word "obey" from the ceremony.[19]

The serene little lady in the plain dress and white bonnet who sat next to Elizabeth was Lucretia Mott, the most famous Quakeress in America. Older than her companions, Lucretia and her husband, James, had been converted to the antislavery cause by the preaching of Long Island Quaker Elias Hicks ten years earlier. James had sacrificed his prosperous cotton business on that account, and Lucretia, a notable preacher in her own right, had been one of the speakers at the first meeting of the American Anti-Slavery Society in Philadelphia in 1833.[20]

These two strong-minded women, along with Ann and the other American ladies, provided Phillips' moral reinforcement when he sought to have their credentials recognized. As it turned out, he needed a more tangible kind of support. Almost as soon as the convention opened, an English delegate jumped to his feet and made some oblique remarks about the "goddess delegates." [21] Phillips countered by moving that his fellow delegates admit to the convention "all persons bearing credentials from any antislavery body," [22] and the debate began in earnest. One after another the English abolitionists rose, appealing to the American ladies to respect English customs and "the teaching of the Word of God" respecting "the particular sphere in which woman is to act." James Birney, leader of the Weld-Tappan delegation, anxious to compensate in London for the defeat his faction had suffered in New York a few weeks earlier, reminded the delegates that many American abolitionists themselves were bitterly opposed to the idea of women delegates.[23]

There were a few affirmative voices. George Thompson was mildly in favor of Phillips' resolution, and George Bradburn, a blunt-spoken giant of a man from Nantucket, probably did more harm than good when he leaped up to announce that, if the Bible sanctioned the slavery of women, the best work a man could do for humanity would be "to make a grand bonfire of every Bible in the universe." [24]

Meanwhile, the subjects of the controversy, furious

but helpless, peered out at the drama from behind the curtain at the end of the hall. Most of them came from Massachusetts and Pennsylvania. Some had been driven into the streets of Boston by the Garrison mob in 1835. Others had participated in the women's antislavery meeting in Pennsylvania Hall in 1838 and had seen the hall burned to the ground after their meeting. Lucretia Mott's house had narrowly escaped destruction at the hands of the Philadelphia mob of that year. She herself had been attacked by rioters during a lecture tour in Delaware and had watched one of her male companions carried off to be tarred and feathered. Women of this sort felt that they knew more about their "rightful sphere" than the gentlemen then expounding it so pompously from the convention floor.

In the end, Phillips' motion was decisively defeated, and the ladies remained in their little coop for the duration of the convention. Garrison, delayed at sea and arriving after the issue had been decided, solemnly refused to take his place on the convention floor and sat with the rebuffed ladies as a spectator.

That Phillips was a hero with the ladies is evident from the frequent reference in Lucretia Mott's diary. One day Wendell was eloquent in his support of the women delegates; another day he made a thrilling speech on the British India question—always he was persuasive, sensible and in the right, a man, like his wife, with "whole-souled" convictions, who thought that emancipation should be universal.

For all its high moral earnestness, the record of this great meeting of humanitarians has its amusing and certainly its human aspects. Most of the Americans had never been abroad before, and they were torn between their Americanism, their reforming zeal and their desire to behave like typical tourists. When the venerable Thomas Clarkson, a pioneer with Wilberforce in the antislavery movement, visited their quarters, the American ladies delightedly swarmed over him, snipping off most of his hair

for keepsakes. They were obviously excited by their prox-
imity to the great men and women of England, and they
fairly swooned when an exotic figure like Lady Byron
joined their group.

On the other hand, they were all Americans, and
American reformers at that. George Bradburn had hardly
disembarked at Liverpool before he began to complain
about the service: there was too much of it, and he couldn't
tell the servants from the aristocrats. Lucretia Mott was
unhappy at the sight of such capable men reduced to the
menial role of domestics. They visited Windsor Castle,
and her husband described it as "one of the many monuments of the extravagance and folly of the English nobility." They were not to be intimidated by the pretensions of the Old World. After being introduced by Lady
Byron to the English poet, Tom Campbell, Lucretia noted
testily in her diary: "Much fuss made with Campbell—a
poor Imbecile—he spoke of our poets unhandsomely—replied to nicely by H. B. Stanton who quoted our Whittier." [25]

There were some who became dazzled by the glitter
of the English nobility despite themselves. Garrison, who
had come a long way since his days as a Newburyport ap-
prentice, must have been showing the effects of this when
he sat for the painter, Benjamin Haydon, after having
visited the Duchess of Sutherland. Haydon jotted in his
diary: "Household and Duchess bewildered his republican
faculties." [26]

Haydon's role at the convention is a story in itself. An
intimate of such literary giants as Wordsworth and Keats,
Haydon was a lusty, expansive fellow who liked to think of
himself as "a man with air balloons under his armpits and
ether in his soul." [27] Commissioned to paint the world
antislavery convention, he sat in an anteroom adjoining
the auditorium and sketched the delegates while they made
history. He was originally asked to put in 103 heads, but
this was later changed to 134. "Rather a joke," he noted

in his diary, "but if they like, they shall have heads all over like a peacock's tail." [28]

While the delegates on the convention floor were denouncing prejudice against color, Haydon was quietly putting them to the test in his studio. As the more important dignitaries sat for him personally, he would offer each of them the place of honor in his picture—beside a woolly-headed Negro. He noted scornfully in his diary that the usual reaction was that the gentleman concerned "sophisticated immediately" and urged "the propriety of placing the negro in the distance as it would have much greater effect." [29] Only Garrison appears to have received the proposal with immediate enthusiasm.

Wendell Phillips was probably too recent an addition to antislavery ranks to warrant special consideration by the official painter. At any event, he does not appear in Haydon's account. The most important result of the convention for Phillips was that it introduced him to English abolitionists and marked the beginning of his association with American feminists. Like the other delegates, however, he and Ann were swept up in the round of social activity which accompanied the convention. Elizabeth Pease and her family were their closest friends in London, and through her they met a laughing Irishman, Richard Webb, and his wife, Hannah, the leading spirits among a group of Dublin reformers devoted to such a variety of good causes they were once described as "anti-everythingarians."

Probably the most celebrated person whom Phillips met at this time was Daniel O'Connell. The great Irish political leader who had led the drive which resulted in the Catholic Emancipation Act in 1829, permitting Irish Catholics to sit in Parliament, had been a frequent visitor to the antislavery convention. He had just begun to renew the agitation to repeal the union between England and Ireland when Phillips went to Conciliation Hall to hear him speak. O'Connell was approaching the end of his life;

his face was lined; his mouth drooped with age, but on the platform he remained masterful—proud, scornful, defiant —still Ireland's "Darlin' Liberator," perhaps the most powerful orator in the language and the man whom Gladstone called "the greatest popular leader the world has ever seen." [30]

Unlike most Bostonians who began life on Beacon Hill, Phillips was always friendly to the Irish, and this attitude can probably be traced to that day in the summer of 1840 when he sat with the crowd in Conciliation Hall and watched O'Connell refuse a large contribution to his cause from a New Orleans slaveowner. "Old Ireland is very poor," he said, "but, thank God, she is not poor enough to take the unpaid wages of anybody." [31]

The excitement of the convention was too much for Ann's health, and by the end of June she was frequently confined to her room. It was decided to pursue health on the continent once again, and they set out to sample the salubrious waters of the famous German spas. At Kossingen, however, Ann seemed only to grow weaker, and they quickly moved on, much to the disgust of their doctor, a "formal, routine sort of German physician" who "announced the odd proposition, at least to American ears— that all sick people had to do was to submit quietly to orders." After stopping at Frankfurt, where they saw the Gutenberg Bible and Ann excitedly touched her fingers to the sacred shoes of Martin Luther, they moved south through the lush, vine-covered Rhine Valley and down the Neckar River to Heidelberg "with its rich old ruin of a castle breathing all sweetly of olden times," then on through Switzerland to Italy for the winter.

Phillips had now been in Europe more than a year and a half, and the charm of the old world was beginning to pall. The Puritan in him rebelled against the dilettante pleasures of expatriate life. He had seen too many monuments, too many quaintly antique villages, too many Alpine peaks and waterfalls. When he jokingly passed on to Elizabeth Pease the story about the American who refused to visit the site of a famous European cataract for fear "such curiosity would seem a reflection on Niagara," he was able to smile more out of sympathy than condescension. Obediently following Ann to a famous mist-covered waterfall in Switzerland, Wendell found that his own power to marvel was exhausted. All he could think of was "a man standing up there and throwing over shovels full of powdered sugar." [32]

From Naples in the spring of 1841, Phillips was describing their journey as this "melancholy tour" which constantly threw up to them "the painful contrasts . . . wealth beyond that of fairy tales, and poverty all bare and starved by its side." He had roamed among the ruins and visited the splendors of Rome and Florence, but these served only to quicken a sense of duty. "The Apollo himself," he wrote to Garrison, "cannot dazzle one blind to the rags, want and misery which surround him. Nature is not wholly beautiful. For even when she marries a matchless sky to her bay of Naples, the impression is saddened by the presence of degraded and suffering humanity." [33]

These sobering thoughts were called forth by an awareness that he had reached a turning point in life. He knew what his mother and the rest of his family expected of this journey: that he would come back refreshed and cured of all his radical fancies. He could sympathize somewhat with his mother's warnings that he was in danger of being carried away by a new and momentary excitement. He knew also that this would have to be a year of decision. He was almost thirty years old, with an invalid wife to care for. Aside from the personal satisfaction that his labors with the abolitionists had brought, he had come to recognize his own exceptional gift for oratory, the one almost indispensable talent for success in American public life. The decision was not simply whether the abolitionists were right or wrong but whether he should give his life to the cause of antislavery in America. By April 1841 he had thought the matter through, and he was able to write candidly to Garrison of this reappraisal: "I recognize in

some degree the truth of the assertion that associations tend
to destroy individual independence; and I have found difficulty in answering others, however clear my own mind
might be, when charged with taking steps which the sober
judgment of age would regret,—with being hurried recklessly forward by the enthusiasm of the moment and the
excitement of heated meetings. I am glad, therefore, to
have the opportunity of holding up the cause, with all its
incidents and bearings calmly before my own mind; . . .
of being able to look back, cleared of all excitement,
though not I hope of all enthusiasm . . . upon the course
we have taken the last few years; and . . . I am rejoiced
to say that every hour of such thought convinces me more
and more of the overwhelming claims our cause has in the
life-long devotion of each of us." [34]

These were his thoughts as he and Ann waited out
the winter and early spring of 1841. And, occasionally,
while meandering through the narrow-vaulted streets in
Naples, he would catch a glimpse of a dusky African face
and be reminded that it was time to go home.

6

The Church, the Negro and the Irishman 1841–1850

The trip back to Boston aboard the Caledonia in July 1841 was not very pleasant. Richard Webb had come down to see the Phillipses off at Liverpool, and Ann wrote him later that the stateroom he had seen turned out to be their "sick room for 13 days and nights." In moments of desperation she and Wendell had even sampled the medicinal properties of the whiskey jug which Webb had provided. Whenever he could, Wendell left his bunk to pace the deck and preach abolition. The passengers, wealthy merchants and slaveholders for the most part, were apparently not impressed with the young, seasick reformer, for Ann wrote that the captain was the only man to give him a sympathetic hearing.[1] Phillips was already learning that the abolitionist's path was a lonely one; he would soon discover that he could not raise his hand to help the slave without at the same time separating himself from his class, his family and his church.

At first it was good to be back. After two years abroad there was plenty to talk about, and the Phillips' summer house on Nahant was overflowing with the families of Wendell's brothers and sisters, all anxious to hear the latest news of Europe. Being part of the family routine again was pleasant. "We rise about seven," Ann wrote to Elizabeth Pease, "breakfast at half-past. Wendell rows the boat for excercise; bathes. I walk with him in the morning; dine at two; in the afternoon we ride with Mother; tea at seven; in the evening we play chess or backgammon with her, or some brother and sister come to spend the night, and we dispute away on the great questions." [2]

Once the novelty of their return began to wear thin, however, and all the anecdotes relating to their journey had been told and retold, Wendell and Ann found that they had come home to an alien household. Whenever the family discussions touched on abolitionism, they were looked upon "as heretics and almost infidels." [3] The old matriarch, Sarah Walley Phillips, was still revolted by the subject, and the rest of the family was growing up in her image. If Wendell had not realized it before, he must have seen now (with what sense of melancholy or horror we can only imagine) that most of the shades of proslavery opinion corrupting the North were represented in his own family. Not that any of the Phillipses would have explicitly defended slavery; it was just that each member of Wendell's family found some good reason for not denouncing it. For his mother it was enough to know that the antislavery cause was violently controversial and could put the family name in a bad light. Wendell's older brother Thomas, clerk of the municipal court in Boston, undoubtedly looked on the whole subject with the wary eye of the politician trained to skirt divisive moral issues. Another brother, George William, a thriving Boston lawyer already established in a handsome estate in Saugus, probably saw the abolitionists as seditious agents attempting to undermine the country's prosperity. As if this were not enough, his pontifical brother-in-law, the Reverend George Washington Blagden, was convinced that the abolitionists were lacking in Christian charity.

The situation was difficult enough, Ann confessed in a letter to Elizabeth Pease, when Wendell was on the ground, but when he was off lecturing for two or three days it was almost intolerable. There were too many Phillipses around, and she discovered that she had almost nothing in common with any of them except the one she had married. "I do not feel right in this atmosphere," she

complained, "and like Rip Van Winkle am ready to
exclaim 'I'm not myself. I am somebody else—that's me
yonder.' " [4]

Wendell's mother had expected him to return from
Europe a changed man, ready to settle down and be a
proper Bostonian like his father, but the society of Nahant
and Beacon Street interested him no more now than it
had two years earlier. On August 2 the Massachusetts
Anti-Slavery Society held a public meeting in Chardon
Street Chapel in Boston for the purpose of welcoming
Phillips. After the meeting Wendell, Samuel May, Maria
Weston Chapman and the Weston sisters, fierce abolitionists all, had tea together and spent the evening in
Parkman's Hall, where the leaders of Boston's colored
population had assembled to honor David Ruggles, a
prominent Negro publisher from New York. Describing
the affair to Elizabeth Pease, Phillips mentioned the gay
banners, "showy dresses, happy faces—eyes brighter than
they'd ever been before. . . . The colored people seemed
living the whole night in Elysium, having got above the
murky atmosphere of . . . prejudice." [5] It was his for-
saking Boston society for this kind of Nigger Hill society
that Beacon Hill could never forgive and Sarah Walley
Phillips could never understand.

In November 1841, Wendell and Ann moved to
Boston to live in a narrow, three-story brick house on
Essex Street which Ann had inherited from her father.
Neither the house nor the location was fashionable.
Thomas Wentworth Higginson remembered the place as
"plain and bare without and within . . . almost home-
less outside the walls of Mrs. Phillips' apartment." [6] It
was intentionally small—kitchen and dining room on the
first floor, study on the second, bedrooms on the third—
lest there be any temptation to entertain.

From the moment they moved in, Ann began to spend
more and more time in her room. So far as her health was
concerned, the trip abroad had been a failure. As her old
complaints continued to hang on—headaches to prevent

her from reading, rheumatism so painful she was forced to ask Wendell to answer her personal correspondence— she began to retreat more and more from society. Her letters at this time express a growing preoccupation with her own unhappiness and despair that the rest of the world could not understand her misery. Even before leaving England she had confided to Elizabeth Pease that since her illness "the world has worn quite another aspect to me, for many that I thought friends have fallen off, and many have misunderstood the nature of my state of health so much that there is no pleasure in communication with them." [7] Shortly after moving into the Essex Street house she complained that all of her time was spent shuttling between bed, sofa and rocking chair in her own room. She was unable to read, write, see company or make calls, and she wryly advised a friend that good health was "as hard to regain as lost virtue." [8]

Year after year the same melancholy note is sounded in all her letters; the girl who had so indignantly objected to being seated behind a curtain at the world antislavery convention a few years before was now voluntarily shutting herself off from the rest of the world. "I have been miserably sick the last 2 years and am sadder and more careworn. . . . It is my own fault though, for if I had perfect trust in God I should not repine as years (oh! how many) passed in sickness." [9] In February 1845 she wrote, "I have had a dreadful winter, so sick that life is a burden to me, I do not know what to do. I am tired of suffering. I have no faith in anything." [10] And the next year, "I grow sicker every year, Wendell lovelier, I more desponding. . . . For his sake I should love to live, for my own part I am tired. . . ." [11]

Despite the few girlish enthusiasms that remained— for flowers in her room, spring birds outside her window, the lilting serenade of organ music drifting up from the street—Ann's mood was frequently melancholy. "I never ask anyone to write me" she told Helen Garrison, "because I know I shall not answer and I do not like to appear ungrateful." [12] And in the midst of her friend's loneliness, during one of Garrison's extended trips to England, Ann's cheerless counsel was: "We *should* love them dearly for that is right; but always bear in mind that the Lord gave and the Lord *may* take away." [13]

Except for one brief period in 1848, Wendell was usually in radiant health. It must have been difficult, therefore, for him to realize that he was married to a chronic invalid, that there would probably be no children, that he must always go alone to the antislavery meetings and celebrations. Not that he ever showed these feelings. Melancholy and despair were alien to his temperament. He always lived on hope for the future, whether the cause was social reform or Ann's health. They began to accumulate a library of "cure" literature. "We are beginning to look somewhat like Hydropathy with hope," he wrote to Elizabeth Pease in 1844.[14] Two years later they were trying mesmerism, and Ann reported that "the poor, devoted Wendell is caught one hour of his busy day and seated down to *hold my thumbs.*" [15]

Every summer Phillips would virtually call a halt to all other activity so that he could take Ann off to a country house, away from the heat of the city. One July afternoon in 1846, when they were staying in Natick, Edmund Quincy came by for a visit. He found Wendell trying to fight off boredom by picking blackberries, and Ann in her customary condition. "His wife looked to me," Quincy wrote to a friend, "better than I ever saw her, which was very few times in my life. But they told me she was very ill. It is one of those mysterious complaints in which organic disease is mixed up with a good deal that is imaginary. But this is a dead secret, for neither of them would ever forgive such a suggestion. The end of it will be, I have no doubt, what a physician said of a connexion of my own in somewhat similar condition . . . Long Life!" [16]

Quincy was right; despite her countless infirmities, Ann Phillips was to outlive her husband. The only

contemporary medical report on her condition from the
family physician suggests that she suffered from "some
defect in nervous organization." [17] Others besides Edmund
Quincy spoke less mysteriously of a *malade imaginaire,*
but no one dared to mention that possibility to Wendell.
A later generation of physicians would probably classify
Ann Phillips as "neurasthenic" or "constitutionally inad-
equate." Such a person is easily fatigued, attacked by an
enormous variety of aches and pains, subject to periodic
bouts of melancholy and simply not fit for the stress of
normal living.[18]

In the absence of a fuller medical record, it is fruitless
to probe deeply into the causes of Ann Phillips' illness. It
is important, however, to understand the effect of her
sickness on Wendell. Phillips' Victorian biographers are
very sentimental on this point and insist that the man's
lifelong devotion and personal care of his invalid wife
prove that the marriage was idyllic. The modern observer
is more tempted to emphasize the tragedy in such a situation and to look for side effects on Phillips' own personality and career. Certainly from 1841 until he died in
1884, nothing loomed larger in Wendell's mind than the
fact of his wife's illness. He would never accept a lecturing engagement without first consulting her, and sometimes he would find her condition so precarious that
for months at a time he would refuse to leave Boston
for any reason. Although on some occasions in her
correspondence Ann sounded the note of the petulant
invalid, as for example when she wrote to Elizabeth
Pease that Wendell was so busy "that we seem to have no
time to think of health," [19] everything indicates that the
married life of Wendell and Ann Phillips was one of love
and understanding. It was, however, a very restricted and
private life. There were no parties and no house guests,
for they excluded themselves absolutely from social life
of any kind. In a marriage without children, and perhaps
without sexual satisfaction, Wendell and his wife would
ultimately come to find one of their strongest bonds in

the fact that they were able to bear the burden of her affliction together.

Another bond was to be found in Wendell's career as a reformer. Because he was denied many of the satisfactions of married life, Phillips had more energy to pour into reform efforts. It would be wrong, however, to consider this as an escape from his wife, for it was she who had helped to show Wendell the rich possibilities of such a career, and despite her physical complaints she continued to take a militant interest in abolitionism and feminism. Edmund Quincy, who probably saw as much of Ann during the 1840s as any of Wendell's friends, nicknamed her "The Countess" and frequently remarked that she could be as vigorous and sprightly in conversation as her husband and just as strong-minded.[20]

Moving into their new house was hectic for the Phillipses, as might be expected for any young couple establishing their first home. Wendell liked to putter and did most of the minor carpentry himself. He was less successful in dealing with the servants. The cook took sick, and the maid, an intractable young lady who "like the zebra appeared to be beyond taming," presented problems completely new to his experience.[21] Things soon settled down, however, and a domestic routine began to develop. Ann spent most of her time in her sunny third-floor apartment, tending her flower box or, when her eyes felt strong enough, reading the *Liberator* and *Anti-Slavery Standard*.[22] She and Wendell took their meals over a tiny table in her room and talked to each other in French. When Wendell was not off lecturing or at a meeting, he stayed in his study, trying to keep up with the numerous British and American journals to which he subscribed. He continued his studies in history and biography, kept up his Latin to the extent of reading one classic a year and began to compile a library of antislavery literature that would soon be the envy of every abolitionist in Boston.[23]

If the Essex Street place was not fashionably located,

from a Beacon Street point of view, it was certainly a convenient house for an abolitionist. A five-minute walk to the south brought Phillips to Francis Jackson's door and the home of Mary and Sam May on Hollis Street. Lloyd and Helen Garrison lived nearby on Dix Place, and a little farther to the north were Ellis Loring's house on Winter Street and the Chapman's residence on Chauncy Street, a favorite meeting place for abolitionists. Theodore Parker's house on Exeter Place was almost in Phillips' backyard.

For some time after his return from Europe, Phillips continued to give part of his time to the practice of law, probably as much to help his younger brother, Grenville, get established as for any other reason.[24] Most of the money he earned at this time, however, came from lecturing fees. Phillips had begun to develop his reputation as a lyceum speaker even before he was married, and his lecture entitled "The Lost Arts," destined to become one of the most frequently repeated lectures in American history, was already widely known in New England. Drawing on his experiences abroad, Phillips had prepared other lectures, including a very popular one on "Street Life in Europe," and within two months of his return to Boston he was confronted with more lyceum requests than he could handle.[25] He tried to make these lectures entertaining and instructive, reserving his radical abolitionist opinions for the antislavery platform. The result was that, as his fame as an orator grew, whenever he visited a given community more and more people came to hear him, no matter what subject he considered. Before the decade was out, Phillips' eloquence alone did much to enlarge the audience for abolitionists in New England.

In 1843, Phillips was appointed to the executive committee of the American Anti-Slavery Society, and the following year he took over the duties of recording secretary. This committee, which met twelve to twenty times a year and was dominated for the most party by Bostonians like Garrison, Phillips, Edmund Quincy, Francis Jackson and Maria Chapman, transacted all of the business for the society and supervised the editing of the *National Anti-Slavery Standard,* which was published in New York. Becoming more and more engrossed in abolitionist work, Phillips served as general agent for the society throughout most of the 1840s. In this capacity he supervised the work of lecturing agents in the field, arranged for their payment and drew up their itineraries. If he didn't know already, Phillips soon found out that no one could get rich by being a professional abolitionist lecturer. Although salaries varied slightly from year to year, a typical agent in the field might get twelve dollars a week, with the understanding that he pay his own expenses or raise half his salary in donations.[26]

Not long after he and Ann returned from Europe, Phillips was invited to tea at the house of an eminent Boston minister. The other guests were three Negroes— the abolitionist Lunsford Lane, Frederick Douglass, the celebrated escaped slave, and a third, very black man by the name of Jones. The hostesses for this occasion were the minister's two abolitionist daughters. Before the guests sat down to table, Abbott Lawrence called. Lawrence was a very wellborn Bostonian who would one day side with the abolitionists but who was not yet converted. Lawrence was first introduced to Phillips and responded with a low bow and "How do you do, sir." Then came the light-complexioned Douglass; Lawrence bowed again and said, "How do you do." He was followed by Lunsford Lane, ten shades darker; Lawrence bowed without speaking. Finally the coal-black Mr. Jones was presented, and Abbott Lawrence "turned on his heel," insulted.[27]

In later years Phillips would tell this as a humorous anecdote. The experience at the time, however, served only to confirm his opinion that one of the most important goals for New England abolitionists was to combat racial prejudice and to improve the condition of northern Negroes. He had first enlisted his own efforts in this behalf back in 1839, when he had supported the petition of a group of Salem ladies urging the legislature to repeal the law prohibiting marriage between Negroes and whites. The petition had caused quite a storm in the legislature, and some idea of the low esteem in which Massachusetts Negroes were held at this time can be deduced from the language of the Judiciary Committee, to which the petition was referred. "Lest future historians should form an erroneous estimate of the manners and morals of the age," wrote the lawmakers, "it is desirable to afford these persons, styling themselves ladies, an opportunity to reconsider their opinions on matrimonial and constitutional rights and remove their names from the petition." [28] It was not enough to quash the petition; it had to be ridiculed as well. During each of the following two years, new attempts were made to repeal this odious law.   In 1841 the senate passed a repeal measure that was voted down by the other house after a violent debate, in the course of which one representative said he "would rather follow his daughter to the tomb than have her marry a black man." [29] The law was finally repealed in 1842, largely through the efforts of the abolitionists, and during the early and middle 1840s Wendell Phillips played an important role in the continuing struggle to win the rights of citizenship for northern Negroes.

That there should have been so much controversy over a bill to legalize intermarriage is not surprising when one considers the wide range of humiliation that New England Negroes were expected to endure at the time. In Rhode Island, for example, a Bastardy Act provided that no unmarried colored woman could charge any white man with begetting her child. The act was repealed in 1844 by the margin of a single vote. [30] Negroes were kept out of the public schools altogether or provided with inferior segregated facilities. The color line was as rigidly drawn in the churches as anywhere else. In 1835 a prosperous Boston Negro purchased a pew on the floor of Park Street Church. His fellow worshipers promptly nailed up the door of the pew, and the trustees refunded his money and ejected him from the congregation.[31]

To Phillips, the practice of such discrimination was as sinful as slaveholding—and for the same reason. The Negro, as Garrison loudly proclaimed in the *Liberator,* was a brother and a man, equal in the eyes of God and deserving equal treatment at the hands of men. This argument for equality was primarily moral. Most of the abolitionists cared little for "scientific" treatises on racial equality, but they were ready to admit that, whatever its cause, prejudice involving color was a real force which could not be disposed of lightly. Some of them knew this from personal experience. A staunch abolitionist like Henry Bowditch could honestly recall that his first public appearance on the streets of Boston beside Frederick Douglass, most famous of all the escaped slaves, had been painful. He had invited Douglass to dine with him, and he confessed that throughout their trip from Marlboro Chapel to Bedford Street he had been nervous and afraid that he might encounter friends along the way. "It was . . . somewhat like a cold sponge bath" he said, "that Washington Street walk by the side of a black man, —rather terrible at the outset, but wonderfully warming and refreshing afterwards."[32] Maria Chapman admitted in an editorial in the *Liberator* that social intercourse with Negroes seemed to be difficult for most white people, but abolitionists should know that the real reason for this was a fear of what others would say. She advised her readers to heed Franklin's warning that "The eyes of other people are the eyes that ruin us."[33]

Except for a tendency to think of Negros as being naturally more imitative than whites (a common fallacy at that time), Phillips was inclined to credit the Negro with all of the ability of the white man. He did not share Harriet Beecher Stowe's belief in the superiority of the mulatto over the black man, and he emphatically disagreed with Theodore Parker's contention that the Negro lacked courage. He eventually prepared a popular lecture on the career of Toussaint L'Ouverture to prove his position. In his judgments of individual Negroes, Phillips strove to be objective. Charles Remond, a Negro leader from Salem, was a long-time friend and a prominent lecturer for the Garrisonians. Phillips appreciated Remond's talents and his service to the cause but felt that he tried too hard to imitate the manners of his white friends. After Remond returned home from an extended lecture tour in England, Phillips complained in a letter to Elizabeth Pease that "English and Irish flattery" had ruined him "for sober matter of fact home toil," and he concluded with the unsentimental observation that Remond had "some foolish ways." [34] This judgment was probably reinforced a few years later when he heard that Remond and another antislavery lecturer in upstate New York had sold a blind horse to a faithful abolitionist and were "more notorious as horse jockeys than as abolitionists." [35] For Frederick Douglass, who had come out of slavery in 1838 to become one of the most dynamic of abolitionist orators, Phillips had unqualified praise. "Language, taste, fancy-eloquence-vigour of thoughts, good sound common sense—manliness are all his," he wrote to Elizabeth Pease. "He never thinks of his color and we never do. He is one of our ablest men." [36]

Phillips' experience in Europe—the sight of a Negro guard at Napoleon's Tomb, Negroes and whites mixing freely together in the Tuileries, colored priests assisting with the mass in St. Peter's—had strengthened his resolve to help the Negroes in Massachusetts when he returned.[37] It was this resolve that brought him before a committee of the state legislature in February 1842.

It was the practice of many New England railroads at this time to provide separate cars for Negro passengers. In July 1841, David Ruggles, a Negro leader in New York, was thrown off a car on the New Bedford line for trying to sit with white passengers. Two weeks earlier he had been assaulted by the captain of a boat running from New

Bedford to Nantucket for attempting to purchase a ticket
with first-class privileges.[38] This was the typical treatment
for Negroes who attempted to cross the color line in public
transportation.

Phillips had traveled with Negroes and knew at
firsthand something of their humiliation. Thus, when he
represented the abolitionists before the Committee on
Railroad Corporations, he must have spoken with real
conviction. In urging the state to prevent railroads from
running segregated cars, he presented an argument which
sounds familiar to modern ears. The speech is a lawyer's
brief, clear-cut, well reasoned, with cases cited to support
two contentions: first, that the state has a right to control
the railroads in such matters; second, that the individual
citizen has a right to equal treatment by a common carrier.
"These corporations are public servants," he argued, "and
are therefore bound to serve in accordance with the laws
of the Commonwealth. . . . It is as *public highways,*
that they hold their various privileges and immunities. It
is not as individuals that they should be dealt with . . .
but it is as corporations, existing for the public service
and the public good. . . ." [39]

Four days after this speech the committee brought to
the legislature a report which followed Phillips' reasoning
very closely. Although the recommended bill prohibiting
discrimination was stalled in the senate, the abolitionists
won a clear-cut victory when the railroads, under threat
of compulsory legislation, voluntarily stopped discriminating against Negro passengers in Massachusetts.[40]

It was natural that Phillips should have been drawn
also into the fight for equal rights in public education.
In February 1846 a group of Boston Negroes petitioned
the Boston School Committee for the abolition of separate
primary schools for colored children. The majority of
the members of the primary school committee showed
little patience with the petition. Separate schools for
Negroes in Boston dated back to 1812. The separation was
not made because of prejudice against color, the commit-

tee maintained, but on the basis of the natural differences between the races. "The distinction is one which the all-wise Creator has seen fit to establish and it is founded deep in the physical, mental, and moral natures of the two races. No legislation, no social customs, can efface this distinction . . . we only state a notorious and undeniable fact." [41] In vain did two lonely members of the committee, Edmund Jackson and Henry Bowditch, protest that other towns in Massachusetts had successfully integrated their schools, that the degraded condition of Negroes did not warrant, but resulted from, segregation. One does not argue with "notorious and undeniable" facts.

Phillips first attracted public attention in the struggle against segregated schools in Boston in August 1846. After the legality of separate schools had been challenged, the school committee asked for an opinion on the subject from the city solicitor. The *Liberator* for August 28, 1846, printed a copy of the solicitor's report and followed it with a long critical essay by its own legal authority, Wendell Phillips. The solicitor had found that under state law the Boston School Committee had a right to regulate city schools in any reasonable manner, so long as this regulation could be justified as being in the best interests of the children concerned. He decided that segregation could be so justified. Phillips, speaking now more as the wrathful moralist than the sober lawyer, prefaced his remarks with a few words calculated to destroy the city solicitor, a hapless gentleman by the name of Chandler. "We were among those," he began, "who mourned the death of the late able city solicitor, John Pickering . . . he had one marked characteristic, preeminently fitting him for public life—an unbending integrity." Then, before closing with the issue itself, he shot a blast at the school committee, saying, "It has long been one of the avowed evils of our city and town organizations, that some important powers are necessarily committed, at times, to very small men." So far as the

meat of the argument was concerned, Phillips attempted
to show that segregation was based on an assumed
difference between the races, that if the implicit assumptions of this were pursued logically, they would lead to a
rigid caste system comparable to that in India.[42]

It is important to notice Phillips' tactics in dealing
with this question. Although he did not ignore the issue
at hand, or the specific arguments of his opponents, he
struck out at the public personalities involved with all of
the invective and sarcasm at his command. While discussing Chandler's opinion, for example, Phillips remarked, in
passing, that legal reputations have a way of tarnishing
when confronted with cases involving slavery and Negroes.
"Even Story," he said, "sullied at last the lustre of a long
life by a decision, the infamy of which even his large
services cannot hide."

The allusion was to Judge Story, Phillips' former law
teacher and Supreme Court Justice, for a decision regarding fugitive slaves. Story had recently died, but his star
still hung bright on the Boston horizon, and the local
press was quick to retaliate for this slur on his memory.
"The ruthless intolerance of Mr. Phillips," wrote an anonymous correspondent to the Boston *Daily Advertiser*, "is
stronger than death and more pitiless than the grave."
Phillips replied with a statement indicating the philosophy
which would guide his criticism of public figures from that
time on. "If to criticize freely the actions of public men
after their death be ruthless and intolerant, how is history
to be written. . . . He wholly forgets the distinction between public and private men. The sanctity of private
life is not to be violated either before or after death. But
when a man puts on the robes of office, his acts become
the property of the nation, and every man, on fitting occasion, may summon them to the bar of public opinion." [43]

In addition to his reference to Story, Phillips had
mentioned also "the timid silence of Horace Mann" on
the segregation issue. Mann, secretary of the Massachusetts
Board of Education and already famous for his pioneer-

ing efforts in public education, refused to rise to the bait. A year later the publication of the board's annual report brought Mann under Phillips' fire again. In a long letter to the *Liberator,* Phillips asked how Mann could reconcile the high-minded language of his report with the fact that a part of Boston's citizenry were arbitrarily denied their right to equal opportunity in education. Phillips believed he knew the answer: Mann was trying to avoid con-troversy; he was compromising with the truth. "Horace Mann represents quite a large class who think they worship Truth," Phillips contended, "but honestly deem it best to sacrifice one half of their deity to secure the rest. . . . Mr. Mann's timidity proceeds not from want of courage, not wholly from want of sincerity, but from want of faith. He is a politic man and stands weighing out the blood and morals of a despised class, buying, by his indifference thereto, well-ventilated school houses! new school books! physiological seats! broad playgrounds! and philosophical apparatus." [44]

Still, Mann held his peace, quite a feat in view of his own contentious personality and the fact that Phillips repeated his attack again in 1848.[45] He did not forget Phillips, however, and the two men, each a reformer in his own right, clashed bitterly a few years later.

Phillips had no personal animosity toward Horace Mann; he had never even met the gentleman, and in a letter to Elizabeth Pease four years earlier he had written, "I shall send you if I can find it *Mann's* 4th July oration on the state of this country—tis glorious." [46] To him the issue was very simple. Horace Mann, in his position of authority and prestige, could have done much for Negro students in Boston, but, because he was "a politic man," he kept silent. One of the great weaknesses of a democratic society, Phillips was beginning to see, was its tendency to produce politic leaders who shunned moral issues. The task of the reformer was to expose the leader and to force the issue.

His participation in the crusade for Boston Negroes

demonstrated to Phillips, twenty years before emancipation, that the Negro issue in America involved far
more than the abolition of slavery. The boy who had
grown up on Beacon Street when it was considered great
sport to stone Nigger Hill youngsters off the Common had
become the Negro's champion. Conscious of this role, he
was always careful to live out his convictions. When
traveling by train with a Negro, Phillips would insist on
sitting in the Jim Crow car with his companion. Once on
a steamer to New York, when Frederick Douglass was
denied a cabin, the Brahmin and the black man spent the
night together walking the deck. "He was one of the few
public men," Douglass recalled, "who remembered those in
bonds as bound with them." [47]

Negroes did not compose the only suppressed class in
Boston in the 1840s. The great influx of Irish immigrants
had already begun; by 1855 one out of every four
Bostonians would be able to boast of his birth on the
Emerald Isle. Phillips and Garrison saw at once that they
could strengthen their position in Boston immensely if
they could persuade the Irish to support the antislavery
crusade. The fact that Daniel O'Connell, still the great
hero of the American Irish, was an outspoken opponent
of slavery provided an opening wedge. In December 1841,
Charles Remond returned from England with a petition
containing the signatures of 60,000 Irishmen, including
those of O'Connell and Father Mathew, urging the American Irish to cooperate with abolitionists. A great meeting was held in Faneuil Hall for the purpose of receiving
the petition. Phillips gave the address and poured out all
his eloquence, invoking the memory and example of great
Irishmen like Burke and O'Connell, together with "a
long line of Popes from Leo to Gregory," to show that
America's Irish should support abolitionism.[48]

It was a shrewd attempt, but it was doomed from the
beginning. The temper of the immigrant was opposed
to that of the reformer. He had been taught to respect
distinctions of rank, to respect social institutions, to find

solace for his own miseries in religion. As a new arrival
to this country, he had no desire to attack an institution
which half the states supported, and, as an unskilled
laborer himself, he had no love for the Negro with whom
he competed in the labor market.

After the Irish press in Boston and New York had
begun to attack the abolitionists, Phillips' estimate of
Irishmen began to decline. They were an illiterate mass,
he confided to a friend in Dublin, manipulated by scheming leaders "to secure offices for hungry demagogues."
Still, there was strong sentiment in America for O'Connell,
and, if he would send "a startling scorching bitter unspar-
ing pointed rebuke . . . laugh, hoot, scorn, hiss, spit at
the recreant Irishman" who supports the slaveholder, all
would not be lost.[49] O'Connell kept silent, and by June
1842 the exasperated Phillips was referring to "his little
soul . . . the tool of bar room demagogues." "Well we
can do without him," he wrote to Richard Webb. "Anti-
slavery kisses no man's toe." [50] A year later O'Connell was
suddenly restored to grace. His strong statement against
slavery brought Phillips back to the platform in Faneuil
Hall in November 1843 to propose three cheers for Pope
Gregory and announce, "I cannot spare all O'Connell to
Irishmen. He belongs to the race—to liberty." [51]

Phillips' vacillating opinions as to the worth of
O'Connell are characteristic. He could never judge a man
except by a single standard, his own measure of the man's
value to the cause which Phillips served. This inability
to appreciate the essential complexity of human beings,
which would have been fatal to him as a novelist, or even
as a politician, did not hurt Phillips as a reformer, but it
did lead him to make preposterous estimates of men who
did not agree with him.

The campaign to lure Boston Irishmen into the anti-
slavery campaign continued rather fitfully throughout the
decade. In the summer of 1849 there was a brief flare-up
of excitement when Father Mathew came to town.

Mathew, world famous for his temperance work in Ireland and England, had been one of the signers of the anti-slavery petition in 1841. His hold over the Irish in America was so powerful that in one section of Boston thirteen of sixteen grog shops closed down after his visit.[52] When Phillips and Garrison tried to get Mathew to throw his influence against slavery, however, they were disappointed. His was a temperance mission, he said, and could not be jeopardized by association with other, more controversial matters. So far as Phillips was concerned, there was a simple explanation for Mathew's reluctance— it was Horace Mann all over again except for the clerical collar—the priest lacked principle and sought to "sacrifice one moral cause for another." [53]

Their attacks on Father Mathew did not improve the reputations of Phillips and Garrison among the Irish. Calling the former a "Termagant" philanthropist, and the latter "a fierce hearted son of an Inquisitor," the Boston *Pilot* blasted the attempt to lure "the amiable and moderate Father" down the false road of antislavery agitation.[54] To another man it might have been a depressing experience—this inability to get the oppressed of one class to help those in another—but Phillips was not a man to brood over defeat. The important thing for him was always to keep going forward. One of the reasons for the recalcitrance of the Irish he attributed to the unwillingness of the Catholic Church to risk its prestige by taking sides on the explosive slavery issue. It was a part of the great national hypocrisy perpetuated by churches of all denominations in America, this refusal to admit the sin of slavery, and the fight against it would go on no matter what became of Father Mathew.

A few weeks after his return from Europe, Phillips had written to his friend Richard Webb in Dublin that the Garrisonian abolitionists were planning to campaign against every church "which does not bear public, faithful, and constant testimony against slavery." Agitation over the right of petition was beginning to pall, he said, "but we can terrify the church the moment we begin to move." [55]

Organized Protestantism had long been a favorite target for Garrison, and his intemperate attacks upon it had helped to bring about the split in the antislavery movement in 1840. The causes of this resentment against what Maria Chapman harshly called "the black-hearted ministry" [56] are not hard to understand. Almost all of the abolitionists had enlisted in the cause through religious motivation, yet the churches seemed to want no part of the crusade. When Samuel May, himself a Unitarian minister, looked back on the problems which abolitionists faced in the 1830s and '40s, he concluded that "the most serious obstacle" had been "the conduct of the clergy and the churches in our country." [57]

During the early years of the New England Anti-Slavery Society, Boston churches would not allow their meetinghouses to be used by abolitionists. In some cases, announcements of antislavery meetings could not be read from the pulpit. So difficult was it to get a white minister to open an antislavery meeting with a prayer that the abolitionists in Boston had to rely heavily on the blessings of Father Snowden from Nigger Hill. Snowden was a kind of colored Father Mapple, who specialized in unsophisticated but vigorous prayers that went directly to the point: "O God! We pray that that seven-headed, ten-horned monster, the Colonization Society, may be smitten through and through with the fiery darts of Truth, and tormented as the whale is between the swordfish and the thresher." [58] It was appropriate that abolitionists be prayed over by a Negro, but this did not lessen their fury against the recreant preachers in pulpits once manned by Cottons, Hookers, Mathers and Mayhews.

Phillips and the other New England abolitionists believed that the failure of the Northern churches to come out against slavery could be explained in two ways. First, individual ministers were afraid to speak the truth and

risk offending wealthy parishioners who feared that abolitionists would disrupt business. Secondly, churchmen in
the North, whatever their own doubts about slavery, did
not want to alienate their slave-holding brethren in the
South. This was understandable from an intellectual point
of view, but from a moral point of view, from a religious
point of view, it was incomprehensible. The abolitionists'
duty, then, was to rebuke the "black-hearted ministry" as
vigorously as they did the slaveholder.

Although most of the abolitionists around Garrison
were either transcendentalists or Calvinists, they felt particularly grieved by the refusal of the Unitarians to come
to their aid. Boston was the Unitarian stronghold, and
Unitarians represented themselves as the most liberal of all
denominations, yet with very few exceptions they refused
to cooperate with abolitionists. "A more pitiful class of
men could hardly be found in any country," declared
Edmund Quincy bitterly in 1844. "They have the united
faults of a small established priesthood and of an dissenting
chapelocracy. The Unitarians are the rich and well educated as a general thing. They have men to preach to them
who can write essays that will not shock their taste, and
with the tacit understanding that they will never preach
anything that would make them uncomfortable. . . .
They are of that incongruous class of hybrids, radico-con-
servatives, their radicalism consisted only in rejecting the
five points of Calvinism. . . ." [59] Quincy's estimate
seemed to have been borne out at the annual meeting of
the denomination that same year, when Samuel May could
not even get his fellow Unitarian ministers to pass a resolution declaring slavery un-Christian. The principal objec-
tion to the resolution was that it would offend Southern
Unitarians by appearing to identify the denomination
with what one minister called the "diabolical spirit" of
William Lloyd Garrison.[60] If the abolitionists received
such a cold reception from Unitarians, who had little support in the South, what could they expect from the stronger
sects, the Methodists, Baptists and Presbyterians?

Stephen Symonds Foster, a raw-boned New Hampshire farmer who had forsaken a career in the ministry for the itinerant life of an antislavery lecturer, delivered up the most radical indictment against the churches for the Garrisonians. Foster, who took pride in having been mobbed and jailed more frequently than any other abolitionist, was lecturing in Nantucket in 1843. In the course of his remarks he said "that the American church and clergy, as a body, were thieves, adulterers, manstealers, pirates and murderers—that the Methodist-Episcopal Church was more corrupt and profligate than any house of ill fame in New York—that the Southern ministers of that body were desirous of perpetuating slavery for the purpose of supplying themselves with concubines—that many of our clergymen were guilty of enormities that would disgrace an Algerine pirate!" Foster didn't get to finish the speech and was lucky to escape from the island with his life. Later, however, he made a fuller statement on the subject and published it in a sixty-four-page pamphlet entitled *The Brotherhood of Thieves or A True Picture of The American Church and Clergy.* The pamphlet, like a good many examples of abolitionist propaganda, is not as wild as its title suggests. After defending his strong language by comparing it to the language which Jesus used to chastise the Pharisees, Foster presented the essential case of the abolitionist against the church in America. Slavery, he pointed out, is stealing, the stealing of a human being's freedom. He provided statistics to show how many ministers and church members owned slaves and were thieves to this extent. He proceeded to indicate the ways in which the churches of the North supported those in the South—hence the "Brotherhood of Thieves." [61]

Wendell Phillips' attitude toward the church was far different from that of Foster, a man who had come to have little faith in organized religion, slavery or no slavery. Phillips had been brought up an orthodox believer in the Old South Church, whose meetinghouse had played such an illustrious role in American history, and he had been taught to take his religious obligations seriously. "For the church," he later recalled, "I had been bred to an unmixed and unlimited respect. I supposed that under its altar was enshrined all American virtue, and that almost all that was good in our institutions had grown up under its influence." [62] As he was drawn into the ranks of the antislavery cause, he was amazed to find the church, which wielded such enormous power over public opinion ("The eloquence of Webster or of Clay is but a whisper compared with the daily droppings of the New England pulpit!"), [63] remaining silent. Only gradually did it dawn on him that, although the church retained its influence, it had lost its spirit, that churchgoing America remained unregenerate because slavery was so bound up with the economic welfare of the country that it intimidated politicians, congregations and ministers alike. His mistake had been in putting slavery off at a distance, in seeing "the trunk of the tree growing out of Southern soil, without the slightest conception that its broad reaching roots . . . penetrated every altar of New England." [64]

There is an interesting element of personal drama in Wendell Phillips' war against the churches of New England. Since 1831 his sister Miriam had been married to the Reverend George Washington Blagden, minister to the Old South Church, where the Phillipses had been members for generations. Blagden came from Washington, D. C., and had attended Yale, where as an undergraduate he had distinguished himself by helping the administration put down a student riot. He had been a friend of the standing order ever since. [65] On April 8, 1847, Blagden preached a Fast Day sermon entitled "A Discourse on Slavery," in which he argued: The position of the abolitionists is unscriptural, slavery being recognized in both the Old and New Testaments; the truly Christian position is to attack sin wherever it is found; slavery can be attacked to the extent that it encourages sin, but the institution itself cannot be recklessly denounced as un-Christian.

About the sins of slavery, Blagden had this to say: "They form a theme for passionate declamation and oratorical display, which affords one of the best opportunities that has ever been offered, for public speakers of warm feelings and vivid imaginations to distinguish themselves. Too many, I fear, have eloquently exposed and deprecated the evils without troubling themselves to go into that patient study of the whole subject which alone can lead to those proper distinctions between things that differ, that can effect any permanent remedy." [66] Blagden addressed this admonition to his congregation, but he was almost certainly thinking of his brother-in-law Wendell Phillips.

Wendell, however, would not have been at hand that morning to hear these condescending words, for he had withdrawn from the church—like every other good New England abolitionist—several years earlier, probably in 1842. In endorsing this campaign to make people "come out" of the churches, he still professed to believe "that both church and ministry are appointed of God." He left the church to worship in his own parlor for the same reason which led him to break with his family and would soon bring about his personal secession from the Union. He did not even attempt to justify the step on the ground that it would help free the slave. With Phillips it was simply a moral obligation to renounce any person and organization not arrayed against the national sin. "I was not sent to abolish slavery," he said. "I was sent to DO MY DUTY." [67]

So far as his clerical brother-in-law was concerned, Wendell preferred to claim his kinship with the Reverend George Phillips, who had come to Massachusetts in the *Arbella* in 1630 to put the Atlantic Ocean between himself and a corrupt church.[68]

7

Phillips and the Cranks
1841–1850

Wendell Phillips was thirty-three years old when
Abby Folsom called him an "ass." It happened at an
abolitionist meeting in Boston's Marlboro Chapel in May
1844. The hall was crowded, and Phillips had been explaining the financial plight of the antislavery society when
Abby took over the pulpit and began to harangue the
audience with her own ideas on free speech and female
democracy. When Wendell heard the voice reaching up
like a cracked trumpet to overpower his own, he stopped
talking. Abby was a notorious figure at reform meetings
in Boston. Some of the reformers referred to her as "an
innocent monomaniac"; to everyone else she was just plain
crazy. Her monomania, if that was what it was, consisted
of a compulsion to enter public meetings, seize the platforms without invitation and speak her mind as long as
her own inspiration or the patience of the audience allowed. She couldn't be hissed down; this was tried once,
and a Boston paper remarked, "They might as well have
drowned a leviathan in a mug of hard cider." The only
solution was to let her run down or to throw her out.
Phillips saw that, on this occasion, Abby was prepared for
a long siege. As he approached to escort her out of the hall,
she began to sink to the floor. Stephen Foster ran up and
slipped a chair under the sagging but still vocal woman,
and Phillips, Foster and another abolitionist carried her
away. As they reached the door, Abby bellowed out that
she was more blessed than the Master: "He had but one

ass to carry him and I have three." Once outside she said
God had been glorified enough for one day and that she
would go home. She shook hands with the befuddled
Phillips and left.[1]

There were a great many exotic characters like Abby
Folsom associated with the antislavery movement, and in
the decade of the forties Phillips came to know most of
them. Some of them, like Abby, plagued the movement;
others contributed to its vigor. The spirit of reform and
change was sweeping over the land in those days, and every
new idea, no matter how fanciful, was sure to get a hearing.
It was almost as if this generation of Americans, like Adam
in the garden, was seeing the world for the first time and
was prepared to name everything anew. Crusty old John
Quincy Adams expressed well the mood of the time when
he confided to his diary in the summer of 1840:

> A young man, named Ralph Waldo Emerson . . . after failing
> in the everyday avocations of a Unitarian preacher and schoolmaster,
> starts a new doctrine of transcendentalism, declares all the old revela-
> tions superannuated and worn out and announces the approach of
> new revelations and prophecies. Garrison and the non-resistant aboli-
> tionists, Brownson and the Mount Democrats, phrenology and ani-
> mal magnetism, all come in, furnishing each some plausible rascality
> as an ingredient for the bubbling of religion and politics.[2]

A few months after Phillips had come back from
Europe, a great congress of reformers met in the Chardon
Street Chapel in Boston, and he had an opportunity to
observe the people with whom he had cast his lot. A little
paper in Hingham captured the spirit of the occasion.

> Since the day of Pentecost, we don't believe such a conglomera-
> tion of strange tongues has ever been known. All sorts of things were
> said by all sorts of persons on all sorts of subjects. Clergymen were
> there as well as laymen, Trinitarians and Unitarians, Transcendental-
> ists and Latterists, Universalists and Calvinists, Methodists and Bap-
> tists, Atheists and Deists, Mormons and Socialists, white men and

black men, men with beards and men without, No-money men and Anti-prosperity men, Cape Cod Come-outers and Latter Day Saints, Jews and Quakers, Dialists and Plain Speakers, Unionists and Perfectionists, Non Resistants, Abolitionists, Women Lecturers, Owenites, Grahamites, and all the *Ists* and *Ites,* the contented and discontented *ons* and *ans* that make up this queer compound called the world.[3]

Although Phillips was not an actual delegate to the Chardon Street convention, he soon became acquainted with the type. Many of them helped swell the ranks of Garrison's following. Phillips must have realized that Tappan and Birney were more than half right when they observed that Garrison had siphoned off all the cranks in the movement for himself. Certainly the gallery of eccentrics was colorful and full: Father Lawson with his long white beard and scythe and a compulsion like Abby Folsom's, Charles Burleigh with his rich-flowing tresses and beard to cultivate the resemblance to Christ, Henry C. Wright and his cold-shower-bath cult and a host of nameless zealots sustained by free love, faith healing and Dr. Sylvester Graham's diet of coarse bread and fruit.[4]

Wendell Phillips was as complete and devoted a reformer as any American has ever been, but he was never really at home with some of his stranger associates. He could sunder the ties which once bound him to Beacon Street society, but he could not destroy what Beacon Street had given him. He could devote his career to the people, but he could never really be one of them. Brahmin born and bred, Brahmin he would die; it was not easy for him, especially at the beginning, to be intimate with those whom, had they not been reformers, he would never have met. Of course, he could never admit this in public. "It is no sacrifice to me," he told a meeting of abolitionists on his return from Europe. "It is a delight—it is a privilege to act with such men as one meets in the anti-slavery cause." [5] Phillips' wife and his most intimate friends knew

better. "Poor Wendell," Miss Weston wrote to her sister
after having dined with Wendell and Ann, "told his trials
in going about the country—that he had to sleep with all
the cause, that he had slept with Douglass, to say nothing
of Foster." [6]

Phillips was most intimate with a small group among
the abolitionists which termed itself "The Boston Clique."
Maria Chapman ("The good Lord uses instruments for
His purpose I would not touch with a fifty-foot pole")[7] and
her sisters, Anne and Caroline Weston, and Edmund
Quincy were the other members of the group. Quincy, the
elegant descendant of a family almost as famous as the
Adamses, had also come into the cause after the Lovejoy
murder. He was a blue blood through and through, and,
except for James Russell Lowell, whose reform instinct
was always a little tepid, and Whittier, who served the non-
Garrisonian camp, Quincy was one of the few really accomplished antislavery writers. Not included in the Boston Clique but still representative of Boston wealth and
society were Francis Jackson and Amasa Walker, prosperous merchants, and two lawyers, Samuel Sewall and Ellis
Loring.

An English visitor to Boston who saw Phillips and
Edmund Quincy walking together down Park Street once
remarked that they were the only men he had seen in this
country "who looked like Gentlemen." [8] This helps to
explain why, of all the abolitionists, Phillips probably felt
most easy with Quincy at this time. The two had known
each other at Harvard, where Edmund's father, Josiah
Quincy, one of the most renowned men in the Commonwealth, had been president. Bred like Phillips out of an
aristocratic background, Edmund had been proceeding
rather aimlessly in life as a literary dilettante until the
Lovejoy affair swept him into the antislavery cause. A
genteel man with long sideburns and steel-rimmed spectacles, he lived with his family in a handsome estate in
Dedham. He was independently wealthy and quite conscious of his social position. "There is nothing in this

country except anti-slavery, that is worth a gentleman's notice," he once told an English friend. "Our politics are a kennel in which the dirtiest dog that rolls in it gets the most bones." [9] Phillips and Quincy hit it off well together because each recognized the other was a gentleman.

Although he was personally more intimate with Quincy, Phillips worked more closely with Garrison than with any other person. Garrison, whose shining pate and benign, bespectacled appearance reminded his friends more of Mr. Pickwick than the incendiary pictured by his enemies, was a true product of the age. He could not be happy unless he was reforming someone. Once on a trip through the White Mountains, he and Nathaniel Rogers noticed that the third member of their party, also an abolitionist, was smoking a cigar, desecrating "his *anti-slavery* mouth . . . with a stupefying tobacco weed." They kept after the hapless offender until the cigar tasted so bad he threw it away, promising to break the habit. "A revolution," exclaimed Garrison, swinging his cap over his head, "a glorious revolution without noise or *smoke* . . . antislavery wants her mouths for other uses than to be flues for besotting tobacco smoke." [10]

Still, for all his incorrigible reformer's zeal, Garrison was a shrewd professional journalist with an eye for the news value of the spectacular. In the same issue of the *Liberator* which carried Henry Wright's argument for "the immediate abolition of the army and navy," he also printed the following grisly notice: "MURDER—an awful murder was committed in a small town called Williamsport, Pa., by an Irishman named Lawrence Tierney, who beat his wife to death and then roasted her body by a slow fire." [11] Another time, under the bold headline MASTURBATION, he reviewed a book entitled *The Water Cure For Debilitated Young Men,* saying "It indicates a foul state of society, when the vice of self pollution, and the crimes of fornication and adultery, are deemed too indelicate for direct investigation. . . ." [12]

Unlike Phillips and Quincy, Garrison was in no sense

an intellectual. He was a reformer-journalist, and his approach to problems was usually simple and extreme. "Garrison is so used to standing alone," Lowell once complained, "that, like Daniel Boone, he moves away as the world creeps up to him, and goes farther *into the wilderness*. He considers every step a step forward, though it be over the edge of a precipice." But even Lowell admitted that Garrison, with all his faults, was an extraordinary man, and he predicted that posterity would "forget his hard words and remember his hard work." [13]

Phillips and Garrison worked closely, but they were too busy to see each other very much socially. So little did the two meet at each other's homes that it once took Phillips more than an hour to find his way to Garrison's house on Pine Street for tea.[14] Still, the relationship between the families was affectionate, and Wendell and Ann always took a close interest in the Garrison children. "Those unruly boys need somebody to take them in hand," Wendell wrote to Helen Garrison in the summer of 1847, when he and Ann were summering in Natick, and Garrison was off on a lecture tour. "Get . . . me to box their ears once or twice and then they'll begin to value their non-resistant mother and father." [15] The Phillipses were always especially proud of Wendell's namesake, young Wendell Phillips Garrison, and ultimately they financed the boy through Harvard.

Garrison was much closer to the cranks than Phillips, always fighting on several fronts at once. Wendell did not participate in his friend's campaigns for pacifism and against the Sabbath, nor did he share his enthusiasm for the community experiments in utopia then dotting the New England landscape. He recognized Garrison's foibles and knew him well enough to laugh over his idiosyncrasies. He knew, for example, that Garrison was a robust hypochondriac and, despite the wrathful tone he sounded in the *Liberator,* an essentially gentle man, easily flustered by domestic crises. "Did you hear the good story about his being found after the accident?" Phillips wrote to a friend

after Garrison had overturned the family carriage. "Mrs.
G. sitting on a bank holding Charles Follen—her mother
leaning against a fence—Wendell Phillips floundering
still in the mud—and WLG himself so overcome he could
do nothing but sit on a stone and cry like a child." [16]

In moral matters, however, and this was what really
counted, Phillips found his friend's judgment "almost
faultless." It was Garrison who had showed him what to
do with his life, and Phillips never forgot this. In January
1846, in a brief note to the Garrisons thanking them for a
holiday gift, he expressed his feelings as sincerely as he
could. "Though differing in some points, we are glad to
have always been together in action—that our slightly
different paths lead always to the same point. I owe you
Dear Garrison more than you would let me express—and
my mother and wife except, more than to any other one.
Since within the sphere of your influence I trust I have
lived a better man." [17] Phillips was a Calvinist and did
not expect perfection in his friends. When their common
friend Elizabeth Pease professed alarm over Garrison's
attacks on Biblical inspiration, he suggested that she expected the upright spirit "without the alloy." "Garrison
is not the only man who sins! or holds erroneous opinions!"
Until he found a man "whose works are more mighty and
his errors lighter," he was content to do battle at Garrison's
side.[18]

Garrison, for all his eccentricities, cut a pale figure
compared with some of the more notable antislavery lecturers who worked with Phillips. Henry C. Wright had
been a hat maker and theology student. In addition to
abolitionism, the bristly haired Wright lectured on spirit-
ualism, nonresistance, cold-water cures and birth control.
He was the author of *The Unwelcome Child or The Crime
of An Undesigned and Undesired Maternity* and *A Kiss
For a Blow or a Collection of Stories for Children; Showing Them How To Prevent Quarrelling.* An ardent pacifist, Wright had a gift for the most blistering kind of invective, and when ex-soldier Zachary Taylor was nomi-

nated for the Presidency, Wright dubbed him "The Blood-
hound Candidate" and urged Garrison to follow up with
a cartoon in the *Liberator*—"bloodhounds in pursuit of
Indian women and children, tearing them to pieces, and
all of them having the face of Zachary Taylor." [19]

The most effective woman lecturer in the Garrisonian
ranks, and a particular favorite of Wendell's, was Abby
Kelly. A Quaker and former schoolteacher in Worcester,
Abby was the first woman to follow the Grimké sisters in
lecturing against slavery to mixed audiences. She was a
handsome, masculine-looking woman, gifted, as Garrison's
seagoing brother, James, observed, "with stentorian lungs
which would put some of our Naval Boatswains to the
blush." [20]

Two of the most intrepid reformers of the day joined
forces when Abby married Stephen Foster. Probably more
than any other man, Foster was responsible for the reputation enjoyed by the radical New England abolitionists
as fanatical wild men. As a grown man of twenty-five,
Foster had left his father's New Hampshire farm to enter
Dartmouth. While at college, he went to jail for refusing
militia service. After a short stay at Union Theological
Seminary, Foster left the church and devoted himself to
the antislavery cause. His mission was to bring the crusade into the churches, and he decided that, if the churches
would not invite him to address them or to use their meeting houses for antislavery meetings, he would speak to
them without invitation.[21]

One Saturday in 1842, Foster and three abolitionist
comrades arrived in Lynn, Massachusetts. They tried to
get a meeting house for an antislavery meeting the next
day but were refused. On Sunday morning, Foster attended the service in the Congregational church. After
the hymn the congregation sat down, but Foster remained
on his feet and launched into an antislavery lecture. Despite the admonitions of the enraged minister, Foster continued to lecture as he was carried out of the church face
down by three muscular parishioners. Once on his feet

again, he set off across the common to the Baptist Meeting House. The Baptists threw him down the steps. Foster ignored his bruises and torn clothing and joined the Meeting of the Friends nearby. In the ensuing scuffle, the Quakers, who had had enough inspiration for one morning, tore off part of his coat. Foster, who believed in non-resistance, left them with a few gentle words and went back to the Baptists, who kept him locked up in a dark closet under the staircase for the duration of the service.[22]

Stephen Foster soon became a notorious figure for his efforts to force abolitionism in the churches. He was invariably thrown out of the churches he entered, and what meetings he held himself were frequently mobbed. He had the true martyr's spirit and entered the churches, as he said, armed only with the naked truth of God. The scars and prison sentences resulting from his efforts he wore as so many badges of honor. Foster's remarks in a letter to a friend in January 1842 suggest the evangelical zeal and the spirit of martyrdom which characterized most of Phillips' co-workers.

I am now laid on the shelf for the winter. Possibly even for a longer period. Indeed, when I dare look on my shattered form, I sometimes think prisons will be needed for me but a little longer. Within the last fifteen months four times have they opened their dismal cells for my reception. Twenty-four times have my country-men dragged me from their temples of worship, and twice have they thrown me with great violence from the second story of their build-ings, careless of consequences. Once in a Baptist meeting house they gave me an evangelical kick in the side, which left me for weeks an invalid. Time out of memory have they broken up my meetings with violence, and hunted me with brick bats and bad eggs. Once they indicted me for assault and battery . . . twice have they punished me with fines for preaching the gospel; and once in a mob of two thousand people have they deliberately attempted to murder me. . . . Still I will not complain, though death should be close on my track. My lot is easy when compared with that of those for whom I labor. I can endure the prison, but save me from the plantations.[23]

They must have presented a queer picture on the platform together—Foster with his simple clothes and great gnarled farmer's hands and his ungainly manners, Parker Pillsbury, the massive-shouldered teamster from New Hampshire who worked with Foster, the ferocious Henry Wright, Charles Burleigh with his beard and hair looking as if he had just stepped out of the Book of John, and Wendell Phillips. At least the critics of the anti-slavery movement found it incongruous. A reporter from the hostile New York *Observer* went away from a meeting in 1845 with the belief that only Hogarth could do justice to the grotesque figures assembled there. But Phillips, the reporter said, was "a gentleman in address and education, a speckled bird in the party to which he belongs and the only man for whom you feel any sympathy." [24]

Certainly Phillips never consciously held himself apart from these people. He was fond of them all, especially Abby Kelly and Henry Wright, but he was an intellectual agitator, not an evangelist. He could confront hostile audiences, even survive the splattering of rotten eggs, but he could no more allow the mob to lay hands on him than he could fly. He did not believe in nonresistance, for one thing, as his later support of John Brown and his own habit of carrying a pistol testified. But there was more to it than this—the aristocratic background again. Phillips had the habit of always treating his opponents as if they belonged to an inferior social class. It was this aloof, patrician air that set him off from the others. "He seemed like some English Jacobite nobleman," Higginson said, "carelessly taking snuff, and kissing his hand to the crowd, before laying his head upon the block." [25]

Not all of the abolitionists in New England liked the idea of a "clique" of Boston aristocrats in a policy-making position. Rumblings of discontent were heard shortly after Wendell and Ann returned from Europe. Tickets had been sold at twenty-five cents apiece to the celebration honoring them. Phillips considered this a bad idea because it played into the hands of those disgruntled persons

"trying to get up a feeling against the Board as if *aristocratic* and exclusive." [26] Theoretically, Phillips was always
a great enemy of aristocracy, but in practical matters too
much democracy could be a foolish thing; Abby Folsom
proved that! Before the 1840s were over, a second grievous
split occurred within the ranks of New England abolitionism when Nathaniel Rogers, eloquent editor of the
Concord, New Hampshire, *Herald of Freedom,* broke
with Garrison. The superficial issue was over the ownership of the paper, whether it rightly belonged to Rogers
or to the New Hampshire Anti-Slavery Society, but the
deeper issue was revealed by Phillips in a letter to Richard
Webb. Rogers was one of the extremists, a "no-organiza-
tion" man who believed that "any man has a right to speak
anywhere on any topic at any time." This doctrine had
great appeal for some of the uneducated people in the
movement who were abolitionists primarily for the notoriety they could get out of it. The disaffection arose,
according to Wendell, because the Boston Clique, who
lived "in brick houses—in broadcloth—and have been to
college," dared to take issue with a crowd-pleaser like
Rogers.[27]

Ideologically as well as socially, Phillips could be distinguished from others in the movement. He liked Foster
personally ("a devoted, noble, single-eyed, pure, eloquent,
John-the-Baptist character"), but he thought his ideas
wild and illogical. The churches had rights also, and
Phillips admitted the justice of the criticism that Foster
could not consistently disrupt church meetings yet complain when hecklers came to disrupt his own meetings.
In other words, although Phillips was radically opposed
to the existence of a proslavery church, he did not want to
impose his ideas on the subject on an unwilling audience.
Because of this position, he was frequently invited to lecture in places where abolitionists of the Foster-Pillsbury
stripe would never have been tolerated.[28]

Regarding the utopian schemes which attracted so
many abolitionists, Garrison included, Phillips was defi-

nitely skeptical. When his friend John Collins quit his post in the antislavery organization to found a community at Skaneateles based on communal property and free love, Phillips had little hope for its prospects. "I hope his heart will one day bring his head right," he wrote to Elizabeth Pease. "His Community, I fear will be still more an utter failure than its principles merely would lead one to expect and that is saying a good deal." [29] His principal criticism of the community principle was that it killed individual development. Sooner or later, the able members would derive all the benefit while the drones did all the work. To this extent, the experiments at Brook Farm, Skaneateles, Fruitlands and the rest represented "the double refined essence of aristocracy." [30] Still, Phillips was not a carping critic. He rejoiced in the spirit of change and the willingness to experiment with social institutions, which filled the air. When he humorously described a friend who gave up milk because "he wouldn't rob the cow" or one who went straight from an ascetic community into the Odd Fellows with the conviction that nature now demanded ritual, it was always without malice.[31]

• A part of his conservatism in such matters was undoubtedly the result of his religious orthodoxy. Many of Garrison's supporters were transcendentalists, but Phillips, although he had great admiration for Emerson as a man of letters, had little patience with the mystical, esoteric atmosphere in which the Sage of Concord lived. In the summer of 1842 he gleefully passed on to Elizabeth Pease a story printed in the Boston *Post* about Emerson and Margaret Fuller at a dance recital by Fanny Elssler. "A lady and gent admiring Fanny at the theatre remained sometime silent. At last at the performance of some grand pas, 'Margaret,' said he, 'This is *music*.'—Fanny jumped more nimbly still.—'Ralph,' continued the lady, 'this is *religion!*'" It was an uproarious story, Phillips thought. "If you have seen enough of their cant, for with all their truth they have cant in perfection, you will roar and roll at the resemblance—could you only know the parties it would be better still." [32]

Until the Civil War, Phillips would always think of abolition as the most important business in his life. He was, however, sympathetic toward many other reform movements and willing to help in them so long as the cause of the slave was not jeopardized. He would lecture on temperance but would not agree with Foster that the anti-slavery society should refuse money from men in the liquor trade.[33] He was always opposed to capital punishment, and, when a colored sailor by the name of Washington Goode was sentenced to death for murder in 1849, Phillips was one of many Boston reformers who participated in the fruitless attempt to save his life. He lectured on prison reform and occasionally contributed something to the *Prisoner's Friend,* a journal in which Quincy was interested. Toward the end of the 1840s his name, along with that of Ann Phillips, began to appear more and more frequently as a sponsor of petitions for female suffrage.[34] In an article in the *Liberator* in December 1849 he made his position on this issue clear, saying: "Though the Anti-slavery cause has never adopted nor endorsed the rightfulness of such a measure, and numbers among its friends many who would doubt its utility, it will still, in future years, be thought an honor due to the Antislavery Agitation that it has given, incidentally, so much assistance to various other reforms." [35]

The fact that moral reformers seemed to spend so much of their time and energy reforming each other was a source of some disillusionment to Phillips. He had been in Europe when the split in the American Anti-Slavery Society had occurred in 1840, and he was thus spared much of the almost incredible bitterness which had resulted, a bitterness so deep and enduring that two years later, when all of the abolitionists in Boston were agitating for the freedom of a captured fugitive slave and Rev. Nathaniel Colver suggested that it might be a good time for "new" and old "organization" abolitionists to make up their differences, Garrison said "Mr. Colver, I should deny my God if I said I could act with you in the sense of approving you." [36] Phillips was sure that the Garrison wing of the antislavery movement was in the right, but he was more concerned with the factional disputes which seemed to keep cropping out even among the ranks of the faithful. More than a mere agitator himself, he was even during the 1840s becoming a philosopher of reform, and he knew that reformers would always be "a discordant host, fighting under different banners, moved by various impulses, erratic, seeking different objects . . . chafing against arrangement and combination by virtue of those very mental characteristics that lead men to new ideas." [37] Yet New England abolitionists insisted in adding to all these natural disadvantages an affection for anarchy among their own affairs and a tendency to squabble among themselves, which Phillips found particularly irritating. In the spring of 1845, after he had devoted almost five full years exclusively to the antislavery cause, he wrote to Richard Webb, "I'm more and more pained every day to see how, in reform movements specially, there lacks a rigid sense of common honesty." [38]

Such moments of disenchantment might be expected in any career. That they occurred so seldom during Phillips' first decade as a reformer suggests that he had found his true calling. He was able to retain a sense of detachment (a rare virtue among reformers) without losing his enthusiasm. He knew that reformers could be as ridiculous as other people, that too much moral earnestness could be laughable. Therefore, he could laugh when he heard about the battle of the sexes at one of Emerson's and Alcott's clubs. The members voted down a proposal to insert the word "women" in the constitution and then turned around and passed a resolution to the effect that "men" meant "all human beings." "What it means after the first vote," Phillips chortled to a friend, "no one seems able to tell." [39]

Now, a little detachment is a good thing for any man, but too much detachment is the ruin of a reformer, and Phillips was a good reformer. He was not, for example, like James Russell Lowell, another Boston aristocrat serving the antislavery cause. Lowell, who wrote for the *Anti-Slavery Standard* in New York, was a poet who suffered from a bad case of overdetachment. He had the unhappy capacity to realize "That Zachary Taylors are no more out of the order of nature than Henry C. Wrights"—that even slaveholders were human. "If you prick them do they not bleed?" he asked. "If you tickle them do they not laugh? If you poison them do they not die?" [40]

Phillips might have agreed with the sentiment, but he would hardly have thought the point worth making. In the spring of 1849, the board of the American Anti-Slavery Society decided that Lowell's pen was not stinging enough, and they took measures to ease him out of his five-hundred-dollar-a-year job. It is appropriate that Wendell Phillips, a bad poet but a good partisan, should have been commissioned to write the letter of explanation. [41]

8

No Union with Slaveholders
1841–1850

In the spring of 1846 Phillips was asked by the secretary of Harvard's class of 1831 to fill out a questionnaire. Under the section marked health he wrote that his health was excellent but that he was growing bald. Under occupation he said he had prepared for the law with Judge Story, "but grew honest and quitted what required an oath to the Constitution of the United States." Asked to note any *other remarks* that might be interesting to his classmates, he wrote:

Nothing but that I am a teetotaler and against capital punishment. I believe in animal magnetism and phrenology. I advocate letting women vote and hold office. My main business is to forward the abolition of slavery. I hold that the world is wrong side up and maintain the propriety of turning it upside down. I go for Disunion and have long since abjured that contemptible mockery, the Constitution of the United States. My surprize is that a quiet moderate halfway sort of sim sam fellow like myself should have somehow the reputation of a fanatic—and my heart beats high with joy whenever I meet a classmate. Three cheers for the class of 1831.[1]

More than a few of the other members of the class of '31, at least those who had not seen Phillips since college and were out of touch with affairs in Boston, must have blinked when they read these words. This was obviously not the same man, not the Phillips who had led the aristocratic clique at Harvard and argued so eloquently for social rank and stability!

Closer friends would not have been surprised, for they had watched his radicalism develop over the last five years. By early autumn in 1841, Phillips was regularly seen on lecture platforms with acknowledged fire eaters like Foster, Pillsbury, Burleigh and Abby Kelly. He lectured so frequently that by March 1842 his throat gave out, and he was forced to cancel some engagements.[2] No man who traveled in such company could countenance moderation in attacking slavery, nor could he escape being tagged as a radical himself.

It was not, however, his association with other agitators, or his participating in the campaign to help Negroes, or his assault on the Church, or the vehemence with which he lashed out at slavery that was primarily responsible for Phillips' growing notoriety in the 1840s. It was his assault on the North itself and the Federal Union. The ordinary citizen in the North in 1840 had never seen a slave. He had little to do with free Negroes and was usually too concerned with his own problems to worry about the plight of 600,000 black men in the South. In Phillips' eyes this man was as guilty as the slaveholder, because his silent acquiescence made slavery strong. "Northern opinion, the weight of Northern power, is the real slave-*holder* of America," he said to a Faneuil Hall audience in February 1842. "Her presence in the Union is the Carolinians' charter of safety. . . . This very fact, that our hands rust the fetters of the slave, binds us to raise our voices the more earnestly on his side. That *Union* which takes from him the power of physical resistances is bound to exert for him all the weight of a correct public opinion."[3] Phillips believed that the Southern slaveholder, living in the midst of a potentially explosive social situation, was protected by the Federal Union with its guarantees against insurrections within the states. Therefore, the Northerner who did not give a fig for slavery, by his very indifference strengthened the grip of the master on his whip.

Now, the implications of this position were ominous
from the beginning. If Northern opinion was "the real
slaveholder of America," and if it was the duty of every
slaveholder to repent immediately, then every Northerner
had a moral obligation to immediately raise his voice
against slavery, and, if the Union made slavery strong, the
only consistent moral position was to work for destruction
of the Union. Phillips always prided himself on being
morally consistent, and he was not reluctant to follow
these implications to their logical conclusion. At an anti-
slavery meeting in Worcester on February 16, 1842, he
proposed that petitions be circulated "asking Congress to
take measures for the immediate dissolution of the Union."
The proposal was based on the assumption that the Union
resulted originally from a compromise between the Northern and the slaveholding states, that the North was thus a
slaveholder also and that it was "the duty of every
Christian to withdraw from a government which upholds
iniquity." [4] By April, the *Liberator* was asserting that
every abolitionist's duty was to work for the repeal of the
Union, and Garrison was invoking the language of Isaiah
in castigating the American Constitution as "a covenant
with death and an agreement with hell." Among the rank
and file of the Garrisonian abolitionists there was considerable reluctance to accept so extreme a position, and
Phillips, who was already becoming known as the philosopher of the movement, was giving lectures designed to
document the assertion that the American system was
really the system of slavery. More persuasive than any
lecture, however, was the arrest of George Latimer in
Boston in October 1842.

Latimer was a Negro who said he had been freed by
the will of his former master. He was seized by a man
from Norfolk, Virginia, and kept in the Boston jail while
the alleged owner prepared to present the evidence of his
ownership before a court. On the basis of previous de-
cisions relating to the remission of fugitive slaves, Chief
Justice Shaw of Massachusetts denied Latimer a writ of
habeas corpus and trial by jury.

As soon as the news of Latimer's jailing spread, Boston
was thrown into a turmoil. The *Liberator* called Stratton,
the constable who had arrested him, "a two-legged blood-
hound" and ran a long article on Boston "the Slave-Catch-
ing City." The Southerner did not have to send to Africa
for his merchandise any longer; there was "a new Congo,
another Guinea, opened to his adventure in the city of
Boston." [5] Henry Bowditch and some friends formed a
Latimer Committee and published a paper, the *Latimer
Journal and North Star,* which reported every development of the case, and they opened a headquarters at Washington and West streets, where they labored day and night
to collect signatures for petitions of protest. A few intrepid
antislavery ladies tried to recruit a cordon of women to
surround the jail; this failing, they reluctantly contented
themselves with selling trinkets to raise funds for the Latimer Committee.

That November, Wendell Phillips addressed a protest meeting in Faneuil Hall. The auditorium was
jammed, and the crowd surged ominously before the
platform. Most of the Boston abolitionists were there,
and friends had driven in from as far away as Brook Farm
in Roxbury. Not everyone in the audience came for the
same purpose, and the undercurrent of hostility became
apparent in the derisive shouts which accompanied Phillips to the platform, but he had not come to mollify anyone. Boston, once a town of proud and freedom-loving people, was sending a human being back to slavery, and those
responsible for it were in the hall before him. "*You* are
the guilty ones," he said. "The swarming thousands before
me, the creators of public sentiment, bolt and bar that
poor man's dungeon tonight." He said he was speaking
to "the white slaves of the North," and when they hissed
him he said it showed the only courage they were capable
of. Men who venerated a Constitution which threw the
weight of the government behind the slaveholder when he
came to claim his property might shake the chains which
bound them to slavery; they could do no more. "There
stands the bloody clause—you cannot fret the seal off the

bond. The fault is in allowing such a constitution to live
an hour." So far as he was concerned, the Bible out-
weighed the statute book. "When I look upon these
crowded thousands and see them trample on their consciences and the rights of their fellow-men, at the bidding
of a piece of parchment, I say, my CURSE be on the Constitution of these United States!" The crowd was howling
now. Phillips looked at the hecklers, calmly, disdainfully.
"Those who cannot hear free speech had better go home,"
were his parting words. "Faneuil Hall is no place for
slavish hearts . . . I record here my testimony against
this pollution of our native city." 6

In the eyes of many Bostonians, Wendell Phillips
had gone to the Latimer meeting a misguided philanthropist. He came away a maniac. One paper, referring to
him as a "former gentleman," wrote "Never did we hear
such a volley of blackguardism and shameless abuse as
came from the lips of this fanatic madman. Our readers
will scarcely believe it, yet we assure them that WENDELL
PHILLIPS had the audacity, the shameless self-degradation,
to CURSE THE CONSTITUTION OF THE UNITED STATES in the
Cradle of American Liberty before an assemblage of
American citizens." 7

Even though Latimer ultimately went free (a group
of abolitionists purchased his freedom from the man
claiming ownership), the incident hardened Phillips'
opposition to the political system which would have sent
him back to slavery. In January 1843 he proposed to a
meeting of the Massachusetts Anti-Slavery Society that the
federal compact involved both North and South "in
atrocious criminality—and should be completely an-
nulled." The resolution passed, and Edmund Quincy
wrote to a friend afterwards "We dissolved the Union by a
handsome vote." 8

For the rest of the decade Phillips thought that his
most important duty was to publicize and dramatize the
moral case against the federal government. With the other
associates of Garrison he strove to show wavering aboli-

tionists that the same reasoning which led them to reject
a church tolerant of slavery applied even more eloquently
to a proslavery political system. So far as the general
public was concerned, Phillips attempted to do what he
had done before so successfully at the time of Lovejoy's
death: to show that the abolitionist position grew out of
American principles. The Declaration of Independence
asserted the principle that any government destructive of
man's God-given rights should be resisted. The original
compact of the American government, based on a compromise with the slave states, was destructive of these
rights. Therefore, argued Phillips, in attacking it abolitionists were merely pursuing the revolutionary tradition
of their fathers.

This argument for disunion rested largely on the
assumption that the Constitution, which bound the states
together, was a document supporting slavery. Many abolitionists took the contrary position, arguing that the word
"slave" did not appear in the Constitution, that positive
guarantees such as those included in the Fifth Amendment
more than balanced those sections in the document which
seemed to sanction slavery; that, in any event, slavery could
not endure without positive congressional enactments
supporting it. In taking this position, men like the prominent New York philanthropist Gerrit Smith contended
that the correct position for the abolitionist was to work
through politics for the constitutional destruction of the
wicked institution.[9]

Phillips had no patience with this position. In September 1844, he had a bitter skirmish with Smith in the
columns of the *Liberator*. He followed this with what he
and the Garrison abolitionists hoped was the definitive
statement on the subject: a solidly written, carefully
documented, 123-page pamphlet entitled *The Constitution a Pro-Slavery Argument*. The essay was intended to
show that the Constitution was really "a compromise
between slavery and freedom," to prove "the melancholy
fact that willingly, with deliberate purpose, our fathers

bartered honesty for gain and became partners with tyrants that they might share in the profits of their tyranny." To make his case, Phillips offered in evidence Articles I and IV of the Constitution, with their references to the use of the slave population for representation in Congress, the power of Congress to suppress insurrections, the protection given to the slave trade, the return of fugitives and the guarantee to protect individual states against domestic violence. In addition, he cited an array of evidence from the debates in the Constitutional Convention and in the state ratifying conventions to show that the men who framed and accepted the Constitution understood it to be a document which recognized and protected slavery.[10]

Righteous men, Phillips believed, would have nothing to do with a proslavery constitution. This principle delivered the finishing blow to his own halting legal career; he simply withdrew from a profession which required him to take an oath in support of the Constitution, but even this kind of consistency did not go far enough. Phillips took the final step at the New England Anti-Slavery Society convention in May 1844, when he voted to support a resolution declaring it to be "a gross departure from abolition principle for any abolitionists to throw a ballot for any office under the state or United States Constitution." [11]

The overwhelming majority of Northerners, including those opposed to slavery, found this position absurd. By refusing to vote, Phillips and Garrison were withholding their support from slavery's enemies as well as from its friends. This was carrying the moral argument to a foolish and impracticable extreme. For his part, Garrison was more concerned with proclaiming the doctrine than justifying it. Again it was left to Wendell Phillips to make the case for the radicals. This he did in a thirty-nine-page pamphlet entitled *Can Abolitionists Vote or Take Office Under the United States Constitution?*

Phillips' defense of the doctrine was based on two large assumptions, the first relating to the nature of government, the second to the nature of man. He had come a long way in his thinking about government since his college eulogies of Edmund Burke, and now he sympathized with those thinkers at the opposite end of the political spectrum. "Government is precisely like any other voluntary association of individuals—a temperance or anti-slavery society, a bank or railroad corporation. I join it, or not, as duty dictates." Phillips maintained that, because representative government is the form of political organization ordained of God, the majority must rule, but he was careful to draw a distinction between the duty of the minority to submit and its right to obey. "If the majority set up an immoral Government, I obey those laws which seem to me good, because they are good—and I submit to all the penalties which my disobedience of the rest brings on me. This is alike the dictate of common sense, and the command of Christianity." [12] This definition of a man's duty to his government bears strong echoes of Calvin. It is based on the assumption that man is a religious being whose first duty is to the higher law of God. "God never made a *citizen,* and no one will escape, as a man, from the sins he commits as a citizen." [13] In America in 1845, the man who did his civil duty by voting sinned, because he was helping to put men into office whose sworn duty it would be to uphold a constitution which sanctioned slavery.

In the forty years of life which remained to him, Phillips never once doubted the soundness of his stand in 1845. At the time, men found it ridiculous for two reasons. In the first place, it was self-defeating. How could abolitionists ever hope to accomplish their goal if they refused to participate in the political process? In the second place, it was almost impossible for a man to take this position and remain morally consistent. Even some of Phillips' admirers felt this way. To be consistent, they argued, he should leave the country altogether; he had no right to stay and criticize, for by his very presence he was participating in the social sin he found so monstrous.

In a lengthy letter to Charles Sumner, Phillips attempted to allay these objections. "Holding that honesty
and truth are more important than even freeing slaves—
and that duties never can really conflict—we take the position you've taken the trouble to read about." He agreed
that he should try to influence the government for the better. "But I must exert that influence through *right* means.
. . . Mark the difference between *speaking* and voting or
taking office—I speak for the changing of laws, all the time
washing my hands of them." The important thing to remember, Phillips lectured his politically ambitious friend,
was that moral responsibility takes precedence over civil
responsibility. "Can the well being of any machinery of
man's devizing (i.e. Govt.) justify the *individual* in doing
what he thinks wrong? Is not the *man,* God's creature,
above all organizations—which are man's creations? . . .
I will use all and any influence for the reform of Govt.
which conscience tells me is right, but I will neither steal,
rob, enslave or murder to support constitutions or qualify
myself for office." Phillips believed that every man had to
make his own compact with government. Good Calvinist
that he was, he did not expect Utopia. The City of God
was not to be found among men, and he realized that a
man's choices were always limited by the social and historical situation in which God placed him. Man had to
live in the world, but he did not have to collaborate with
the devil, which is what Sumner and all other "good citizens" were doing. "What right *you* have to set up a Govt.
and *force* me to pay taxes, and then tell me I must leave
the country or be guilty of all the sins you incorporate into
your Govt. I confess I cannot see. The God who made the
land is *my* God as well as *yours*—how, when and where he
gave you and your friends the exclusive right to dwell here
and make Govt. which should so compromise all others
born here, whether they agreed to it or not, as to make
them sinners, I can't see. To live where God sent you and
protest against your neighbor—this is certainly different
from *joining him* in sinning, which the office holder of
this country does." [14]

Although this position was condemned in the public mind from the beginning, Phillips did as much as any one could do to persuade people that it was the true position. Even more important than his ability as a pamphleteer (he wrote relatively little) was his ability to dramatize the issue from the lecture platform. Although he was not to become nationally famous until the fifties, Phillips' stature as an orator was growing steadily, and by the mid-forties he was being acclaimed by all who heard him, friends and enemies alike, as one of the outstanding speakers of the age. In the spring of 1843, John Neal, who was reporting an antislavery meeting in New York, set down his impressions of Phillips' platform personality. Neal, no reformer himself, had been dozing in the audience when he noticed that "a gentleman with light hair, and countenance remarkable for its intellectual expression took the platform: as his bearing gave promise of something above the ordinary eloquence of such meetings, we resolved to stay a few minutes longer. But Mr. Wendell Phillips had scarcely opened his lips when we were wide awake, and listening to a burst of eloquence very startling. The man was faultless in his elocution,—graceful in his action—and his argument was sustained with a language vivid, and full of that generous power of feeling which is the life and soul of true oratory—the speech was every way worthy the best orator of any nation." [15]

Because of his reputation as a speaker, Phillips was constantly sought after by lyceums throughout the North. What time he could spare from his abolitionist activities he devoted to lyceum platforms, although the latter were a secondary consideration. He thought of the lyceum as a path to an audience which he might someday reach on the antislavery issue. Since the lyceum was not intended to be a forum for reformers, it was natural that his appearance on such a platform would occasionally arouse antagonism. The most notable example of this occurred in Concord between 1842 and 1845.

The Concord Lyceum, one of the oldest and most celebrated in the nation, had expressed its opposition to the abolition movement at meetings in 1833 and 1835. When it was announced on December 19, 1842, immediately after a lecture by Horace Greeley, that Wendell Phillips would address the next meeting on the subject of slavery, John Keyes, one of the town's stalwart citizens and a power in the lyceum, offered a resolution that since the lyceum was "established for social and mutual improvement the introduction of the vexed and disorganizing question of abolitionism should be kept out of it." [16] The resolution was tabled, and Phillips gave the lecture on December 21. A little more than a year later he returned to the Concord Lyceum. In the intervening months his radicalism had become even more pronounced, and one of his listeners reported that for an hour and a half the speaker "gave us all his treason against Church and State." The reaction of the audience was so vigorous that the next session of the lyceum was to be devoted to a discussion of the speech. Phillips appeared at this meeting and heard himself denounced as an arrogant stripling and a leader of "silly women." His reply, given extemporaneously and reported in the *Liberator,* gives a good insight into the temper of his thinking at this time. Accused of attempting to subvert the very institutions which protected his own liberty, Phillips said "My liberty may be bought at too dear a price. If I cannot have it except by sin, I reject it; but I would not so blaspheme God as to doubt the safety of obeying Him." So far as the stripling and the silly women were concerned, "Our pulpits are silent. Who ever heard this subject presented before the movement of the silly women and the striplings?" [17]

A good many members of the lyceum remained unconvinced, and when on March 5, 1845—after a lecture on the less controversial subject of "Water"—it was again proposed that Phillips be invited to deliver an address on slavery, tempers began to fray. The motion was carried by a narrow margin, whereupon John Keyes and Reverend Mr. Frost resigned as curators. The president quit the chair, and the meeting was thrown into momentary con-

fusion until a temporary chairman could be chosen. Ralph
Waldo Emerson and Henry Thoreau were elected as the
new curators.[18]

Phillips' lecture on March 11 must have been impressive. "Have you ever heard W. Phillips ?" Emerson wrote
to a friend the following day. "I have not learned a better
lesson in many weeks than last night in a couple of hours."
Emerson was still tepid on the subject of abolitionism; it
was not until 1850 when the Fugitive Slave Law made him
a reformer in spite of himself that he really espoused the
movement. Consequently, it was Phillips the orator who
impressed him most. "The core of the comet did not seem
to be much, but the whole air was full of splendours. One
orator makes many, but I think this the best generator of
eloquence I have met for many a day. . . ." [19]

Thoreau, even more impressed than Emerson, reported the lecture for the *Liberator*. "We must give Mr.
Phillips the credit for being a clean, erect and what was
once called a consistent man," wrote Thoreau.

> He at least is not responsible for slavery, nor for American
> Independence; for the hypocrisy and superstition of the Church, nor
> the timidity and selfishness of the State; the indifference and willing
> ignorance of any . . . in this man the audience might detect a sort
> of moral principle and integrity, which was more stable than their
> firmness, more discriminating than his own intellect, and more grace-
> ful than his rhetoric, which was not working for temporary or trivial
> ends. It is so rare and encouraging to listen to an orator who is
> content with another alliance than with the popular party, or even
> with the sympathizing school of the martyrs, who can afford some-
> times to be his own auditor if the mob stay away, and hears him-
> self without reproof, that we feel ourselves in danger of slandering
> all mankind by affirming that here is one who is at the same time an
> eloquent speaker and a righteous man." [20]

Phillips' encounter with the standing order in Concord suggests that, despite his avowed Calvinism, he was
closer to the transcendentalists at some points than he

would have liked to admit. He was able to capture Emerson's enthusiasm, not only because of his eloquence (Webster possessed as much and Emerson would soon pour all his contempt upon him), but also because he spoke as the man of principle, anxious to give voice to his private vision of the truth no matter what the cost. "Let us affront and reprimand the smooth mediocrity and squalid contentment of the times," Emerson had said in "Self-Reliance." Perhaps he felt that in Phillips he had finally found an orator willing to take this advice.

There was also a great similarity between the ideas Thoreau would express in his famous essay "Civil Disobedience" in 1849 and the ideas which Phillips was dramatizing in 1845. Thoreau preached the higher law and said that every man more right than his neighbors constituted a majority of one; Phillips maintained that every man should choose his own government, "each for himself, each acting by the light of his own conscience." [21] Thoreau refused to pay taxes to an immoral government, and Phillips cursed the Constitution. The great majority in Massachusetts, of course, looked on Phillips as a dangerous visionary and Thoreau (if they knew him at all) as an ill-tempered crank, but the majority saw only the institutions and not the spirit of the age.

The persistence of Phillips and Garrison in attacking the Constitution and the federal government was especially irritating to the anti-Garrisonian abolitionists. After the antislavery movement had split in 1840, the anti-Garrisonians had begun to devote more and more of their time to politics, attempting to work through the two major parties or through the infant antislavery Liberty party, first organized at a meeting in Albany in 1840. To these men the doctrine of disunion seemed grossly impractical, and they chafed under the realization that, even though Phillips and Garrison spoke only for themselves, the furor which their extreme position aroused tended to stamp every abolitionist with fanaticism.

Phillips had been in Europe when the Liberty party was organized, but he wasted little time after his return in condemning it. "A third party is full freighted with dangers," he wrote to a friend in Pennsylvania. "The real progress of our cause is to be looked for from those who keep aloof—who have rid themselves not only of *old* parties—but of *parties* themselves—who feel that the real opposition to our enterprise lies deeper than the reach of the ballot box." [22] Nevertheless, the word somehow got around among the Garrison people that Phillips was a friend of that party, and his name actually appeared on the ballot as a nominee for alderman in the Boston elections of 1841. Lydia Maria Child, the tenacious editor of the *National Anti-Slavery Standard* who was always on the lookout for backsliders, wrote an open letter which began "Wendell Phillips are you a liberty party *man* or a liberty party *tool?*" Phillips quickly reassured his friends that his name had been used without his consent and that, if he had to choose, he would rather be a "tool" than a "man," since "The last would imply want of principle; while the other would argue only want of sense." [23]

Phillips rejected the overtures of the Liberty party leaders because he was convinced that moral principles could not mix in American politics, the whole business of which was to avoid moral issues and throw up a false image of national majesty before the eyes of the people. So far as he was concerned, the Bunker Hill celebration in the summer of 1843 dramatized this essential truth. John Tyler, the President of the United States, was to be an honored guest. Tyler was a slaveholder, and the prospect of his coming, attended perhaps by his own bond servant, to dedicate the most famous American monument to liberty must have given Phillips a certain grim satisfaction. It seemed to prove that no good could ever come to abolitionism from political leaders. Phillips was commissioned by the New England Anti-Slavery Society to wait on the President when he visited Boston and prevail upon him to free his slaves. Tyler, who had enough troubles of his own at this time, saw to it that Phillips was refused an interview.[24]

The great Daniel Webster gave the oration at Bunker

Hill and was fulsomely applauded by the Boston press. Phillips' reaction was expressed by Maria Chapman in the *Liberator*: "It is not possible that the late celebration on Bunker Hill can have been either pleasing to God, or honorable to the people of the United States. Failing in these particulars, it is to be regarded as an audacious exhibition of national hypocrisy, equalled by nothing in history [embodying] all forms of national dissimulation, cant, bombast and impudence." Maria was editing the *Liberator* at this time, dipping her pen into the same bitter ink that Garrison used, and before she finished blasting this monument to American hypocrisy she had even lashed out at the sacred memory of George Washington, "a warrior and a slaveholder" whom Americans had made "more than a rival of Christ." [25]

Phillips' confidence in the rightness of his position did not blind him to the fact that the tide of the times was running against him. In the elections of 1842 the Liberty party emerged holding the balance of power in Massachusetts, and by 1844 the political efforts of abolitionists were showing significant results throughout the North. The more effectively Phillips operated on the antislavery lecture platform, the more support he seemed to stir up for the politicians. "The new converts run right into Liberty Party and become almost wholly hostile to us," [26] he complained in a letter to Elizabeth Pease. The cause was obvious; it lay in the American's veneration for the ballot box as one of his God-given rights. The high moral position in which Phillips rejoiced was contrary to the national character, and he agreed with Garrison's exasperated remark that if the Asiatic cholera were to invade American shores every four years it would do less damage than Americans do to themselves in every national election.

Still, Phillips was shrewd enough to see what was happening to American politics. As early as 1844 he predicted that the Liberty party would grow until it became profitable for one of the major parties to absorb it. In a surprisingly prescient letter to Richard Webb in October of that year, he seemed to foresee the ultimate development of the Republican party. "I think they are fated to grow," he said of the Liberty party men, "till some political convulsion shakes the whole country into two great parties (which will come soon) of North and South—slave and *Antislave*. Then they will merge into the common mass, some few of their cunning leaders . . . will secure prominence and office, the rest be forgotten. . . . I always said they would grow, till they grew fat enough to make it worth while for one of the great parties to eat them." [27]

The fact that their numbers were dwindling, as more abolitionists succumbed to the lure of politics, did not sap the faith of those who remained with Phillips and Garrison. It is in the nature of the reformer to feel surer of his path the lonelier it becomes. At a meeting in August 1844, Charles Burleigh referred to the radical abolitionists as "this battalion of the sacramental host of God's elect," and Garrison cried out "We have been maligned—deceived—betrayed; thousands have fallen away from us, enraged and disappointed at the stern requisitions of antislavery principle, and the impracticability of defeating those who rely upon it as a guiding star; but still the cause is only the more potent for such desertions. Abolitionists! angels are looking down upon you in joyful approval." [28]

If Wendell Phillips thought the angels were smiling at him, he did not say. Perhaps he was aware of the implications involved in his decision to spurn politics. It was almost certain that if he sought a political career he could have been successful. His social position in Massachusetts, his education, his remarkable oratorical skills, his ability to earn the respect even of his critics could easily have won him a national reputation as a leader among political abolitionists. He knew he was giving up all this by staying with Garrison, and there were times when he could even admit that it was a hard decision to make. When his old friend George Bradburn deserted Garrison for the Liberty party, Phillips could understand the defection. "He is a clever man," he wrote to a friend in October 1844, "but sore

tempted—I acknowledge politics is a sore temptation to
me, at least." [29] He deliberately resisted the temptation by
going all out to defend the proposition that the true moral
reformer could only soil himself and his cause by mixing in
politics. "The politician," he said in a speech in May 1845,
"must conceal half his principles, to carry forward the
other half—must regard, not rigid principle and strict
right, but only such a degree of right as will allow him at
the same time to secure *numbers*. His object is immediate
success. When he alters his war cry, he ever looks back over
his shoulder to see how many follow." The reformer, on
the other hand, worships truth; "his object is duty, not
success. He can wait, no matter how many desert, how few
remain; he can trust always that the whole of truth, however unpopular, can never harm the whole of virtue." [30]

Meanwhile, his old schoolmate, Charles Sumner, was
rapidly gaining prominence as a public figure in Massachusetts and would by the end of the decade represent the
antislavery sentiment of Massachusetts in the United States
Senate. Seeing his friend's political star rising, and his own
extinguished before it had a chance to shine, made Phillips wonder about his own career. Writing to congratulate
Sumner for the Fourth of July oration which was being
acclaimed from all sides, Phillips revealed some of the
doubts in his mind in the summer of 1845. "As I closed
the last page," he wrote, "I could not help thinking how far
ahead you had strode of the [class] of 32–33 and wondering,
at the same time, whether I had been all that time seated
still, playing with pebbles?" [31]

Phillips was never one to waste his energy in brooding. He had committed himself to the unpopular cause,
and he stuck with that cause. By the early spring of 1845
he was becoming optimistic. The church was splitting into
Northern and Southern sections, a development in which
he rejoiced, and the annexation of Texas in March, which
had struck a severe blow at the hopes of antislavery Whigs
and Liberty party men, was beginning to make Northerners reconsider the appeal for disunion. "Men who would

have whispered Disunion with white lips a year ago now love to talk about it," he wrote to Elizabeth Pease in January 1846. "Many leading men will talk as we were once laughed at for talking a while ago." [32]

This momentary jubilation was tempered with sorrow over his mother's death shortly before. Although Sarah Phillips had never reconciled herself to Wendell's career, the emotional attachment between mother and son had been close. "We differed utterly on the matter of slavery," he confided to a friend, "and she grieved a good deal over what she thought was a waste of my time—and a sad disappointment to her—but still I am always best satisfied with myself when I fancy I can see anything in me which reminds me of my mother." [33]

For Sarah Walley Phillips the final irony may have been the realization that her death would make Wendell all the more secure in his career as agitator and reformer. His share of the family inheritance totaled about $20,000, which, together with his wife's property, made him *"very well to do,"* according to Quincy. A few years later his name appeared in a book dealing with the fifteen hundred wealthiest men in the Commonwealth. Although there is reason to believe that he and Ann were never as wealthy as some people believed, Wendell obviously did not have to worry about making a living now. This economic security, reinforced by the social confidence which his family background provided, made it all the easier for him to immerse himself in unpopular causes as long as he lived.[34]

The advent of the war with Mexico in May 1846 provided more ammunition for Phillips to fire at the politicians. The abolitionists had been united in opposing the annexation of Texas because it involved adding new slave territory to the Union. So far as they were concerned, the war with Mexico which followed was caused by the slave power which sought to acquire Texas and to wrest even more land from Mexico for the expansion of slavery. Back in 1843 a group of Northern congressmen had signed a statement declaring the efforts then in progress to annex

Texas unconstitutional and unworthy of a free people's support. Representative Briggs of Massachusetts had been one of the petitioners. In 1846, Briggs, as governor of Massachusetts, was asking his fellow citizens to support the war against Mexico. That afforded an instructive example, according to Phillips, of what politics did to a man. He might begin with a principle or two, but eventually the need for popular support and the requirements of his "oath" of office would wreck him. Briggs became a loyal governor by being a moral traitor.[35]

In September 1846 the temper of antislavery agitation suddenly quickened in Boston, and Phillips was allowed to preach his radical gospel before one of the largest audiences ever assembled in Faneuil Hall. The opportunity came about when an escaped slave, known only as "Joe," was discovered on the brig *Ottoman* in Boston Harbor. He fled to the shore but was pursued and captured by the ship's captain and promptly sent back to slavery on a boat bound for New Orleans. Bostonians of every shade of antislavery sentiment were aroused by the incident and held a mass meeting in Faneuil Hall to protest the "kidnapping" on Massachusetts soil. The meeting was held on September 24, and the hall was packed. Phillips sat on the platform and heard John Quincy Adams, who presided, denounce what had happened in a voice choked with indignation. The other speakers included Charles Sumner, who was making his first public appearance on an antislavery platform, Theodore Parker and the fiery Samuel Gridley Howe.

Those present were preparing to pass a resolution which would make it impossible for any Negro to be apprehended in Massachusetts and returned South except by established legal processes. Phillips opposed the resolution as a halfway measure. It did not go far enough, because under the Constitution any escaped slave would still have to be returned if a master showed proof of ownership. The outrage was not that "Joe" was sent back "illegally" but that he was sent back at all. Massachusetts needed a new

Declaration of Independence to free herself from the obligations of enforcing unjust laws. "This is the time,"
Phillips insisted, "for Faneuil Hall to say, not that we will
never permit the slave hunter, or his agents, to take up
without legal warrants his slave escaped from bondage, but
to say that he shall not take him—warrant or no warrant. . . . The time has come when self-respect, duty to
the slave, and duty to God, demand of us to announce
that, Constitution or no Constitution, law or no law,
humanity shall be paramount in Massachusetts." [36]

The men who had come to Faneuil Hall that afternoon were all sympathetic with the antislavery cause, and
they listened attentively. They were not, however, prepared to follow his advice. Wendell found this reaction
more and more common in the months that followed. He
was heartened to see the steady increase in antislavery
sentiment but disheartened to discover how few converts
he could win over to his own ranks. Men continued to
think that they could be abolitionists and politicians at
the same time. The Whig party in Massachusetts, for
example, was splitting over the slavery issue, but, to Phillips' disgust, men like Sumner, Howe and Charles Francis
Adams no sooner left the Whigs than they began to form
a party of their own.

Phillips watched this politicking from the sidelines.
The true abolitionists' role, he thought, was not to win
votes but to stir up the public conscience. "We must speak
strongly," he had advised the Garrisonites in December
1846, "because the crisis demands plain talking. Remember this is no evil which lynx-eyed ingenuity has discovered. We are not going about with a lamp at mid-day,
in order to ferret out some little local evil. Every sixth
man is a slave. The national banner clings to the flag-
staff, heavy with blood. This sin concerns the interests of
the country, the purity of the religious, the integrity of the
political character of the nation. The evil is tolerated because the conscience of the nation has been put to
sleep." [37]

In attempting to waken the nation's conscience, Phillips became increasingly merciless in his pursuit of public personalities, and he insisted that the abolitionists direct their official resolutions at persons rather than principles. "Let those who like the work of preaching abstractions do it," he told the delegates to the Massachusetts Anti-Slavery Society in January 1848. "For myself, I have never been able to find an abstract sin. When I have met sin, it has always been embodied." Despite the Puritans' maledictions on Catholicism, the shadow of the inquisitor had loomed large over New England in the seventeenth century. Phillips was a Puritan several generations removed, and, for all his love of liberty, there seemed at times to be a touch of the inquisitor in him. His two favorite whipping boys at this time were Governor Briggs and Robert C. Winthrop, the Whig representative from Boston, who, as Speaker of the House, had looked with friendly eyes on the war against Mexico. "Like a Grand Jury for Christendom," Wendell intoned before a gathering of abolitionists, "we summon the slaveholder, and his apologists and instruments before us . . . whenever we find a governor, a mere professor and not a doer of the truth, a hypocrite in his pretended zeal for liberty, a deceiver of the people, we nail him to the counter as base coin; and whenever we find a South Carolina Speaker in the garb of a Boston boy, we nail *him* right to the floor of Faneuil Hall, and leave him there." [38]

As the election of 1848 approached, Phillips continued to plead for disunion as the only course for moral men to follow and the only sure cure for slavery. Anti-slavery politicians were setting themselves an impossible task. Given the Constitution and the difficulties of amending it, there could be no hope for abolishing slavery constitutionally. Meanwhile, every citizen participated in the national sin so long as he remained loyal to the Union. Without the strength of federal union to protect it, Phillips was convinced that slavery would gradually disappear. "Slavery in this country will never be abolished at a blow," he insisted. "It will crumble piecemeal—state by state—perhaps, county by county. . . . But to clear the North from sin, the plan must be general and finished at once." Beneath all this lay the dark implication that once the North separated from the South the slave would be free to rise up and break his own bonds. Although Phillips purported to see "nothing but disaster in slave risings," he made it clear that Americans, so free with their means in supporting the struggles then going on for freedom in Poland and Greece and South America, could not forever withhold their support from "the three millions, whose prison-door [their] strong arms alone has kept bolted for fifty years." [39]

The election of 1848 seemed to give a striking reproof to Phillips and Garrison. The political abolitionists continued to increase in vigor and in numbers. The Free-Soil party, organized that August in Buffalo, attracted large numbers of dissatisfied voters from the two major parties and was strong enough to swing the balance in the election to the Whigs. Meanwhile, the persistent moral blindness of the nation as a whole could be seen in the fact that the new President, Zachary Taylor, was himself a slaveholder.

Phillips was spared the vexation of witnessing the last weeks of the campaign. At the end of August, while visiting in Lynn, he was stricken with an attack of dysentery which almost proved fatal. He had always been careful about his health, and his friends sometimes likened him to an athlete in training. The sudden shock at the prospect of losing him was staggering. "I could not tell, and cannot bear to think, what we should do if Wendell Phillips were to die," wrote Samuel May. "To me the loss would be greater than that of Garrison even, if I may speak of my individual grief and loss; I cannot estimate or compare the degree of loss to the cause." Wendell's physician, Dr. Reynolds, prescribed enormous doses of laudanum and morphine, and when Edmund Quincy visited Phillips he could hardly recognize his friend. It was not until October, when Wendell had returned to his home on Essex Street and was seen occasionally in his carriage, that his friends began to breathe easily again.[40]

It was January 1849 before Phillips was fully back in health. He had become by now a little more sanguine about the political developments of the last few years. He introduced a resolution before the meeting of the Massachusetts Anti-Slavery Society, which said, "We look upon the Free Soil movement as the unavoidable result of our principles and agitation, and hail it so far as its formation gives proof of the wider spread of a degree of antislavery feeling in the community." It remained, however, a "free-soil" and not an antislavery party, because it was not "pledged to trample underfoot the compromizes of the Constitution." [41] This was a pretty feeble endorsement, which is exactly what Phillips intended. A few months later he publicly reprimanded Charles L. Remond when the latter admitted having voted for the Free-Soil candidate for governor. If a man had to mix in politics (Phillips could see that his friend Sumner labored under such a compulsion), he might as well be a free-soiler, but the true abolitionists should "stand aloof from all such organizations." [42]

Despite his failure to win new disciples for the Garrisonites, Phillips could look back on his efforts between 1840 and 1850 with some satisfaction. He had helped to win important victories for the Negro in Massachusetts; he had exposed a complacent church and had watched a rising antislavery sentiment in the country play havoc with the old political alignments. In retrospect, Phillips could see that the war with Mexico, immoral though it was, had proved a blessing in disguise by creating a situation in which no amount of campaign oratory could keep the slavery issue out of national politics. Ever since 1846, the Congress had been paralyzed in its efforts to take action regarding the territory acquired from Mexico. Southern leaders demanded the right to take slavery into this territory, and the extremists underlined their demands with the threat of secession. Northern politicians, aware of the growing weight of antislavery opinion among their constituents, insisted that slavery be contained within its present limits. Sectional feeling ran so high that when Congress convened in December 1849, it took three weeks and sixty-three ballots to elect a Speaker of the House. The wrangling became so bitter that on one day alone, reported Robert C. Winthrop, three fist fights broke out on the House floor.[43]

Phillips welcomed these developments. He didn't expect the politicians to solve the problem, at least not in any moral sense, but the fact that the crisis existed at all, he believed, was due substantially to the efforts of the abolitionists who devoted themselves solely to the work of publicizing the evil of slavery.

Most encouraging of all, the people of Massachusetts appeared to have demonstrated convincingly that they would tolerate no slave hunting on their soil. Phillips seemed to have found new evidence of this when he introduced "Box Brown" to a Faneuil Hall audience at the end of May 1849. Brown was a slave who had escaped by being nailed up in a box and shipped North. After presenting Brown to the wildly applauding audience, Phillips reminded his listeners that the escape had been against the law. Their cheers, then, were a sign of moral progress in Massachusetts. "We say on behalf of this man, whom God created, and whom law abiding WEBSTER and WINTHROP swore should find no shelter on the soil of Massachusetts—we say that they may make their little motions, and pass their little laws, in Washington, but that FANEUIL HALL REPEALS THEM, in the name of the humanity of Massachusetts." [44]

9

The Fugitive Slave Law and
Thomas Sims   1850–1851

For Phillips the early fifties were years of domestic felicity and national disaster. In the fall of 1849 he and Ann adopted Phoebe Garnaut, orphaned daughter of the woman who had nursed Wendell through his nearly fatal illness. The presence of this vivacious teen-aged girl made life at 26 Essex Street considerably brighter. When Wendell was off lecturing, Phoebe's sunny influence helped overcome Ann's loneliness, and the challenge of supervising the girl's education kept Ann from brooding over poor health. Whatever peace of mind Wendell may have derived from this, however, was shattered when Congress passed the Fugitive Slave Act. He had boasted that Faneuil Hall would repeal every proslavery law that came out of Washington. During the next few years he was to make increasingly desperate appeals for disobedience while the people of Massachusetts coolly allowed the Fugitive Slave Act to be dramatically enforced in Boston.

From Phillips' point of view, 1850 began auspiciously. California, grown weary of waiting for Congress to act, had taken matters in her own hands, called a convention, adopted a constitution and now stood petitioning for admission to the Union as a state. A national crisis resulted because California's constitution prohibited slavery, and her admission to the Union threatened to destroy the equal balance between slave and free states. Pleased by anything that brought attention to the slavery issue, Phillips welcomed the crisis but not the way the politicians set about to cope with it.

On January 29, Henry Clay appeared in the Senate with a proposal which, he said, could resolve the issue threatening the Union. To satisfy the demands of anti-slavery elements in the North, he proposed that California be admitted as a free state and that the slave trade be prohibited in the District of Columbia. To appease the South, he proposed that the rest of the territory acquired from Mexico be organized without mention of slavery and that Congress enact an effective law for the return of fugitive slaves. In the famous "Great Debate" which followed, the three giants of American politics, Clay, Calhoun and Webster, made their last appearance together before the Senate.

From January until March, Phillips followed the reports of these ancient statesmen as they played out their roles. As a young enthusiastic Whig fifteen years earlier, he had been dazzled by Henry Clay, but the Great Kentuckian's luster had long since dimmed. Judging everything, as he now did, according to its approximation of absolute justice, Phillips could find little good in a man who built his whole career on compromise, and he dismissed Clay as "beyond redemption." [1]

John C. Calhoun's speech was read before the Senate on March 4. The old South Carolinian's body was dying, but his will blazed as defiantly as ever. He would have no compromise: the South must have equal opportunity to Western territory; antislavery agitation must be stopped or the Union was at an end. For all "the abomination of his pro-slavery doctrines," [2] Phillips had always respected Calhoun. "There are two men in this country rigidly consistent," he had said a few years earlier, "John C. Calhoun and William Lloyd Garrison." [3] What Phillips admired was Calhoun's devotion to principle, his refusal to bow down before the political god of expediency. This, together with his threat of secession—to Phillips not a

threat but a consummation devoutly to be wished—made
him a much more palatable figure than Clay.

Of the three statesmen, Phillips had always reacted
most strongly to Webster. Like most Harvard students,
he had idolized Webster and rarely missed an opportunity
to hear the great man argue a case or expound in Faneuil
Hall, and he could for years afterward declaim whole pas-
sages from Webster's earlier speeches. He knew the majestic figure that Webster cut on the platform and how,
to New England audiences especially, he was the incarnation of the powerful young American nation. Webster
seemed to have been hewn out of the granite of the New
Hampshire hills where he was born, and he always dwarfed
his audience. The sparks shot from his cavernous eyes,
and when the musical thunder of his voice evoked the
memory of Concord and Lexington a man could almost
hear the musketry and smell the powder.

Although Phillips never ceased to think of him as a
goliath, he had grown sour on Webster's public career
during the forties for the same reasons that turned him
against Clay. Webster was too successful a politician to
have ever taken a consistent antislavery position. Although
he had spoken brilliantly against the slave trade and at
one time had said he would never support the extension
of slavery, Webster was always quick to disavow abolitionism and assure the South that he meant no harm to slavery
where it already existed. Long a national ornament of the
Whigs, Webster's strongest support came from the business community of Boston, which was deeply involved in
the Massachusetts textile industry and thus anxious to
maintain cordial relations with the South. Webster was
supposed to represent the Commonwealth, but, as far as
Phillips was concerned, he took all his orders from State
Street and went to Washington with Boston inscribed on
one side of his banner and Richmond on the other.[4]

On March 7, Webster rose in the Senate to answer
Calhoun. The purpose of this speech, his last great effort
before the Senate, was to survey the history of the slavery

controversy in America, to point out the sources of the
inflamed feelings in both sections and to oppose the idea
of secession. Although he did not say it in so many words,
Webster implied that he would support Clay's plan, and
he contended that the whole argument about slavery in
California and New Mexico was an academic one because
slavery would automatically be excluded there by the
geography and climate of the country. Webster was as
hard on the abolitionists as he was on the incendiaries of
the South. They made the mistake, he said, of treating
ethics as a branch of mathematics and deluded themselves
into thinking that "what is right may be distinguished
from what is wrong with the precision of an algebraic
equation." Their fanatical assault on slavery called up
an equally extreme response on the part of slaveholders
and thereby endangered the Union. If bloodshed was to
be averted, each section must conciliate the other. As a
gesture of conciliation, he would support the passage of a
fugitive slave law.

Webster was wildly applauded in the Senate, and this
applause re-echoed through the columns of most of the
Whig papers in the country. In New York the price of
United States bonds, which had been falling, turned
sharply upward, and a group of grateful businessmen gave
Webster an expensive gold watch and chain. From New
England came a public letter of commendation containing
the names of several hundred prominent Bostonians, including merchants, ministers and other professional men.[5]

This was not all that Webster heard from New England. Outside of Boston, the press was largely critical of
his speech, and the abuse he received at the hands of Massachusetts reformers was extraordinarily bitter. The explanation for this is simple: these men felt betrayed.
Whittier, who was inspired to characterize Webster in the
famous poem which begins:

> So fallen! so lost! the light withdrawn
> which once he wore!

The glory from his gray hairs gone
Forevermore!

said he had composed the lines in one of the saddest
moments of his life "in tones of stern and sorrowful rebuke." Emerson, who after reading Webster's famous
reply to Hayne in 1830 had written in his journal, "the
beauty and dignity of the spectacle he exhibits should
teach men the beauty and dignity of *principles*," now
wrote that the word "liberty" in Mr. Webster's mouth
sounded like "love" in the mouth of a whore, and he said
in a public address, "All the drops of his blood have eyes
that look downward." [6]

On March 22, Phillips wrote in an extra edition of
the *Liberator* a long review of Webster's speech. The
article, surprisingly sober and analytical in tone, probably
reflects the constraint under which he labored whenever
he tried to put words on paper. He took up Webster's
speech point by point and attempted to show where it was
inconsistent with earlier speeches in which Webster had
supported the Wilmot Proviso. It was not, however, the
inconsistencies which Phillips deplored but rather the
fact that Webster seemed to be oblivious to the importance
of slavery as a moral issue. "Daniel Webster has spoken
for three hours on slavery," Phillips wrote, "and no mor-
tal man can tell whether he loves or hates it." Because
Webster was unable to face up to the great issue of the
day, Phillips continued, he forfeited his title to statesmanship and became "a mere advocate, now of a tariff, now of
a bank, now of this great interest, now of that; and if he
was not fed for his arguments he ought to have
been. . . ." [7]

Three days later, at a protest meeting in Faneuil Hall,
Phillips dropped all pretence of objectivity. Likening
Webster's speech to the situation which would have ex-
isted if Sam Adams "had gone over to the British or John
Hancock had ratted," he disposed of the whole thing by

saying: "I care not whether I am able to answer that speech or not. . . . I care not for the argument. He gave comfort to the enemy, and that is treason." [8]

Phillips had the crowd with him, but when he went to New York to address the annual meeting of the American Anti-Slavery Society on May 7, the situation was far different. As a traditional Democratic stronghold and as the greatest shipping center on the Atlantic coast, New York was more openly sympathetic with the South than most Northern cities, and there was a growing resentment in many circles over the abolitionists' being allowed to hold their annual meetings there. Early in May, the New York *Globe* and Bennett's *Herald,* printed a series of inflammatory articles about the coming meeting. Referring to Garrison as a Boston "mulatto" and to Phillips as a white man "merely from blood," the *Globe* reminded its readers that they were coming to urge the destruction of the Union. "No public building, no, not even the streets, must be desecrated by such a proposed assemblage of *traitors.*" The *Globe* made sport of the celebrated goal of emancipation by describing the "emancipated" Negro in Santo Domingo ("black, ignorant, brutal, bloodthirsty, lustful, vain and stupid") and then launched into a tirade against the abolitionists:

What are the designs of these men? To have immediate emancipation or disunion. To incite the Negroes of the Southern States to rise upon their masters, to butcher them in cold blood, to violate and use their wives and sisters and daughters as the innocent victims of negro brutality, to scatter fire, rapine and murder all through the South. The interests, the prosperity, and the happiness of the South are tied up in the destiny of New York and the North. Her safety, her security, is a part of our own. Her white men, her white women are our own flesh and blood . . . and if they perish by the mad acts of fanaticism, our heart strings are cut too.

Now was the time, the *Globe* said, for all good men to come out and join a riot. "Let the merchant, whose

fortunes are interwoven with the South, leave his counting room or his store, and go forth in support of his rights.
Let the mechanic, the laborers, and every honest citizen
who values the honor of the city and the safety of his
race leave his work for one or two days, and devote
them to his country. . . . Let the mad fanaticism which
will cover the country with blood be rebuked and
silenced. . . ." [9]

The *Globe* had its way, but not immediately. The
meeting was convened in the afternoon of May 7 in the
Broadway Tabernacle, a large square auditorium at
Broadway and Anthony Street which was used also for revival meetings. Phillips was on the platform along with
Quincy, Frederick Douglass, Francis Jackson and others
as Garrison opened the proceedings. When Garrison was
suddenly interrupted, for no apparent reason, by a burst
of applause from the gallery, Phillips knew that trouble
was ahead. A few minutes later, a beefy-faced man in the
audience jumped up, shook his fist at Garrison and berated him for making unflattering remarks about President Zachary Taylor. This was Isaiah Rynders, better
known as Captain Rynders to his followers. Rynders, a
former boatman on the Hudson, professional gambler
and weigher for the Custom House in New York, specialized in breaking up meetings for Tammany Hall.
Although he had been charged with bribery and arrested
for assault, there was still a place for Rynders in the politics of New York, and he and his men had come to the
Broadway Tabernacle to turn this meeting into a riot.

There was no time for Phillips to speak, so he had to
sit on the platform and watch Garrison struggle through
the afternoon, coping with an almost constant stream of
interruptions and heckling from the floor. At one point,
when Rynders made a particularly menacing gesture, an
enthusiastic young abolitionist jumped to his feet and
threatened to kill him, which only added to Garrison's
worries, since he was a pacifist.

For Phillips the high point of the afternoon came

after a seedy fellow with a dirty bandage on one hand, who introduced himself as "Professor" Grant, got up and delivered a long speech purporting to show that Negroes were closer to monkeys than to the human race. When he was done, Frederick Douglass stood up. Flawlessly dressed, and with magnificent presence, he advanced to the front of the platform and said: "The gentleman who has just spoken has undertaken to prove that the blacks are not human beings. He has examined our whole conformation, from top to toe. I cannot follow him in his argument. I will assist him in it, however. I offer myself for your examination. Am I a man?" The speech caused a sensation, and, as Douglass stood his ground answering the taunts from the audience with deliberation and good humor, Wendell heard Captain Rynders grumble that Douglass was "only half a nigger and didn't count."

The next morning Rynders and his men were on hand again. Samuel May tried to sell some antislavery pamphlets but was hooted down. Then Charles Burleigh, "The Hairy Man," began to speak. Burleigh, a nonresistant who wore a kind of biblical tunic, a long, flowing beard and his hair in ringlets, was made to order for this crowd. "Say, old Dad," someone yelled, "how much do you owe your barber?" They let him go on, then someone else shouted, "Say, old leather-lungs, old Jerusalem, why don't you shut up and let some other nigger speak?" Rynders even came up on the platform and stroked Burleigh's beard.

Then it was Phillips' turn. He had endured the ridicule quietly like the others, knowing that the mayor had refused to send any police to help maintain order and that Rynders was trying to provoke violence so that he could turn the meeting into a Donnybrook—but now Phillips began to abuse the audience. In a scornful voice he asked the Southerners to identify themselves, and he denounced the rest as rabble. Amidst the confusion of the cheers and hisses he heard someone yell, "Say, Garrison, you've given us a white-washed nigger instead of a real black one." Then someone else shouted, "Put him out, put the red-head down; we won't listen to him." [10]

These words were still ringing in his ears when the meeting adjourned. It was the first time he had been howled down by a mob.

For a while it appeared that the abolitionists would be unable to find a platform for their most eloquent voices. The annual meeting was forced to adjourn amid great confusion, and attempts to find another hall were unsuccessful. Finally, Henry Ward Beecher came forward and offered his church, and Wendell lectured there before an audience of about two thousand. Beecher made it clear that he was acting in the interests of free discussion rather than radical abolitionism, and Phillips responded with a muted speech, endeavoring to demonstrate that abolitionists were not as mad or fanatical as the New York press represented them.[11] The philanthropist Lewis Tappan, who had long since broken with the radicals, heard the lecture and described it to a friend, saying "Mr. P. made a good impression. Still his *destructive* scheme is not liked. He purposes to destroy the Government and the churches, but proposes nothing to take their place." [12]

Wendell, who never learned to wear a muzzle gracefully, was probably happy to leave New York and get back to Boston and to the New England Anti-Slavery Society, which met from May 28 to May 30. Despite the temporary setback in New York, he was able to tell his audience in the Melodeon that 1850 promised to be a good year for abolitionists. His optimism was stimulated by the debate over the proposed Fugitive Slave Law. If the law passed, the abolitionists would for the first time have a popular argument against the Constitution. When slavery actually placed "its vile hand on the Northern freeman for the service of the Southern shareholder," the slumbering conscience of the North could be brought alive.[13]

In anticipating the way in which the Fugitive Slave Law might be exploited as an issue, Phillips was relying heavily on the fact that fugitive slaves had been befriended in Massachusetts for more than half a century. In 1843 the Commonwealth had passed a Personal Liberty Law, which denied the use of state officials or facilities for the recovery of slaves in Massachusetts, and by the end of the decade the fugitives were becoming so numerous that Lowell complained in a letter to a friend that he was "positively beflead with runaway slaves" seeking contributions to buy their wives.[14] The *Liberator* office at 21 Cornhill Street was frequently used as a stopping place for fugitives passing through Boston, and a storeroom over the office was always kept full of clothes and disguises. Most of the runaways came as stowaways on boats out of Southern ports. While in Boston, they were usually kept with some family on Nigger Hill, then assisted to a safer spot in New Hampshire, Maine or Canada.

Exactly how much Phillips had to do with fugitive slaves before 1850 is difficult to discover. Considering his wife's illness, it is doubtful that his house on Essex Street was a regular stop on the Underground Railroad. As a leader of the abolitionists, however, Wendell must have been informed about runaways passing through Boston, and he was undoubtedly generous with financial assistance when it was needed. He must have been familiar with the more celebrated spots along the route: the secret vault in the cellar of Stephen Foster's "Liberty Farm" in Worcester, the tunnel which ran from Squire Walcott's cellar in Natick to the railroad embankment near by and the false bottom in the wagon which Israel How Brown regularly drove from South Sudbury to Fitchburg.[15]

After September 18, 1850, Israel How Brown and Squire Walcott and Stephen Foster and Wendell Phillips and everyone else who helped escaped slaves became criminals. The Fugitive Slave Act, one of the five laws making up the famous Compromise of 1850, was stringent enough to satisfy the most rabid proslavery men in the South. It placed the entire responsibility for apprehending fugitives on the Federal government and provided special United States commissioners to issue warrants for the arrest of fugitives and certificates for their return. Anyone guilty of obstructing the process was liable to a fine of $1,000 and six months imprisonment. The bill also stated that an affidavit on the part of the claimant would be accepted as evidence of ownership and that alleged fugitives would be denied the right to trial by jury and the right to give evidence in their own behalf. The commissioner was to receive ten dollars when a certificate was granted for the return of a fugitive and only five dollars when the certificate was refused.

The response was what might have been expected. Southerners hailed it as a long-overdue gesture from the Federal government to protect Southern property. Political leaders of both the Democratic and Whig parties hailed it as part of a compromise designed to admit California as a free state, solve the problem of slavery in the West and soothe sectional antagonisms. Meanwhile, the *Liberator* tauntingly announced that more and more fugitives were coming through its offices on Cornhill Street, and abolitionists of all kinds, united for the first time in ten years, denounced the law as immoral.[16]

On October 14, a mass meeting was held in Faneuil Hall to protest the new law. Charles Francis Adams presided, and the meeting was controlled and attended largely by political abolitionists who felt that all means short of violence should be resorted to in order to repeal the law. Frederick Douglass reported on the consternation which the law had caused among the colored people in the North who felt that the new law brought every Negro within reach of the slave catcher. Then Phillips urged the public to nullify the law. Reminding his audience that those who helped slaves still had the right to a jury trial, he said, "We must trample the law under our feet." [17]

A vigilance committee was organized after the meeting for the purpose of thwarting the execution of the Fugitive Slave Law in the vicinity of Boston. Ultimately, it had more than two hundred members. The committee

publicly condemned the law as unconstitutional and unjust, professed its belief that no one in Boston would be
mean enough to support it and advised the fugitive slaves
and colored inhabitants of Boston to remain in the neighborhood, "for we have not the smallest fear that any of
them will be taken from us and carried off to bondage."

Phillips was appointed to the executive committee,
and he plunged into his new duties with enthusiasm.[18]
Popular repudiation of the law was what he had hoped
for, and he was happy to be able to cooperate with others
in the work even though most of them did not subscribe
to his radical theories about the Constitution and the
Union.

Returning to Boston, Phillips found his friends on
the Vigilance Committee facing their first challenge. A
Mr. Hughes and a Mr. Knight had come to Boston as
agents of a slave owner in Macon, Georgia. They carried
warrants for the arrest of William and Ellen Crafts, a
Negro couple recently escaped from slavery. The committee moved swiftly. Making sure that the Crafts were
safely hidden away, the vigilantes launched a campaign
to drive Hughes and Knight out of town. The two visitors
found that whenever they walked down the street they
were accompanied by a group of well-dressed men who
shouted, "Slave hunters, slave hunters, there go the slave
hunters!" When the Southerners were heard to call
William Crafts a thief, the legal subcommittee swung into
action and had them arrested for slander, but they were
quickly bailed out. Finally, the committee appointed
Theodore Parker (the Crafts were members of his congregation) to prevail upon the slave catchers to leave town.

Phillips had come to know Parker quite intimately
since 1847, when the latter had moved into a house on
Exeter Place, almost in the Phillips' backyard. Phillips
could not agree with Parker on theology (Parker was so
radical that he had even broken with the Unitarians) or
on the importance of politics to the antislavery effort, but
he was impressed by Parker's zeal and his insistence on

the practical applications of religion. Like everyone else, Phillips was amazed at Parker's knowledge. He had mastered more than a dozen languages and was always carrying on several monumental research projects at the same time. An impressively homely man with a massive, bald dome, Parker, who was brought up on a farm, retained something of the farmer's unsubtlety in his manner and appearance. His approach to every congregation and audience was blunt. He laid them under siege and always called in the heaviest artillery at hand. Among church people, Parker was noted for preaching a gospel of love, but Hughes and Knight would never have believed that; it took only a single interview for him to put the fear of God into them, and they packed their bags and were off.[19]

Phillips was obviously happy at these developments. Boston was acting as he had hoped. The slave interest was getting a taste of the treatment it had been meting out to abolitionists for years—with one difference: there had been no violence in Boston, no horsewhippings or shootings. The slave catchers simply found themselves frustrated by a public opinion which refused to support an immoral law.

Two weeks later, however, Phillips was hooted down by a mob again, this time in Faneuil Hall. The abolitionists had planned a meeting to welcome George Thompson after a fifteen-year absence. Thompson had gone on to make a political career for himself since Phillips last saw him and was now a member of Parliament. His welcome on the part of the general public in Boston, however, turned out to be as unfriendly as it had in 1835. The hall was jammed by a delegation of Webster Whigs whose purpose was to spoil the meeting. Not even Phillips, whom the hostile press described "as almost the only man of the Garrison gang whom the masses will ever hear," was allowed to speak. He tried until he was hoarse, but the crowd only hooted, broke into a chorus of "Yankee Doodle" and cheered for Daniel Webster. To compound the confusion, Abby Folsom jumped up in the gallery and harangued the audience. Finally, the captain of the police arrived to adjourn the meeting. This was the final blow to Phillips, not only because the police had made no effort to stop the riot but also because the captain's name was Sam Adams! [20]

Not even an antiabolitionist riot in Faneuil Hall could discourage Phillips. The riot represented "the last spasms of defeated Whiggery—Webster Whiggery," he told an audience in Lynn ten days later, but that could not stop the fury over the fugitive slave issue. "Oh no! This chasm in the forum all the Clay in the land cannot fill. This rent in the mantle all the Websters in the mill cannot weave up. Perpetuate slavery amid such a race as ours! Impossible!" [21]

As the agitation over the Fugitive Slave Law continued, Phillips began to find his position as a spokesman for the radical abolitionists less lonely than it had been a few years earlier. More and more people, whether they agreed or not, were willing to listen to what he had to say, and, despite his notorious reputation as a radical, lyceum requests continued to pour in. "As a popular speaker, we doubt if there is his superior in the country," wrote a reviewer who heard one of his lyceum lectures about this time. "If he had only flattered the prejudices and opinions of the majority, instead of denouncing them, if he had only just kept pace with public opinion—we venture to say not a man in New England would, at this time, have more admirers." [22]

Another new development, although he may not have been conscious of it himself, was that Wendell had begun to grow out of Garrison's shadow. The two men were still fast friends, and their families saw as much of each other as they ever had. When Garrison needed two hundred dollars to meet household expenses ("Everything is absorbed on bread and butter"), it was natural for him to turn to Phillips for a loan. [23] For his part, Wendell continued to delight in the progress of Wendell Phillips Garrison ("my little namesake . . . an embryo edition of ten years old"), who had already learned to set type and was publishing a paper of his own.[24] Moreover, Phillips never forgot that Garrison had been the great awakener, and at a soiree on January 24, 1851, celebrating the *Liberator*'s twentieth birthday, he eulogized Garrison as the man who "taught us how we intensify this life by laying it a willing sacrifice on the altar of some great cause."[25] Nevertheless, at the annual meeting of the Massachusetts Anti-Slavery Society a few days later, and in the months and years which followed, although Garrison remained the nominal head of the radical abolitionists, more and more of the rank and file looked to Phillips for leadership.

Meanwhile, a new flurry of excitement broke out in Boston in the middle of February when an escaped slave, known as Shadrach, was arrested in the Cornhill Coffee House, where he was working. Marshal Patrick Riley had no sooner taken Shadrach to the courthouse when a group of lawyers from the vigilance committee, headed by Richard Henry Dana, showed up to act as counsel. The hearing was postponed for a few days, and Dana made his way through the crowd of Negroes who had quietly gathered around the courthouse and returned to his office across the street to plan the case. A little later, he heard a yell outside. Looking out the window, he saw the courthouse doors burst open. "Down the steps came two huge Negroes bearing the prisoner between them with his clothes half torn off, and so stupefied by the sudden rescue and the violence of his dragging off that he sat almost dumb, and I thought had fainted; but the men seized him, and being powerful fellows hurried him through the square into Court Street where he found the use of his feet, and they went off toward Cambridge, like a black squall, the crowd driving along with them and cheering as they went."[26]

That was the last Boston ever saw of Shadrach. He was taken out of the state by way of Concord and Leominster, where Mrs. Jonathan Drake, a zealous abolitionist determined to get all the satisfaction out of the occasion that she could, dressed the fugitive in a bonnet, took him to church and introduced him to her friends as "Mrs. Brown." [27]

Repercussions of the Shadrach incident were felt far outside Boston. President Fillmore issued a proclamation urging support of the laws and ordered the United States Attorney-General to prosecute all obstructionists. Henry Clay, whom the *Liberator* described as "with one foot in the grave, and just ready to have both body and soul cast into Hell," rose in the Senate to urge the passage of an even more stringent fugitive-slave law.[28]

Phillips rejoiced when he heard about Shadrach and agreed with Garrison that the rescue should be distinguished from the kind of mob action which so frequently harassed abolitionist meetings. "The rescuers were not activated by a lawless spirit," Garrison wrote in the *Liberator*, "but by a deep and commendable sympathy with a wronged and outraged man . . . by a love of liberty . . . by a clear appreciation of justice—by the spirit of the revolutionary motto, 'Resistance to tyrants is obedience to God.' " [29]

If public opinion showed signs of regeneracy in Boston, it remained as corrupt as ever in other parts of the state. Wendell learned this just two days after the Shadrach affair, when he accompanied George Thompson to Springfield. A mob, encouraged, Phillips thought, by the local Whig merchants and leaders of the Democratic party, was waiting for them and refused to let the scheduled meeting take place. Thompson, who was hung in effigy from the limb of one of the big elms in Court Square, had to dodge a shower of rotten eggs and spend the night in a hotel room with shattered windows. When Phillips tried to lash back at the crowd, they brought in a fife-and-drum corps to drown him out.[30]

Phillips found this experience exhilarating, in keeping with the stepped-up tempo of his life at this time. When he returned to Boston, the city was still buzzing over the Shadrach case, and he heard that nearly a hundred Negroes had fled the city in the last few days. An old Ne-

gro woman of seventy came to him for advice. Although
she had been free all her life, she was afraid of being
arrested and sent into slavery by mistake. Many fugitives living in Boston for some time now were setting
out for Canada, leaving their jobs and their families behind. The vigilance committee was meeting every night,
and Phillips felt gratified to be part of a movement which
could measure its work in tangible results. He exulted at
the stories of successful escapes. "The way we get news of
warrants is surprising," he wrote to Elizabeth Pease. "One
officer was boasting to one of our members, whom he did
not know to be such, that now they had a fellow in sight,
and he would be arrested by one o'clock. Our friend
lounged carelessly away, told what he'd heard, and by 12
the poor fellow described was steaming it on iron lines to
Canada. Another at work on a wharf, came out of his employees store, saw his old master before him—dived into
the cellar, up the back door, and he's not been heard tell
of . . . since." [31]

For all his stern moralizing, there was something of
the romantic in Wendell Phillips. Had he been born in
Europe, he would probably have been one of those gallant
young men anxious to shed blood for liberty in the revolutions of 1848. He hinted as much in a letter:

> The long evening sessions—debates about secret escapes—plans
> to evade where we can't resist—the door watched that no spy may
> enter—the whispering consultations of the morning—some putting
> property out of their hands, planning to incur penalties, and plan-
> ning also that, in case of connection, the Government may get noth-
> ing from them—the doing, and answering no questions—intimates
> forbearing to ask the knowledge which it may be dangerous to have
> —all remind me of those foreign scenes which have hitherto been
> known to us, transatlantic republicans, only in books.[32]

Phillips believed that Southern leaders realized the
impossibility of getting all their fugitives back. When the
two slave catchers Hughes and Knight had been turned

out of town by Parker, one of them had grumbled: "It isn't the niggers I care about, *but it's the principle of the thing.*" All the South wanted, Phillips thought, was one fugitive from Boston "to show the discontented ones at home that *it can be done.*" [33] Wendell knew that Washington had sent out special orders that the law be enforced. He knew that the political authorities in Boston were friendly to the federal administration and that most of the merchants in town were disgruntled at the prospect of permanently alienating the South. Despite this, he clung to the hope that Boston would flout the law. What happened to Thomas Sims on the eleventh of April destroyed this hope.

Sims had been in Boston about a month and was staying at a boarding house for Negro sailors when he was arrested on April 3. The next morning he appeared before Commissioner George T. Curtis and was represented by a battery of lawyers from the vigilance committee who secured a twenty-four-hour postponement. Meanwhile, Sims was kept a prisoner in the courthouse.

When Phillips came down to the courthouse, he found it surrounded by an iron chain and guarded by three hundred policemen, most of them specially sworn in by Marshal Tukey for the job. A pack of bloodhounds was kept in readiness near by. The chain, which hung about four feet from the ground, was designed to keep a hostile crowd, or any would be rescuers, from approaching the courthouse, but Wendell saw it as a symbol of the chains which fettered every citizen in a nation corrupted by slavery. When he heard that Lemuel Shaw, Chief Justice of the Supreme Judicial Court of Massachusetts, had crawled under that chain on his way to court, Phillips was glad that he had given up his own legal career.

Although the hearing before Commissioner Curtis on Saturday, April 5, seemed to prove that Sims actually was a fugitive, another postponement was obtained, to Monday, to allow the defense to prepare their case challenging the constitutionality of the law.

On Saturday evening, the members and friends of the vigilance committee held a public meeting on Boston Common. Samuel Gridley Howe presided, and Phillips was the first speaker. Comparing the policemen around the courthouse to British redcoats, he said "If Yankee ingenuity cannot drive a four-wheeled wagon load of slaves through any law which drunken legislators can make, let us hide our heads.—One thing is certain, Courts obliged to sit guarded by bayonets will not sit long in Massachusetts." How should the law be opposed? To the Negroes in the audience he said "Should any officer under this law or any other, attempt to take wife or relative into bondage, I should feel justified by every law of God and man, in shooting that officer." He appealed to all the citizens of Boston to make public opinion clear, to surround the courthouse in angry thousands and, without resorting to violence, "throw every obstacle in our power in the way of the execution of this law. Block the wheels of Government so far as we can. . . ." [34]

As the trial dragged on, every passing day seemed to seal Sims' fate. Boston merchants were still convinced that their prosperity depended on maintaining cordial relations with the South. One businessman told Phillips that if the abolitionists got their way grass would grow on Milk Street and Boston would go bankrupt. Wendell began to sense the public's complacency about the matter when he heard an acquaintance say that "he thought a little blood would do good—a little of Theodore Parker's blood."

Phillips addressed another meeting in Tremont Temple on April 8, but most of his time was spent consulting with the other officers of the vigilance committee. When two of Father Snowden's sons were arrested for being in the vicinity of the courthouse with firearms, Phillips supplied their bail. The usual orderly regimen of 26 Essex Street was turned upside down, and Ann was as excited and involved in what was going on as Wendell. "I never saw anything equal to Ann Terry's guts," wrote Deborah Weston to her sister. "They were up night and day and one night, when a row was strongly anticipated, she aided Wendell with the knowledge that if he got off alive, he was to run for Halifax and she was to join him there or in England." Phillips was apparently pushing the other members of the vigilance committee to make some attempt to free Sims, and whenever he was called out at night the house was left open and Ann took over, roaring down instructions from her third-floor bedroom like a sentry.[35]

By the middle of the week, carpenters were busy putting up a shack on the deck of the brig *Acorn* tied up at the end of Long Wharf. The word soon got around that the shack was for Sims, and the vigilance committee began to meet in more frenzied consultation than before. It was obvious that there would be no popular protest from Boston, but Phillips continued to hear reports that one hundred men from Plymouth County and two hundred more from Worcester were about to descend on the city, muskets in hand, to effect a rescue.[36] He waited, but no one came. Meanwhile, he thought that the captain of the *Acorn* could be bribed to let Sims off at Hyannis, but to his disgust several of the members demurred because bribery was immoral.[37] On Friday, Commissioner Curtis gave his opinion that Sims should be returned to Georgia, and that night the members of the vigilance committee, unable to agree on any plan of action, returned to their homes in despair.

About four o'clock on Saturday morning, while Phillips was still in his bed, Marshal Tukey assembled his company of policemen in front of the courthouse and marched Thomas Sims through Court Square, across the pavement marking the spot of the Boston Massacre, to the head of Long Wharf, where he was put on board the *Acorn*. Sims was the first Negro ever to be returned to slavery from the soil of Massachusetts. Six days later, on April 19, he was publicly whipped in Savannah.

10

Kossuth, Horace Mann and
Anthony Burns   1851–1854

Phillips had thought up until the last minute that the people of Massachusetts would rise up and refuse to let Sims be re-enslaved, but in the end the man had been taken away almost without protest. He could have been dragged away at high noon, Wendell now believed, "and not a dog would have wagged his tongue." [1] It was not the United States commissioner, or the marshal, or the government in Washington, but the general corruption of public sentiment in Massachusetts that had re-enslaved Sims. The effect of the experience on Phillips was to redouble his efforts at regenerating public opinion. During the next four years he was to see the tide of popular sentiment turn sharply against slavery. He was even to find himself temporarily on the side of the majority in Massachusetts, only to succumb once again as the organized powers of government combined to send another celebrated fugitive in Boston back into slavery.

The key to understanding Phillips' words and actions during this period is to be found in his thinking about the importance of public opinion. Concerned with the subject ever since Lovejoy's death, he had gradually developed a theory of American political institutions which now underpinned his strategy as a reformer. His basic assumption was that the American system was a government not of laws but of men. Public opinion was sovereign, and the function of the statesman was not to direct or control public opinion but to represent it. It followed from this that the creative power in American society lay with those who tried to shape public opinion. "No matter where you meet a dozen men pledged to a new idea,—wherever you have met them, you have met the beginning of a revolution." Abolitionists, therefore, need not fret over their slender ranks. Webster could have his little joke about their "rub a dub dub" agitation and dismiss them as a handful of noisy fanatics, but they had already made enough of a dent in public opinion to mortally wound him and the party he represented.

There was nothing sentimental in Phillips' conception of the masses. He saw public opinion in America as a massive, amoral potential. It was public opinion that had mobbed Garrison and murdered Lovejoy. It was public opinion that resisted the Fugitive Slave Law and would one day, if properly shaped, destroy slavery. The function of the agitator, however, was a necessary part of the democratic process and would not stop with the abolition of slavery. "Eternal vigilance is the price of liberty: power is ever stealing from the many to the few. The manna of popular liberty must be gathered each day, or it is rotten. . . .   Only by continual oversight can the democrat in office be prevented from hardening into a despot: only by unintermitted agitation can a people be kept sufficiently awake to principle not to let liberty be smothered in material prosperity." [2]

Phillips' concern with the importance of public opinion helps to explain why he followed with growing impatience the publicity given by the American press to Louis Kossuth in the summer and fall of 1851. Kossuth was a Hungarian and one of the great revolutionary leaders in the nineteenth century. As the leader of those revolting against Austrian domination, he had captured the American imagination. The natural sympathy of Americans for popular revolutions elsewhere had been stimulated further by the fact that Austria had bluntly told the United States to keep her nose out of European affairs. President Fillmore had retaliated by offering Kossuth, who was now a refugee in Turkey, safe passage in an American warship. Kossuth accepted and landed at New York on December 5, 1851, where he was received with a tumultuous public celebration. Kossuth was an eloquent orator, and wherever he traveled in the United States he was greeted with tremendous enthusiasm.

To Phillips it was a sour spectacle. The same people who threw eggs at George Thompson were pelting Kossuth with laurels. In speech after speech the Hungarian lauded Americans for their love of liberty, the freedom and perfection of their nation. He had never heard, it seemed, that one out of every twenty human beings in America was a slave. When the abolitionists reminded him, he said he could not interfere in matters of "domestic" policy. This was the gist of Phillips' criticism in a speech in Boston on December 27. He had as much affection for the course of republicanism in Europe as any man; what he objected to in Kossuth was the way he endorsed "the great American lie" by allowing the American people to indulge in an orgy of patriotic high-mindedness.[3]

The speech on Kossuth, which is one of his more eloquent efforts, shows how profound Phillips could be in his criticism of American institutions. He recognized that a patriotism blind to national sins was idolatrous, and he knew how enthusiastically men can indulge their idealism when their self-interest is not involved. The political slavery of Hungary was a bad thing, but, in trying to save Hungary, Kossuth was helping the American people to live comfortably in their hypocrisy and draining off precious moral energy for a cause far less worthy than antislavery.

Phillips' frequent assault on public personalities during these years was a calculated part of his campaign to prod the public conscience. "The great mass of the people," he said, "can never be made to stay and argue a long question. They must be made to feel it through the hides of their idols. When you have launched your

spear into the rhinoceros hide of a Webster or a Benton,
every Whig and Democrat feels it. It is on this principle
that every reform must take for its text the mistakes of
great men." [4]

Phillips gave a practical demonstration of what he
meant in a Faneuil Hall speech on January 30, 1852. His
subject was the surrender of Sims, and his purpose was to
indict publicly everyone who had a part in returning Sims
to slavery. He accused the merchants of complicity. "I
feel that these peddling hucksters of State and Milk Streets
owe me full atonement for the dishonor they have brought
upon the city of my birth." He disposed of the mayor.
"He was only the easy and shuffling tool of the moneyed
classes, and therefore too insignificant to be remembered
with any higher feeling than contempt." He described
Rufus Choate, a Webster man and one of the most illustrious lawyers in the country, who had recently defended
the Fugitive Slave Law in Faneuil Hall. "He struck me
like a monkey in convulsions." [5]

There were many even among those generally sympathetic with the abolitionists who could not abide such
language. It was too harsh, too personally offensive, too
lacking in Christianity, but Phillips, always deaf to such
criticism, scorned "this effeminate Christianity" which
would let millions suffer to spare one man's feelings.

Phillips' enemies would have admitted that, as an
assassin of public reputation, he was perfectly impartial.
Even Charles Sumner was beginning to wince under the
lash. In the fall of 1850 a coalition of Free-Soilers and
Democrats had come into power in Massachusetts, and
Sumner had been sent to the Senate. Sumner's instincts
on the slavery issue were unimpeachable, and Phillips rejoiced to see him in the Senate. He was distressed, however, by the frenzied politicking behind the scenes. The
bargain struck between the Democrats and Free-Soilers
was public knowledge: the Democrats were to take the
bulk of the state offices, including the governorship, while
the Free-Soilers were to get the senatorship vacated by

Webster. Phillips suspected that the price was too high. Not only was the new governor, George Boutwell, a man of tepid antislavery sentiment, but it had taken twenty-six ballots and more than three months for the legislature to elect Sumner. The issue had still been in doubt at the time of the Sims case, and, even though Sumner had served as counsel to Sims, Phillips believed that Free-Soil men had been too timid in the crisis. "I think they sacrificed Sims to the election of Mr. Sumner," he said. "Sims and silence elected Charles Sumner." [6]

Two months after Sumner had gone to Washington, Wendell wrote him a short note of congratulation. "Great accounts come floating here of your triumphant success in Washington, social and otherwise. In all that raises you . . . none finds less surprise or more pleasure than yours most truly Wendell Phillips." [7] This was in February 1852. Despite these generous words, Sumner was already beginning to find out how difficult it was to try to be a reformer and a politician at the same time. The abolitionists had sent him a petition appealing for the release of Drayton and Sayres, two men convicted in the District of Columbia for promoting the escape of twenty-six slaves. Acting on his own discretion, Sumner did not present the petition to the Senate but proceeded privately in his efforts to free the men. The abolitionists in Massachusetts were annoyed at this show of independence, and Phillips found that wherever he went to lecture he was asked "by free soilers as well as our folks" if he trusted Sumner. Although his answer was always in the affirmative, Wendell was growing impatient with Sumner's caution. "Let us still believe the event will justify us in trusting him," he told an audience on April 12, "spite of his silence there for four long months, silence when so many ears have been waiting for the promised words."

Sumner, who was always sensitive to criticism, wrote Phillips to inquire why his popularity among the abolitionists was waning. His letter found Phillips in a testy mood. "Though Kossuth's welcome roars through our

streets I may as well sit down and answer you," he replied
to Sumner, "especially as your Free Soil friends have sent
me no tickets of admission to the State House, not thinking it delicate perhaps to suppose me willing to look at
him!" Garrison had been blasting Sumner in the *Liberator,*
and Phillips tried to explain this away by passing on his
remark "I should never let a Whig sit there silent 4½
months—why shd I let him?" and reminding Sumner that
Garrison had never known him personally. Phillips knew
Sumner, trusted him, and would continue to trust him,
"at least till the end of the session and listen then to his
explanations." [8] Sumner could no longer be looked on
merely as an old friend. He had become a public figure,
and Wendell would judge him accordingly.

Although Sumner might prove to be a problem in
Washington, Phillips found himself faced with a more
urgent problem at home. Despite all his ministrations and
the advice of a multitude of doctors, Ann was sicker than
ever this spring. Perhaps the excitement of the Sims case
had been too exhausting. Whatever the cause, she was in
almost constant misery, so doubled over with pain she
could not walk. In desperation, Wendell decided to take
her for an extended water cure at an establishment in
Florence, Massachusetts. June and the early part of July
were devoted to preparations for the move, and Wendell
did little lecturing. As usual, he spoke at the Fourth of
July celebration which the abolitionists sponsored every
year at the picnic grounds in Abington—only this time he
appeared on July fifth, because an exasperated Whig had
hired the place the day before just to keep the abolitionists
out.[9]

Wendell and his wife arrived in Florence sometime
in the middle of July. Because Ann was almost totally
incapacitated, the trip was a major undertaking, and Wendell hired a private railroad car for the occasion. He
described the journey in detail to Helen Garrison: "I am
happy to tell you that we got to Springfield very comfortably. I brought Ann down in my arms. She rode to Depot

door, opposite to it stood our car, to which she walked—
four or five seats in it had been taken out to accomodate
our baggage—& the more to receive the bed—so I and all
my baggage—consisting of bags, band boxes, baskets,
bundles, trunks, tubs, carpet bags & chairs, one wife & one
domestic—got into this car, locked ourselves in and
started." That night they stayed in a hotel in Springfield.
The next morning their car was hitched to the Northampton train, and an hour later Ann was on her way by
carriage to the tiny village of Florence two miles away,
Wendell following, like a teamster, with a wagonful of
luggage.[10]

Once they were established in their new quarters at
the sanatorium, Dr. Munde examined Ann, announced
that all her pains were a good sign because they showed
"an active system" and began the treatment. She was
doused in tubs of cold water, wrapped in wet sheets and
packed in mud. This was to continue more than a year.

Meanwhile, Wendell, who confided to friends that
he was the only one who really felt that the "cure" would
help, was stuck in an isolated village with nothing to do.
Fortunately, the silk factory across the street from the
hotel burned down shortly after they arrived, and Wendell was able to supervise the rebuilding job from his
front porch. Except for this, he reported to the Garrisons,
life was pretty dull. He slept until 10, weighed himself
four times a day, ate three times a day, waited for the
mail and knitted mittens in the evening. "We've erected
a new flag staff in town," he wrote in one letter. "The
old one blew down, overcome with the weight of its honor
in welcoming Kossuth—then I've ascertained that they've
no fine needles at the store, though they boast an excellent
assortment of cowhide boots and axe handles . . . our
cat caught a mouse Saturday evening and the Macomber
baby cried lustily half an hour Sunday morning. We have
waffles & highbush blackberries for breakfast three morn-
ings out of five and the only saddle horse here is so hard a
trotter that I do not yet see any prospect of my getting

many rides. Yesterday morning I picked up all the scraps
of paper in the garden and today the stage was ten minutes
late." [11]

Occasionally the monotony would be broken by an
invitation to lecture in an adjoining town. His lectures
in Northampton drew the biggest crowds there since Jenny
Lind. To his surprise, he was invited to address a society
at Williams College. Being met at the station at Wil-
liamstown with a span of horses, he was "smothered in
with 12 Judges, three Governors & lots of DD's. They are
the bluest of the blue Connecticut orthodoxy up there—
how they ever came to let the young men invite me I cannot tell." Except that his mention of Theodore Parker's
name made everyone shudder, he made a good impression.
The lecture, entitled "The Duty of a Christian Scholar
in a Republic," was an early version of the lecture he
would give nearly thirty years later at Harvard amid a
blaze of publicity.[12]

Phillips read the papers avidly and tried to be of what
influence he could, despite his isolation. When the reports
of Sumner's first antislavery speech in the Senate came in,
he sent off a letter of congratulations, tempered with
criticism. Sumner was commended for demanding the
repeal of the Fugitive Slave Law but reprimanded for
taking the position that harmony could be restored by
putting the slavery question into the absolute control of
the states.[13]

Sometime in September, Edmund Quincy came to
Florence for a visit. He found Ann in good spirits but
too weak to stand and with her spine "crooked almost
. . . to deformity." Wendell seemed to spend most of
his time in his wife's room, and Quincy suspected that
such confinement jeopardized his health. Most of all,
Quincy regretted that his friend was forced to be out of
action so much of the time. "It does seem," he wrote to
Richard Webb, "as if God had given him his great powers
for something better." [14]

On October 24 the news of Webster's death reached

Florence. The bells in the meeting house mournfully tolled the event, and one of the greatest funeral processions in the history of Massachusetts began as thousands of men and women set out on horseback, on foot and in every kind of conveyance to catch a last glimpse of the great Daniel, laid out in an open coffin in front of his house in Marshfield.

Back in Boston, the abolitionists were frustrated beyond all endurance. Webster dead seemed to be even more beguiling than Webster alive, and the radicals were afraid that the moral lesson they had tried to burn into the public mind after he had supported the Fugitive Slave Law would be erased in one great eulogistic orgy. The refined Edmund Quincy spoke for the most vehement of them when he wrote that he was nauseated by all that had been made of Webster's "opiated piety on his deathbed & all the blasphemous twaddle that has been vomited forth from so many pulpits over this hoary reprobate . . . as Milton says 'it is enough to give a vomit to God himself.' " [15]

It was probably Quincy who asked Phillips to write a piece on Webster for the *Liberty Bell,* and Wendell, happy to have something to do, quickly accepted. He thought about the thousands of sermons which would be preached in the meeting houses of New England to honor the memory of the man who had secured the passage of the Fugitive Slave Law. "One would think our priests were awe struck," he wrote, "or beside themselves with gratitude that the Great Man condescended to die a Christian." He thought about the three great political leaders of the day—Calhoun, "the pure manly uncompromising advocate of slavery," Clay, "the secret facile and therefore more dangerous, ally of Calhoun," and "Webster, the greatest orator, the greatest lawyer, the greatest mind" ("in simple intellect no American has ever equalled him"). In the end, Phillips decided, Webster had been a casualty of American institutions. Devoured by political ambition, blasted by the curse of political expediency,

Webster had been one of the majestic figures of the century, but he illustrated what happened when the Puritan spirit was extinguished in the Yankee. (How high was the higher law he had demanded? Was it higher than the Blue Ridge, higher than the Alleghenies?) Despite this moral blind spot, Webster had become a great American hero. Because of this, Phillips had bitterly denounced him in his lifetime and would continue to denounce him long after he was laid in the grave.[16]

The election results in November seemed to confirm Phillips' prejudices about Webster. The Whigs again went down to defeat, a fate reserved, he hoped, for all political organizations that tried to temporize on the slavery issue. The fact that a Democratic President, Franklin Pierce, was being sent to the White House with strong Southern support did not bother Wendell, for he felt that the destruction of the Whigs presaged the coming of two great sectional parties which would mean "the beginning of the end" for the Union.

As winter came upon them, Phoebe Garnaut joined the Phillipses at Florence, and Wendell helped to while away the time by giving her lessons in French, Latin, arithmetic and geography. Ann had found the noise of the hotel too irritating, and they had moved to a little cottage which stood on a corner of the grounds facing a waterfall. When the snow came the other patients had snowball fights and went sliding, and Ann looked wistfully out at them from her second-floor window.[17]

Phillips returned to Boston briefly in January 1853 to lecture on the "Philosophy of the Abolition Movement." In this speech he reiterated the necessity for abolitionists to stand apart from all other organizations and parties and to criticize friends and foes alike whenever the cause demanded it. He mentioned Sumner's conduct in the Senate as an example. Sumner's aid to the cause he freely admitted; on the other hand, he felt that, to the extent that Sumner was following the Republican line and agitating for the abolition of slavery only in the ter-

ritories, he was derelict in his duty. In the same manner
he criticized other antislavery men in Congress, including
Joshua Giddings and Horace Mann.[18]

Sumner quickly wrote for an explanation, and Phillips replied by reminding him that, as an officeholder,
sworn to uphold the Constitution, he and Phillips were
sometimes working at cross purposes. Like every other
radical, Wendell was directing his appeal at the people
of Massachusetts, and when they threw Sumner's speeches
defending political action in his face he had to demur or
give up the argument. Although there appeared to be no
way to reconcile their differences, Wendell still thought
that he and his friend could help each other. As a senator,
Sumner could reach people who would never listen to
Phillips. On the other hand, Phillips believed that the
agitation of the radicals sustained the militant kind of
public opinion that would keep Sumner in office.[19]

Phillips had said he did not believe that the politicians
he mentioned would be offended by his criticism, but in
this he was disappointed. Even Sumner was more hurt
than he realized, but the real trouble came with Horace
Mann. Moving from education to politics, Mann had
been in the House of Representatives since 1848 and had
earned a reputation as one of the most outspoken anti-
slavery men in Washington. Phillips had chided Mann
for putting the Constitution above the Higher Law. Mann
replied in the form of a public letter to Phillips, and a
heated controversy began.

Mann would probably have ignored Phillips' remarks
if he had realized how bored Wendell was in his village
retirement. It was not that Phillips disliked Mann or
even felt any violent disagreement with him. His attitude
toward Mann was almost exactly like his attitude toward
Sumner. It was just that Mann was there, and he wanted
to argue. The controversy helped to keep Wendell occupied from February to June.

The *Liberator* published the correspondence between
the two. It began with a restatement of all the old argu-

ments regarding the Constitution and slavery and the propriety of an antislavery man participating in politics. Both disclaimed any intent to damage the other personally, but before long Mann was finding it "hard to believe that any man at once honest and intelligent" could say what Phillips did, and Wendell was charging his opponent with having obstructed the integration of Boston schools some ten years earlier. This led Mann to accuse Phillips of championing the Higher Law while carrying on as if he believed in "a lower law," and he said he found in one of Phillips' letters "Seventy-five substantive errors and misstatements, moral and logical." [20]

Phillips took an infuriatingly lofty tone. "Mr. Mann indulges in epithets and insinuations, which may 'catch the ears of the groundlings,' but it would not become me to notice them." [21] In private, however, he was more zestful. "I'll teach him that the Garrisonians never go out, even on the most gala occasion, without their pockets 'full of rocks.' I look on the fight as the test question of my speech. If I floor him no other man will relish disputing my positions." He didn't think much of Mann's ability in debate, and he told Quincy that Theodore Parker had worked over one of Mann's speeches three times in an unsuccessful attempt to prune out the "gnarls and knots." [22]

By June the controversy had begun to pall. Friends of both felt that the prolonged debate had done the cause more harm than good, and Phillips himself had lost his appetite for it. "I hardly read the Mann letter," he wrote to Quincy in June, "it's so weak and trashy. He does not understand the subject he is talking about." [23]

The controversy between Mann and Phillips reveals not only how cantankerous an idealist can be but also the tremendous gap which still separated Phillips from the majority of people in the North. Even though the Fugitive Slave Law had brought radicals and antislavery politicians into closer cooperation, they were still far apart on many important points. It was impossible for Phillips to

give any politician unqualified praise without surrendering his own position regarding the Constitution and the
Union. It was equally impossible for any man to stay in
politics and subscribe to Phillips' views. Although he
recognized this last point, Phillips felt that the politicians
owed a greater debt to the radicals than they acknowledged. It was Garrison and his supporters who had begun
the transformation of public opinion which the politicians
now represented. Their function was to represent this
opinion, to try and institutionalize it in law. He objected
when they presumed to go beyond this point and define
the limits of the entire antislavery effort, to judge the very
men who had made their position possible.[24]

The Phillipses returned to Boston in late September.
Even though the long stay at Florence had made no appreciable change in Ann's health, they were both glad to
be back at Essex Street. Garrison and the others were
happy to find Wendell in their midst again, and several
of the abolitionsts got together at the Antislavery Bazaar
and gave him a bronze statuette as a token of esteem. It
cost one hundred dollars and portrayed "a woman of color
with two white children on her lap."[25] This kind of appreciation was all the reward that Wendell needed, and
he threw himself back into the routine of antislavery
work.

Ever since 1850, Phillips had felt that, despite momentary diversions, the political currents in the nation
had been moving in the right direction. The uproar over
the Fugitive Slave Law, the disintegration of the Whigs
and the rise of the political antislavery movement had all
been good omens. In January 1854, the encouraging trend
was reversed by Stephen Douglas' proposal in the Senate
to organize the Kansas and Nebraska territory with or
without slavery according to the will of the inhabitants.
The implication was that the Missouri Compromise, which
since 1820 had kept slavery out of the territory north of
the 36th parallel, would be repealed.

Phillips believed that this proposal was a deliberate

attempt to propitiate the South by throwing the West open to slavery. He was dismayed when the bill passed the Senate in March, but he consoled himself with the knowledge that it had served to sharpen sectional antagonisms. The Massachusetts senate had been unanimous in voting a resolution of protest to the Kansas-Nebraska Act, and a remonstrance signed by some three thousand New England ministers and sent to Congress indicated that even the sluggish churchmen were beginning to clank their chains. A change in public opinion was apparent when he addressed an antislavery meeting in New York in the Broadway Tabernacle, where Captain Rynders and his gang had created such a shambles a few years earlier. Now, the big crowd on hand listened attentively while Phillips poured invective on the Northern politicians. At this time, with the public temper noticeably more sympathetic to the radical abolitionists, the fugitive-slave controversy which had been smouldering since the Sims case, burst forth again.[26]

Ever since the return of Sims, Phillips had been doing what he could to defy the Fugitive Slave Law. Even when tucked away with Ann at the sanitorium, he had not neglected his responsibilities as a member of the vigilance committee. Whenever he would get information from a Southern correspondent about a fugitive en route to Boston, he would pass on the word to a friend on the committee. The confidant was usually Austin Bearse, a rugged sea captain who had learned about slavery at first hand as a mate on ships plying the slave trade between Southern ports. Bearse was now a general agent for the vigilance committee. He served as doorkeeper at the secret meetings, and he used his yacht, *The Wild Pigeon,* to help carry fugitives to safety. Phillips had sent the following letter to Bearse on January 10, 1853:

DEAR FRIEND

When my little colored boy arrives, I wish you to take charge of him, and keep him till you can get some *safe* way to send him to the Cape. You know it is not safe to have colored children travelling about alone, so be very careful that you get him a safe conveyance. He is to be sent to J. E. Mayo, Harwich, to stop at the Union Store there. If Mr. Mayo is not there, Captain Small will attend to him. You must write to Mr. Mayo *two days before he will arrive,* telling him when *to expect him. Pay postage on your letters.* His name is Bernardo. I shall direct the Bath people to have him left at 21 Cornhill. So tell Wallcutt about him and let him attend to Bernardo till you arrive. *Write me of his arrival the moment he comes.* Charge expenses to me.

Yours truly

WENDELL PHILLIPS

Bearse followed the instructions carefully, and Bernardo was spirited away to freedom without mishap, one more example of the efficiency of the Underground Railroad, which, the abolitionists boasted, could get an escaped slave from a border state into Canada in forty-eight hours.[27]

The trial of Anthony Burns put an end to all boasting. Burns was a Negro tailor who worked in Coffin Pitts' clothing store on Brattle Street. While walking home on the evening of May 24, he was suddenly seized by a half-dozen men who darted out of an alley near Peter Brigham's saloon. They hustled him swiftly down the street to the courthouse, where he was clapped into a barricaded room and soon after confronted by his old master, Colonel Charles F. Suttle from Virginia.

Phillips heard the news sometime the next morning, a Thursday, and immediately went off to an emergency meeting of the vigilance committee in Tremont Temple. The members of the committee were agreed that Burns could not be sent back to slavery, but they could not decide on a way to save him. One party wanted to attack the Courthouse and take the prisoner by force. Phillips considered this impractical and urged that they wait until the fugitive slave commissioner brought in his decision. If he ordered Burns to be returned, then the committee and all the friends they could rouse should surround the courthouse, jam the streets and frustrate the order by making it clear that it could be executed only over the bodies of Boston citizens. Phillips apparently thought that one of two things would happen if it came to this. Either the authorities would give in to such massive resistance and release Burns, or they would try to take him through the crowd, and in the ensuing confusion he could be rescued. The debate was long and spirited, and it was only after the committee had adjourned and met again that evening that the members were able to decide for the latter plan. They also agreed to hold a mass meeting in Faneuil Hall the following night to stir up popular support.[28]

When Wendell went home he found Ann waiting up for him, anxious to know every detail of what had happened. She had heard about the man only this morning, but she was as distraught about the matter as if Anthony Burns were a close relative. "You will see by the papers that a fugitive is arrested here," she had immediately written to her cousins in Weymouth. "Do for mercy sake both of you come into town & give yr advice & counsel. Do stir up Weymouth for if this man is allowed to go back *there is no* antislavery in Massts—We may as well disband at once if our meetings & papers are all talk. . . ."[29]

An eclipse of the sun was expected on Friday. Phillips must have been struck with the grim appropriateness of God's timing in blotting out the sun over Boston. The day was not meant for philosophy, however, but for action, and early in the morning he, accompanied by Coffin Pitts and the Rev. Mr. Grimes, minister to Boston's colored congregation, went down to the courthouse to see Anthony Burns. When they were turned away by the guards at the door, Phillips took a carriage to Cambridge to visit Edward G. Loring, the fugitive slave commissioner, who was also a lecturer at Harvard. If Loring was cool in receiving Phillips, there was a reason. On at least one occasion Wendell had said in public that it would have "a wholesome effect" if one of the commissioners were to be shot on the bench.³⁰ Loring agreed to give Wendell a letter permitting him to see the prisoner, but as he handed it to him he said "Mr. Phillips the case is so clear, that I do not think you will be justified in placing any obstacles in the way of this man's going back, AS HE PROBABLY WILL!" Wendell listened to this in amazement, and he remembered the words later with bitterness. It was clear that Loring had prejudged the case before the evidence was in and was determined to send Burns back to Virginia.³¹

Letter in hand, Phillips clattered over the Charles River bridge a second time and went back to Court Square. This time he got by Watson Freeman, the pockmarked United States marshal who had helped to engineer the kidnapping of Burns, and was allowed to see the prisoner. Slavery had left its mark on Anthony Burns. He had on one cheek a large scar which looked like a brand; one hand was scarred, and the other had been broken and never set properly, so that a piece of bone stuck out. He was obviously dejected and frightened, unwilling to say or do anything to make his condition more miserable than it already was. It was said that he had admitted being Suttle's slave and was willing to go back with him. Phillips asked him if this were true and if he wanted counsel to represent him before the commissioner.

It must have been a baffling experience for Anthony Burns. First he was seized like a common thief, thrown into jail, brought face to face with a man who claimed him as absolutely as if he were a horse or a cow; now he was being solicitously waited on by a gentleman who said he wanted to set him free again. Phillips finally got him to accept a lawyer, then left to help prepare his defense.³²

Apparently, Wendell never thought of taking the case himself. He still did not feel that he could appear before a court in good conscience, but Richard Dana could, and it was to him that Phillips went for help. Dana was one of those who had been swept into the antislavery ranks by the Fugitive Slave Law. Ten years earlier he had thought the abolitionists "a nest of ignorant, fanatical,

heated, narrow-minded men," but he had since become
an ardent Free-Soiler and had served as counsel for
Thomas Sims in 1851.[33] His blood was as blue as Wendell's, and he had seen more of the world. He had gone
to sea as a young man and could remember what it was
like to scrub a deck, reef a sail and pack a hold with filthy
California hides. He had written it all down in a famous
book, *Two Years Before the Mast,* and had then gone on
to make a distinguished career in the law. A short, stocky
man with curly hair, Dana was known in the courts as the
seaman's champion. He had been one of the first to hear
about Burns' arrest and had interceded in his behalf to get
a postponement. Dana told Phillips he would be happy
to take the case.

After he left Dana, Phillips composed the following
placard and had it posted about the town.

THE FUGITIVE SLAVE—TO THE PUBLIC

Anthony Burns, the alleged fugitive, this morning stated to us that
he was arrested upon the false charge of robbing a jeweler's shop!
That the statement that he wished, or is willing to return to slavery

'IS A LIE!'

That he never so stated to any person. He has given us full power,
under his own hand and seal, to act as his attornies, and has requested us to do everything in our power to save him from going
back to slavery.

COFFIN PITTS
WENDELL PHILLIPS[34]

The rest of the day Wendell spent conferring with
other members of the vigilance committee. Among other
things, they were furious to discover the kind of men
Marshal Freeman had called on to guard the courthouse.
During the Sims trial any number of respectable citizens
had been willing to be deputized by the government, but
the sense of the community now, fired in part by the

controversy over the Kansas-Nebraska Act, was overwhelmingly opposed to Burns' arrest. Consequently, the marshal was forced to scour the saloons to make up his posse of more than a hundred men. Many of these were rounded up by a notorious character called Louis Varell, the king-pin of the Boston underworld, who operated a brothel and gambling hall and had recently been tried and acquitted for murder. The deputies bore Louis' stamp of approval, and almost half of them had criminal records. These men, armed with billies, cutlasses and revolvers, now stood guard over Burns and would sit in the courtroom throughout the trial. The sight of such people posing as respectable upholders of law was too much for the vigilance committee, and they retaliated by spreading posters about the town.[35]

MURDERS THIEVES AND BLACKLEGS
Employed by Marshal Freeman!!

MARSHAL FREEMAN has been able to stoop low enough to *insult even the United States Marines,* by employing MURDERERS, PRIZE-FIGHTERS, THIEVES, THREE CARD MONTE MEN AND GAMBLING HOUSE KEEPERS to aid him in the rendition of Burns. . . .[36]

Wendell came home late Friday to find his wife, attended by Anne Weston, wringing her hands with excitement, while Phoebe peered at the sun through a piece of smoked glass. After a hurried supper he and Anne Weston went off to Faneuil Hall. Posters advertising the meeting had been scattered throughout the city during the day, and by eight o'clock the hall was full.

The men on the platform represented a good cross section of the antislavery population in the Boston area. The chairman was George Russell, former mayor of Roxbury, assisted by several gentlemen who had been on the Governor's Council in the past. Two charter members of the vigilance committee, Samuel Gridley Howe and Henry Bowditch, were there, also Robert Morris, a Negro lawyer. Several speakers were scheduled, but the two men the crowd really came to hear were Phillips and Theodore Parker.

In the calm, scornful manner which his audiences had come to expect, Phillips recounted the events of the last two days. When he talked about Burns' arrest and the appearance of Colonel Suttle, he lingered over the word "master" until the crowd cried "No! No! He has no master." Explaining the unsuccessful efforts that members of the vigilance committee had made to get Burns released on a writ of replevin, he said "when law ceases in the city of Boston, it is time for the sovereignty of the people to begin." How did he expect the people to assert their sovereignty? On this point he was not precise. His reported remarks suggest that he wanted them to mass around the courthouse during the trial and thereby discourage any attempt to send the fugitive back.

See to it every man of you that loves Boston, that you watch these things so closely that you can look into that man's eyes. (Applause) When he comes up for his trial, get a sight of him. (Renewed applause.) When he comes out of his trial get a sight of him. (Great cheering.) Whenever he stands in the streets of Boston don't lose sight of him—I don't mean to (Enthusiastic cheers.) I tell you, fellow citizens, there is nothing like the mute eloquence of a suffering man to stir your hearts to do your duty as children of Faneuil Hall (Applause). I want you to see him every man of you. I want you to be wherever he is, and I will trust the result (Cheers) . . . Faneuil Hall is not here. I do not know these pictures; I do not know these walls. Faneuil Hall is up in the purlieus of that Court House, where tomorrow, the children of Otis and Hancock are to prove that they are not bastards. (Applause) . . . My resolution is, for me, that I will try to behave in this case, so that we shall wipe off the stain of Thomas Simms, so that no kidnapper shall again dare to show his face in the city of Boston. Make your resolution as I do. See that man for yourselves; and never lose sight of him, so long as his feet rest on Massachusetts soil. Who says aye to that? [37]

When Phillips sat down, Theodore Parker got up to speak. If not in style, Parker's speech was like Phillips' in substance. The honor of the community was at stake, and he proposed, at the end, that the meeting adjourn to meet in Court Square the next morning. As he finished a voice from the floor called out "Why not tonight?" This call was quickly taken up by others, and Parker's voice was overwhelmed by the clamor for immediate action.

Seeing that Parker was losing control, Phillips again jumped up. The crowd was turning into a mob, and he did not want that. His voice rang out, and the uproar died down. What was desired, he argued, was not a mob action under cover of night but a great public demonstration in the light of day before the very eyes of the officers of government.

> . . . it is in your power so to block every access and exit from the Court House, that it shall not be possible to carry him out of it except by your permission. You can do it. Five hundred resolute men among you can do it. . . . all that is asked of us, fellow citizens, is not to baulk their efforts by the utterly useless, harmful, fatal step of showing ourselves a tumultuous, aimless, purposeless mob. . . .

Even while he was talking, however, a man who had been struggling to get to the front of the hall suddenly yelled, "A band of Negroes is breaking the door to the Court House." This broke up the meeting. About two hundred men rushed out of the hall in the direction of Court Square.

Dismayed and confused by what was happening, Wendell stood on the platform and watched his audience pour out. Then he and Edmund Quincy walked Miss Weston and Phoebe back to Essex Street and gave a full report of the evening's activities to Ann, whose sympathies were completely with those who had wanted to assault the courthouse. The next morning (Saturday), they learned that the assault, led by Thomas Wentworth Higginson, had been made. It was repulsed, and one of the guards was killed.

Once again the abolitionists had demonstrated their inability to work together in a practical emergency. Phillips felt his part in the failure keenly. The attack on the courthouse, planned by Higginson and some others, had never been discussed by the vigilance committee. According to the plan, when the Faneuil Hall audience was sufficiently excited, there was to be a signal from the floor, seconded by encouragement from the platform, and the entire crowd was to be swept off to the courthouse en masse. But there had been bungling all around, and Phillips, not having been informed of the plan, had tried to prevent its execution.[38] People were already saying that, if the entire crowd had been led into Court Square, Burns would have been freed. Even if he had known about it, however, it is doubtful that Phillips would have acted differently, for he faced a real dilemma. Ever since Lovejoy had been killed, Phillips had been protesting against the American mob. His whole purpose was to replace the mob with an enlightened, disciplined public opinion. He knew that a great crowd, inflamed by passionate oratory and suddenly dispatched on an assignment of violence, was a mob—whatever its goal. What he wanted to see was a popular uprising of citizens, each of whom had soberly consulted his conscience and was prepared to restrain his government from sending another human being back to slavery. Phillips, in other words, was a moralist above everything else and would probably have been a dismal failure as a practical revolutionary. His hero, Samuel Adams, would not have had his compunctions about the use of mobs.

On Saturday morning when Phillips came down to Court Square, he found the military taking over. The mayor had ordered out two companies of artillery, one at city hall, the other at the courthouse. At the same time, Marshal Freeman had brought in two companies of

United States Marines and was acting with the confidence
of a man who has all the power of government on his side.
Before the day was out his position was further reinforced
by a telegraph from Washington. "Your conduct is approved," wired President Franklin Pierce. "The law must
be executed."

Wendell went to an antislavery meeting in Tremont
Temple and found Higginson there, holding a cloak over
his mouth to hide the cutlass wounds he had received the
night before. The abolitionists were paralyzed with indecision, and, since the case had been postponed until
Monday, Phillips spent the rest of the day consulting with
friends and preparing a prayer about Burns which would
be sent to all the Boston churches on Sunday. He heard
a rumor to the effect that some of Batcheleder's friends
(Batcheleder was the man who had been killed) had sworn
to mob him, but he paid no attention to it. He told Ann
there was nothing to worry about. That night after supper
he went out again, and Ann went to bed. She was roused
suddenly by someone beating on the door. Phoebe Garnaut went down, opened the door and found Theodore
Parker, who had just heard that the Phillips house was
about to be sacked. He wanted to take Ann to his place
for safety, but she would not leave until Wendell came
home. When he returned, a hurried consultation took
place and finally Ann's maid, Polly, who was frightened,
and Phoebe, who was furious at the prospect of missing
some excitement, were taken away to a friend's house for
safekeeping. Wendell also sent along some personal valu-
ables, including his father's portrait. By this time other
friends had arrived, and one of them ran off to give the
alarm to Wendell's brothers and sisters who lived nearby.
One brother-in-law, the Rev. George Blagden, who had
given Wendell over to the Devil years ago, apparently did
nothing. The second, Dr. Edward Reynolds, came down
to the house but, finding it full of abolitionists, retreated.
Wendell's older brother, Tom, however, went to the
mayor, who promised that the police would keep a special

eye on 26 Essex Street. The trouble never materialized, and the night passed quietly.

Anne Weston and Wendell and Ann Phillips spent Sunday together in watchful waiting. One encouraging sign was the news that many ministers usually silent on slavery matters had mentioned Burns in their sermons.

On Monday morning, business almost stopped in Boston. A great crowd gathered outside the courthouse. Many in the crowd were apparently heeding Phillips' plea and swore that they would stand there, morning and afternoon, as long as the trial lasted. People from the country and outlying towns were flocking into the city, and the police had all they could do to keep a path open through the street for traffic.

Most of the abolitionists were shut out of the courthouse, and even some of the judges who were trying other cases found they could not pass the barrier which the military had set up. Wendell, however, acting as Burns' agent, was allowed free access to the court, and he spent the three days when the case was actually tried shuttling in and out. On Monday, it was rumored that Colonel Suttle had agreed to sell Burns, that he would not take him back to slavery no matter what decision Judge Loring brought in. By Wednesday the abolitionists' hopes were rising. Dana had been able to produce several witnesses who swore that Burns had been in Boston at a time before that set by Suttle as the date of his escape. Phillips sat in the court exultant while this took place, then "sweat like rain" while Seth Thomas, counsel for Suttle, cross-examined one of the Negroes who had given this testimony. Meanwhile, the word in the streets was that Suttle had instructions from Virginia not to sell Burns at any price. Everything, therefore, would hang on Loring's decision, which would be given on Friday.

The New England Anti-Slavery Society was holding its annual convention in the Melodem. Phillips missed the first sessions but appeared Wednesday night to give a short, fighting speech violently denouncing the officials who were

holding Burns. When he mentioned the name of Benjamin
Hallet, the district attorney, he paused and asked for a
glass of water. Stephen Foster handed him one, and he
rinsed out his mouth, spat the water on the floor and went
on with the speech.[39]

On Friday morning the citizens found more soldiers
in their city for the purpose of preserving the peace than
had been seen since the Revolution. A veritable army
was parading on Boston Common. At the request of the
United States Government, Mayor Smith had called out
the First Battalion of Light Dragoons, the Fifth Regiment
of Artillery, the Fifth Regiment of Light Infantry, the
Third Battalion of Light Infantry and the Corps of Cadets.
In all there were twenty-two companies and a total force
of more than a thousand soldiers, each supplied with
eleven rounds of live ammunition.[40]

At nine o'clock Anthony Burns was brought into the
court room for the last time. Judge Loring appeared on
the bench and read the fateful opinion. Rejecting Dana's
argument that the law was unconstitutional, Loring told
the court that the claimant need establish only the fact
that his alleged property had once been held in slavery and
had escaped. This Colonel Suttle had done. The only other
question was whether the man before the court was the
actual Anthony Burns in the record. This, he decided, had
been established by the prisoner himself in his conversation with Suttle immediately after his capture; therefore,
Loring would grant the certificate that would return
Burns to slavery.

As word spread that Burns must return to Virginia,
a huge mass of people began to descend on Court Square.
Some crowded the sidewalks and lined the streets leading
from the square to the wharf; others stood on rooftops or
leaned out of windows along the route of the procession.
Perhaps twenty-five thousand came to see the last rites
administered to Burns' freedom. Not all were abolitionists, of course. Some were just drawn by the excitement, and others had come to give a cheer for Marshal

Freeman and District-Attorney Ben Hallet. The great majority, however, were there to mourn the event, many of them in response to the vigilance committee's final broadside:

> Let there be no armed resistance; but let the whole people turn out, and line the streets, and look upon the shame and disgrace of Boston, and then go away and take measures to elect men to office who will better guard the honor of the State and Capitol.[41]

About two o'clock, the twenty-two companies of militia marched down from the Common and formed lines on both sides of the street. Then Anthony Burns appeared, smartly dressed in a new suit contributed by his guards. In the center of a square of armed deputies, he began the march down State Street to the steamer *John Tyler* tied up at Long Wharf. Some of the store fronts which the procession passed had been draped in black by their owners, and suspended over the corner of Court and Washington streets was a large coffin, labeled "liberty." After they put him inside a cabin aboard the steamer, a reporter got in to see the prisoner. "There was lots of folks," Anthony Burns is reported to have said, "to see a colored man walk through the streets." [42]

Phillips looked on more in sorrow than in rage. For the second time in three years, Boston, the city that had once rocked the cradle of liberty, had allowed a human being to be condemned to slavery. Heretofore he had always taken the long view, always insisted that every temporary defeat could be used to hasten the inevitable victory. Now his optimism deserted him. National politics was completely in the hands of the slave power, and Phillips expected a further expansion of slave territory so as to include Cuba and Mexico. "The future seems to unfold a vast Slave Empire," he wrote to a friend, "united with Brazil and darkening the whole West. I hope I may be a false prophet but the sky was never so dark." Others were encouraged by the change in public sentiment

between 1851 and 1854 and by the opportunity to exploit
Burns' martyrdom, but Phillips could not "forget the man
in the idea." He could not think of Anthony Burns sym-
bolically; he remembered him only as a frightened black
man, with a scarred face and broken hand, who needed
help. Wendell had promised to help him and failed.[43]

Meanwhile, word was out that District Attorney Ben
Hallet had sworn to prosecute whoever was responsible
for attacking the courthouse. The rumor was that Phillips,
Parker and Higginson would be arrested and tried for
inciting a riot. If convicted, they would face a heavy fine
and a year in jail. Parker had already decided that if he
went to prison he could use the time to prepare a volume
of sermons, write his memoirs, complete the first volume
of the "Historical Development of Religion" and study
Russian.[44] Higginson, who had actually led the assault in
which a man had been killed, was not quite so serene and
wrote Phillips for advice. Replying both as a lawyer and
as an abolitionist, Wendell told Higginson to plead not
guilty and to argue *"the higher law"* before a jury. "If
with this banner nailed yet to the mast, you face a jury with
success, you not only help the agitation by a trial, but by
beating the government, a great point." Although Phillips obviously did not believe that a jury would ever convict Higginson, he seemed to enjoy seeing the man squirm,
and he could not resist a parting jibe: "That you did not
tell me and thus give me a chance to help you instead of
making a fool of myself in Faneuil Hall, I will never forgive you—but I'll say nothing about it till we are both in
jail—then we can discuss it at our own leisure." [45]

The threat of an indictment did not bother Phillips,
and he continued to conspire against the Fugitive Slave
Law at every opportunity. Late one night in October,
1854, he and Samuel Gridley Howe went down to the harbor and, with the help of Austin Bearse and his brother,
rescued a Negro who was being kept prisoner in a ship
just about to return to the South. The fugitive, who had

apparently been discovered as a stowaway on the voyage north, was still clad in a tow cloth when Wendell took him by carriage to Lewis Hayden's home. Two weeks later, disguised as a woman, he was taken across the border to Canada.[46]

On November 20, Phillips set off on a lecture tour which took him through sixteen cities in three weeks. He had always been unwilling to be away from home for any extended period and had never lectured in the West. The rapid completion of new railroad connections now made such a trip feasible, and he visited Cincinnati, Cleveland and Detroit for the first time. When he returned in the middle of December, he was arrested.

Ben Hallet had carried out his threat but not without difficulty. The first grand jury charged with finding bills against those who had obstructed the Fugitive Slave Law had refused to indict. A second jury had responded with indictments against Parker, Higginson, Phillips and others who had been active in Faneuil Hall the night the courthouse was attacked. The abolitionists were jubilant at having more attention drawn to themselves and at the possibility of turning Parker and Phillips into martyrs.[47] Their enemies, oppressed by the prospect of two such men in the witness stand arguing their case before a jury, were just as relieved when the case was dismissed on a technicality. Wendell took the whole thing in stride and didn't even bother to come to court for the trial (on April 3, 1855), but Parker, who apparently had his heart set on being convicted, wrote and published an incredibly long and furious essay in his own defense.[48]

Phillips was willing to let Parker spell out the defense because, while the government was trying to convict him for breaking the law, he was prosecuting the man who had upheld it. The need of the hour, Phillips had told an audience on January 25, was for an example of genuine antislavery sentiment, "a commonwealth or a city that should be a model for the world." [49] Perhaps Massachusetts, still burning with humiliation over Anthony Burns, could provide the model. With this in mind, Phillips led the fight to get rid of Judge Loring.

As a fugitive slave commissioner, Loring held a Federal appointment and was beyond the reach of the abolitionists. He was also a judge of probate in Massachusetts, however, and as such was subject to removal by the governor. On February 20, Phillips appeared before a legislative committee to argue for Loring's removal. His case rested on two points. The first was that the state constitution provided that a judge did not have to be guilty of a crime in order to be removed; he could be removed for any reason on appeal of both houses of the legislature to the governor. Massachusetts judges, in other words, were subject to the sovereignty of the people. The second point was that Loring should be removed because he had brought dishonor on the people of Massachusetts by his handling of the Burns case. He had ignored the Personal Liberty Law of 1843; he had prejudged the case (Phillips recited his own conversation with Loring as evidence); he had been high-handed in dealing with the evidence, having accepted the word of slavecatchers over that of local witnesses, and having admitted only that part of Burns' testimony most damaging to his case.[50]

One of the interesting aspects of Phillips' campaign against Loring is that it brought him into conflict with Richard Dana. As counsel for Burns, Dana had been dismayed with Loring's decision, but he leaped to his defense now, fearing that the independence of the judiciary was at stake.[51] The sight of Dana and Phillips tilting at each other over Loring is a wonderful example of New England individualism in practice. It also reflects the wide divergence in temperament and opinion among those in the antislavery ranks. Each man acted consistently with his own principles, Phillips according to his belief in the sovereignty of public opinion, Dana in the belief that a people cannot remain free if their judges are subject to the fickle currents of popular enthusiasm.

After a long debate the legislature voted to remove Loring, but, to Phillips' intense disgust, Governor Gardiner refused to act. The agitation was continued during each succeeding session, and Loring was finally removed by a Republican governor, Nathaniel Banks, in 1858. It was a cruel fate, perhaps, for a man who was merely trying to interpret and uphold the law, but Phillips had no sympathy. When someone criticized him for exposing his private conversation with Loring he replied icily, "I have no *private* conversation with slave commissioners. My interview with Mr. Loring was an official one." [52]

Phillips did not hound Loring out of office for reasons of revenge but because he wanted to show up the commissioner as an example of the invasion of Massachusetts by the slave power. He did not care about Loring as an individual. This air of detachment, the refusal to be distracted or to become too personally involved, was the product of unrelenting self-discipline. Wendell knew how a reformer's power could be vitiated by sentimentalism or bitterness. The rendition of Burns had tested this discipline. It had taken him three months to feel able once again to think "more of the 3,000,000 [slaves] and less of the individual." [53] Consequently, he had no tears to spare now for a man who accepted an office which required him to surrender human beings into slavery.

The Eloquence of Abuse
1854–1856

In October 1855 a group of Wendell's friends got together and commissioned sculptor John A. Jackson to do his bust in marble. Plaster copies were made available at ten dollars a head. Phillips was in his prime now, forty-four years old, somewhat fleshier and balder than before but with the same sandy sideburns curling down below his ears. Striding across the Common or down Washington Street, erect and vigorous, with a broad-brimmed soft felt hat pulled down rakishly over one eye, he was as well known to Bostonians as any man in the city. When Harriet Beecher Stowe visited Boston a few months earlier, she had noticed that he was drawing larger crowds at his lectures than ever before. A sign of the times, she thought; the antislavery tide was rising "slowly, surely and with resistless regularity." [1]

Although the gap separating Phillips from the broad sweep of Northern opinion steadily narrowed during the last half of the decade, it was not his ideas that were changing. On July 4, 1854, he had attended an antislavery picnic at Framingham and sat on the platform applauding while Thoreau read his marvelous essay on "Slavery in Massachusetts" and Garrison publicly burned a copy of the Constitution of the United States. Garrison's gesture, widely reported in the press, went far to disrupt the temporary alliance which the fugitive slave cases had created between the radicals and the political abolitionists. For his part, Phillips was glad to see the politicians go their own way. The return of Anthony Burns to slavery had made him all the more convinced that disunion was the only way out. It was true that Sumner was beginning to talk more and more like a radical, but his voice was a lonely one, and Phillips looked forward to the day when Massachusetts might be cured of the madness of sending anybody up to Washington.[2]

Except for the work of Sumner and a few others, the moral level of politics in Washington remained abysmally low. In the most encouraging political development of the day, Free-Soilers and antislavery Whigs and Democrats in several Northern states were beginning to form a new party, which they called Republican. Wendell had seen this coming years before, and he welcomed it, believing that the Union would eventually be shattered by the conflict between two great sectional parties. The fact remained, however, that the slave power, represented by Franklin Pierce's administration, was still firmly entrenched in Washington and had won impressive victories with the passage of the Fugitive Slave Law and Kansas-Nebraska Act. Meanwhile, the political abolitionists were floundering in a sea of intrigue and associating themselves with issues that had no moral justification. A glance at Massachusetts politics was enough to convince Phillips of this. The coalition of Free-Soilers and Democrats which had put Sumner in the Senate in 1851 had been defeated in 1852, and the Whigs had controlled the state until the election of 1854, when the Free-Soilers were carried into power again, this time on the coattails of the Know-Nothing party. The Know-Nothings, a political phenomenon in America during the mid-fifties, owed most of their success to the clever exploitation of anti-immigrant, anti-Catholic prejudices. By cooperating with them, the political abolitionists were able to send another strong antislavery man, Henry Wilson of Natick, to the Senate.

Phillips was glad to see Wilson take his place beside Sumner. "If a man could get it honestly, who would not covet to stand in the position Henry Wilson occupies

today—a great nation for his audience, and the conscience
of Massachusetts at his back?" The trouble was, you could
not get it honestly. To get elected, you needed to connive
with bigots, and once in office you were sworn to support
the rotten system which protected slavery.[3]

The leader of Know-Nothingism in Massachusetts was
Governor Henry J. Gardner. A Boston dry-goods merchant who was also a skillful politician, Gardner played
all the angles, trying to make himself attractive to every
element in the state except the Irish. When campaigning,
he always managed to make a few antislavery sounds, but
his strength lay in his appeal to nativism. It was Gardner
who had blocked the abolitionists' efforts to remove Loring, and Phillips lashed into him with language far more
vituperative than any he had employed in his speeches
against the judge. "Our course is a perfect copy of
Sisyphus. We always toil up, up, up the hill until we
touch the soiled sandals of some Governor Gardner, and
then the rock rolls down again. Always some miserable
reptile that has struggled into power in the corruption of
parties—reptiles who creep where *man* disdains to climb;
some slight thing of no consequence till its foul mess blocks
our path; and dashes our hopes at the last minute." [4]

There was an enormous difference in Phillips' opinion
of Henry Gardner, who merely dabbled in antislavery
politics for personal gain, and the way he looked at sincere
antislavery political leaders in Washington like Sumner,
Wilson, Joshua Giddings, John P. Hale and Salmon P.
Chase. But even these men, he thought, had to be kept
under careful surveillance, lest they stray too far from the
moral principle which was the taproot of every true reform
movement. It was their timidity which irritated him most.
When he lectured at Dartmouth on the same program
with Chase, the senator from Ohio who was one of the
leading Republicans in the country, Phillips was able to
get a firsthand view of Republicanism in action. The
speeches of both men were enthusiastically received, and
in the evening they were serenaded by the students and

called out to speak again. Phillips, who had earlier addressed his audience on the duty of the scholar to become an agitator, never forgot the experience. "We stood under the stately elms of the old college. The moon shone down upon us—it was a solemn hour, almost up to midnight; the young men were roused to extraordinary enthusiasm by the presence of a man who stands out prominently, in a political sense, before the nation, and he said—Gentlemen, I pledge my life, I ask you to pledge yours to this— *No* slavery,—*no slavery*—outside the slave states. (! ! !) That was all!" If this was to be the extent of the Republican crusade, Wendell decided that he preferred the less popular, but infinitely more zealous, company of the reformers.[5]

Despite his radicalism, it was true, as Mrs. Stowe observed, that Phillips was reaching a wider audience than ever before. With the improvement of train service beyond the Alleghenies, it was now feasible to make quick trips to the West, and Phillips lectured in Detroit for the first time in 1854. From this time on it became customary for him to spend as much as four of five months of each year on tour, and by the end of the decade Phillips, whose presence on the program was enough to assure almost any lyceum a successful season no matter how large a deficit other speakers might incur, was widely acclaimed as the outstanding orator in the nation.

Although the abolitionists sometimes wished that Phillips would spend less time giving popular lectures and more time abolitionizing, Wendell always looked on the popular lecture as a means to an end. He would agree to give his chatty "Street Life in Europe" to a conservative audience in order to "get *within the enemy's works.*" If he made a good impression, his listeners might come another time to hear him lecture on slavery. On some occasions he would agree to lecture on a noncontroversial subject only if his sponsors made it possible for him to give an antislavery lecture in the same auditorium.[6]

The sources of Phillips' power on the platform were

deceptive. Those seeing him for the first time were invariably surprised to discover that he was not an orator
in the grand manner. An Andover student, hearing that
Phillips was to lecture in Boston, made a twenty-two-mile
pilgrimage on foot to hear him. At first the trip seemed
hardly worthwhile, for Phillips stood on the platform, one
hand lightly resting on a table, talked for about twenty
minutes and suddenly sat down. When the astonished
young man consulted his watch he found that he had been
listening for an hour and a half.[7]

There was, as the Andover student discovered, nothing ponderous about Phillips as a speaker, no bombast,
no flights of empty rhetoric. He spoke almost conversa-
tionally; his appearance was invariably one of calm poise,
and he relied little on the kind of theatrics that led Henry
Ward Beecher to auction off a slave girl from the pulpit.
"The most prolonged applause could not disturb a muscle
in his countenance," one listener remembered, "and a
storm of hisses seemed to have as little effect on him." [8]

Webster, with his bull-like body and cavernous
smouldering eyes, could overpower an audience with sheer
physical magnetism. Phillips did not have this power. He
was a man of almost average height, rather slightly built
with finely drawn features which most easily lent themselves to expressions of scorn and resolution. What everyone did notice about him was his aristocratic bearing. "I
think he has more culture," Emerson confided to his journal, "than his own, is debtor to generations of gentlemen
behind him." [9] Born in a Beacon Street mansion, the son
of Boston's first mayor, bearing the name of one of New
England's first families, Phillips came as close to being a
native-born aristocrat as any American could. His assurance on the platform was undoubtedly related to the fact
that he did not have to make a name for himself. He had
a way of treating his opponents as if they were socially
beneath him as well as morally loathesome.[10] Because of
this he was nearly immune to criticism and absolutely in-
vulnerable to a heckling audience. He would never lose

his temper but would reply to his critics in a tone so witheringly contemptuous it was like a shaft of air blown off an iceberg. Neither rotten eggs nor brickbats could startle him, and hissing so consistently aroused him to his best effort that his admirers sometimes sat in a back row and hissed merely to make him warm to the subject.[11]

As early as 1844, Emerson, who always rated eloquence among the noblest of human talents, wrote in his journal: "I wish that Webster and Everett and also the young political aspirants of Massachusetts should hear Wendell Phillips speak, were it only for the capital lesson in eloquence they might learn of him. This, namely, that the first and the second and the third part of the art is, to keep your feet always firm on a fact." [12] The meaty eloquence that Emerson admired was perhaps a product of Phillips' legal training under Judge Story at Harvard. Even at the height of his career as a radical and propagandist, he never lost the ability to make the lawyer's case. And in his most inflammatory speeches, when logic was a secondary consideration ("Heat not light," he once said, "was what men wanted"), Phillips usually carried the understanding as well as the heart of his audience. "His speeches were a succession of propositions that appeared so nearly self-evident," an Oberlin professor recalled, "that you were only too glad to accept them and move on to the coming triumph." [13]

Not only were Phillips' feet firm on fact; they were also firmly anchored in the rocky soil of New England. He almost never employed a classical allusion in his speeches, but he was always careful to sprinkle his remarks with rustic anecdotes which could drive home a point to the most unsophisticated ear. For example, in 1859 when he wanted to impress on his audience the fact that no mån in Massachusetts would help to return a fugitive slave, and a voice from the audience interjected the remark that a United States marshal in Worcester had expressed his willingness to do just that, Phillips instantly rejoined by telling the story of "the Cape Cod captain who had the

steamer that runs from Hyannis to Nantucket, and in the
cabin was a notice that no gentleman was expected to spit
on the carpet. One day the captain went up to a man and
remonstrated with him for disregarding the notice. 'Lord
captain,' said he, 'I ain't a gentleman.' I am not sure that
a United States marshal comes up to my statement when I
said no *man*." [14] Homely, but to the point, like the story
of the bear who ventures into a settler's cabin and finds
a kettle boiling on the stove. It burns his nose and in a
fury he hugs it and is scalded to death. Just so, Phillips
said, "the Democratic party clasped slavery everywhere,
and the more it has howled; and it will die with the hot
doctrine in its arms." [15] His stories usually had a local
flavor; they were about the sea captain in Hyannis or the
lawyer in Worcester County or, when he wanted to make
a point about fast-talking politicians, about "the man in
West Bridgewater who said that another man's wife lied.
The husband of the woman came to him and said, 'You
say my wife does not tell the truth; I want you to take it
back.' 'Now,' said the other, 'tell me, doesn't your wife
talk faster than lightning?' 'Yes, but what has that to do
with it?' 'Well, I maintain there is not truth enough in
the world for her to speak it all the time, fast as she
talks.' " [16]

By far the most sensational characteristic of Phillips
as a speaker was the contrast between his perfectly controlled, poised, almost dispassionate manner and the inflammatory language he employed. It was the apparent
effortlessness of his delivery that impressed many listeners
the most. "Staples said the other day that he heard Phillips speak at the State House," wrote Thoreau in his
Journal. "By thunder! he never heard a man that could
speak like him. His words come so easy. It was just like
picking up chips." [17] In an effort to explain how the
speaker remained somehow detached from his own eloquence, another observer compared him to "a cold but
mysteriously animated statue of marble." [18] Time and
time again when Phillips was on tour, talking before new

audiences, the reporter would register the audience's surprise. "They had conceived him to be a ferocious ranter and blustering man of words. They found him to be a quiet, dignified and polished gentleman and scholar, calm and logical in his argument." [19]

One of the reasons why abolitionist meetings in the middle and later 1850s began to draw impressively large crowds, as the critics of the abolitionists pointed out, was that for many people an antislavery meeting had all the elements of a theatrical performance. The star performer was usually Wendell Phillips, and his stock in trade, according to the unconverted, was "personal abuse." To the abolitionists themselves, he was, as his publisher later remarked, the greatest "master of invective" in the nineteenth century.[20] With sublime confidence, almost as if he were reading from a sheaf of statistics or reciting a series of scientific facts, Phillips would take the platform to announce that Daniel Webster was "a great mass of dough," Edward Everett "a whining spaniel," Massachusetts Senator Robert C. Winthrop "a bastard who has stolen the name of Winthrop" and the New England churches an ecclesiastical machine to manufacture hypocrisy "just as really as Lowell manufactures cotton." It was the way Phillips uttered his epithets that fascinated most critics. The shrewd Scottish traveler David Macrae, who had been led "from the ferocity of his onslaughts on public men and public measures . . . to form a false conception of his delivery," noted with surprise that vehemence and declamation were replaced by sarcasm, "cold, keen, withering." Macrae was impressed by the relentless manner in which Phillips pursued his opponents. "He follows an enemy like an Indian upon the trail. . . . When he comes to strike, his strikes are like galvanic shocks; there is neither noise nor flash but their force is terrible." [21]

A writer for an English paper, contrasting Phillips' speeches with "the rounded periods of Mr. Seward" and "the finished artistic rhetoric of the patriotic Mr. Everett," noted one quality which grated on European ears, and that was "the concentrated bitterness, the intense spirit of hatred with which they are frequently suffused." [22] Because Phillips did not like to talk in general terms about issues, because he always took dead aim on personalities and heaped "the concentrated bitterness" of his rhetoric upon the heads of men prominent in public life, and because the people turned out in droves to hear him, Robert C. Winthrop believed that Phillips had "gradually educated our people to relish nothing but the 'eloquence of abuse.' " [23]

No matter how bitter, how merciless, how seemingly vindictive his assaults on individuals, Phillips always felt justified in what he was doing. He did not think of himself as an ordinary lecturer or orator but as a kind of minister to the public, preaching the gospel of reform. "An aggressive Christianity," he contended, "the Christianity that attacks everything and everybody until it secures something no longer capable of being found fault with—that is the element of all reform." [24]

It was not only a strong sense of religious duty which sustained Phillips' "eloquence of abuse"; there was also his American heritage. Consider, for example, the following passage from a speech which he gave on July 4, 1859:

> Here under the blue sky of New England, we teach the doctrine, that whenever you find a man downtrodden, he is your brother; whenever you find an unjust law, you are bound to be its enemy; that Massachusetts was planted as the furnace of perpetual insurrection against tyrants [loud applause] that this is a bastard who has stolen the name of the Winthrops [tremendous cheering]—been foisted into the cradle while his mother was out [loud laughter and applause], that the true blood of the Bradfords, the Carvers, the Endicotts and the Winthrops crops out in some fanatical abolitionist, whom the church disowns, whom the state tramples underfoot, but who will yet remodel both, by the potency of that truth which the elder Winthrop gave into our hands, and which we hold today as an example for the nation. [Prolonged applause] This is my speech for the Fourth of July.[25]

This passage, a typical example of Phillips' rhetoric, illustrates his fondness for invoking the spirit of the American past (which for him was identical with the New England of the Puritans and the Revolutionary fathers) to justify his own position, and it undoubtedly helped his audiences tolerate his radicalism. Not only could they enjoy the vulgar satisfaction of seeing great men cut down to size, but all of this might be done within the honorable bounds of the American tradition.

Although possessing a demagogue's vocabulary, Phillips was an intellectual, a profound student of American history who believed that his own radicalism could be justified by the theory on which American political institutions were based. He paused once in the midst of a blistering denunciation of Henry Gardner to lecture his audience on this point.

> Do not say I am personal in speaking thus of Governor Gardner. O! no not personal. To the making of a person there must be a heart. He is a mere mask, a phantam, a nightmare. . . . Do not blame me when I speak thus of Henry J. Gardner. What is the duty of the minority? . . . What is the duty of a minority in this country? A minority has no right to rebel. . . . The majority have said the thing shall be so. What is our duty? It is not to resist, it is to convert. And how shall we convert? If the community is in love with some monster, we must point him truly. The duty of a minority being to convert, every tool which the human mind knows, it is their right and duty to use; a searching criticism, pitiless sarcasm, bitter invective, rigid analysis of motives, constant recurrence to the admitted facts of a man's career,—these are our rights, if our function is to save the people from delusion.[26]

What Phillips is saying here is that the revolutionary in America, without recourse to the barricades, must content himself with an explosive rhetoric which will destroy a corrupt, reactionary public opinion and replace it with a public opinion capable of sustaining the rightful order of things. Thus, Phillips could advise the reformer "never to be silent, never to be appeased, never to be anything but implacable." There was to be no escape, not even in the grave. "He is an apostate to New England," Phillips said, seven years after Webster's death, "who lets these bones rest in peace. Not until I can take the evil that he did, and cover it forever with the green sod that covers him, shall I cease to criticize him." [27]

Believing that extravagant language was morally justifiable, Phillips made it his weapon. He liked to tell the story of the South Carolinian who had moved to New England and become an abolitionist. Visiting Paris on business, the new convert was approached by an old acquaintance from South Carolina who began to talk to him about the possibility of sponsoring a world convention to defend slavery. Anxious to find some way of making his own position clear without wasting time arguing over it, the abolitionist said, "Perhaps you don't know me. I was born in Charleston, South Carolina, it is true; but I board with Garrison, and am engaged to be married to Frederick Douglass's sister." The statement, Phillips pointed out, was a literal lie, with the essence of emphatic truth in it, and it had the desired effect of immediately routing the slaveholder.[28] In defending the extravagant statement, Phillips would have denied that he was sacrificing the means to the end. Words were made to be used, he often said, and reformers were obliged to tip their vocabulary with the sharpest flint if they hoped to pierce the calloused conscience of an indifferent public. "Our rhetoric is learned from the New Testament," he said. "There a truth is nakedly stated; its limitations, qualifications and conditions left to the good sense of the reader. That is the way to reach the mass." [29]

What sets off Phillips from the other lecturers within the Garrisonian camp, such colorful individuals as Parker Pillsbury and Stephen and Abby Kelly Foster, is that Phillips alone was consistently recognized as great even by those who most hated his ideas. After hearing him declare, in what was perhaps an unconscious parody of Webster's

famous words, that he hoped to witness before he died
"the convulsion of a sundering Union and a dissolving
church," a New York reporter remarked that Phillips'
sentiments "however repugnant to general opinion were
expressed with a clear and lofty eloquence and extraordinary felicity and beauty of illustration." [30]   In Boston
where Phillips was loved and hated the most, a writer for
the *Courier* made the same point in blunter language.
"It is a dish of tripe and onions served on silver," he wrote,
"or black-strap presented in a goblet of Bohemian glass.
. . . Mr. Phillips thinks like a Billingsgate fishwoman,
or a low pothouse bully, but he speaks like Cicero." [31]

For all this modern Cicero's eloquence, however, it
was not words but events that lay behind the fast-swelling
antislavery tide in the winter of 1855. The events were
not even taking place in New England, a fact which Phillips noted when he said that if the Pilgrims of 1620 were
to return they would not be found in Plymouth but in
Kansas.[32]   He was referring to the armed struggle then
going on between the proslavery and antislavery factions
to control the territorial government in Kansas. New
England was contributing largely to the number of anti-
slavery settlers, and, although the number of outright
abolitionists among these was probably small, the few
Garrisonians who trickled into the area soon found that
talk and high principles would not be enough to win the
day in Kansas. Charles Stearns, for example, a good abolitionist and pacifist, had gone out to the newly established
town of Lawrence as a storekeeper. Reporting to Garrison
late in 1855, Stearns wrote that the town was full of armed
men, that entrenchments ran in front of his door and that
his store was serving as a morgue for the body of a friend
killed in the fighting. In these circumstances, Stearns felt
that his pacifism had to be reinterpreted. "God never
made these fiends," he wrote, referring to the proslavery
men from Missouri, "they are the Devil's pawn, and are
to be killed as you would kill lions and tigers. I have
always said I would shoot a wild beast. If I shoot these

infernal Missourians, it will be on the same principle."
Nonresistance was dear to him as ever, "with this proviso
—it does not apply to wild beasts." A Christian was
directed to turn the other cheek to any man but not to any
murderous ape, and Stearns' last shrill words were, "We are
surrounded by *drunken* ourang-outangs." [33]

There is a certain pathetic comedy about this idealistic New Englander's thrust into reality. The insistence
on self-justification, the hysterical rhetoric, the fantastic
logic—everything that was foolish about the abolitionists
—seems to be represented here.

Phillips' attitude toward Kansas at this time was am-
bivalent. He still felt that disunion might be achieved
without violence, and he did not like the prospect of fighting in Kansas because "the moment you throw the struggle
with slavery into the hands of the barbarous West, where
things are decided by the revolver and the bowie knife,
slavery triumphs." [34] The age of bullets was over, he
thought, and the fate of slavery was to be decided in the
East, where the wealth and power of the country lay.
Nevertheless, on August 24, 1855, he subscribed $100 to-
ward a rifle fund for the New Englanders in Kansas.[35]

As Phillips moved through the early months of 1856,
he continued to preach disunion and to urge Massachusetts to repudiate a federal government which was supporting the proslavery government in Kansas. On May 19
there occurred in Washington an event which rocked the
nation and greatly enlarged the audience for his radical
pronouncements. Charles Sumner stood up in the Senate
to deliver a long address on Kansas. He had written
Theodore Parker earlier that he was about to pronounce
"the most thorough philippic ever uttered in a legislative
body," and he was as good as his word. In language extraordinarily bitter for the Senate, Sumner abused by
name those of his colleagues who supported the proslavery
element in Kansas. He was particularly vituperative in
his attack on Senator Butler from South Carolina and
Stephen A. Douglas. He described Butler as a chronic
liar whose chivalrous airs were in the hire of a mistress

who, "though polluted in the sight of the world, is chaste
in his sight—I mean the harlot, Slavery!" In the debate
which followed, he referred to Douglas as a "noisome,
squat and nameless animal." Three days later Preston S.
Brooks, representative from South Carolina and Butler's
nephew, strode into the nearly deserted Senate chamber
and, while Sumner was seated at his desk writing, beat
him into unconsciousness with a cane.[36]

Mass meetings were held throughout the North to
protest the assault on Sumner, and Phillips addressed one
of these in Boston. Referring to the Senate as a "chamber
of Assassins," he tried to dramatize the incident so as to
promote his own doctrines. "Where are we?" he demanded.
"Just where we were twenty years ago, battling for the
liberty of speech on the Senate floor. Once we had no
men to speak. Now the men are brave enough, but speak
at risk of assassination. . . . If a coward and brutal bully
of South Carolina is a fitting member of the House of
Representatives, then it is not fit that any decent son of
Massachusetts should sit there by his side." Even in the
North there had been criticism of Sumner's inflammatory
speech, but Phillips announced that he had read it "with
an unmixed approbation." He had nothing but the
"uttermost contempt," he said, for those members of the
press in Boston who criticized Sumner's language "while
he lies thus prostrate and speechless—our champion beaten
to the ground for the noblest word Massachusetts ever
spoke in the Senate." [37]

Phillips saw at once that Sumner was worth more to
the radical cause wounded than he had been whole. Here
was a martyr whom the entire state could rally around.
The two words to be spoken now were Sumner and Kansas; the moral to be told was that barbarism in Kansas
and barbarism in Washington were one and the same, that
the only recourse of Massachusetts was to cut herself off
from the evil.

Sumner, meanwhile, was languishing in Washington,
unable to work, searching for the vigor which had been
so suddenly shattered. Realizing that he would be in-

undated by a flood of letters, Wendell did not write his
friend until the middle of July. Assuring him "how ten-
derly we bear you in our heart of hearts," Phillips
cautioned Sumner about returning to the Senate before
he had fully recuperated. "Let this session go by. Be
sure Massachusetts will give you six more years to work
in. You have done more than your share in this session's
fight. Enough to satisfy the most impatient spirit. Come
home and rest." [38] A month later he wrote in a similar
vein, advising Sumner that his reputation had never been
higher and that progress could be made even though his
voice was still. "The cause goes well. The idea grows—
we thank God that he has given us such texts." [39]

Much to Phillips' disgust, the attack on Sumner had
the effect of making abolitionists even more political-
minded than before. As the national election of 1856 drew
near, there were three parties in the field, the Democrats,
the Know-Nothings and the Republicans. For their first
presidential candidate, the Republicans had chosen John
C. Fremont, the celebrated and dashing explorer. Anti-
slavery voters were working enthusiastically for Fremont,
and even Garrison felt called on to make a statement to
the effect that he would, if he were a voting man, choose
Fremont over Buchanan, the Democratic candidate. Fremont feeling was running so high among the radicals that
a man from East Bridgewater wrote an angry letter to the
Liberator complaining that he could not tell the difference
between an abolitionist meeting and a Fremont rally.[40]

Sympathizing with the abolitionist from East Bridgewater, Phillips believed that the enthusiasm for Fremont
was naive. He recognized only one encouraging thing
about the election, and that was the sectional character
of the Republican party. "It is a Northern party against
the Southern . . . the first crack in the iceberg is visible;
you will yet hear it go with a crack, through to the
centre." [41] Fremont himself, Phillips thought, was an unknown quantity. Because he had successfully battled
snow and starvation in the Rocky Mountains, abolitionists
somehow assumed he would lead the struggle against

slavery.[42] The Republicans, however, as skillful at con-
niving as the next party, were struggling to dissociate
themselves from the abolitionists. Phillips could speak
with experience on the latter point because he was approached by one enterprising politician who actually suggested that he help Fremont by getting Garrison to
denounce him in the *Liberator!* [43]

Phillips compensated for his aloofness toward the
Fremont campaign by showing a passionate interest in
the state election, where Henry Gardner was running for
a third term as governor. Gardner, the man who had saved
Judge Loring, was the villain of the hour. "A consummate
hypocrite," Phillips called him, "a man who, if he did not
have some dozen and distinct reasons for telling the truth,
would naturally tell a lie. . . . My mission today is to
say to any Free Soiler who hears me, Save me from Governor Gardner." [44]

The Republicans in Massachusetts, however, had no
intention of saving Phillips from Gardner, for they knew
that, although he was the Know-Nothing candidate for
governor, many of his supporters were also supporting
Fremont for President. They were loath to oppose
Gardner and risk alienating these voters and losing the
state for Fremont. On the other hand, they knew that if
they supported Gardner they would alienate many Republicans in the West who despised Know-Nothingism.
They responded to this dilemma by not nominating a
gubernatorial candidate of their own and by leaving
Gardner strictly alone during the campaign—another
miserable example, Phillips thought, of the politicians'
habitual practice of sacrificing principle to expediency.[45]

As it turned out, Gardner won and Fremont lost.
The dismal prospect of another Know-Nothing administration on Beacon Hill and another Democratic administration in Washington was sweetened somewhat for
Phillips by Charles Sumner's return to Boston. The senator, who came home to cast his ballot, made a triumphal
entry on November 3. In a carriage drawn by six gray
horses and followed by a procession more than half a mile

long, he wound slowly through streets hung with flags,
strewn with bouquets and crowded with thousands of
waving, cheering spectators. At the foot of the steps leading to the State House, Sumner attempted to make a
speech, but he was too feeble and could only hand his
manuscript to a reporter; whereupon he was escorted
through the immense crowd to his mother's house on
Hancock Street.[46]

Wendell was gratified to see his friend honored so
handsomely. The only sour note of the entire spectacle,
aside from the fact that Governor Gardner had spoken the
official words of welcome, was struck when the procession
passed by the great Beacon Street mansions which remained shuttered and mute, a grotesque reminder of the
perversity of Boston's aristocracy.

Phillips spent two hours with Sumner and found that
he was still far from a complete recovery. His conversation was as brilliant as ever, but he was easily fatigued and
showed only a fraction of the awesome mental powers of
old. "With *constant rest* and *great care,* I think he may get
entirely well," Wendell wrote to Elizabeth Pease. "His
brain is as an arm would be recently broken and just growing together—with just prospect of being strong sometime
—but it cannot lift a 50 pound weight today." [47]

Convinced that the assault on Sumner had made the
people of Massachusetts more amenable to radicalism,
Phillips spent the winter of 1857 and 1858 hammering
away at his favorite themes. Let Massachusetts throw her
whole weight to upset the Union, and let the slaveholders
stew in their own juice. If people scream treason, remind
them that "Treason runs in the blood that flowed out on
Bunker Hill." And if they cry impossible, remind them
that "the blood and genius of the genuine Yankee are constitutionally orderly and he does not need a government." [48]

In March two events occurred to help Phillips make
his case to the North more plausible. On March 4, Buchanan, in his inaugural address, denounced the agitation
against slavery, thus insuring that the antislavery voices in
the North would be shut out of the national councils for

another four years at least. Two days later the Supreme Court handed down the Dred Scott decision, which declared that any attempt to shut slavery out of the territories by federal law was unconstitutional and that the Negro was not considered a citizen under the Constitution.

For more than a decade, Phillips had been preaching that the slave power controlled the nation, that there could be no escape from it within the nation. Most of his listeners had demurred. If they were opposed to slavery at all, they preferred to rely on the Constitution and the political process. All the evidence, Phillips believed now, showed that these people were wrong. Slavery, which had long dominated politics and filled the presidential chair, now controlled the highest court in the land and interpreted the Constitution so as to protect its own interests. In these circumstances Phillips never felt more sure of his own commission. "I must raise you to the level of disobeying what the country says is Law," he told an audience in May. "I must make you willing to go behind a parchment and say what is Justice. I must raise New York, Massachusetts, Ohio and Wisconsin to the level of being glad of being called Traitor." [49]

The tune was the same, and, although more and more lips were beginning to hum the melody, Phillips became increasingly frustrated over the next two years. He hoped that the assault on Sumner and the Dred Scott decision would encourage the people of Massachusetts to transform themselves into a collective abolitionist, but the most they could accomplish was to go Republican in the state elections of 1857. It was a victory of sorts, certainly, to see Henry Gardner knocked off his perch on Capitol Hill, but the new governor, Nathaniel Banks, was hardly a radical improvement. Banks was a typical example of the American success story. Beginning as a two-dollar-a week mill hand in Wrentham, he had gone a long way in politics on a nickname (the "Bobbin Boy"), a slogan ("Success is a duty") and a sure instinct for straddling touchy issues. Beginning his career as a Democrat, he had at one time or another taken almost every position on

slavery possible for a Massachusetts man and had finally
ended up as a Republican by way of the Know-Nothings.[50] "Nobody," Phillips moaned, "can charge Mr.
Banks with ever having made an enemy by doing anything." [51]

No matter how hard he tried, Phillips could not carry
his point about Banks and the other Republicans. The
great majority of people sympathetic with the abolitionists
insisted on seeing these men as their rightful leaders.
Phillips would never forget or forgive the wealthy friend
who said he had given $5,000 to the Fremont campaign
and had nothing left for the radicals. This experience,
multiplied many times during the winter of 1857 and 1858,
when the antislavery societies were feeling the added pinch
of a national depression, helps to account for the air of
injured martyrdom that so often characterized his speeches
at the time. After "Twenty years of incessant sacrifice," he
said, "the treasury is empty, the hand is tired, the toil of
many years has gained but little." [52] That little, however,
was precious and should be guarded tenaciously against
malicious enemies *and* mistaken friends. More and more
he began to talk like the enthusiast who is blessed by having been persecuted. "God grant," he said after he heard
a young abolitionist make a speech, "that our battered
bodies may fill up the gap and give him an easy road to
walk."

Phillips' state of mind was not helped by the wave
of religious revivals sweeping across the country. He
found it hard to understand how a minister like Henry
Ward Beecher could preach abolitionism (with all that
this implied in the way of criticizing the church) and at
the same time participate in the revivals which sent "a
slave-hunting, woman-whipping, soul-selling people" flocking back to the church deluded into thinking they were
truly Christian.

Although Phillips would have thought it a sin to lose
hope, the prospects for halting the advance of slavery
seemed bleak in the spring of 1858. In Washington, Pres-

ident Buchanan ("The lees of a wornout politician") was throwing his support behind a proslavery constitution for Kansas. Freedom was lost there, Phillips believed, victim to an imperialistic slave power which would soon spread out to Cuba and Central America with a new slave trade.[53]

With the collapse of any effective political resistance to slavery on a national level, Phillips felt that the best way to thwart the slave power was through state action in the North. He wanted Massachusetts to pass a law which would free every fugitive entering the state and imprison any judge who attempted to enforce the act of 1850. As a nonvoter, Phillips did not feel that he could in conscience sign the petition for such a law, but this did not stop him from endorsing it on the platform. "I will call every Free Soiler a liar and a hypocrite who refuses to sign that petition, or, in yonder State House, refuses to vote for such a law. No man can stand under the United States Constitution without being a kidnapper, who is not willing to vote for that law." When he appeared before the state Committee on Federal Relations to plead for the petition, he based his case on the assumption that Massachusetts was not "a mere bob to the kite of the Constitution" but a sovereign power, responsible to God for defending the rights of man. The legislators, impressed by Phillips' rhetoric but not by his argument, rejected the bill.[54]

Almost everywhere he looked in the autumn of 1859, Phillips found reason to be dismayed. Proslavery politicians were entrenched not only in Washington but in all the offices of the federal government and in American embassies all over the world. The West was lost, and the majority of people in the North didn't seem to care. The great crusade had stalled once more, and Phillips must have realized that it was not for a Boston Brahmin, a thinker and a talker like himself, to get it started again.

It took a lean, leathery man fresh from the wars in Kansas to do that.

12

"A Lord High Admiral of the Almighty": Phillips and John Brown 1856–1859

Phillips probably met John Brown early in 1857, and he must have seen him several times thereafter. Like everyone else, Wendell would have been struck by Brown's appearance. If Garrison sounded like a prophet, John Brown looked like one. He was not yet adorned with his famous patriarchal beard, but there was something about the wild, bristling, gray hair, the taut mouth and the intensity of the glittering gray-blue eyes to suggest a man inspired or, perhaps, possessed.

Phillips would have insisted on the former word. There was every reason for him to be impressed by Brown. Wendell was probably present the night Garrison met Brown in Theodore Parker's parlor and tried to convert him to pacifism. A quaint sight this, each man a visionary in his own right, fantastically impractical yet in deadly earnest. Garrison quoted the New Testament; Brown countered with the Old. Dialectics was not the old man's specialty, but Phillips would have sensed the wonderful simplicity in his argument when he insisted that, if slavery was as evil as Garrison said, a man should act as well as speak against it.[1] Brown had already acted, and he carried mementoes with him to prove it—a double-edged dirk taken from a "Border Ruffian" after the skirmish at Black Jack and a length of the chain used to secure his son, who had been captured by federal troops and driven

like an animal across the Kansas prairie. Here was a man
as good as his word. He dealt in deeds, not in a mouth-
ful of rhetoric or a handful of type. Phillips was obviously
fascinated when he heard Brown talk of his adventures,
especially after the celebrated raid into Missouri, which
had resulted in the freeing of eleven slaves. After shep-
herding the Negroes safely up to Canada, Brown had
stopped at Cleveland and advertised two horses for sale.
The horses had been taken in the raid, but Brown advertised the sale over his own name and calmly stood by
the auctioneer's stand advising all bidders of the "defect"
in title. Wendell was delighted with the story and with
the nonchalant way in which the old man admitted that
the horses brought a good price.[2]

The impression which Brown made on the intellec-
tuals in and around Boston was remarkable. "A man of
rare common sense and directness of speech, as of action,"
Thoreau described him, "a Transcendentalist above all,
a man of ideas and principles."[3] "A man to make
friends," wrote Emerson, wherever "courage and integrity
are esteemed."[4] Even that shrewd and conservative merchant prince Amos A. Lawrence was struck by Brown's
"severe simplicity of habits . . . his determined energy
[and] deep religious faith."[5] Brown obviously exhibited
qualities which appealed strongly to men nurtured in the
traditions of New England. To Phillips he seemed to be
the incarnation of the "Puritan principle." He had utter
faith in his own mission. He refused to quibble, would
reveal his exact plans to no one and merely asked others
to trust him as he trusted himself. He did not stop to ask
what the people thought, or what the Constitution said, or
what the consequences might be; he saw his duty and was
willing to act accordingly. For more than a generation,
Phillips had been urging the people of New England to
fall back on their Puritan heritage, and it was almost as
if this man was a second Cromwell raised up in answer
to his prayers.

When Brown came to Boston in 1857, his professed

purpose was to collect funds to maintain a company of soldiers to fight for freedom in Kansas. His real purpose was to get backing for a raid in the South which, he hoped, would spark a general slave insurrection and thus bring down slavery. Eventually, Brown's closest supporters were let in on this general plan, although he never revealed the particular plans which took him to Harpers Ferry. It is difficult to discern exactly how much Phillips knew about Brown's project. The group closest to Brown included Samuel Howe, T. W. Higginson, Frank Sanborn, Gerrit Smith, Theodore Parker, Frederick Douglass and George Stearns. Although Phillips' monetary contributions to Brown seem to have been limited to a gift of twenty-five dollars toward a purse raised to help him buy a farmhouse, he was very intimate with this secret committee, and he was invited to attend the meeting held in Canada for the purpose of organizing Brown's expedition. Without being informed of the exact details, Phillips knew that a direct assault on slavery was being planned somewhere in the vicinity of Harpers Ferry.[6]

In principle, Phillips would have been sympathetic with any attempt to stimulate a slave insurrection, since he believed that every slave had a moral right to rise against his master. In practice, however, there is reason to believe that he might not have supported Brown, had he been fully informed in advance of the event. It would not have been the extremism but the impracticability of Brown's plan that would have disturbed Phillips. In the summer of 1858, Lysander Spooner sent Phillips a copy of a circular advising the slaves and nonslaveholding whites in the South to rise up against the slave owners. Spooner was planning to have the circular distributed throughout the South, and he asked Phillips' opinion. Wendell sympathized with the idea and agreed with Spooner that slavery was a state of war that justified any amount of violence on the part of those in bondage, but he thought it impossible that Spooner's scheme could muster enough support "to save the attempt from being ridiculous." [7]

Once the raid on Harpers Ferry had become history, however, Phillips leaped to applaud it. There is no question but that he was much more influential in defending Brown than he had been in supporting him beforehand. Garrison, whose initial reaction to the raid was a mixture of horror and guilty admiration, assured the readers of the *Liberator* that "an enterprise so wild and futile" could not have had the support of any of the respectable abolitionists.[8] Documents captured in Brown's headquarters in Virginia soon proved this to be wishful thinking, and before long the whole country knew that all of Brown's most important backers were leaders in the antislavery movement. It was a moment of crisis for these men; John Brown was being tried for treason, and they were accessories to the fact. Frederick Douglass left for England. Gerrit Smith, the highly unstable humanitarian and Free-Soiler in New York State, temporarily lost his mind. The erratic Samuel Gridley Howe, after making a clumsy and not very honorable attempt to exonerate himself, scurried off to Canada, as did George Stearns and Frank Sanborn. Only Higginson, displaying the same kind of courage which had sent him crashing against the doors of Anthony Burns' prison, stood his ground. Now that the "secret committee" was exposed and its members too scattered or paralyzed to act, Phillips moved into the foreground. He and John Andrew, a prominent Republican lawyer soon to become governor of Massachusetts, supplied legal advice to the conspirators and arranged for Brown's counsel in Virginia. On October 21, three days after the raid, Phillips sent an unsigned letter to Sanborn in Canada telling him that the wounds that Brown had suffered when captured had not been fatal. "Old man will probably recover," he wrote, "and I live in hope we'll see him again yet. Be sure we'll leave no stone unturned." The next day he wrote again urging Sanborn's immediate return, because "We are in motion with fresh plans and need your counsel and knowledge of men and means."[9] The new plans apparently involved a fantastic scheme cooked up by Lysander Spooner to kidnap Governor Wise of Virginia at Richmond, carry him off in a fast steamboat and hold him hostage until Brown was released. To carry out the plan would require the purchase of a boat, and it was estimated that the cost of the whole expedition would be ten to fifteen thousand dollars. When Phillips was approached for help, he said he would favor the plan "if our men will go." He was referring to members of the vigilance committee. The project fizzled out when it became obvious that the money could not be raised.[10] That Phillips could consider it even for a moment suggests his highly excited state of mind and his hope that the Union was about to fall apart.

Phillips made his first public statement on John Brown in Henry Ward Beecher's church in Brooklyn on the first of November. Unlike Garrison, who wrestled with his conscience and finally decided that Brown, justified "by the code of Bunker Hill," could be placed on a moral level with Moses and Joshua but below that of Jesus and Peter,[11] Phillips praised Brown without qualification. The lesson of the hour, he said, was insurrection. America had been ecstatic over a Hungarian rebel like Kossuth; now let her honor the revolutionary spirit in her own land. Lashing back at those who complained that Brown had broken the law, Phillips maintained that the principles of law did not obtain in a slave society any more than in a community of pirates. "Virginia is only another Algiers," he said. "The barbarous horde who gag each other, imprison women for teaching children to read, prohibit the Bible, sell men on the auction block, abolish marriage, condemn half their women to prostitution, and devote themselves to the breeding of human beings for sale, is only a larger and blacker Algiers." Since one on God's side was a majority, John Brown was clearly in the right and Virginia in the wrong. Therefore, Phillips assured his cheering audience, "John Brown has twice as much right to hang Governor Wise, as Governor Wise has to hang him." [12]

In this matter, however, not right but power would decide, and Phillips must have known that Brown's execution was inevitable. On November 19, he participated, along with John Andrew and Emerson, in a mass meeting in Boston for the purpose of raising money for Brown's family. John Brown went to the gallows on December 2. That night a huge crowd assembled in Faneuil Hall for a memorial service. In front of the speaker's stand stood a massive likeness of Brown, and on each side was a placard bearing his words. One of the placards read, "What is life at best to me, so long as I hold a commission direct from God Almighty to act against slavery?" [13]

Wendell Phillips was one of John Brown's pall-bearers. Mrs. Brown, who had claimed her husband's body in Virginia, brought it to Philadelphia, where Phillips joined her in preparation for the long, mournful journey to the family homestead at North Elba, an isolated hamlet in the Adirondacks. John Brown's wife, a large, strong-bodied woman, was no stranger to sorrow. The daughter of a blacksmith and almost completely uneducated, she had borne her husband thirteen children. Seven had died in childbirth, one had been killed in Kansas and two at Harpers Ferry. For three painful days the little funeral party traveled north. Wherever they stopped for food, groups of people clustered around to offer sympathy. After crossing Lake Champlain on the second day, they stopped at Elizabethtown, and a number of volunteers sat up all night in the courthouse to guard the coffin. Phillips did not record his impressions of this journey, but it must have made a profound impact on him. He had never met Mrs. Brown before, and he may have felt uncomfortable, an alien intruding on the privacy of another's grief. It must have been a silent procession, the bereaved widow lost in her own thoughts and Phillips, who had been asked to give the oration over John Brown's grave, groping for language worthy of such a moment.[14]

On the evening of the third day, after covering the last twenty-five miles over nearly impassable mountain

roads, the party reached the farmhouse at North Elba.
The next day, Brown's coffin was placed on a table before
the door, and Phillips addressed the mourners in the
crowded little house. There were four widows present,
Mrs. John Brown, the wives of Oliver and Watson Brown
and the widow of another raider, William Thompson.
Phillips' brief and simple speech was addressed to them.
Harpers Ferry had not been a disaster, he told them; John
Brown had not failed—he had actually struck the blow
which would finish slavery in Virginia. "True the slave
is still there. So, when the tempest uproots a pine on your
hills, it looks green for months,—a year or two. Still, it
is timber, not a tree. John Brown has loosened the roots
of the slave system; it only breathes,—it does not live,—
hereafter." He had fulfilled his mission and now slept
secure "in the blessings of the crushed and poor." Those
who remained, who had sacrificed neither blood nor kin,
must take a new baptism. "How can we start here without
a fresh and utter consecration? These tears! How shall
we dare even to offer consolation? Only lips fresh from
such a vow have the right to mingle their words with your
tears. We envy you your nearer place to these martyred
children of God." The grave was dug in the shadow of a
huge boulder near the house, and as the coffin was lowered
into it the members of a neighboring colored family sang
some of the hymns that John Brown had liked.[15]

The eulogistic note that Phillips sounded at North
Elba was far from being unanimous in the North. Northern Democrats were quick to exploit Harpers Ferry for
partisan reasons; Republicans were just as quick to disown
it, and moderates of all political persuasion shrank back
from it in horror. The week after Brown was buried,
Phillips spoke in New York at a meeting to raise money
for his family, and the anti-Brown sentiment was so strong
that seventy-five policemen were needed to keep order.[16]
Brown was now beyond reprisal, but Wendell Phillips, the
agitator who had made Brown possible, was still available.
When he lectured on Staten Island, a group of proslavery

men tried to kidnap him, and he escaped through the
good graces of a fast carriage and the twenty armed abolitionists who guarded the hall.[17] At the same time, back in
Massachusetts, Caleb Cushing, former attorney general
under Pierce and the most eloquent Democrat in the
state, told a crowded audience in Faneuil Hall that Phillips was a monomaniac preaching a gospel of hate, a
"drunken mutineer" who had seized control of the political opinion of Massachusetts.[18]

Within a few weeks after Harpers Ferry, the problem
of evaluating John Brown and his champions became so
buried in legend and rhetoric that it was almost impossible
for anyone to give a balanced judgment on the subject.
To many, Brown was a deranged fanatic who would stop
at nothing, not even murder, to attain his goal. To Phillips, he was a "marvellous old man, a hero and saintly
martyr to the cause of liberty." Although the truth lies
somewhere between these extreme interpretations, it is
important to discover why Phillips took the position he
did.

When Phillips thought of Brown, he remembered
the man he had met, his simplicity, sincerity and single-
ness of purpose. Everything that he heard about Brown at
Harpers Ferry and beyond, including the legend of
Brown's kissing the slave child on his way to the scaffold,
fit perfectly with this image, and he accepted it without
question. Whatever he knew about Brown's earlier life
he picked up in conversation with Mrs. Brown or with
Higginson, who carried on an extensive correspondence
with the Brown family. All of the details and anecdotes
would have been favorable—about the devoted family
man who liked to sing hymns at his fireside with a daughter on each knee, the scrupulous manager of tanneries who
would turn a customer away if he detected the slightest
defect in his stock, the shepherd so tender with his flock
that he would take a chilled lamb into his own kitchen
and bathe it in a tub of warm water.[19]

The John Brown whom Phillips did not know was

the man who came from a family riddled with insanity. His maternal grandmother and his mother had both died insane. Two aunts and three uncles on his mother's side were intermittently insane, as were his sister, one of his brothers and six first cousins.[20] Many friends who had known Brown and his family sent in affidavits to this effect in an attempt to save him from the gallows, but Phillips blinked at the evidence and tried to laugh it away. "You remember the madman in Edinburgh. A friend asked him what he was there for. 'Well,' cried he, 'they said at home that I was mad; and I said I was not; but they had the majority.' Just so in regard to John Brown. The nation says he is mad." [21]

The John Brown whom Phillips did not know was the man who had experienced nothing but frustration and failure during the first fifty-five years of his life. He had tried several occupations including farming, tanning, sheepraising, wool brokerage and land speculation, and had failed at them all. His early reputation for honesty had been challenged. He was accused of embezzlement, and from 1820 to 1845 he figured in twenty-one lawsuits in Portage County, Ohio.[22] This is the man who, Phillips said, "must have lived wholly for one great idea," the man in whose every word and every deed "there does not seem to have been a trait that we cannot, with a whole heart, honor." [23]

The John Brown whom Phillips did not know was the man who on the night of May 24, 1856, led an armed party into a proslavery settlement in the Pottawotomie country in Kansas, dragged five defenseless men from their cabins and shot and hacked them to death in cold blood.[24] Whether John Brown himself actually pulled a trigger or swung a cutlass is debatable, but there is no question about his responsibility for the murders. During his trial he denied that he had anything to do with the killings, and this was enough for Phillips, who insisted in his speeches that Brown had not been within "twenty-five miles" of Pottawotomie.[25] The man who had super-

vised the butchering of five helpless men became Thoreau's "angel of light," the man who, Emerson predicted,
would make the gallows "glorious as the cross," the man
who, Wendell Phillips asserted, had "unfolded trait after
trait of earnest, brave, tender Christian life."

What John Brown had done at Harpers Ferry spoke
so loud that Phillips could not hear what was said about
the rest of his life. Emerson and Thoreau fell in love with
Brown for his personal accomplishment, because he was
the transcendentalist, the man of principle, in action.
Phillips fell in love with him for what he had done for the
cause. Many men had talked as if slavery were the greatest
curse on earth; Brown had *acted* as if it were. Harpers
Ferry was the legitimate offspring of speeches that Phillips
had been giving for a generation, and he knew it. How
many times had the word "disunion" dropped from his
lips? Brown had done more for disunion in two days than
Phillips had in twenty years. Wendell could see the evidence wherever he looked. Yesterday he had been mobbed
for preaching abolition; today insurrection "was the lesson
of the hour," and the North held mass meetings to honor
John Brown. The South was hysterical. The Southern
press incorrectly identified Brown with all Northern abolitionists and Republicans, and advised Southerners to take
radical means to ensure their own security. The result was
a wave of scare rumors about new raids and slave upris-
ings, the creation of vigilance committees, the lynching of
innocent people, the rupture of traditional ties between
the two sections and the enhanced prestige of those Southern radicals who wanted secession. All of this made Phillips jubilant, and it was impossible that he should not
have rejoiced in the man who had done such work.

For almost a quarter of a century, Wendell Phillips
had labored to create in America a public opinion that
would destroy slavery. During this time he had learned
that people in the mass are more responsive to symbols
than to arguments. Elijah Lovejoy had been a symbol of
the tyranny which slavery exerted over free speech. Web-

ster was a symbol of cupidity in politics; Anthony Burns
was a symbol. The assault on Sumner was a symbol of
Southern barbarism, and the Dred Scott decision a symbol
of slavery's stranglehold on the national government.
Phillips had found each of these symbols useful in his
attempt to reshape the thinking of America, but he knew
that John Brown would be the most powerful symbol of
all. Brown had assured himself of immortality, not only
by what he did at Harpers Ferry, but also by his heroic
conduct after he was captured. From the moment he was
arrested until the trap was sprung on the Charleston gallows, Brown acted more like a saint than a condemned
man. His testimony at the trial, including the famous
speech which has become a permanent part of our literature, his deportment in the prison, and his letters to
friends and family, all spoke eloquently for a man of
courage and dignity. God had chosen John Brown to
supply the text, Phillips thought, and it was left to others
to preach the sermon. In Phillips' sermons, Brown became
a symbol for divine judgment, "the impersonation of God's
order and God's law," "a Lord High Admiral of the Almighty, with his commission to sink every pirate he meets
on God's ocean of the nineteenth century." [26]

Wendell Phillips was so dazzled by what John Brown
had done for the cause that he could not see the man as
he actually was. He saw the man inspired, the "angel of
light," but not the man possessed, the angel of destruction.
For once, Phillips' Calvinism failed him; he was so anxious
to find the hand of Providence at Harpers Ferry that he
could not tell the awful difference between the wrath of
a man called Brown and the wrath of God.

13

Under the Flag   1860–1861

"Suppose men say we do nothing but scold our neighbors; suppose men say we do nothing but exhaust the vocabulary of abuse; suppose men say we do nothing but manifest the morbid bitterness of our own envious spirits,—such things have been said before. The old, old party from which we spring [the Puritans] bore the same calumny in their day; yet they saved England and survived."[1] Phillips spoke these words at an American anti-slavery meeting in the spring of 1860. He was convinced that the future lay with the moralists and not with those who would try to repeat the work at Harpers Ferry. John Brown had burned his way into the Northern heart; the abolitionists must exploit with speeches and pamphlets the advantage he had provided with powder and shot. To do this, they must remember that the hands of the North were not yet clean enough to clasp and that they, as custodians of the American conscience, could never afford the luxury of popularity. This was the advice he gave to others. In attempting to follow it himself during the ensuing months, Phillips had to steer a course through some of the stormiest seas in his whole career.

Although he had decided years before that politics was the plaything of the devil, that did not keep Phillips from taking an intense interest in the presidential campaign of 1860. He was encouraged by the sectional split within the Democratic party, but his chief interest lay in the Republican convention which met at Chicago on May 16. The leading contender for the nomination was the cultivated senator from New York, William Seward. Ever

since 1850, when he had denounced the Fugitive Slave
Law in the Senate, Seward had been a power among anti-
slavery politicians. He and Phillips had met for the first
time in 1855, when they lectured from the same platform
in Plymouth.² Unlike Sumner, Seward, a slight man with
a sallow, wrinkled face, a rasping voice and an unending
supply of cigars, looked every inch the politician. On
slavery, however, Seward was as sound as any man in public life. His famous declaration that an "irrepressible conflict" existed between North and South was exactly the
word that Phillips wanted to hear spoken in high places.
True, Seward had backed off and sounded much more
conciliatory now that he was straining for the Republican
nomination, but Phillips thought that his recent speeches
were probably "as good as any Pres T. [*sic*] candidate
could make." ³

As it turned out, Seward had not changed his tune in
time. After leading on the first two ballots in the convention, he lost the nomination to a less controversial
politician. Once again, the Republicans had shied away
from supporting a man who might possibly be linked with
the abolitionists. Phillips knew little about Lincoln and
was not impressed by what he did know. "The ice is so
thin," he announced to a Boston audience, "that Mr. Lincoln, standing six feet and four inches, cannot afford to
carry any principles with him on to it." ⁴ He was apparently referring to the position which Lincoln had taken
on slavery during his debates with Stephen A. Douglas
in 1858. In response to a series of direct questions, Lincoln had finally admitted that he did not "stand today
pledged" to abolish slavery in the District of Columbia
and was not opposed to a fugitive slave law or to the internal slave trade. Any one of these opinions was bad
enough; taken together, they suggested that Lincoln was
a faceless candidate, pliable and evasive enough for professional politicians but deserving the scorn of honest men.
Lincoln was ready to be President but could not make up
his mind "whether it is right to sell babies by the pound,

and upon an auction block," beside the Capitol of the United States. "Who is this huckster in politics?" Phillips asked. "Who is this county court advocate? Who is this who does not know whether he has got any opinions?" The answer, obviously, was that Lincoln was a nobody whom the Republican papers would be able to mold into whatever likeness they chose, the blander the better.

If we are to understand the role which Phillips set for himself at this time, we must separate the man from his rhetoric and read his speeches not, like some historians, as "a kind of grandiloquent, self-righteous raving," [5] but in the light of the purpose which informed them. Evaluating the four presidential candidates by their relative merit, Phillips had to put Lincoln at the head of the list. Breckinridge, the proslavery choice of the Southern Democrats, was unthinkable. Stephen Douglas, nominated separately by the Northern Democrats, was a notorious trimmer whom Phillips could never forgive for having sponsored the Kansas-Nebraska bill. John Bell and Edward Everett, running on a conciliatory Constitutional Union ticket, represented the dying gasp of the Whigs, a last desperate attempt to maintain the unholy alliance between Northern capital and Southern cotton. Lincoln was the most antislavery of any candidate and deserved to win. Phillips was disheartened, however, to see how little of the radical sentiment in the North had rubbed off on the Republicans. They wanted to be known as the party of principle but were terrified by the abolitionists and the prospect of being tarred as "Black Republicans." As their standard-bearer, Lincoln was scrupulous to keep his principles well in hand, willing to admit that slavery was wrong and should be kept out of the territories but too timid to say the institution was evil and should be destroyed. Confronted with this situation, Phillips could not support Lincoln or any other candidate. His duty was to make sure that the people were not beguiled by the political squabble into forgetting the profound moral issue. He was carrying out this duty, he thought, when he denounced Abraham Lincoln as "The Slave-Hound of Illinois."

Phillips first employed the epithet in an article in the *Liberator* in June. He was referring to a bill sponsored by Lincoln in the House eleven years earlier, which would have required city authorities in Washington, D. C., to return fugitive slaves escaping into the district. He cited the *Congressional Globe* as the source of his information, but he neglected to point out that the whole bill, of which he had cited only one provision, was intended to provide for the gradual abolition of slavery in the District of Columbia. The extravagance of Phillips' language was offensive to many. Horace Greeley berated him for not printing the entire law, and Phillips immediately asked the *Liberator* to do just that, thereby keeping the issue before the public all the longer. When Joshua Giddings wrote to say that Wendell's criticism was unfair, he replied that slave-hunting was slave-hunting no matter who encouraged it. He felt that as an enthusiastic Lincoln man, Giddings, like so many others who called themselves abolitionists, was unwilling to admit that if Lincoln disavowed these sentiments he stood to lose thousands of badly needed votes. "They rejoice that he can ride on two horses, beguiling Republicans by his ostentatious and superfluous endorsement of the Declaration of Independence, and winning conservatives by his alacrity in the slave hunting service of 1849." [6]

Of course, Lincoln was not, nor had ever been, a "Slave Hound," and Phillips, satisfied by the blood he had drawn from the moralists in the Republican party, was willing to change the metaphor to "Constitutional Hound." He would make a rhetorical but not a moral distinction. The man who upheld the hunting of slaves because of the Constitution was as guilty as the man who ran slaves for money. Phillips' purpose in attacking Lincoln so savagely in the first place was simply to dramatize the rottenness of the American conscience by showing that only a "Slave Hound" could be elected President. [7]

The air was full of election oratory in the summer and early fall of 1860, but, except for these early blasts, Phillips' voice was not heard. Ann had fallen into one of her periodic crises, and Wendell, much to the distress of his friends, shut himself in with his wife and was not seen on a lecture platform from the middle of June until November. He tried to convince himself that the enforced rest was good for him ("I am idle as the trees and grow fat like them"),[8] but he was obviously glad to get back before an audience and help welcome the results of the election. "For the first time in our history," he announced on November 7, "the *slave* has chosen a President of the United States." This statement, which must have startled many listeners who remembered how Phillips had treated Lincoln a few months earlier, was not as inconsistent as it sounded. Without being a good candidate, Lincoln had been the best candidate, and Phillips was willing to accept a half-victory over no victory at all. It was not the man but his being voted into office that was significant. "Not an abolitionist, hardly an antislavery man, Mr. Lincoln consents to represent an antislavery idea. A pawn on the political chessboard, his value is in his position; with fair effort we may soon change him for a knight, bishop or queen and sweep the board. This position he owes to no merit of his own, but to lives that have roused the nation's conscience, and deeds that have plowed deep into its heart." [9] Not only the slave but Garrison, Phillips and John Brown had elected Abraham Lincoln.

Phillips greeted the results of the governor's race in Massachusetts with unqualified enthusiasm. John Andrew had been elected, and Phillips said "For the first time within my memory we have got a man for Governor of Massachusetts, a frank, true, whole-souled, honest MAN." The statement was worthy of a Republican party worker, but Phillips was quick to point out that he retained all his old skepticism about politics. The average Republican was still too vacillating a creature to offer much hope for moralists. He cited Seward as an example.

At first glance, Seward appeared to have spoken more courageously against slavery than any other famous political figure, but, tracing his erratic course before, during and after the Republican convention, Phillips found that he had balanced every radical pronouncement with blandishments about national harmony and the Union. Seward's radicalism, it turned out, was only an appearance; the man really had a conscience like the famous Damascus blade, "so flexible that it could be placed in a sheath, coiled like a snake." [10] With a Republican administration waiting to take office for the first time in Washington, this was no time to relax. What was needed now more than ever was a vigilant antislavery public opinion to keep Lincoln, Seward & Co. morally honest, and Wendell directed all his efforts to this end.

He had a new platform from which to speak now, one that had formerly belonged to Theodore Parker. In the spring Parker had died in Florence, Italy, struck down by tuberculosis in his 50th year. Phillips knew that Parker's loss to the cause could not be estimated. In addition to being one of America's most celebrated ministers and scholars, Parker had been an enormously skillful writer and pamphleteer, and his close ties with Republican leaders helped to give him an audience inaccessible to Phillips and Garrison. More than this, Phillips mourned him personally. He and Parker had been neighbors and comrades for a decade. Glancing out his back window, Wendell had been able to look across to Parker's study, where frequently the light would burn all night in testimony to Theodore's prodigious capacity for work. Phillips was a Calvinist and Parker a radical Unitarian, but they never talked about that. It was enough for Phillips that Parker wanted to make Christianity work, and, though he admitted that he hardly knew what Parker's religious beliefs were, Phillips zealously defended his friend against his enemies among the conservative Unitarians ("the little worms that run about on the surface of corruption call themselves the children of Channing") and said he would feel surer of his own faith if he could find a Parker preaching it.[11] In his will, Parker left to his "much valued friend, Wendell Phillips," an eleven-volume folio edition of *The English State Trials*. He could not properly bequeath him the pulpit he had occupied, but his congregation did that for Parker when they asked Phillips to fill their pulpit for the first time on November 18.

Parker had been so popular as a preacher that his congregation (the members preferred the name "fraternity") had been forced to vacate their church and move into the Music Hall, a huge barnlike auditorium used by its owners the other six days a week for concerts and dance recitals. The Music Hall, for all its ugliness, represented a major capital investment, and the proprietors had always been uneasy about letting a controversial figure like Parker take it over. When they heard that Phillips had been invited to preach, they were extremely reluctant to rent the hall, and it took several hours of persuasion and a $50,000 bond to convince them.[12]

The proprietors had reason to be apprehensive. With the election of Lincoln, who had not secured a single electoral vote in the South, the nation had plunged into the gravest crisis in its history. Exactly one week after the election, the South Carolina legislature unanimously called for a state convention to decide on secession, and it was apparent that several of her sister states were prepared to follow her out of the Union. Confronted for the first time by secession as a near fact and not a threat, people in the North were excited and confused. Phillips and the other radicals wanted the South to break away, but majority opinion in the North saw only disaster in disunion. The onset of what seemed to be a sharp business panic aggravated Northern discontent. The stock market was wobbling; money was tight, and Northern financiers and merchants were appalled at the prospect of what might happen if the South decided to withold its newly harvested cotton crop from Northern mills. In Boston, where commercial interests were extremely influential and where the Democrats and the Bell-Everett Constitutional Union party were strong, there was a powerful sentiment for stifling any further agitation of the slavery issue, even if this meant forcibly putting a muzzle on Wendell Phillips.

The reception that Phillips received on his first appearance in the Music Hall was orderly. It was no novelty for him to preach a sermon, since almost all of his lectures had been sermons of one kind or another. His theme for the occasion was the pulpit, and what he had to say amounted to an apology for Parker's career and his own. The greatness of Theodore Parker's fraternity, he said, derived from their scouting of metaphysics, their agreement on a common moral purpose and their willingness to listen to anyone with a genuine message. For this they had been denounced as infidels by the orthodox denominations and practically excommunicated by the Unitarians, but they still retained their pulpit. The pulpit would never need a church; it would flourish wherever the moral energy of the people was expressed, not in Solomon's Temple but where Jeremiah and Isaiah spoke, not in King's Chapel but on Cornhill Street where Garrison published the *Liberator,* not in the Old South but in the Music Hall with Parker and Wendell Phillips.[13]

Two weeks later, Phillips found his pulpit in a Negro church on Joy Street, and the circumstances were far less pleasant. It was the anniversary of John Brown's death, and a group of Negroes had organized a meeting in Tremont Temple to celebrate the event. When an invasion of Bell-Everett men prevented the speakers from being heard, they adjourned and announced an evening meeting to be held in the Joy Street church. That afternoon 500 posters appeared on the streets:

Citizens of Boston!—the sympathizers of JOHN BROWN say they will hold a meeting at Martin's Church in Joy Street, this Monday evening, Dec. 3d. UNION MEN, shall IT be allowed? LET BOSTON SPEAK.[14]

In the evening the church was jammed, and a crowd of several thousand sullen Union men was milling around the Joy Street area. Phillips mounted the pulpit and gave a short, biting speech in which he attacked Mayor Lincoln for being too pusillanimous to prevent riots, and he praised the fact that a Negro church existed in Boston and was not run by State Street. Although he gave no quarter in his speech, Wendell had some misgivings about the wisdom of trying the ugly mood in the city with an evening meeting. His apprehensions were realized after the meeting broke up, when several Negroes were assaulted with stones and clubs. Rightly guessing that he was the game they were really after, Wendell slipped out a rear door and had climbed the hill to the Common before the mob caught up with him. By this time about forty friends had formed a tight cordon around him, and he was escorted across the Common to Essex Street while the frustrated rioters straggled in the rear, yelling threats and insults.[15]

Phillips was scheduled to preach a second time in the Music Hall on December 16. At first he believed that, since he was to speak on Sunday, there would be no trouble. Once his subject was announced, however, and it became generally known that he would speak on "Mobs and Education," rumors that a new riot was being planned circulated so freely that even the police began to organize for a crisis, and Phillips finally agreed to place himself in the hands of a bodyguard. On the appointed day, some thirty-three hundred people pushed their way into the Music Hall and took every inch of available space. No one had any illusions about this being a conventional religious service. There were seventy-five police in the building, stationed in the lobby and near the front of the hall, while more than twenty armed volunteers sat behind Phillips on the platform.[16]

Phillips played on two related themes. He began by discussing the theory of the American mob. He felt that he was something of an expert on the subject, having been

brought into the abolitionist fold by the Garrison and
Lovejoy mobs and having been confronted by many mobs
himself. The mobbing of abolitionist meetings, he said,
illustrated the tyranny with which the majority could
threaten liberty in a democracy. In America, where most
able men were lured from political careers into commerce, the danger from mobs was particularly acute, because government could not supply the leadership to cope
with them. Hence, the futility of the Boston mayor in the
present crisis.

So much for theory. In the second part of his address,
which most of the people had come to hear, Phillips concentrated on personalities. Taking his text from a psalm
of David ("Why do the heathen rage and the people imagine a vain thing?"), he turned his attention to the men
who had disrupted the John Brown meeting. Never, not
even in the most wrathful sermons of Theodore Parker,
had the heathen been so mercilessly flayed. The leader
had been Richard Fay, a lawyer with wealthy family connections, and his colleagues, including Thomas Perkins,
a broker, Jonas French, a former aid to Governor Gardner,
and Rufus Choate, Jr., were mostly young merchants,
clerks and lawyers.[17] Phillips had been furious to hear
the Boston papers refer to this new generation of whiggery
as "gentlemen," and he denounced them with the scorn
of a man who had lived on Beacon Street long before the
Whigs were born. "Narrow men, ambitious of office,
fancying that the inheritance of millions entitles them to
political advancement. Bloated distillers, some rich, some
without wit enough to keep the money they stole. Old
families run to seed in respectable dullness . . . Trading
families, in the third generation, playing at stock-jobbing
to lose in State Street what their fathers made by smug-
gling in India. . . . Snobbish sons of fathers lately rich,
anxious to show themselves rotten before they are ripe.
. : . The whole led by a third-rate lawyer broken down
to a cotton clerk borrowing consequence from married
wealth. . . . These are the men, this is the house of
nobles whose leave we are to ask before we speak and hold

meetings. These are the men who tell *us*, the children of the Pilgrims, the representatives of Endicott and Winthrop, of Sewall and Quincy, of Hancock and Adams and Otis, what opinions we shall express and what meetings we shall hold." [18]

Phillips got some hisses for his efforts, but the audience, for the most part, was friendly and frequently laughed at the picture he painted of men "whose souls are actually absorbed in pricing calico" undertaking to limit free discussion in Boston. After the speech, however, a policeman told Wendell that there would be trouble outside. By denouncing one mob, Phillips had raised another, and as a result he would have to run the gantlet if he wanted to get home. The narrow passageway connecting the Music Hall to the street was only fifty yards long, but it took the police (two hundred strong by now) fifteen minutes to fight their way through the mob. Once out in Winter Street they formed a wall around Phillips and marched him down Winter to Washington Street and down Washington to Essex Street. The mob kept lunging for Phillips, but the police held their ranks, and Wendell himself went along with a smile on his face, as coolly as if he were out for a Sunday morning stroll. For some hours afterward the police kept a guard in Phillips' house, and that evening several young friends, armed with revolvers, spent the night in his parlor. Wendell brought out an ugly-looking pike formerly belonging to John Brown which, he said, he would use if anyone tried to storm the house.[19]

The fact that Phillips could not make a speech in Boston without risking his life vividly illustrates the anxiety which gripped the North as the new year approached. South Carolina had taken ten other states out of the Union with her, and plans were already being drawn for the government of the Confederacy. In Washington, a bumbling lame-duck President complained that he was powerless to do anything to avert disunion. Business was bad in Northern cities, and the future looked even worse. Nathan Appleton's letter to a gentleman in South Caro-

lina urging reconciliation was widely printed in Boston
and elsewhere as the sensible voice of the North. Emphasizing the beneficial economic ties uniting the sections,
Appleton dismissed the abolitionists as a noisy minority
and said "every man of common sense" knew that the
abolition of slavery was "an utter impossibility." [20] This
was the high ground taken by friends of the Union.
Where the lower ground lay was pointed out by the press
in editorials about the danger of agitating the slavery issue
in such a crisis. Taking the hint, the rank and file among
the Democrats and Bell-Everetts pledged themselves to
shut Phillips up.

One day in late December, Maria Chapman called
at Essex Street and found Ann trembling over a neatly
packed box addressed to Wendell. Afraid that it might be
filled with explosives, she peered timidly under the lid,
right into the face of a dead cat. With such warnings becoming more common, and, with a new mayor coming into
office, Wendell's friends became extremely fearful for his
safety. Mayor Wightman, who had been elected by the
factions that wanted Phillips silenced, made clear his unwillingness to give him the protection of the city.[21] Phillips' friends, therefore, decided to take over the responsibility of the police themselves. Whenever he gave a lecture in or around Boston, a self-appointed bodyguard
went with him. Some of these militant admirers were
old-line abolitionists; a good many were Negroes, and
some, like the youthful Oliver Wendell Holmes, Jr., were
enthusiastic idealists from Harvard. In addition, a Boston
German club mounted a regular guard of four men, which
was sometimes posted in a print shop near the Essex
Street house and sometimes in the Phillips parlor. Wendell himself never left home without a pistol in his pocket,
and he assured his friends that he would not hesitate to
use it. "I can see over my shoulder," he said, "and before
a man can touch me I shall shoot." [22]

Phillips' next appearance in the Music Hall was on
January 20. Speaking on "Disunion," he abused everyone, especially Seward, who wanted to conciliate the

South. Rather than do anything to keep the slave-holding states, Phillips said, the North should "build a bridge of gold and pay their toll over it." Mayor Wightman had reluctantly ordered a detachment of police to preserve order, not because of any affection for Wendell but because he knew that Governor Andrew was to be in the audience.[23] Still, there was the usual brawl in getting Phillips back to Essex Street. Sam Howe, who interrupted a letter he was writing Sumner to join the other members of Wendell's bodyguard, returned to describe what had happened. "About fifty hard-fisted and resolute Germans went ahead and pushed the mob to the right-left. Then followed some fourty [*sic*] or fifty determined antislavery Yankees, who arm in arm and close ranks preceded and followed Phillips. A hack had been got ready at the back door, but to my great joy, it was decided to go boldly out at the front door & by Winter & Washington Streets. . . . It was a hard struggle down Winter St. & through Washington St. as far as the corner of Bedford St. The mob pushed against us, howling & swearing & clamouring,—a few resolute fellows pushing us against the wall, & evidently longing for a stop or melee in which they could get a lick at Phillips; who however bore himself very resolutely & bravely. Our course was to bear on steadily, saying nothing. At the corner of Bedford St. there was some obstacle, & a sudden stop; & you may judge of the purpose when I tell you that I came near being thrust into Browns windows & one man near me was actually pushed & jarred against the huge plate glass so hard that it was smashed in. At last we got to Phillips' door & way was made for him to get in. Then there was groaning & hooting & other disgraceful acts, before the crowd dispersed." [24]

Phillips gave one of his most memorable performances three days later in Boston's Tremont Temple. The occasion was the annual meeting of the Massachusetts Anti-Slavery Society. This time, Wendell heard, his opponents were ready for anything and, if they could not stop the meeting any other way, would stop it with bloodshed. Although he came to the platform that morning with a pistol in his pocket, Phillips was relying on other weapons. Garrison was home ill, and Wendell knew that he would be the chief target for all the Union men in the hall. Looking over the audience, he could see that the gallery was full of noisy boys, and he guessed that a good many Boston shopkeepers had closed for the day and sent their clerks and apprentices to swell the ranks of the trouble-makers.

James Freeman Clarke was the first speaker. He was heckled all the way, but he managed to finish. The Union men were saving their heavy ammunition for Phillips. When he stood up, the groans and hisses grew so loud that he had to space his remarks a sentence at a time, but there was no mistaking what he had to say. "We came here today to let Washington see what Boston thinks of this crisis, and we want her to declare that, Constitution or no Constitution, Union or no Union, against the law or with it, the Southern states, so long as they be slave states, shall be shovelled out of this Union." When the uproar became too great for him to continue, Phillips took off his coat and prepared for a long siege. Then in the next lull he broke in with "I would not give slavery a spoonful of earth to stay in the Union—not one; not a blade of grass, nor relinquish a single principle." They tried to stop him by singing, and he shouted back, "That is the death knell of slavery—don't you hear it? That is the maniac singing in his chains." When the crowd seemed to be getting the best of him, he ignored it and began to speak in a low voice to the reporters who were stationed directly below him. This tantalized his hecklers into yelling for him to speak louder. When he responded they listened, and for half an hour he kept them under his spell. As soon as he sat down the spell was broken, and Emerson, who succeeded him, was handled so roughly that he didn't even finish his remarks.

A second session was held in the afternoon. By this time the meeting had created so much excitement that representatives of almost every group in Boston were to be seen milling around inside the hall or on the steps outside. The *Traveller* ticked off the list: "Breckinridges, negroes, Douglas men, Garrisonians, Bell men, North Streeters, Beacon Streeters, John Brown's men, ministers of the Gospel, pick-pockets, reporters, teamsters, dry goods jobbers, loafers, brokers, rum-sellers, ladies, thieves, gentlemen, state officers, boys, policemen." It was such a motley group that one gentleman stopped on his way into the building, looked around uneasily, took off his hat and announced to everyone in earshot that he was "neither an abolitionist, a rioter, nor a pick-pocket" but was going in to see a man on business.[25]

Somehow they got through the afternoon program but not until the mayor had ordered the police to clear the galleries. Wendell saw, however, that the mayor could not be relied on to protect the evening meeting, and, as soon as the afternoon session adjourned, he and George Smalley, a young Boston lawyer who had recently flocked to his banner, went to see the governor. Phillips had come to respect Andrew during the John Brown crisis, and he knew that, despite his obesity and innocent, almost childlike appearance, Andrew was a resourceful and decisive man. Finding the governor in his office, Phillips told him what had happened and asked him to send state troops to guarantee the abolitionists their right to free speech and assembly. Andrew was attentive but said he could not legally justify the action. Phillips insisted that the power was inherent in the governor, but Andrew would not budge. Phillips turned and strode out of the office. His image of the new governor came crashing down. The "frank, true, whole-souled, honest MAN" had turned into a mere politician like all the rest. As they walked out of the State House, Wendell told Smalley that he would "never again speak to Andew as long as I live." When they got back to Tremont Temple that evening, they found themselves locked out. The building had been shut by order of the mayor.[26]

The Tremont Temple meeting meant both victory and defeat for Phillips. It was a personal victory for him to have tamed that wild and vicious crowd. It was a defeat to see the proceedings finally disrupted. This was a victory for slavery, and a newspaper in Atlanta confirmed it by printing a letter from Boston. "A John Brown meeting cannot be held in Boston now," their correspondent wrote, "no more than it could in Atlanta. We have got a most powerful organization here that will be heard from in due time. . . . Tell the people of Georgia not to be too rash. Tell them to bear with us a little longer and all will be well." [27]

The men who tried to mob him were not, of course, the only people who disagreed with Phillips. Most of the Republicans took Lincoln's position that the South could not secede, and Horace Greeley, whose New York *Tribune* was, perhaps, the most influential Republican paper in the country, accused Phillips of being too doctrinaire. He was a "close communion reformer" who insisted that everyone "take the wine from his cup or go to hell." Gentlemen who began by ignoring citizenship, Greeley wrote, were "not the best judges of those who still recognize political relations." [28]

It would have been impossible, however, for Phillips to have taken any other course. "All my grown-up years," he told an audience in New Haven, "have been devoted to creating just such a crisis as that which is now upon us." [29] Having agitated for disunion for more than twenty years, he could not regret it now. His reason for wanting to let the Southern states secede was a moral one. The South would take the sin of slavery with her, permitting the Northern states to organize a new government based on justice, and the great American hypocrisy would be ended. He tried to support his moral appeal with rational arguments. The North today, he said, stood in the same position with respect to the South that the colonies had been in with respect to England. The separation of the colonies at the time of the Revolution had struck a great blow for liberty, not only in America but in the world; so would the separation of the Northern and Southern states. He argued also that a Southern confederacy was bound to fail; Louisiana was tied to the West by the Mississippi River; the deep South would reopen

the slave trade and drive the border states into the arms
of the North. The fear that disunion would bring depression upon the North, he said, was based on a myth;
not Union but Yankee ingenuity was the mother of American trade and prosperity. Phillips had convinced himself
that disunion meant abolition. While other men looked
about them and saw only disaster, Phillips gloried in the
new dawn. The crisis had come about because the American people had finally grown decent enough to refuse the
concessions the South demanded. After disunion there
would be no obstacle to the full expression of Northern
antislavery sentiment, and this onslaught from without,
together with the weaknesses within the South, would soon
bring about the end of slavery. "Northern pulpits can-
nonading the Southern consciences; Northern competition
emptying its pockets; educated slaves awaking its fears;
civilization and Christianity beckoning the South into
their sisterhood. Soon every breeze that sweeps over Carolina will bring to our ears the music of self-repentance,
and even she will carve on her Palmetto, 'We hold this
truth to be self-evident—that all men are created
equal.' " [30]

No matter how many reasons Phillips could find to
justify himself, his position had always been one difficult
for others to understand, and it became increasingly
difficult after Lincoln's inauguration. The new President
had made it clear in his inaugural address that, while he
would do nothing to threaten slavery within the states,
he would not countenance secession. Meanwhile, the
South continued to demand the surrender of federal forts
and arsenals on its soil, and the threat of civil war increased. Phillips thought that Lincoln was trying to tam-
per with Providence. "Disunion leaves God's natural laws
to work out their own solution," he said on April 5. "Let
us stand out of God's way, and His divine laws will have
free course." [31]

Then came Fort Sumter. South Carolina had fired
the first shot, and the Civil War was unleashed. The
South had solved Lincoln's torturous problem for him

by introducing force. The question concerned no longer
the theoretical right of secession but whether the Federal
government was prepared to defend its property and citizens. Lincoln declared that insurrection existed and called
for volunteers. Instantly, the confusion and hesitation
that had characterized opinion in the North was swept
away in a great wave of patriotism. The Union was no
longer an abstraction but something which men would
fight to preserve.

The booming echo of South Carolina's shore batteries
was soon drowned out in Boston by the fife and drum and
the thunder of marching feet. The towns and villages
eagerly responded to Governor Andrew's call for troops,
and every incoming train brought a fresh load of soldiers
into the city. The parade of the companies through the
winding streets down to their headquarters at Faneuil Hall
seemed endless, while up on Capitol Hill the halls of the
State House were piled high with knapsacks, overcoats,
blankets, rifles and boxes of cartridges. The American
flag flew from every mast, and almost everyone among the
thousands of Bostonians thronging the streets proudly
displayed a red-white-and-blue rosette on his breast. Unanimity ruled the day. Boston banks offered to lend the
state $3,600,000 in advance of legislation. The Demo-
cratic Boston *Post* appealed for the defense of "our noble
Republican Government." Daniel Webster's son, Fletcher,
announced he would head up a regiment and was
cheered by a great crowd in front of the Old State House.
A shoemaker in Hingham heard the roll of drums outside
his door and rushed off to enlist, leaving his shop un-
locked and his leather still soaking in the tub. Conciliation was an insulting word now, and when the captain of
a barque out of Savannah tied up at a Boston wharf and
tried to fly a secession flag an angry crowd pulled it down
and tore it to pieces.[32]

Phillips had not prepared himself for this day. He
was accustomed to being out of step with the mass of the
people, but he had never felt as isolated before. In the

past he had always been able to accept events and make them work for his own end. How could he do this now? He had thrown his whole weight behind the agitation for peaceful destruction of a Union he despised; now he was confronted by a war to preserve the Union. If he supported the war, he violated his own principles; if he opposed it, he not only gave comfort to the South but threw away his last hope for exerting influence in the North.

Phillips sat in his study and pondered his position. He consulted his friends and then went into the streets and talked with the men who had been trying to mob him. Wherever he went he found the same unanimous enthusiasm. Those who could not march themselves were cheering on the parade; everyone was ready for war. One afternoon he walked into Smalley's law office looking haggard and distressed, and he complained that his friends expected him to do the impossible, "to renounce my past, thirty years of it, belie my pledges, disown every profession of faith, bless those whom I have cursed, start afresh with a new set of political principles, and admit my life has been a mistake." That evening Smalley called on Phillips at home. He found him sprawled out on the parlor couch asleep. When he woke up, Wendell announced, without further discussion, that he would speak in the Music Hall next Sunday (April 21, nine days after the attack on Sumter) on the subject of the war.[33]

The word spread rapidly. Phillips had kept Boston in convulsions all winter with his oratory about disunion. What would he say now? Rumor had it that he would announce his conversion to the cause of the Union, and when the audience streamed into the hall and saw the platform decked with flags the rumor seemed prophetic. Wendell took the pulpit and announced that his text was taken from Jeremiah: "Therefore thus saith the Lord: Ye have not hearkened unto me in proclaiming liberty everyone to his brother, and every man to his neighbor: behold I proclaim a liberty for you, saith the Lord, to the sword, to the pestilence, and to the famine." There could hardly

have been a listener in the hall who did not know what
to expect after this.

Those who had come to enjoy the spectacle of Phillips making a public recantation were disappointed.
"Many times this winter," Wendell began, "I have counselled peace,—urged as well as I knew how, the expediency of acknowledging a Southern Confederacy, and the
peaceful separation of these thirty-four states. One of the
journals announces to you that I come here this morning
to retract those opinions. No, not one of them! I need
them all,—every word I have spoken this winter,—every
act of twenty-five years of my life, to make the welcome
I give this war hearty and hot." It was as abrupt and
simple as that, no apologies, no quibbling. Yesterday
the government had been an agreement with Hell; today
it was "the Thermopylae of Liberty and Justice."

Most of Phillips' reasons for justifying the war were
ordinary enough and similar to other abolitionists'. The
struggle was between civilization and barbarism. It might
have been resolved peacefully, but the South had deliberately chosen war, despite the long history of Northern
appeasement. The question of secession posed a delicate
problem, because Phillips had often urged Massachusetts
to secede, and, less than two weeks before, he was quoted
as saying "on the principles of '76" Lincoln had no right
to maintain soldiers in Fort Sumter. The right to secession existed, he said now, but it was a revolutionary
and not a legal or constitutional right. The Southern
states could not justify their action on this ground because they were not acting as a people (Negroes being
denied a voice in the matter), but as slave-holding oli-
garchies.

Throughout his speech Phillips stressed his hope for
the future. He did not deceive himself, he said, into
thinking that the North was suddenly become abolitionist;
that party was as tiny as ever. Nor did he overlook the
fact that the majority of the people flocked to the flag
under the enthusiasm of the moment and that the pa-

triotism of State Street was related directly to the economic interest of the North. He found his encouragement in the hope that there was coming into prominence in the North a new class, composed of

the cordwainers of Lynn, the farmers of Worcester, the dwellers in the prairie,—Iowa and Wisconsin, Ohio and Maine,—the broad surface of the people who have no leisure for technicalities, who never studied law, who never had time to read any further into the Constitution than the first two lines—"Establish *Justice* and secure *Liberty*": they have waited long enough; they have eaten dirt enough; they have apologized for bankrupt statesmen enough; they have quieted their consciences enough; they have split logic with their Abolition neighbors long enough; they are tired of trying to find a place between one-forty-ninth and forty-eighth corner of a constitutional hair; and now that they have got their hand on the neck of a rebellious aristocracy, in the name of the PEOPLE, they mean to strangle it.

The war, Phillips had decided, would be something more than a war of civilization against barbarism, freedom against slavery. It would be a national atonement for the sins of seventy years, and the result was as sure as the will of God. After the smoke and the carnage, "The world will see under our banner all tongues, all creeds, all races,—one brotherhood,—and on the banks of the Potomac, the Genius of Liberty, robed in light, four and thirty stars for her diadem, broken chains under her feet, and an olive branch in her right hand." [34]

The cheers were deafening. No hisses now, no need for the bodyguard and police escort. The villain had become a champion, and the men who had mobbed him before would now willingly carry him back to Essex Street on their shoulders. His tongue was on their side. The eloquence of abuse had taken the field against their enemies. For the first time in twenty-five years, Wendell Phillips was in danger of becoming popular.

14

Phillips and Lincoln: Early War Years 1861–1863

Wendell Phillips was fifty years old when the Civil War began, and his reputation as the most eloquent spokesman for the abolitionists, which had been rising steadily for more than a decade, was greater than ever. A quarter of a century spent in agitating unpopular causes had left its mark, and for the first time people noticed that Phillips was beginning to look like a reformer. At the Harvard commencement in 1861, Wendell fell in with his old friend Lothrop Motley, who had become famous as a historian and diplomat. A mutual acquaintance, happening upon the two men in deep conversation, was struck by the difference in their appearance. Motley, fresh from years of gracious living abroad, had a genial visage reminiscent of "smiling vineyards," while Phillips' face was "as sharp and militant as a fortress." [1]

Phillips would have been flattered by the comparison, for militancy, he believed, was exactly what the hour demanded. Because slavery was destined to be cut down by the sword, there could never be peace or union until one government, respecting the freedom of all men, ruled from the Gulf of Mexico to the Great Lakes. In trying to ascertain what he could do to help lead the nation to this Promised Land, Phillips found that his choices were severely restricted. He was shut out from the army (his friend Higginson would soon lead a Negro regiment into the field) and from political office by his refusal to take an oath under the Constitution. The American Anti-

Slavery Society wanted to send him to England in an effort to strengthen ties between British and American abolitionists and influence British opinion to favor the Northern cause, but he believed it more important to stay home and make Americans accept the war as an instrument to free the slaves.[2]

During the months after Sumter it was possible to distinguish several major groups competing for public support in the North. At one extreme were the radical abolitionists led by Phillips and Garrison. Tiny in numbers, they were extremely vocal and tireless in their agitation. Phillips represented their sentiment when he warned that the war would leave the "bloodiest stain on the century" unless it was prosecuted for the purpose of destroying slavery.[3] At the opposite extreme were the Democrats, who supported the war with various degrees of enthusiasm but refused to recognize its antislavery character and still hoped for reconciliation with the South. Obviously, Phillips could not support this party, although he was willing to see individual antislavery Democrats appointed to public office.

The Republicans, despite their victory in the election, were already beginning to divide into factions. The moderates, led by Lincoln, controlled the Administration, opposed the extension of slavery, hoped for its gradual extinction, preferably through colonization schemes, rejected emancipation as a military goal and considered the war as a struggle for the supremacy of the Union. Some of these Republicans, like Lincoln himself, sincerely hated slavery, and some, like the recruiter in Terre Haute who tried to get public support by bragging, "I hate a nigger more than I hate the devil," seemed to prefer slavery to abolitionists and free Negroes.[4] So far as Phillips was concerned, there was little to choose between the moderate Republicans and the Democrats.

The radical Republicans in Congress, who seemed to be gaining in power, offered more hope. Some of these, like Charles Sumner, George Julian and Owen Lovejoy (brother of Elijah Lovejoy), were abolitionists in politics with close personal ties to the reformers. Others, like Ben Wade and Zachariah Chandler in the Senate and Thaddeus Stevens in the House, were hard-bitten politicians anxious to assure the future domination of their party by crushing the South and the Democratic party. They were far from being Boston gentlemen or spotless reformers, but there was a colorful brashness and purposefulness about them that Phillips found attractive. "Old Ben" Wade from Ohio, for example, had been one of the first outspoken antislavery senators. A short, powerful man with a bulldog's jaw and courage, he had hurled, after Sumner's beating, ferocious taunts at his Southern colleagues. When it seemed certain that he would be challenged to a duel by Senator Toombs of Georgia, Wade announced that his choice of weapons would be squirrel guns at twenty paces. Toombs promptly forgot the challenge, and the whole North chortled. "Zach" Chandler, who became Wade's crony on the influential Joint Committee on the Conduct of the War, was a grim, transplanted Yankee merchant who had made a fortune in Detroit before going into politics. A shrewd political boss who knew the connection between free liquor and political votes, Chandler had also been free with his money in supporting the Underground Railroad and the war in Kansas. In 1861 he had helped to smash the efforts of the peace commissions, and his remark that "without a little blood-letting the Union was not worth a rush" had brought him national notoriety. Thaddeus Stevens was the Republican floor leader and chairman of the Ways and Means Committee in the House. An acidulous man with a long history of political controversy behind him, Stevens had one of the sharpest tongues in Washington. After Webster made his famous speech on the Compromise of 1850, Stevens growled, "As I heard it I could have cut his damned heart out." Stevens had a clubfoot, a handsome mulatto housekeeper whose precise duties were a source of constant speculation among his enemies, a sure hand for poker and an all-encompassing hatred for slavery and the South.[5]

Phillips felt a kinship with the radicals in Congress and did all he could to keep up their truculence. When a report was circulated about a colonel of the First Massachusetts Regiment returning an escaped slave to his Virginian owner, Wendell sent a scathing letter to Charles Sumner, demanding that the officer be reprimanded, cashiered or at least denounced from the Senate floor. "This much is *due*," he concluded, "to the hope held out that this Govt. means *freedom* by this war. . . ." [6]

Sumner, who was Phillips' closest friend in Washington and his only intimate contact in Congress, was frequently barraged by letters of this sort, but Wendell was not above trying to wheedle him in matters of patronage. Some of his requests were on behalf of relatives; others, as in the case of the appointment of a Boston postmaster, were frankly political. "I have no right to any influence in your *Republican* appointments," he assured Sumner, "& certainly should never ask anything for one of *my* party. But to you my old friend may I not be allowed to say how *glad I* should be to see *Phelps* where he wishes to be and deserves to be." [7] For all his outward spurning of the institution, Phillips knew instinctively that the first law of politics was to reward one's friends and punish one's enemies.

Like everyone else, Wendell had his own ideas about how the war should be run and how long it would last. The South, he advised, should not be underestimated; she was too desperate and determined to be put down by any half-hearted Northern effort. Nevertheless, with decisive planning on the part of the government and decisive action on the part of the army, Phillips thought the war could be won in two years or less.[8]

On July 22, Boston papers carried the frightening reports of the Northern rout at Bull Run. In the first major engagement of the war, the South had gone a long way toward verifying its assumption that the North had

neither the taste nor the talent for battle. On the Monday
after Bull Run, Phillips, along with James Freeman
Clarke and W. H. Channing, was visiting John Murray
Forbes' estate at Milton. It was "a sad feast," Forbes recalled. "Channing almost cried, and all were in the
depths except Phillips, who strictly insisted that it was
just what we wanted, and was perhaps the best thing that
could have happened." [9]

Phillips' optimism was partly a product of his Cal-
vinistic faith in Providence and partly the result of his
belief that the people in the North needed to be jolted out
of their complacency. Bull Run had resulted from their
lack of an acute sense of moral purpose. There were too
many disloyal office holders in Washington, too many
former slave chasers trying to get commissions in the
Union army, too many morally confusing examples like
that of the Massachusetts officer surrendering a fugitive
in Virginia. Phillips called on the public to help dispel
the confusion, "to visit every man, no matter what his
position or his courage, with public rebuke, that fails
in the great question of the hour." What might this mean
in practice? He spelled it out in language that was almost
certainly seditious. "If you have any influence, therefore,
on members of Congress, on editors, on the creators of
public opinion, on your neighbors, on the rank and file
of your army, teach them that with Massachusetts bayonets, it is better to be insubordinate, and shoot a colonel,
than it is, unasked, unauthorized, and Heaven-damned, to
turn themselves into hunters of slaves." [10]

The events of the following weeks and months made
Phillips sound more and more waspish. When the House
and Senate passed resolutions that the war was intended
only to preserve the Union and not for the purpose of
interfering with slavery, it appeared that Bull Run had
demoralized rather than strengthened the moral purpose
of the North. Reminding his listeners that Greece had
fallen "because leaders and peoples were both rotten,"
Phillips ominously predicted that another six months

without a Northern offensive would find Europe recognizing the Confederacy and the war all but lost.[11]

The one bright star on the horizon during this gloomy summer was John C. Fremont. As the commanding general of the Western Department with headquarters in St. Louis, Fremont issued a military proclamation on August 30, declaring martial law in the strife-ridden border state of Missouri and freeing all slaves whose masters were resisting the government. Fremont had long been a favorite of the abolitionists, and his action, which was also received with great popular enthusiasm, took them by storm. Phillips applauded as loudly as the rest. Here was a man who deserved to be a leader because he was willing to "launch a thunderbolt" and proclaim emancipation. Lincoln, however, thought otherwise. Apprehensive of what such an announcement might do to the wavering border states, and feeling that a general had no right to meddle in the political business of emancipation, he revoked Fremont's order and recalled him from his command, replacing him with General Halleck who promptly directed his troops to turn away all fugitive slaves. Fremont's thunderbolt had been about as effective as a pop gun.

The melancholy summer turned into an even more melancholy autumn. George B. McClellan, the dandy little general who had taken over the army on the retirement of the ancient Winfield Scott, preened his moustaches, posed like Napoleon and trained his army. McClellan did everything but fight. He had the Napoleonic ego and the Napoleonic stance without the Napoleonic talent for winning battles. Meanwhile, the "rattlesnake flag" of the Confederate army still flew within sight of Washington, and Phillips brooded over the possibility that a dark conspiracy in the nation's capitol was paralyzing the war effort.

The President's message to Congress in December, in which Lincoln emphasized that his purpose was to prevent the war from degenerating into "a violent and remorseless revolutionary struggle," was to Phillips a confession of the futility of the first six months of the war. Victory without revolution would mean the Union restored with slavery, bloodletting with no atonement. Lincoln, however, seemed to have the people with him on this issue. Even the Republicans in Massachusetts were afraid to talk about a war to free the slaves, and at their convention in Worcester they would not support Sumner's appeal for an emancipation policy.[12]

Confronted with this depressing train of events, Phillips did the only thing he could do—he made speeches. Some years before, he had prepared a lecture on Toussaint L'Ouverture. He dug it up now, refurbished it and delivered it wherever he could. The great Santo Domingo leader, "an unmixed negro with no drop of white blood in his veins," was a symbol for Phillips of the capacity of the Negro race, and Phillips always tried to leave his audience with the impression that the story of Toussaint, a man with Napoleon's courage, Cromwell's zeal and Washington's nobility, was proof enough that the American Negro would acquit himself well after emancipation.[13]

When he spoke directly about the political situation at this time, Phillips tried to soften his remarks somewhat so as to appeal to as broad an audience as possible. In New York, long a battleground for antislavery lecturers, he said he did not look on the war as an abolitionist but as a citizen. He argued that slavery had caused the war and that any attempt to reconstruct the Union without first destroying slavery would be not only immoral but economically disastrous. He tried to paint the purpose of the war on the broadest possible canvas, showing it to be a part of the continuing struggle between democracy and aristocracy which went back to the French Revolution and beyond. What was needed, he concluded, was leadership capable of dramatizing the cause and unleashing the energies of the people. "I demand of the government a policy. I demand of the government to show the doubting infidels of Europe that democracy is not only strong

enough for the trial, but that she breeds men with brains
large enough to comprehend the hour, and wills hot
enough to fuse the purpose of nineteen millions of people
into one decisive blow for safety and for Union." [14]

Although Phillips' patience with Lincoln's government was almost exhausted, he looked to Congress with
new hope. When the House repudiated Lincoln's message
to Congress by refusing to readopt a resolution defining
the purposes of the war purely in terms of restoring the
Union, and when Ben Wade, Zach Chandler and George
Julian emerged as the leading members of the newly organized Joint Committee on the Conduct of the War,
Phillips was considerably cheered. It looked as if Congress
might be able to lead the nation into the Promised Land
after all. He sent off another letter bucking up Sumner.
"Don't let others steal all your laurels when you have
stirred the game by bagging it themselves," he said. "Go
forward with your bill for total Emancipation." [15] In his
speeches he began to demand that Congress abolish slavery. The constitutional authority could be found, he believed, in the provision "which says there shall not be
nobles in any state." His remarks about Lincoln became
increasingly abusive. Lincoln was trying desperately to
keep the radicals in his own party in check so as not to
affront the slave-holding border states and drive them out
of the Union. It was unfortunate, Phillips said, to have a
President who was "a Kentuckian" at heart when what
the nation needed was "an unmixed loyal Northern
man." [16]

Despite the radicalism of such remarks, Phillips had
the ear of the North as he never had before. He received
almost two hundred invitations to lecture during the
winter of 1861-62, and, although the number of people
who actually heard him was probably not more than
fifty-thousand, it is estimated that more than five million
read his speeches in the press.[17] The most impressive example of his popularity came when he visited Washington. On March 16, 1862, Phillips lectured in the Smith-

sonian Institution. The hall was crowded, and many representatives and senators sat on the platform behind him. The incident afforded a dramatic illustration of the change which had overtaken public opinion. A year before, Phillips would not have been admitted to any platform in the city; now the cream of Washington society turned out to hear him and swallowed his criticisms of the government without a murmur.

So successful was the first speech that he was prevailed on to stay over another day and lecture on Toussaint L'Ouverture. He was also the guest at an elegant dinner party held by the Speaker of the House, Galusha Grow, and attended by Vice President and Mrs. Hannibal Hamlin, Mrs. Fremont and Charles Sumner. The next day he was invited to Alexandria to address the troops of the Fourteenth Massachusetts Regiment. The prospect of Wendell Phillips addressing soldiers in the field was full of harrowing possibilities, but his remarks were mild, and he even included some praise for Lincoln's plan to compensate those loyal slave states that would begin to abolish slavery. Whatever the troops may have felt about Wendell Phillips, it made a profound impression on him to hear the roll call of a Massachusetts Regiment and the soldiers singing "John Brown's Body" on Virginia soil. The courthouse in which Brown had been sentenced was now used as a barracks for Massachusetts troops.[18]

Back home in Essex Street, Ann was fretting. It was the first time in years that Wendell had been so far from Boston, and the thought of him so near the Confederate lines, surrounded by immoral political leaders, filled her with foreboding. "Wendell needs *you,*" she scrawled in a hasty note to Garrison; "otherwise you leave him alone with *politicians* & his influence *without* you *must* be comparatively null." [19] Ann's wifely solicitude was charming, but her fears were unwarranted. Everywhere in Washington, Wendell was given a dignitary's welcome. When he was escorted onto the Senate floor by Sumner, at least half the senators in the chamber came up to welcome him, and Vice-President Hamlin left his chair to shake Phillips' hand.

Before he left, Phillips had an interview with Lincoln. One cannot help but wonder what the two men thought as they confronted each other. What did the tall, gaunt, shaggy man, the man with the rustic manner and shrewd genius of the frontier—what did the harried, overworked President think when he met his most celebrated critic face to face? Did he see him as a fastidious reformer from Beacon Hill and marvel at the diversity of a nation which could at the same time honor Phillips and himself? Did he remember that Phillips had called him a "huckster," a "slave hound," a hapless incompetent ("No man can be broader than his cradle")?[20] Did he meet with Phillips because he respected his opinion and influence and sought his advice, or did he think of him as simply another fanatic to be humored? And what did Phillips think of Lincoln? Did he recognize in the flesh the man he had so often described as an honest, well-meaning, "second rate" politician? Did he catch in the face and manner of the man who would soon overwhelm the American imagination any sign of Lincoln's terrible anxieties, of his charity, his resolution, his wisdom?

These questions must be left unanswered. The only report we have of the meeting comes from Phillips. "I told him that if he started the experiment of emancipation, and honestly devoted his energies to making it a fact, he would deserve to hold the helm until the experiment was finished—that the people would not allow him to quit while it was trying." Phillips is reported to have said this in a speech some weeks after the meeting. Another time he said, "The last words of your President to me were 'It is a big job; the country little knows how big.' "[21] These words had fallen on unsympathetic ears. Phillips was not interested in hearing about Lincoln's gigantic task and crushing responsibilities. He wanted results.

His triumph in Washington had revealed him to be the chief moral advisor to the nation, and he intended to play that role to the hilt.

Upon leaving Washington, Phillips set off on a brief lecturing swing through the West, where he had not appeared since 1856. The cheers of Washington were still ringing in his ears when he was hit by an egg in Cincinnati. The slave-holding state of Kentucky lay just across the river, and Phillips had never been popular in Kentucky. After he lectured in Washington, Kentucky's Senator Garret Davis called him a traitor and said he should have been "manacled and confined at Fort Warren or Fort Hamilton." [22] The way many Kentuckians felt about abolitionists can be seen in an editorial taken from a Louisville paper about this time. Discussing what would happen if Lincoln freed the slaves, the editor wrote, "It would take a standing army of two hundred thousand men to retain Kentucky in the Union, and then the soldiers would be compelled to aid in exterminating the black race. If they are emancipated, there is but one thing to be done with them: they must be wiped out—utterly obliterated. It must be a merciless, savage extermination of the whole tribe. There will be no question of humanity, or justice, or mercy. It will be nature's first law—self defense." [23] There were obviously a lot of Kentuckians in the Cincinnati Opera House the night Phillips tried to lecture there. He sensed the ugly mood of the audience but opened, as was his custom, with a defiant statement of abolitionist principles. He had hardly begun when a large boulder came down from the third tier of boxes and crashed into the footlights in front of him. At the same time, two eggs thrown from the second balcony burst on the stage like bombs. Phillips kept on talking, and the eggs kept on exploding. Finally, the men in the gallery made a rush downstairs for the stage crying, "Tar and feather him," "Put the nigger out." While his friends held off the charge, Phillips left through the stage wings and walked out of the building, spattered and stinking but unhurt.[24]

Coming on the heels of his Washington success, what happened to Phillips in Cincinnati dramatizes the conflicting state of Northern opinion toward the war in 1862, and helps to explain why Lincoln was moving so warily around the subject of emancipation. The mob may have been inspired by Kentuckians, but the glaring absence of police protection for the meeting suggested to many that it had strong Ohio support and was sanctioned by the authorities in Cincinnati.

It was a close escape for Phillips (after the riot a bottle of vitriol was found in the lobby of the Opera House), but he took it calmly and said it did him more good than harm. Moving on to the Northwest, through Chicago, Detroit and Madison, Wisconsin, he found a more appreciative audience. "You have no idea how the disturbance has stirred the West," he wrote to a friend in Boston. "I draw immense houses, and could stay here two months, talking every night." Before long he was confessing that Cincinnati had opened his way "to the hearts of the prairies so quickly" that he was almost afraid people would accuse him of having staged the riot.[25]

Back in Boston on April 17, Phillips gave a lecture entitled "Washington and the West." He was full of encouragement by what he had seen, and he announced that "the masses are to settle this question, not the statesmen." The "great West" was on the alert, "fully aware of the magnitude of the struggle" and determined to drive the war to a successful conclusion. Finding that a genuine enthusiasm for the war did exist, Phillips again became more mellow (for a time) in his remarks about the President. Lincoln was not so bad after all. If he lacked anything, it was "neither intention nor capacity" but the power to forge ahead and lead the nation. Together with his new Secretary of War, Edwin M. Stanton, Lincoln would give the nation what it asked for.[26]

As the spring wore on, however, all of Phillips' old frustrations came back. The periods in history which he had studied most avidly were the Puritan Revolution of 1640 and the American Revolution. They had both been glorious struggles over principle. Phillips wanted the Civil War to be a revolution in this heroic tradition, but he could see it in this light for only moments at a time. Then would come the chilling realization that Wisconsin zeal was checkmated by the counting house mentality of State Street, the Cromwellian Fremont was cancelled out by the toothless McClellan, and the Roundheads in Congress were frustrated by Border State insolence and the temporizing of the Boston *Daily Advertiser*. This is how Phillips felt at the end of June, 1862. During the previous two months everything had gone wrong. An attempt to repeal the Fugitive Slave Law in the House had failed. Lincoln had overruled another general who tried to emancipate the slaves under his jurisdiction, and Fremont had resigned. McClellan, meanwhile, who had made one of his infrequent moves in March and succeeded only in capturing a dummy Confederate fort a few miles outside Washington, had finally pushed south almost within sight of Richmond, where he unaccountably stayed for the first three weeks in June, unwilling to commit his army.

On June 29, while McClellan and Lee were fighting a long, indecisive battle in front of Richmond, Phillips poured out his heart in a letter to Sumner. If the war lasted until December, he warned, Europe would come in on the South's side, the struggle would drag on for years, and the blood would be on the government's hands. "Lincoln is doing twice as much today to break this Union as Davis is. We are paying thousands of lives and millions of dollars as penalty for having a *timid* & *ignorant* President, all the more injurious because honest." The radicals in Congress were on the right course, but they must take a stronger tack and refuse money and supplies until the government did its duty. "Make *one* effort more," he pleaded, "to rally your party and save us." [27]

In addition to stronger leadership in the White House, Phillips was convinced that the army needed better generals. "I wish," he wrote plaintively, "*I* could nominate ONE." Whenever he found a likely recruit he would shoot off another letter to Sumner for help. He knew of a certain Captain Pinner, "bred to the business in Prussia," who wanted to be General Clay's quartermaster; he was "the best *quartermaster* in the army & Clay ought to have him." Then there was an aspiring brigadier general by the name of Maggi, who had trained at Turin and fought under Garibaldi and was now wasting away in New Bedford, teaching French and Italian to ladies. Sumner would have to do what he could "for the nations sake to use Maggi. . . . Don't my dear fellow *throw this aside*— put it in your pocket as a *reminder* & go and see Stanton about it." [28] If most of these requests came to nothing, it was probably a good thing. The chances are that Wendell knew very little about the men he recommended. For all his harshness on the lecture platform he was an easy mark for anyone with a sad story or anyone seeking a personal favor. Lincoln was having enough trouble with his generals without this kind of help.

Looking back at the first eighteen months of the war, what exasperated Phillips most was that it had been fought as if slavery did not exist. Because a majority to actively support emancipation could not be found in the North, Lincoln was unwilling to take the initiative and turn a civil war into a crusade for freedom. Phillips' analysis of the situation was perceptive enough, but the prospect of a government so morally becalmed was more than he could stand. He gave vent to his frustration on the first of August when he said publicly that if Lincoln had been a "traitor" he could not have done more to help the South.[29]

Although a careful reading of Phillips' remarks

would have shown that he said also that the President
was "as good as the average North" and "honestly waiting,
like any other servant for the people to come and send
him on any errand they wish," his speech was savagely
denounced in the Northern press. The concensus was
that Phillips was the one whose loyalty should be questioned. "WENDELL PHILLIPS SPOUTING FOUL TREASON,"
screamed a headline in the New York *Herald*. Phillips
was compared unfavorably with Jefferson Davis and accused of discouraging enlistments. One writer predicted
that if Lincoln would put him in prison it would be worth
100,000 men to the Union cause.[30] Even the usually sympathetic Horace Greeley blasted Phillips in the columns
of the *Tribune*. Wendell rode out the storm, more content than he had been in months. His shot had struck a
tender spot, and the violent reaction to it suggested that
the North was beginning to wonder how it could justify
so "wasteful and murderous" a war.

On September 22, after Lee had been turned back at
Antietam, Lincoln finally did something that Phillips
could applaud. In his preliminary Emancipation Proclamation, the President declared that on January 1, 1863,
all slaves in areas still in rebellion against the United
States would be free. It was hardly a radical document.
Lincoln said nothing about slavery in the border states,
and his message implied that, if the South laid down her
arms, slavery would be left untouched. It was enough for
Phillips, however, especially when Lincoln followed it
up a few weeks later by removing McClellan from his
command. "I trust the President," Phillips told a cheering Boston crowd on November 19. "I am not going to
criticize the President. I believe that today he has turned
the corner and recognizes the fact, not simply that the
slaves of rebels, but that *slaves* must be freed." [31]

Phillips' sudden endorsement of Lincoln, and his
enthusiastic response to the Emancipation Proclamation
when it was signed on New Year's Day, elicited many sour
remarks from the opposition press. "The proclamation

may lose us Kentucky," the Boston *Courier* prophesied, "but then it has given us Mr. Phillips. He will doubtless take the field with a formidable army of twenty thousand adjectives." A substantial body of opinion in the North held that Lincoln had violated the Constitution by declaring the slaves free. When Phillips attempted to refute this argument, the New York *Herald* likened his role as a constitutional advisor to that of "Rabelais editing the Confessions of St. Augustine." [32]

Although circumstances seemed to have thrown him into Lincoln's camp for the moment, Phillips had no intention of remaining there. A few hours after the President had signed the Proclamation, Phillips had gone out to George Stearns' house in Medford and presided over the unveiling of a bust of John Brown. That old man also had a face "as sharp and militant as a fortress," and the flood of memories which were unveiled along with his marble likeness served to remind Phillips of his own unrelenting mission.[33] Three days later he was calling the Emancipation Proclamation the "reluctant gift" of Lincoln to the masses and was urging the people to be vigilant lest the government let it remain a paper order.[34] He was like a general in the field, half-afraid of one victory lest it make his troops complacent for the battles ahead.

15

Phillips and Lincoln: Later War
Years   1863–1865

Three weeks after the Emancipation Proclamation was signed, Phillips went to Washington for a second interview with Lincoln. As a member of a delegation of abolitionists including Sam Howe, George Stearns and Moncure Conway, Wendell's mission was to urge on the President the wisdom of appointing antislavery men to administer the subjugated areas in the South. Lincoln had agreed to see the Boston men on the evening of January 24, but he was called away at the last minute to confer with Secretary of War Stanton. Wendell, however, refused to leave the White House without seeing someone, and he managed to get an interview with Mrs. Lincoln. When he rejoined his companions in Willard's Hotel afterward, he was in good spirits and reported that Mrs. Lincoln was hostile to their archenemy, Seward. If he had known that Mary Todd Lincoln had once referred to Seward as a "dirty abolitionist sneak," he might not have been so jubilant.[1]

The next day, Lincoln greeted his visitors with the laughing announcement that the White House was overcrowded because the family cat and the family dog had both sprung litters at the same time. The intended hilarity grated on Wendell's ears, and he immediately opened the interview on a serious note by asking Lincoln about the Emancipation Proclamation. Antislavery people, he said, expected it to be carried out diligently, and he suggested that Fremont be chosen to administer the order

in North Carolina. The President was obviously prepared for this, and he delivered a short lecture on the
hazards of a reformer in politics. When he had issued his
celebrated order in Missouri, Fremont had been operating as a reformer, and now he had to pay the penalty.
The principle involved, Lincoln explained, was that "the
first reformer of a thing has to meet such a hard opposition and gets so battered and bespattered that afterwards,
when people find they have to accept his reform, they will
accept it more easily from another man." Wendell knew
enough about reformers to concede this point, but he
could not reconcile himself to the manner in which the
President justified the appointment of the present military governor of North Carolina, a man by the name of
Stanley, who was a notorious abolitionist-hater. Stanley
had been in Washington when the Proclamation was
issued and had told the President that he "could stand
that." The incomprehensible thing to Phillips was that
Lincoln could blandly admit having appointed a man of
such begrudging loyalty to execute his policy.

At one point during the interview, the President, remembering, perhaps, the abuse that he had received from
Phillips during the past year, said tartly that "most of us
here present have been long working in minorities, and
may have got into a habit of being dissatisfied." Neither
this remark nor anything else that Lincoln said during
the interview helped to break the habit so far as Wendell
was concerned. The meeting ended amicably, but when
he left the White House that evening Phillips had developed grave doubts as to the government's capacity for
the hard days ahead. These doubts were reinforced the
next day, when the delegation gave a dinner for the anti-
slavery members of Congress. Several speeches were made
by important lawmakers, and Phillips was struck by the discrepancy between the critical remarks the radical Republicans made about Lincoln in private and what they said
for public consumption. Even Sumner felt obliged to
wear a muzzle for fear of hurting his influence with the

President.[2] Having just discovered his own lack of influence at the White House, Wendell had no such compunctions, and his speech a few days later was full of condescending remarks about Lincoln. He described the President as "a man born and brought up in Kentucky whose later years have been spent in striking an average between the Republicanism of North Illinois and the border-ruffian democracy of its south." It was too much, Phillips said, to expect such a man to be a statesman and understand "the events amid which God has placed him."[3]

Deeply disturbed by what he had seen in Washington, Phillips returned to Boston where he found McClellan being given the key to the city. Although Lincoln had replaced him and he was now a general without a command, "Little Mac" continued to exert a powerful spell over Northern opinion. Still idolized by the men in the Army of the Potomac and obviously the darling of the Democratic party, McClellan visited Boston at the request of a group of gentlemen who sought to blow new life into the old Constitutional Union party and lay the foundations for a presidential campaign the next year. He stayed at Edward Everett's house, and his visit was a roaring success. Merchants and bankers closed their doors in honor of the occasion; the streets were thronged with people anxious to get a glimpse of the general's carriage, and a public reception in Tremont Temple drew such a crowd that it paralyzed traffic for blocks around.[4]

Phillips had been fighting the perversity of his native Bostonians long enough not to marvel at their latest expression of idolatry. McClellan himself, Phillips realized, was important only to the extent that he provided a focus for the expression of conservative sentiment. Lincoln had told Phillips that he was afraid that the Emancipation Proclamation had done more harm than good in the North. Phillips could not believe that this was true, but he did know that there had been a lot of dissatisfaction in the army and that those soldiers who were grumbling

that the army motto was "First the negro, then the mule,
then the white man" [5] generally stood up for McClellan,
as did the Democratic party and a majority of the Northern newspapers. Obviously, the enthusiasm for McClellan
was directly proportional to the peoples' unwillingness to
see a war for the Union turned into a war against slavery.
So long as the people felt this way, there would always be
a McClellan somewhere on the horizon.

The McClellan affair, coming on the heels of his
melancholy experience in Washington, helped to set Phillips on the course he was to follow over the next two
years in demanding more resolute leadership for the
North. If the North was ever to recognize that it was em-
broiled in a great social revolution and not a mere civil
war, Phillips was convinced, a stronger man than Lincoln must be put at the helm.

Phillips' approach to the public during the spring
of 1863 was shaped by several considerations. He was
aware of the impatience in the North for military victory,
the relatively low esteem in which Lincoln was supposedly
held and the increasing importance of the radical Republicans in Congress. As judicious a witness as Richard
Henry Dana had observed after visiting Washington in
March that personal loyalty to the President was almost
nonexistent. "If a Republican convention were to be
held tomorrow," Dana predicted, "he would not get the
vote of a state." [6] Knowing that a good many substantial
Republicans shared Dana's misgivings, Phillips could
afford to be candid when he faced a Republican audience
in New York City. "I do not believe in the government
at Washington," he announced. "I do believe in the nation, I believe in events. I believe in the inevitable tendency of these coming ten years toward liberty and
Union. But it is to be done as England did it in 1640,
by getting rid gradually, man by man, of those who don't
believe in progress, but believe in the past." Even a Republican President, he implied, might have to be purged
for the sake of progress. The trouble with the North,

Phillips told his politically minded friends, was that it was handcuffed by "negro hatred" and "constitutional scruples," unable to carry through the great social revolution that the times required.[7] Phillips envisaged a bold program in which Emancipation was only the first step. Victory on the battlefield and the destruction of chattel slavery were to be followed by the reconstruction of Southern society around the Negro. To this end, Phillips urged the creation of a Freedman's Bureau and the guarantee of Negro suffrage. With the outcome of the war still uncertain and with the North still grumbling over the Emancipation Proclamation, he served notice that he would accept nothing less than full citizenship for the Negro. He based the demand on his faith in the effectiveness of the democratic process.

> The moment a man becomes valuable or terrible to the politician, his rights will be respected. Give the negro a vote in this land, and there is not a politician from Abraham Lincoln down to the laziest loafer in the lowest ward in this city who would not do him honor. . . . I don't care for his race . . . I don't care for his brains, whether they weigh much or little. He has brains enough to be responsible in the police and criminal courts of his country, and therefore he has brains enough to go to the ballot box.[8]

Although Phillips' program was extreme and sounded hopelessly utopian to many, he was being heard with more respect than ever before. Republicans invited him to address their meetings, knowing that he was no Republican and reserved many of his sharpest barbs for their leaders. Aspiring politicians were now anxious to receive his endorsement. A friend of Benjamin Butler, for example, heard Phillips praise Butler on the lecture platform and immediately sent a report to the general. "Phillips, in these winter months, manufactures a vast amount of popular opinion," he wrote. "No man will speak oftener or to larger audiences in America for the next few months." [9]

Phillips' attitude toward Butler is worth examining. Benjamin Franklin Butler was one of the cleverest politicians Massachusetts ever produced. Long before the Civil War he had attained wealth and prominence from his practice in criminal law and had become one of the leading Democrats in the state. He attended the Democratic convention in 1860 and supported the nomination of Jefferson Davis for President. Like many Northern Democrats, however, he was a strong Union man, and the outbreak of the war found him a brigadier general of militia leading Massachusetts troops into the field. During the war, Butler's reputation skyrocketed, and he became one of Phillips' heroes. It was Butler, alone among the Northern generals, who cut through the red tape and fog of indecision which obscured the Administration's policy toward fugitive slaves. When they came into his lines at Fortress Monroe in 1861, he simply declared them "contraband" and put them to work for the Union cause. The term immediately became famous, and Butler enjoyed a growing reputation as a man who could be trusted to deal decisively with slavery. This reputation was enhanced enormously by his administration as military governor of New Orleans. Acting almost as a law unto himself, Butler assumed the entire financial control of the city, hanged a man for hauling down the American flag and told the high-spirited New Orleans ladies that if they did not stop insulting his troops they would be treated like common prostitutes. All of this, of course, aroused publicity. Large numbers of people in the North were indignant over Butler's high-handed dealings, and there quickly spread rumors that he was looting the city for personal gain. When he was recalled to Washington and replaced by Nathaniel Banks in December 1862, he was probably the most publicized figure in the army.[10]

That Phillips should have emerged as one of Butler's most persistent champions is not as incongruous as it seemed. It is true that Ben Butler was anything but a gentleman reformer. He was an opportunist with an instinc-

tive love of notoriety, and he looked more like a pirate than
a crusader. He was a squat man with a drooping paunch
and a cast in one eye. He did, however, have a reputation
as a man of action. In an army led by men like McClellan,
Burnside (who had lost disastrously at Fredericksburg) and
Halleck (a general of "utter, unredeemed, unfathomable
incapacity," [11] according to Phillips), this was something.
Above all, Butler had shown that he would not truckle
to the South, and his instincts on the Negro question
seemed sound. Phillips was always more interested in deeds
than in motives, and he called Butler the ablest general in
the Army, the only man who had "organized victory." He
exploited Butler's reputation as a symbol for the radical
cause, and in doing this he apparently forgot his convictions about capital punishment. "If I were he and were to
die soon," Phillips told an audience, "I would have a
tombstone inscribed 'I was the only Major General of the
United States that ever hung a traitor; that ever, by the
boldness of my action, and the method of the death, told
the world it was a Government struggling with rebels, with
the right and purpose to put them beneath its laws, at any
cost.' " [12]

It is significant, certainly, that while Phillips was singing the praises of Butler he should have found himself
temporarily estranged from Sumner. The two old friends
were brought into conflict when Sumner backed a Boston
man, Col. T. G. Stevenson, for brigadier general. Stevenson had caused a flurry of excitement by allegedly stating
that he was opposed to drafting Negroes and would refuse
to serve with them. Sumner, presumably persuaded by
the colonel's father (an old-time cotton Whig of some influence in Massachusetts politics), supported Stevenson's
nomination, and his support was supposed to have secured
it. Citing this action in a widely reported speech on May
11, Phillips said it had "materially lessened" his confidence
in Sumner's "intelligence and fidelity." [13] While it is probably not true, as one of Sumner's biographers suggests, that
Phillips broke off relations with Sumner completely, even

to "passing him on the street without recognition," it does appear that during the next several months the correspondence between the two was halted except for a few formal and very chilly letters on Phillips' part. Sumner apparently felt the cut deeply and protested to a friend: "Wendell Phillips *knows* me; he knows me, and he ought not to speak of me as he does." [14]

There is no reason to believe that Phillips took pleasure in denouncing Sumner or that it was petulance on his part. When the Stevenson incident occurred, Massachusetts was training the first Negro regiment to be used in the war. Phillips believed in the use of Negro troops, from both a military and a moral standpoint. To admit the Negro as a soldier was to go a long way toward putting him on an equal basis with the white man, removing the race prejudice which was at the root of Northern inability to act decisively against the South. In dramatizing the forces of prejudice opposing this project, Stevenson had thrown doubt on the whole undertaking. He deserved to be rebuked; instead he was promoted. The effect on the public, as Phillips pointed out, was morally confusing, and the fact that a famous antislavery senator was involved made it all the worse. In reprimanding Sumner, Phillips was reminding both senators and citizens that there could be no victory without justice and no justice without equality. What he wanted was a society which would "punish the Colonel who treads on a negro as severely as if he had wronged a college graduate whose home is on Beacon Street or Fifth Avenue." [15]

Sumner's distress at being attacked by his old friend must have been intensified whenever he thought of his critic's fast-growing audience. The first volume of Phillips' speeches, published in the summer of 1863, sold out in four days.[16] History was catching up with Phillips, and, temporarily at least, he was no longer a lonely agitator but the most popular spokesman for a substantial body of radical opinion in the North.

A reviewer wrote in the *Atlantic* that Phillips' book

revealed a man "given to snap judgments" and "momentary partialities." [17] Nowhere was this shown more clearly than in Phillips' remarks about the Army during the summer of 1863. Frustrated by the lack of a concerted Northern offensive, he declared on July 4 that the government in Washington, "instead of being a machine to carry on this war effectively, is nothing but a great National Committee to manage the next Presidential election." Yet, even as he spoke, Grant was accepting the surrender of Vicksburg and Meade was pinning down a momentous victory at Gettysburg. Phillips joyfully responded to the news of Gettysburg by declaring that the army now had "a *brave,* an *able,* and a *sober* General" in George Meade. The word "sober" was a reference to Meade's predecessor, Joe Hooker. For several months Hooker had been one of Phillips' favorites. "He means to fight; he knows how to fight; and those two are new elements at the head of the army." This is how Phillips talked about Hooker in May, after Hooker's defeat at Chancellorsville.[18] By July, Hooker was out of command and rightfully so, according to Phillips, who now announced that Hooker had been drunk at Chancellorsville. Phillips did not originate the rumor of Hooker's drunkenness, but the fact that he picked it up so casually and gave it the support of his own authority illustrates his growing tendency to employ whatever gossip was at hand for sensational effect. "Let me make the Generals, and I don't care who makes the proclamations," he boasted. "Only let me put at the head of the advancing columns of the Union certain men I could name, and the cabinet at Washington may shut themselves up and go to sleep with Rip Van Winkle till 1872." [19]

Despite the drift to radicalism suggested by Phillips' growing popularity, antiwar sentiment had remained powerful in some sections of the North. In the middle of July, rioting broke out in New York, and for four days mobs terrorized the city, looting buildings and lynching Negroes. On July 13 the riot spread to Boston. As in New York, the action began as a protest to the draft and soon developed into a general riot. When the rioters began to fire the Cooper Street armory, troops were called in from Fort Warren and Fort Independence, and the mob was finally dispersed by cannon shot and bayonet charges. Several people, including a seventy-one-year-old man and a ten-year-old boy, were killed.[20]

That such violent resistence to government policies could take place during wartime served to confirm Phillips in his belief that the nation was suffering from a crisis in leadership, and nothing Lincoln could do would change his mind. In his message to Congress that December, the President seemed to offer encouragement to the radicals by defending the use of Negro troops and declaring that he would stand by the Emancipation Proclamation. Phillips could not have overlooked the latter point, because he received a note to the same effect addressed in Lincoln's own hand. Henry Wright had written to the President asking for a signed guarantee that he would uphold the Emancipation Proclamation. Lincoln's reply, mailed to Wright in care of Phillips at the antislavery office in Boston, read "I shall not attempt to retract or modify the emancipation proclamation; nor shall I return to slavery any person who is free by the terms of that proclamation, or by any acts of Congress." [21] Phillips felt, however, that the President cancelled out these reassurances when he accompanied his message to Congress with a Proclamation of Amnesty and Reconstruction. This document provided for the liberal pardon of rebels and for the re-establishment of state governments in the South on easy terms, and it contained a statement of principle to the effect that the Federal government would allow the states to take the lead in handling the Negro problem.

In his address to Congress, Lincoln implied that the Emancipation Proclamation was subject to judicial review. Ben Butler sent off a hurried note to Phillips: "Have you read the message and proclamation?" Butler asked. "The administration has put the Negro, his liberty, his future, into the hands of the Supreme Court. God help him if he has no other refuge! And yet no one seems to see the point, at least so far as I can see from the newspapers. Will Congress arouse to the question?" [22] Butler closed by saying he had marked the letter "private" because he had no right to discuss such affairs, but felt he could confide in "an earnest man." Coming from Butler, the show of delicacy was amusing, but the general had no need to worry about Phillips, who saw nothing out of place in being encouraged by a high-ranking officer to criticize the policies of his commander-in-chief. If anything, Phillips was flattered to be consulted personally by a potential presidential candidate, and he immediately wrote back to tell Butler that he would follow up his suggestions.[23]

Two weeks after Lincoln's message, Phillips gave a major address devoted almost exclusively to an analysis of the President's policy. Discarding theatrics, he was almost dispassionate in his criticism. Lincoln was trying to bring the South to terms by suggesting compromise. Some compromise, Phillips admitted, was inevitable ("in a nation divided on its own soil, there never was a strife which was not ended by compromise"), but he was afraid that the President, like Daniel Webster in 1850, was willing to cement the Union with Negro blood. Lincoln's willingness to let a panel of judges decide the fate of the slaves was an example. Roger Taney, chief architect of the infamous Dred Scott decision, still presided over the Supreme Court, and the prospect of his revoking the Emancipation Proclamation brought out Phillips' most derisive remarks. "The hot new purpose of today," he said, "just born of long, bitter experience, and tried in fierce battle, is to be tested and measured by the fossil prejudice and iron precedents of a century back—to such a tribunal President Lincoln proposes to submit the final settlement of the war. We are to furl banners and adjourn the fight, not knowing which party has beaten, or how much he has gained, until that Court decides on our measures." Phillips proposed something that the Court could not touch, an amendment to the Constitution prohibiting slavery and providing that no state should make any distinction among its citizens on account of race. In addition, Phillips asked that the government take steps to see that the Negro was not left in a state of vassalage. This could be done (how he would square it with the Constitution Phillips did not say) by the confiscation of plantation lands and their division into 100-acre farms for Negroes and loyal whites. Once they were socially reconstructed, the Southern states could be safely brought back into the Union.[24]

Although Phillips' proposal was about as far removed from Lincoln's as possible, his remarks about the President were surprisingly mild. Lincoln's great weakness, Phillips said again, was his cautious disposition, his insistence on waiting for the people to tell him what to do. Nevertheless, he was careful to praise the President and declared that he had "carved for himself a niche so high in the world's history, that he can well afford to have his faults told."

Phillips' language was becoming more cautious now, possibly because he had begun to realize the extent of his audience and was unwilling to jeopardize his influence with a national election in the offing. His speeches were receiving wide coverage now in both the Republican and Democratic press. The New York *Herald* might write, "We pollute our columns this morning with a speech of Wendell Phillips," but the *Herald* as well as the New York *Tribune* found that what Phillips had to say was newsworthy and would sell papers. As usual, the Democrats tried to make political capital by identifying the Republicans with Phillips' radicalism. Unlike the situation in 1860, however, when the accusation was patently ridiculous, shrewd observers were beginning now to see more and more truth in the assertion. "Emancipation, abolition, confiscation, southern lands for landless Negroes! This is the programme," snarled the *Herald,* predicting that, as usual, the leading Republican papers like the New York *Tribune* and the *Times* would wait a few months "and then follow Wendell Phillips' lead." [25]

The *Herald's* prediction appeared to be borne out in

April 1864, when Lincoln implied that he would favor a constitutional amendment to abolish slavery, something Phillips had been demanding for months. The explanation which Lincoln gave is worth noting, for it shows how accurate Phillips was in his analysis of the President. "I claim not to have controlled events," Lincoln said, "but confess plainly that events have controlled me. Now at the end of three years' struggle the nation's condition is not what either party, or any man, devised, or expected. God alone can claim it." [26] Phillips' only quarrel with this explanation was that the President was giving too much credit to God and no credit at all to the men like himself, who did God's work by forging the controlling events.

To Phillips, the President's remarkable candor was simply an admission of failure in leadership. A man willing to be controlled by events had made an acceptable President in 1861, but the situation now demanded aggressive leadership from men of revolutionary spirit willing to direct policy, control events and reshape the character of the nation. Many of the radicals in Congress were more qualified than the President on this score, and Phillips let it be known that he was willing to work with them to keep the government out of conservative hands. "Now my idea is," he wrote to George Julian, "the Administration has wished many times, but been unable to *resist* the Revolution. It has overborne them. Keep its hand on the helm and it will still overbear all resistance and accomplish its full object. But let such a majority as I have described once get its hand on the helm and the revolution may easily be checked with the aid of the Administration, which is willing the Negro shd. [*sic*] be *free* but seeks nothing more for him, but on the other hand plans how to let the white race of the South *down easily*." Phillips told Julian that he rejoiced "to work in your gang" and intended to use the summer of 1864 to ripen "a public opinion sufficient to control legislative action in this matter of Reconstruction enough to keep it in a safe channel." [27]

During the following months, Phillips was to become more involved in politics than ever. He had long since given up on the Administration, and he believed that either Butler or Fremont would make a better President than Lincoln. In May a group of avowedly anti-Lincoln radicals issued a call for a convention to be held in Cleveland to nominate a candidate for President. Phillips endorsed the convention in a widely distributed public letter in which he accused Lincoln's government of "carrying us to a point where we shall be obliged either to acknowledge the Southern Confederacy or to reconstruct the Union on terms grossly unjust, intolerable to the masses, and sure soon to result in another war." [28] At the same time, Phillips tried to take a more active role in Republican politics. Representing his ward in Boston, he participated in a caucus to elect delegates to the national Republican convention at Baltimore. He opposed the resolution endorsing Lincoln but was overwhelmed by party regulars. He also used his influence in an unsuccessful attempt to lure an anti-Lincoln delegation from Vermont. These failures, demonstrating that he was entirely without *practical* influence so far as the regular Republicans were concerned, caused him to lean all the more heavily on the hope of what might come out of Cleveland.[29] Unable to go there himself, Phillips sent off another letter which made his preference for a candidate clear. "If Mr. Lincoln is reelected, I do not expect to see the Union reconstructed in my day, unless on terms more disastrous to liberty than even Disunion would be. If I turn to General Fremont, I see a man whose first act was to use the freedom of the negro as his weapon. I see one whose thorough loyalty to democratic institutions, without regard to race—whose earnest and decisive character, whose clear-sighted statesmanship and rare military ability, justify my confidence that in his hands all will be done to save the state that foresight, skill, decision and statesmanship can do." [30] Fremont was nominated, and Phillips became one of his most enthusiastic supporters during the ensuing campaign.

In coming out so strongly for Fremont, Phillips was throwing in his lot with one of the most dashing and romantic figures in America. Familiar to millions as "the

Pathfinder," Fremont had made a national reputation in the 1840s by leading the first topographical expeditions into the Rocky Mountains. He had also played an important role in the conquest of California and had been victimized (so far as the public was concerned) in a widely publicized court case. He also struck it rich in California gold. A tall, handsomely bearded man, Fremont came to personify the romance of the West, and his name was linked with that of the legendary mountain man Kit Carson, who had been one of his guides, and with the daring, courage and resourcefulness of the American pioneer.[31]

In 1856, Phillips had derided Fremont as a figurehead chosen because the Republicans were afraid to face up to the slavery issue; now he saw him as the man who had dramatized the demand for emancipation and had become a symbol for thousands of Northerners who wanted to fight the war on moral principles. There were other people, many in high places, who thought that Fremont caused more trouble than he was worth. He had a capacity for stirring up controversy and alienating important people. His abilities as a military strategist were far from outstanding, and an investigation of his command in the Western Division eventually showed up a number of administrative and financial irregularities. When Lincoln removed him from command, however, his troops almost threw down their arms and refused to fight. Fremont had a rare gift in being able to inspire personal loyalty among his followers. He could strike sparks among the masses, and Phillips thought he saw in him the kind of leader he wanted, a man who might be able to control events and lead the nation along righteous paths.

Despite his personal admiration for Fremont, Phillips was never a very good hero-worshiper, and the decision to support Fremont's candidacy was based on several hard-boiled political considerations. In the first place, he and the other Fremont men believed, at least in the beginning, that, even though he was running as a third-party candidate, Fremont had a good chance to win. As evidence of the fact that the people were drifting away from the

Administration, they could point to the election of 1862, in which five key Northern states, carried by Lincoln in 1860, sent Democratic delegations to Congress. Even in Republican-ridden Massachusetts the Republican plurality had been cut in half. Fremont had a strong following among the German population, which comprised seven to fourteen percent of the total population, in several states. In addition, the Fremont men expected that Northern discontent with the indecisive conduct of the war would drive many more people, Republicans and Democrats, into the Fremont party. In the spring of 1864 this was not an empty hope. The Republicans had already shown signs of internecine warfare by allowing a presidential boom to develop for Salmon Chase, and, with Grant's army suffering bloody losses in Virginia, Lincoln's prospects looked dim. Even if Fremont were to be defeated, Phillips felt he must lend his influence to support a party willing to dramatize the moral issues of the war, and he called the provision in the Cleveland platform which promised to secure absolute equality before the law to all men "the high-water mark of American politics." [32]

In supporting a third-party candidate, Phillips naturally drew the fire of regular Republicans. He was also attacked by strongly antislavery Republicans and accused of doing the Devil's work in attempting to divide the Republican party. He replied by saying that, although he was himself not a voter "and could neither give nor take office under the present constitution," he welcomed the opportunity to work with any man, Republican or Democrat, "in securing a union without a slave, and with every man, black or white, equal before the law." True to his best form, he refused to admit any inconsistency in his new position, and he suggested that his critics did not take the trouble to understand him. "Don't abuse my speeches as most men do the Bible, reading it in *verses*," he advised the editor of the *Independent*. "Absorb them in generous paragraphs, and you will see that they are all of a piece—using different means, but always for the same end." [33]

As the summer wore on, Phillips became more and

more engrossed in politics, and he frequently consulted with Fremont. On July 20 he wrote to Elizabeth Cady Stanton that, although he had done everything he could to shape the policy of the party, he was still not ready to call himself "a partisan" of Fremont. He was anxiously looking forward to the forthcoming Democratic convention in Chicago and hoped that the Cleveland platform would serve "as a possible nucleus to which breaking parties may gravitate, for break they must and will." [34] Phillips apparently thought that, just as the Republican party was called into existence by the slavery issue and built on the shambles of the Whigs, so a new party could be created by the issue of the war and reconstruction. This seemed plausible in late July and early August. Grant had lost almost 60,000 men at Cold Harbor in June. The President had pocket-vetoed the Wade-Davis bill, a radical reconstruction measure, and the radical Republicans were grumbling among themselves and covertly discussing the possibility of getting Lincoln to withdraw in favor of someone else. Meanwhile, the Democrats had yet to name their candidate, and Phillips hoped they would recognize that slavery was doomed and would bid for the support of the Fremont faction. He felt that, if the Democrats ignored this possibility and nominated McClellan on a peace platform, they would win, and he could only hope then for "a *live* Republican Party *opposing* McClellan in the chair." Phillips had apparently resigned himself to this gloomy eventuality by late August, but he continued to meet with Fremont. The general might not win the election, but if he did not come out of the struggle a convinced abolitionist it would not be Wendell's fault. "I wish I had more influence with F. and that some men had less," Phillips confided to a friend on August 22. "But I believe in *him*." [35]

When the announcement of Fremont's nomination was first made, Lincoln and his supporters had treated the whole thing as a joke. By midsummer, however, they were taking it more seriously. McClellan promised to run a strong race, and the Lincoln supporters, remembering

what the Liberty party had done to Henry Clay twenty
years earlier, were afraid that Fremont might swing just
enough votes to throw the election to the Democrats.
Fremont was dangerous; it was imperative that a way be
found to get him to withdraw. Zach Chandler was the man
who worked it out. According to the plan, if Fremont
retired he would receive an important military command
and the satisfaction of knowing that his bitter political
enemy, Montgomery Blair, would be removed from the
cabinet. Fremont consulted his advisors. Some of them,
like Whittier who said "There is a time to *do*, and a time
to *stand aside*," counselled withdrawal. Phillips, however,
felt that Fremont should remain in the race, and he made
a special trip to the general's cottage at Nahant to argue
the case.[36] He failed. On September 22 Fremont retired
from the campaign.

Although the evidence indicates that Fremont rejected
a "deal" and withdrew because he feared that McClellan's
election would be bad for the nation,[37] Phillips could
hardly have found his experience as a political advisor very
satisfying. Once again the reformer had been outmaneu-
vered by the politicians. Phillips now lost all interest in
the outcome of the election. His name, however, continued to be heard in campaign orations, since the strategy
of the Democrats was to charge that Lincoln had been
abolitionized and forced to make a war for the Union into
a war against slavery. Robert C. Winthrop, whose unreconstructed Whiggery had taken him into the McClellan
camp, said sarcastically before a huge rally in New York:
"We are assured that a vote for Abraham Lincoln is to
usher the glorious day when the eloquence of Wendell
Phillips may be enjoyed at Richmond and Charleston, as
it is now enjoyed at New York and Boston."[38] At the
same time, Phillips was telling his friends he would "cut
off both hands before unnecessarily doing anything to elect
Mac and one hand before doing the same for Lincoln."[39]

As it turned out, the most eloquent testimony for
Lincoln's re-election came not from the mouths of orators
but on the field of battle. Sherman's victory at Atlanta on

September 2 probably did as much as any one thing to assure Lincoln's re-election. The end of the war was now in sight, and Lincoln's famous remark about not swapping horses in the middle of the stream made sense to a majority of voters.

Once the votes were counted, Phillips wasted no time worrying about what should have been but set about preparing for the future.[40] The chief danger which lay ahead, he wrote to Ben Butler, came from the "too-hasty-peace-makers-on-any-terms." They must be stopped, and popular sentiment must be whipped up for the radicals in Congress—"the earnest men of the times." [41] The first goal was to make sure that the Republicans made good on their pledge to abolish slavery through constitutional amendment. In the early months of 1865, however, when Congress and several states had already ratified the Thirteenth Amendment, Phillips left this behind and began ranging the countryside, stirring up the people to demand a full-scale program for radical reconstruction. With Sherman driving his way north from Georgia through the Carolinas and with Grant crouched at the gates of Richmond, the days of the Confederacy were numbered. The problem was no longer how to win the war but how to secure the peace. On March 1 he wrote Sumner that he had been addressing audiences every night for the past month and found the people distrustful of "all *present* reconstruction" and "enthusiastically ready" for radical leadership. Sumner was back in grace now, largely because of his determined opposition to Lincoln's lenient program of reconstruction in Louisiana.[42]

Lincoln continued to be the chief of the "too-hasty-peace-makers," and Phillips, who had finally come to appreciate the strength of the President's personal following among the people, must have been filled with foreboding by the inauguration and the President's appeal to "charity for all." While Lincoln's thinking at this time was infused with the spirit of the Gospels, Phillips' was Hebraic. He wanted the people to think less about charity and more about justice.

Because he had always had deep misgivings about Lincoln as a President, Phillips received the news of his assassination with mixed feelings. "I was very sad for Lincoln," he wrote to Mrs. Stanton; "twas very, very sad to picture that patient head bowed in death in an instant before that drunken and mad bullet." The event was not without its providential aspect, however. Lincoln had won such trust from the masses that it was difficult to argue against him. "The removal of men too great and too trusted is often a national gain in times like these and it lifts off a weight and lets people develop and think for themselves." [43] The same day that he wrote this letter, Phillips addressed a public meeting in Tremont Temple. While orators and clergymen from every pulpit and platform in the North were joining in a solemn hymn of praise for the martyred President, Phillips came as close as he would ever come to eulogizing Lincoln's memory. "No matter now that, unable to lead and form the nation, he was contented to be only its representative and mouthpiece; no matter that, with prejudices hanging about him, he groped his way very slowly and sometimes reluctantly forward. Let us remember how patient he was of contradiction, how little obstinate in opinion. . . . With the least possible personal hatred, with too little sectional bitterness, often forgetting justice in mercy. . . . if his sympathy had limits recollect he was human, and that he welcomed light more than most men, was more honest than his fellows, and with a truth to his own convictions such as few politicians achieve. With all his shortcomings, we point proudly to him as the natural growth of democratic institutions."

Phillips had spoken his mind about Lincoln when he lived; he was determined to be honest about him in death, and honesty required him to say that, in a sense, it was better for the nation that Lincoln had died. "God has graciously withheld him from any fatal misstep in the great advance, and withdrawn him at the moment when his star touched its zenith, and the nation needed a sterner hand for the work God gives us to do." [44]

16

The Split with Garrison
1865–1867

John Wilkes Booth had unwittingly played into the hands of the radicals. Just as the firing on Sumter had hardened the Northern purpose for fighting the war, so did Lincoln's assassination harden the Northern heart toward the problem of reconstruction. But irony plays no favorites, and no sooner did the radical abolitionists see the gap which had always separated them from the great body of Northern opinion begin to close than they fell out among themselves. Less than three weeks after Lincoln's death, Phillips went to the annual meeting of the American Anti-Slavery Society in New York and heard Garrison, his friend and associate for almost thirty years, say "The old state of things, when we mingled together like kindred drops into one, no longer exists. We are a divided house and it is useless to deny the fact." [1]

Even a slight acquaintance with the personality and character of the men and women in its ranks makes one marvel that the American Anti-Slavery Society did not splinter into a thousand factions long before 1865. Phillips always believed that the vitality of the abolitionist movement depended on the fact that it was made up of men and women of independent spirit. "The moment we cease to criticize each other with the same freedom that we criticize the world," he predicted, "we shall have lost that peculiar character of intellectual life which gives us our efficiency." [2] Although there is a great deal of truth in Phillips' judgment, history tells us that the enthusiastic spirit of self-reliance and self-criticism which sustained the abolitionists in adversity also proved their undoing.

When the political abolitionists broke away from the radicals in 1840, Garrison inherited a band of supporters who were small in numbers, devoted and self-sacrificing, enormously vocal and more or less cranky. Always potentially schismatic, these reformers had stayed together because of their loyalty to a common cause and because differences among themselves were as nothing compared with their differences with the world. As time went on, however, their internal disputes became more pronounced, and two opposing factions developed within the Garrisonian camp. The more conservative faction centered in Boston and counted Garrison, Sam May, Jr., Edmund Quincy, Maria Chapman and the Weston sisters among its leaders. The radicals drew their strength from the provinces and were led by Abby Kelly, Stephen Foster and Parker Pillsbury. In the 1840s the tension between these two groups found expression in the support which Nathaniel Rogers received in his controversy with Garrison and in the Boston abolitionists' repudiation of the tactics employed by Foster and Pillsbury in their assault on the churches. A decade later it cropped up again in a controversy over the attitude the reformers should take toward the Republican party. In 1856, when they enthusiastically came together to pass resolutions in praise of Charles Sumner, a few of the abolitionists raised objections. The fact that Sumner had been hit over the head by a Southern congressman did not alter the fact that he was a politician himself, sworn to uphold a proslavery Constitution. To give unqualified praise to Sumner, Foster argued, was to countenance the lie that politics and morality could mix in a slave nation. Garrison had handled Foster rather sharply at the time, and this served only to accentuate the differences between the two factions.[3] In 1859, Garrison had a falling out with Abby Kelly Foster, when he rebuked her for treating the Republicans as savagely as if they owned slaves themselves. Feeling that her integrity was challenged, Abby refused to accept a place on the board of the American Anti-Slavery Society, and she wrote to Phillips explaining her position. Like many of the abolitionists, Abby subscribed to a kind of syllogistic morality which conceded nothing to circumstance. If, as she believed, slavery still existed because the North supported the Constitution and the Union, and if the North was Republican, it followed that the Republicans were slaveholders and should be denounced as such. Garrison was getting old, Abby confided to Phillips, and "advancing age always tends to conservatism. My constant prayer is to be preserved in the full flower of fanaticism and saved from the beginnings of popularity among a people who participate, though ever so remotely, in holding slaves." [4]

Before 1863, Phillips seems to have played a conciliatory role with respect to the differences among the abolitionists. Although he did not agree with Foster and Pillsbury when they invaded the churches, he refrained from criticizing them, and when Abby Foster and Garrison were feuding he managed to avoid taking sides. On the one hand, he believed that Garrison was wrong in attacking Abby. At the same time, he accused the Fosters and Pillsbury of sulking because the rest of the abolitionists would not share their views. "Your danger and Pillsbury's," he wrote to Abby, "is intolerance—you are leaning to sectarianism and bigotry. You incline to suspect the honesty of those you cannot at once convince to your views." [5]

During the early years of the war the abolitionists were too taken up with the common purpose of making the war an instrument to destroy slavery to worry about their own differences. By 1864, however, the old tensions had reappeared and become too obvious to be ignored. Taking their cue from Garrison, more and more of the abolitionists were coming to feel that, with the Emancipation Proclamation and the growing antislavery character of the Republican party, their mission as members of a separate antislavery organization was practically accomplished. To many of the reformers, this seemed like backsliding, and they did not hesitate to say so. Garrison talked about the "miraculous change" among the Republicans, but Abby Foster insisted that the politicians were willing to move against slavery only because of military necessity. All of the action against slavery so far had been taken "not from the highest but from the lowest motives" and therefore not from motives which could be trusted.[6] That Phillips was more in sympathy with the latter position became apparent at an antislavery meeting in January 3, 1864, when he split with Garrison by supporting a resolution which accused the government of trying to make a fraudulent peace. Garrison accused Phillips of impeaching Lincoln's motives. The man who had once likened the Methodist Church to a cage of filthy birds now protested that he would "always rather err on the side of charitable judgment than of excessive condemnation." After a heated debate the measure passed. It was the first official acknowledgment that Phillips had taken over the actual control of the American Anti-Slavery Society.[7]

Although the decision to spurn politics had been one of the ties binding the Garrisonians together in the first place, it was now obvious that they were splitting along political lines. The New Bedford man who compared Phillips' treatment of Lincoln to the "mocking and unholy abuse of Christ toiling up Calvary or wrestling with his agony in the garden"[8] typified the pro-Lincoln abolitionists who flocked to Garrison's banner. That Garrison was indeed a Lincoln supporter became clear when the *Liberator* came out for his re-election. With Garrison actively endorsing Lincoln, and Phillips doing the same for Fremont, it was hard for any of the abolitionists not to take sides. The tension mounted, and at the meeting of the American Anti-Slavery Society in May there was a flare-up when Phillips began the proceedings with a long, caustic speech attacking the Administration. Garrison again demurred, saying "I do not feel disposed, for one, to take this occasion, or any occasion, to say anything very harshly against Abraham Lincoln." At the business meeting that evening, Wendell first publicly acknowledged that he and Garrison were at odds, by denouncing his endorsement of Lincoln. "I would have sooner severed my right hand than taken the responsibility," he said. "There are no hundred men in the country whose united voices would be of equal importance in determining the future of the government and country. A million dollars would have been a cheap purchase for the Administration of the *Liberators'* article on the Presidency." [9]

There can be no doubt that Phillips and Garrison strained to keep the controversy from degenerating into a personal quarrel. The ties between them were too strong to be easily broken. Whatever their present differences, Wendell continued to look on Garrison as the great awakener in his life. Garrison, on the other hand, was indebted to Phillips in a number of ways. Not only had the most eloquent of all abolitionists never wavered in his loyalty; he had also been generous with his money. Economic crises were frequent in the Garrison household, and it had been a comfort to know that Wendell was always ready to help out. The correspondence between the two families makes it clear that Ann and Wendell were like aunt and uncle to the Garrison children. Their favorite, of course, was Wendell Phillips Garrison, and they had paid his way through Harvard, solicitously watching his progress as if he were their own son. Garrison undoubtedly had these facts on his mind when he wrote in the *Liberator* praising Phillips for "the manly avowal of his convictions" and deploring the talk of a possible "schism" between them. After a particularly sharp encounter during one of the meetings in New York, Garrison wrote to his wife, saying he hoped he had done nothing to offend "dear Phillips." [10] About the same time, William Lloyd Garrison, Jr., assured a friend that, despite their strong opposing convictions, not one "unpleasant personal feeling" occurred to either Phillips or his father.[11]

As the presidential campaign began, however, and the

antislavery societies were transformed into debating societies over the election, it became increasingly difficult to
maintain cordial relationships. Oliver Johnson, who
edited the *Anti-Slavery Standard,* was one of Garrison's
staunchest supporters, and in June he wrote an article in
the *Standard* attacking Fremont. Phillips was infuriated
and demanded a retraction, but Johnson threatened to re-
sign if he could not express his convictions in the paper.
The upshot was a series of meetings of the executive committee of the American Anti-Slavery Society, where Garrison was able to control enough votes to let Johnson have
his way. To make matters worse, Johnson wrote Phillips
a letter in which he said that Fremont was a tool of the
Copperheads out to destroy the Republican Party, "a base
man in affiliation with other base men, and therefore
wholly unworthy of anti-slavery support." [12] Phillips
ignored Johnson's letter but continued to denounce the
Standard. Garrison, meanwhile, began to include favorable notices of Phillips' speeches under his "Refuge of
Oppression" column in the *Liberator,* a space traditionally
reserved for proslavery writers.[13]

Many of their mutual friends were dismayed to see
Garrison and Phillips drawing apart. Wendell Phillips
Garrison, who was now working in New York, was torn by
conflicting loyalties and wrote Phillips to explain why his
sympathies lay with his father. Phillips replied by identifying himself with the "no Union with slaveholders" position, which had been responsible for keeping the abolitionists out of politics in the beginning. "I find no man criticizing me today," he wrote, "who would in his *present mood*
have been an *abolitionist* from 1835 to 1848. The tone is
the Whig voice of 1850." Although Phillips would try to
be tolerant of those who disagreed with him, he warned
his namesake against the danger of strong political loyalties. "Don't let N.Y.K. looseness lead you to imagine that
all the virtue and all the loyalty of the land resides in the
Republican party. I used once, twenty years ago, to have
such a dream of the Whigs. I woke out of it then and

believe now that, all things considered, the rank and file of the parties is about equal." [14]

It pained Phillips to find himself becoming increasingly estranged from his old friends. He tried to pretend that it was only differences of opinion which separated them. "I forgive you for quitting Boston! and being a Lincoln man!!" he wrote to Garrison's son. "Can I express myself more emphatically or select more impressive illustrations of the *strength* of my affections?" The cordiality, however, was somewhat forced, as events soon revealed. In September, Phillips asked that his contribution to the *Liberator* be withheld until after the election.[15] He had refrained from doing much lecturing during the summer weeks, but he was preparing to break silence and make a public statement about the election. "Soon I shall find occasion to say why I still remain reformer and not politician," he wrote to Sam May, "and still trust the old antislavery policy that it's always safe to do right—deeply regretting that some of you cannot any longer dare to stand on the old platform." [16] Neither May nor the other abolitionists backing Garrison could understand Wendell, an advisor to Fremont, when he accused them of being politicians. The most charitable interpretation they could put on Phillips' activity was that his long service as a reformer had blinded him to political realities and duped him into supporting a third party, which courted disaster by threatening to split the antislavery vote. Phillips had a great record as a reformer, but, as May told him, "no man is infallible, no man always right; as it is certainly possible you *may* be wrong, I am convinced that *your* turn to be wrong has come now." [17] Having immunized himself long before to criticism of all kinds, Wendell was not dissuaded by blunt words from friends. He continued to berate the *Standard* ("I consider it a disgrace to the Society and a fraud upon it judged by the last six months")[18] and to talk as if only he and the people standing with him had a right to be called abolitionists in 1864.

On October 20, Phillips gave his first speech in about

four months. As everyone expected, it was an indictment of Lincoln's administration. The President's great fault, according to Phillips, lay in his vacillating course toward slavery, carried on in defiance of the Northern will. Examined in retrospect, the speech appears to have been a very uneven performance. Phillips was at his most persuasive when he contrasted the vast powers which the government had assumed in, for example, suspending habeas corpus, with its faltering action on behalf of the Negro. He was much less persuasive when he tried to show that Lincoln had been lagging behind public opinion. "The North chose war instead of submission as the means to save the Union in 1861 because she perceived that war would practically destroy slavery," Phillips asserted. "But for this motive I do not believe the North would have ever accepted the Southern challenge. All our history shows this. Every man familiar with 1861 one inch below the surface has facts to prove it heaped up and running over." This was not only bad history, as anyone who had lived through the early years of the war knew; it was also a direct contradiction of what Phillips had been saying earlier. Time and again in 1861 and 1862 he had insisted that Lincoln would perform whatever the people told him to do. When Garrison challenged him on the inconsistency, Phillips shrugged it off impatiently. "Can I not grow wiser?" he asked. Another time he said he had simply been more charitable in 1862 than he was willing to be in 1864 and that, in any event, it was better to be right than foolishly consistent. He was convinced that his present evaluation of Lincoln was the correct one.

There had been a time when Garrison proudly printed almost every word that Phillips uttered in public. Wendell's speech on October 20 was one of the last to appear in the *Liberator*. Garrison said he would publish it despite a "great pressure for lack of space." The alleged lack of space did not prevent the editor from condemning the speech as "not only exceedingly ill-timed but severely unjust." [19]

After the election Phillips hoped that the abolitionists would close ranks, but it was too late for that. Although they had proved remarkably tough over the years in the way they had taken criticism from outsiders, the reformers turned out to be surprisingly thin-skinned when they were criticized by each other. Two months after the election, the usually sweet-tempered Samuel May referred to Phillips and his supporters as "seceders" from the antislavery organization, who, having done all they could "to *divide* the *only* antislavery political party of the North," now condemned Garrison and company as "apostates." May said Phillips and Garrison were "alienated" from each other but not yet estranged, though it might well come to that.[20]

It was not so much the heritage of bitterness left over from the presidential campaign that held the two reformers apart; it was the fact that they continued to disagree on what the hour demanded of the abolitionist. The man who had changed the most, certainly, was Garrison. Like a prophet in sight of the Promised Land, he was losing his zeal for righteous wrath and denunciation. He found himself, he said, less inclined to make speeches against slavery, "inasmuch as the people have pronounced slavery accursed, and demand its extirpation." No longer willing to strike out violently wherever he saw the taint of sin, he now wanted to judge public men as fairly as possible, not to endorse anything they did but to recognize the accomplishments amidst the difficulties. He was largely satisfied with Lincoln's approach to reconstruction. He had no substantial fault to find in Louisiana, for example, where Nathaniel Banks was administering a plan of reconstruction according to which Negroes were treated as apprentices to freedom, no longer slaves but unable to vote or bargain for the terms of their labor. With the problem of Negro suffrage Garrison was not much concerned. The right to vote, he said, was "a conventional right of society" and not to be confounded with the natural right of a man to his liberty. When Frederick Douglass called emancipation without the ballot a "mockery," Garrison rebuked him for his "extravagance" and pointed out that Negroes were denied the vote not only in the seceded South but in many of the loyal states also.[21]

Perhaps, as Abby Kelly suggested, Garrison was simply growing old and losing the taste for battle. What we know of Garrison's personal life, that he was not the sour, furious man the columns in the *Liberator* suggested but a man of sweet and genial disposition, makes it plausible that he was happy to retire from the field and surrender his role as excoriator of the national sin, a role which he had assumed only out of duty in the first place. There is another part to the story of his transformation, however, one which can be appreciated only if we understand how essentially different Garrison and Phillips were in personality and motivation. What they had in common was a highly developed moral sense, a fierce hatred of slavery and the compulsion to pursue the course of duty that their consciences discovered. The fact that they conceived of their duty toward slavery in the same way is what held them together for so long. In many respects, however, it was much easier for Phillips to give himself up to a career in reform than it was for Garrison. He did not, for example, have to worry about earning a living, a source of constant anxiety to his friend. Even more significant is the fact that Phillips never had to "make good." His friends talked a lot about Wendell's sacrifice in breaking his Beacon Street ties to go over to the abolitionists. What they (and most of his biographers) failed to understand was that Phillips never really cut away from the aristocracy. Although he scorned Boston society and alienated relatives and family friends, nothing Phillips did could alter his having been born a gentleman. Garrison, on the other hand, came from an impoverished and obscure family, and there is reason to believe that his boyhood experience continued to rankle him as a man. The boy who had waited at the back doors of plush mansions to collect leftovers for his mother's table emerged as a proud, ambitious man, determined to succeed in the

world. When he came to Boston as a young printer in
1827, he made a political speech in behalf of Harrison Gray
Otis and was ridiculed in one of the local papers as a
presumptuous, unknown young man. Garrison wrote to
the paper saying, "If my life be spared, my name shall one
day be known to the world, at least to such an extent that
common inquiry shall be unnecessary. This, I know, will
be deemed excessive vanity—but time shall prove it prophetic." [22] This was before he enrolled himself in the
crusade against slavery. When that time came, however,
and he issued the famous manifesto "I am in earnest—
I will not equivocate—I will not excuse—I will not retreat
a single inch—AND I WILL BE HEARD," the echo of his early
prophecy could be heard clearly.

   This is not to say that Garrison was a charlatan who
simply fastened upon abolitionism as the way to get ahead
in life; it is to say that he wanted to free the slaves and
make a name for himself at the same time. With Garrison
it was Ben Franklin all over again, except that Garrison
was more interested in fame than fortune. He pursued
his calling diligently; he sacrificed himself, and by 1865 he
felt that he had succeeded. Garrison practically admitted
as much when he addressed a meeting in Faneuil Hall
called to celebrate the Thirteenth Amendment, then being
ratified. People who once sneered at him were stopping
him on the street and congratulating him, as if the amendment were a personal accomplishment. Disclaiming any
motive of personal pride, he said he was glad to see that
people had finally come to recognize him as "a true friend
of liberty and humanity, animated by the highest patriotism, and devoted to the welfare, peace, unity and ever-
increasing prosperity and glory of my native land." [23] The
prophecy of 1827 had come true; Garrison was known and
respected. He had achieved his reputation the hard way,
by almost forty years of vociferous dissent; is it any wonder
that he chose not to jeopardize it?

   While Phillips was bludgeoning the public and its
leaders as recklessly in 1865 as he had in 1845, Garrison

enjoyed the benefits to be gained by swimming with the current. One of these came in April, when Secretary of War Stanton invited Garrison to be a guest of honor at the flag-raising service at Fort Sumter. Samuel May took over the editorial duties of the *Liberator* in his friend's absence and pointed up the obvious moral of the occasion. Recalling Garrison's humble beginnings and the long years of his persecution, May wrote "Mr. Garrison is no longer a proscribed, but an honored man—in the land of his birth. . . . He bears a name and has acquired a reputation,—to be enjoyed while yet he lives—which the most greedy of fame might covet." [24]

According to May, Garrison was the prophet who was finally being honored in his own country. According to Stephen Foster, he was a crusader in tarnished armor, willing to come to terms with the devil. Foster, who was never known to make an understatement about anything, was so upset with the *Liberator* by this time that he not only refused to give money to support it but feared that he was committing a deadly sin by paying postage on it when it was sent to him free.[25] With people like this backing Phillips, meetings of the antislavery society became increasingly acrimonious. The argument which triggered the final split was brought about when Garrison and his friends took the position that the American Anti-Slavery Society should be dissolved.

Early rumblings about dissolution had been heard as far back as 1863 from a few abolitionists who felt that their work had about come to an end when the Emancipation Proclamation was announced. In the beginning this group was small, numbering Maria Chapman and her sisters among its most conspicuous members. By 1865, when the passage of an amendment to abolish slavery was clearly imminent, Garrison also was ready to close up shop. In January he proposed to the delegates of the Massachusetts Anti-Slavery Society that, in case the Thirteenth Amendment was passed any time during the year, the board call a special meeting to terminate the society. This touched off a rancorous debate, in the course of which Bronson Alcott, in his most Delphic manner, advised the delegates that if Garrison no longer wanted to lead them they should find another leader. Garrison objected to the distinction being made "between Mr. Phillips and myself, as though I had fallen into the rear, and he was now the 'leader' of the cause." Asserting that he did not "think it any evidence of superior fidelity to the anti-slavery cause to deal in sweeping accusations against President Lincoln" or any other public man, Garrison argued that after the Thirteenth Amendment there would be no antislavery work as such, and the reformers should then "mingle with the great mass of the people, who have accepted abolition, and unite with them in carrying forward the struggle for equal political privileges."

After these remarks, George Downing, a prominent Negro leader from Rhode Island, stood up and pointedly read from the Declaration of Sentiments of the American Anti-Slavery Society three clauses relating to the improvement of the free Negroes. Neither Downing nor other Negroes among the abolitionists felt that the time had come to relax their efforts. This was Phillips' position also, and he sought in vain for a way of expressing it without appearing to be competing with Garrison for leadership of the organization. Garrison had left the hall before Phillips spoke, and Wendell prefaced his address with laudatory remarks about his leadership. "There is nothing more unpleasant to me than any allusion to him and myself as antagonists," said Phillips. "I have never uttered an antislavery word which I did not owe to his inspiration." Nevertheless, he could not go along with his old friend in giving the reins of antislavery reform over to the Republicans. The nation still needed "the constant, incessant, discriminating criticism of the abolitionists as much as ever," if the Negro were ever to receive the justice he deserved. Garrison's mistake lay in equating the Thirteenth Amendment, which would abolish slavery and leave the whole

area of political and social rights untouched, with *"justice
—absolute, immediate, unmixed justice to the negro."* [26]

The rupture came at the annual meeting of the American Anti-Slavery Society in New York on May 9, 1865. Two days earlier, Wendell had delivered a short address before Theodore Parker's old society in Boston. The occasion was ostensibly for the purpose of welcoming the new minister, David Wasson, but Phillips was really preaching to the abolitionists. He found his text in the farewell address which John Robinson had made to the departing Pilgrims at Leyden. "I charge you, follow me no further than you see me follow Christ. God hath yet much truth to break forth from his holy Word. I bewail much the condition of the churches which have made a period in their religion, and will not go beyond the instrument by which they were reformed. Luther and Calvin were shining lights in their day, but they did not exhaust the whole counsel of God. I charge you, it is your church covenant, that you keep your minds open to whatever shall be made known to you from the written word of God." [27]

In the spirit of John Robinson's remarks, "with face set forward and not backward," Phillips went to New York determined to keep the American Anti-Slavery Society alive. Garrison, May, Quincy and Oliver Johnson, the shining lights of yesterday, were determined to retire, and they asked the abolitionists to vote the society out of existence whenever the Thirteenth Amendment became law. Garrison had the executive committee on his side, but the rank and file were with Phillips, and Garrison's resolution lost by a large margin. The nominating committee then brought in its slate of officers and again offered Garrison the presidency. He refused, finding it impossible to accept the nominal direction of an organization which had spurned his leadership. Phillips was elected in his place.

When Garrison announced that he was retiring from the society, Phillips moved a resolution expressing grati-

tude for his services. It was passed by acclamation. It was
not, however, a sweet farewell for Garrison. Having organized the American Anti-Slavery Society in the beginning
and having led it through the vicissitudes of thirty years,
he now found his prestige higher among the public he had
abused than among his old associates. He tried to leave
gracefully, but he felt humiliated, and, when reminded
that Foster and Pillsbury still looked on him as a friend,
he recalled the old maxim, "Save me from my friends, and
I will take care of my enemies." His references to Phillips
were almost as blunt, and he accused him of playing with
the truth in an attempt to paint the government as black as
possible—a bayoneter of presidents masquerading as a
"lifter" of public opinion.[28]

It was, Phillips must have realized, a mixed victory.
The American Anti-Slavery Society would continue to
have an official existence, but it must get along without
most of the old leaders. Estranged from the man who had
made him a reformer in the first place, Wendell found himself accused of having led an anti-Garrison clique into
power. He had begun the fall from grace, Oliver Johnson
wrote in the *Standard*, when he let himself become a political tool for Fremont; now he was the tool of cranks like
Foster and Pillsbury.[29]

Not even the personal friendship of Phillips and Garrison was comprehensive enough to absorb these blows
without injury. Sensing that their old intimacy was gone,
Wendell no longer felt welcome at Garrison's house, and
when Wendell Phillips Garrison was married in November 1865 he sent the bridegroom a note of congratulations
and a check but stayed away from the wedding.[30] Garrison was apparently hurt by this, and when his daughter
Fanny was about to be married he sent Phillips a long,
affectionate letter of invitation. Professing gratitude for all
of his friend's "generous acts of kindness" and pecuniary
aid in the past, Garrison refused to admit that there was
a breach between them. "Though my dear P., you and I
have differed somewhat in our judgment of the bearing of

events and the action of public men," he wrote, "yet it is my comfort and solace to know that in our principles, our desires, and our claims for equal and exact justice to the colored race, as to the white, we blend together as fully as ever. May our friendship be as perpetual as sun, moon and stars, but without the occasional obscuration!" [31]

When he went to the Garrisons' house to attend Fanny's wedding, Wendell noticed that his old comrade seemed more fulfilled than ever before. "It was very pleasant," he remarked rather wistfully to a friend. "I saw Garrison in the hall as I went in. I am very glad his life is ending so happily and so full of honor. He seems wholly at rest. I am very much impressed by his serenity every time I see him. It is as if he were living in an atmosphere of peacefulness." [32]

However pleasant he may have found it to contemplate, Phillips did what he could to shatter Garrison's serenity. A few weeks after Fanny's wedding, Garrison tried to get the Massachusetts Anti-Slavery Society to disband, and Phillips defeated him again, this time even more decisively than in New York. In the course of the debate, Wendell contended that the retired abolitionists were not lifting a finger to help the Negro. Although the times called for unceasing radical agitation, Garrison and his friends were wasting their efforts on philanthropic organizations like the Freedman's Union, concerned with nothing more than "cheap soup and primers." Phillips even implied that his old colleague was being used as a front for churchmen and politicians who had always hated the abolitionists. "All these associations would welcome you to their ranks," he said, "if you would forget certain ugly principles identified with this society." [33]

The accumulating tensions between the two were made even greater by a prolonged controversy over the administration of a bequest left by Francis Jackson. Both Garrison and Phillips sat on the board of trustees, and the former wanted the money for the Freedmen's Union, while Phillips sought it for the *Anti-Slavery Standard* which now was exclusively under the latter's own influence. Phillips said he would rather use the money to attend the theatre than give it to the Freedmen, and Garrison contended that it would be an utter loss to waste it on the "debris" of the antislavery society. The controversy finally went to the courts, and in August 1867, the money was awarded as Garrison wanted. Phillips immediately wrote an article for the *Standard* implying that Garrison had gone back on his word. Garrison took this as a sign that their friendship was finally broken. For several years thereafter, the two were to see very little of each other.[34]

It is always a melancholy prospect to see men of good will, who have long toiled together in pursuit of the same ideal, fall out among themselves. Yet in this case it is easy to understand how it happened. Not only Phillips and Garrison, but all of the abolitionists, had invested too much of themselves in their work to be moderate now; they could not look on the split as a mere difference of opinion any more than they had been able to look on pro-slavery argument as a difference of opinion. It was a moral issue; their integrity was at stake, and thirty years of reform agitation had taught them that there was but one side to every moral question. It is no wonder, then, that old comrades began to treat each other like enemies, no wonder that when Phillips approached Edmund Quincy on the State House steps Quincy turned his back rather than acknowledge the greeting. Once they had "mingled together like kindred drops into one." Now half the men whom Phillips had worked with for thirty years passed him on the street without speaking.[35]

17

Phillips and the Radicals
1865–1870

Like other famous men, Phillips was constantly be-
sieged by autograph hunters. It was typical of him not to
content himself with a simple autograph; he had to accom-
pany it with a moral aphorism. In November 1865, he was
writing "Peace if possible. Justice at any rate." [1] He knew
that his continued militancy would lose him friends and
make him look more like a crank than ever, but he knew
also that any other course was impossible for him. He had
burned his bridges behind him long ago, and he was satisfied with the results. "I do not look back with any regret
on the path—which events rather than my own will selected for me" he wrote in a letter. "If I have not done
all that elsewhere perhaps I might, I have, at least, done
with some degree of efficiency work that few others were
willing to undertake & work indispensably necessary to be
done by somebody." The work was not yet finished, and
he would stick at it until someone younger or stronger
came along to take his place.[2]

"*No Reconstruction without Negro Suffrage.*" This
headline, which appeared in the *Anti-Slavery Standard*
shortly after Phillips became president of the American
Anti-Slavery Society, proclaimed the idea to which
Wendell would commit himself for the next five years.
By restating the old motto "No union with slaveholders,"
Phillips sought to point the direction for a morally justifiable reconstruction program and at the same time to un-
furl a banner to rally faltering abolitionists.[3]

As the end of the war approached, Phillips was as much afraid of Northern complacency as anything else. He found Garrison's view that the nation now subscribed to abolitionist principles both morally pretentious and naive. The North may have won a military victory, but she had fought for selfish reasons, had been pushed into abolishing slavery and would have to be pushed again if the Negro was to get his due rights. While others talked about the wonderful regeneration of Northern opinion,[4] Phillips saw to it that the *Standard* emphasized the existence of anti-Negro feeling in the North. As long as the Democrats in Connecticut, for example, could gain an important political victory by exploiting public opposition to Negro suffrage, and influential papers like the Chicago *Times* were damning the "nigger on the brain" radicals for wanting to enfranchise "an inferior animal," it was absurd, Phillips thought, to interpret victory in moral terms.[5]

Unlike his knowledge of the North, which came from firsthand experience, Phillips had to rely on others for his information about the South. As the nation's leading non-political radical, he received many letters from the South. Some of his correspondents remained anonymous, but they all purported to give him a firsthand account of conditions in the South, and almost all of them told him exactly what he wanted to hear. Phillips had neither the time nor the patience to sift the evidence, and he sent the letters along to Parker Pillsbury, who printed them in the *Standard*. One writer said he had traveled all over South Carolina and met only two loyal whites. "They are *subdued*," he wrote, "not convinced or converted. The only genuine friends of the United States are the blacks, with a *very* few exceptions." [6] Most of the men who wrote these letters were Northerners traveling in the South, and their warning was always the same: Beware the admission of unreconstructed rebels back into the Union! The devil was still alive, licking his wounds and plotting for ultimate victory. This was the impression Phillips wanted to convey in the *Standard,* and its readers, brought up on thirty years of horror tales about the barbarism of slavery, must have responded with a familiar thrill when they read about the cardboard box that was said to have been left outside Charles Sumner's home in Washington. Accompanying the box was a note. "You old son of a bitch, I send you a piece of your friends, and if that bill of yours passes, I will have a piece of you." Inside the box was a freshly cut black finger.[7]

Convinced that the North was still demoralized by race prejudice, and the South "subdued but not converted," Phillips took to the lecture platform to persuade the people that the Thirteenth Amendment would not come close to solving the Negro problem. Although the Constitution now prohibited slavery, the very nature of our federal system of government meant that the freedmen were left to the mercy of the individual states for the protection of most of their rights. Phillips asked his audiences to think about the plight of the Negroes living in the heart of the plantation country. "Can they own land? Can they testify in a court of justice? If a man enters their house and wrongs property and daughters, can they go before tribunals and claim justice with free lips? Can they vote . . . are they citizens? That is for white men at the capitol of the state to say." [8]

Indeed, the white men at the state capitols were already beginning to say what the Negro's rights would be. Governor Humphreys of Mississippi, for example, stated in a message to his legislature that emancipation did not make the Negro a citizen "or entitle him to social or political equality with the white man." As a freedman, Humphreys advised, the Negro would have to be protected in certain civil rights and given equal access to the courts, but as the main source of Mississippi labor he could be controlled by the state and kept in the fields. Most of the famous "Black Laws" drawn up by the Southern states in 1865 and 1866 followed this pattern. They endeavored to protect some of the Negro's rights as a freedman and at the same time secure his subordinancy in the social order. On

the one hand, the Negro was kept strictly apart by pro-
visions against intermarriage and social intermingling;
on the other he was bound closely to his white employers
by laws regulating his labor. In South Carolina the law
stipulated that Negro farm laborers (officially designated as
"servants") be required to labor six days a week from sunrise to sunset, and in other areas in the South the Negro
was not allowed to go out at night without a written permit
from his employer.[9]

The historian, looking back with the perspective of
nearly a century, can see that these laws, not as "black"
as they once seemed, were written by men seeking to define
in legal terms the status of a slave population suddenly
set free. Phillips saw them simply as part of a great Southern conspiracy to acquiesce to the letter of the law without
surrendering the spirit of slavery. Men nurtured in the
traditions of a slave society were reducing the Negro to
serfdom because the Federal government refused to protect
him, and the people of the North refused to give him a constitutional amendment to guarantee his civil rights.

For a few weeks following Lincoln's death, Phillips
nursed the hope that Andrew Johnson might be the man
who would lead the nation to protect and rehabilitate the
Negro. His confidence in Johnson was stimulated in part
by the President's ardent speeches promising punishment
to "traitors" and in part by word he received from Sumner
that Johnson and he agreed completely on Negro suffrage.
"It is a great relief to be so assured in regard to our President," Phillips wrote to Sumner on May 5.[10] A week later
he was on the lecture platform praising the President.
"One of the ablest men born south of Mason and Dixon's
line, there was ground into him early, in the providence of
God, a supreme conviction of the danger of State rights and
caste to this American Union, and he is today naturally
the leader, and perhaps the ablest champion on that question." [11]

The honeymoon between Phillips and Johnson was
over almost as soon as it began. When the President's

plan for the reconstruction of North Carolina was revealed at the end of May, it became clear that, however radical Johnson had sounded at the outset, he was really bent on carrying out the same moderate approach to reconstruction that Lincoln had favored. Lincoln, who believed that restoration was primarily an executive responsibility and that the rebellious states had never been out of the Union, had been anxious to see the Union restored as painlessly as possible with the help of a minority of loyal whites in each state. In pursuing this policy, Johnson recognized the loyal governments which Lincoln had set up in four of the Southern states, and he established provisional governments for the seven remaining states. By December 1865, every Confederate state except Texas had fulfilled the modest requirements which Johnson exacted, and the President felt able to inform Congress that the Union was restored.

Long before he got to this point, Johnson turned up as a villain in the columns of the *Standard*. The Republican party, declared the *Standard,* was being "Tylerized" and was letting a man without "loyalty to Northern ideas" haul it around by the nose.[12] By the end of the summer Phillips was back in the lecture circuit with a speech entitled "The South Victorious." The South, he said, built on the three ideas of slavery, states rights and racial inequality, was supposed to have lost the war, but she was still fastened to the last two ideas as firmly as ever. Johnson, of course, was responsible. Bred in Tennessee, he did not believe in the Negro; "he hates chains and hates black men, equally Yankees, and it cannot but crop out." [13]

Phillips did not restrict his fire to Johnson but blasted away also at the Republicans in Congress who were not yet critical enough of the President. Everywhere he looked, Phillips saw complacency and soft-mindedness. He wrote to Ben Butler that the administration was "sending us over, bound hand and foot, into the power of the rebels" and needed to be "defied and overawed by such an exhibition" as men like Butler and Sumner could provide. Butler was about to be mustered out of the army and return to Congress, and Phillips urged him to begin agitating the issue of reconstruction before Congress met.[14]

When the Congress did meet in December 1865, Phillips was gratified to see the radicals, under Sumner in the Senate and Stevens in the House, frustrate the President's plan by refusing to seat the delegations from the Southern states. A joint committee of fifteen was set up to report to Congress on the matter of reconstruction, and the long, bitter battle between the President and Congress was under way. According to the radical view of reconstruction, the Southern states were "conquered provinces" and must submit to drastic conditions before being allowed back into the Union. Phillips cared nothing for the subtleties in constitutional theory which distinguished the congressional from the presidential interpretation of reconstruction. It was enough for him that Congress was against Johnson and anxious to impose terms on the South. When Sumner turned on the President in December, Phillips congratulated him on having taken the only honorable course. "*All* whose *judgment* you value agree," Wendell assured his friend; the rest were "hypocrites and dupes." [15]

Although they never entered into any formal agreement, Thaddeus Stevens, Charles Sumner and Wendell Phillips were teamed up against the President. "Old Thad" was the most strategically located. As chairman of the Committee of Fifteen, he was the most powerful man in Congress and could practically dictate policy. Clomping through the halls of Congress on his clubfoot or slouched in his seat glowering under a cockeyed wig, Stevens was a man to beware. Without a sentimental bone in his body, Stevens hated slavery and the Democratic Party with equal intensity and was determined to see the Union restored on terms that would not threaten Republican control of the nation. Charles Sumner, Stevens' counterpart in the Senate, was still a dominating figure in Washington. Pompous and doctrinaire, he seemed always to pretend that he stood above the storm and stress of politics. A lot of people couldn't stand Sumner, but to Phillips he was a living relic of the "barbarism of slavery," a man who bore his scars eloquently, the most fervent abolitionist in the Senate and the ablest exponent of Negro suffrage. With Stevens and Sumner holding the reins, Congress was in good hands, but Phillips had lived too long to expect a moral revolution in Washington. The politicians would draw up a program only as radical as they thought the people would support. The task for abolitionists, therefore, was to stimulate a public sentiment which would sustain radical legislation. To this end Phillips took his "The South Victorious" speech wherever he could find an audience. The words differed from night to night, but the theme was always the same. The administration was throwing away the fruits of victory. Andrew Johnson was determined to take the rebel chestnuts out of the fire. The President was flirting with treason. Let him go unchecked and the men who fell at Gettysburg and Antietam and Chancellorsville would have died in vain.

Back in Washington, Gideon Welles, the President's patriarchal Secretary of the Navy, snorted in his beard every time he read a report of Phillips' speeches. A man of "extraordinary gifts," thought Welles, but, thank God, "a useless member of society and deservedly without influence." [16] Andrew Johnson, however, had a different opinion. For months he had endured Phillips' epithets, seen them publicized in papers all over the country and imitated by the members of his own party in Congress. On February 17, 1866, the *Standard* printed an editorial entitled "OUR POOR WHITE PRESIDENT." Johnson, a man who had had to fight for everything in his life, had taken all he could stand. Five days later, on Washington's Birthday, he addressed a group of admirers outside the Capitol. He said the men who were trying to block the restoration of the Union were "as much opposed to the fundamental principles of this Government; and . . . as much laboring to prevent or destroy them as were the men who fought against us." When somebody in the crowd called on him to name names, the President bellowed "I say Thaddeus Stevens of Pennsylvania. I say Charles Sumner. I say Wendell Phillips and others of the same stripe are among them." [17]

Phillips apparently left no record of how he felt at being singled out by the President as a conspirator, but he must have been pleased. Johnson, at least, was being drawn into open warfare, and this was more than the radicals had ever been able to accomplish with Lincoln. While more temperate observers quailed at the prospect of a government paralyzed by the conflict between executive and legislature, Phillips' only fear was that the struggle might be too hastily resolved in the interest of party solidarity. "Now this is no time to consult *harmony*," he wrote Sumner. "Let confusion endure—the nation was never so wise as today and never growing wise at such a rapid rate. We shall have everything only by being in no haste to settle anything." [18] The nation, Phillips thought, would stand behind the radicals. Veterans who remembered the horrors of war, capitalists who wanted assurance that their investment would be secure, loyal men in the South who wanted protection, the masses in the North who wanted to be sure there would never be another civil war—all of these groups would accept radical action in the South, if only Congress would lead them.

Phillips' ideas, however, were ahead of those of most of the radicals in Congress. While the latter were concerned to a great extent with formulating a policy which would cripple the Democratic party and thus secure the indefinite ascendancy of the Republicans, Phillips' goal was suffrage for the freedman. When the joint committee brought a proposed constitutional amendment before Congress at the end of April, he was disgusted because the proposal, intended to prevent any state from discriminating against Negroes in the matter of civil rights, made no specific guarantee of suffrage. Thaddeus Stevens, whose home state of Pennsylvania denied the vote to Negroes, had reported the bill on April 30, and Phillips scratched off a hasty note to him the same day. "I see the report of the Reconstruction Committee. It is a fatal and total surrender. The South carries off enough of the victory to enable her to control the nation, mold its policy and shape its legislation for a dozen years to come. Twenty years of admiring trust in your anti-slavery devotion must be my apology for urging you to protest against this suicidal step. It is not necessary. The country is ready for its duty. It only needs leaders. Do not let the Republican party desert its post. Or, if that must be, let the statesmen, the 'practical statesmen' of the nation be true to their duty." [19]

At the annual meeting of the American Anti-Slavery Society eight days later, Phillips pulled out all the stops. Under his direction, the society accepted a resolution declaring that the President had "destroyed the loyal North; is bent on giving it over, bound hand and foot, into the hands of its once conquered foe; that he should long ago have been impeached for gross usurpation in his manifest use of his high powers to aid Rebellion, and for the treasonable purpose of defeating the secure and peaceful settlement of the Nation."

In his principal address, Phillips said the war had brought about a great social revolution in the South and that it was up to Congress to see that the fruits of the revolution should not be lost. "The national sword must never be sheathed," he said. "South Carolina shall never be shut up like China or Japan against civilization. The doctrine of State Rights, which meant a dúngeon for white men to make victims of black men within is exploded forever.— This is the new dispensation. This is the New Testament, 1860 is the blank leaf between the old and the new." The question of the constitutionality of reconstruction irritated Phillips. Congress had a right "under the War Paper," he thought, to destroy the Old South. "We have conquered not the geographical but the ideal South; its thumb screws and slavery, its no-schools, its white men born, booted and spurred, and its black men born saddled and bridled for them to ride, the South which imprisons teachers, which

denies Bibles, which raises up half its population in con-
cubinage and ignorance, which denies the right of marriage
between men and women—that South we have conquered,
and we have a right to trample it under the heels of our
boots. That is the meaning of the war." [20]

As the summer of 1866 came on, Phillips found himself succumbing to a familiar frustration. It was an election year. The politicians, as usual, were not anxious to
hurt anybody's feelings, and the Republicans were anxious
to maintain as much party unity as possible. When Congress finally passed the Fourteenth Amendment in June,
Phillips was not impressed. The proposed amendment did
not specifically guarantee the ballot to Negroes, but did
provide that a state's representation in Congress be reduced
in proportion to the number of adult males that it disquali-
fied from voting. Phillips found this clause cumbersome
and evasive, a compromise similar in spirit to the old three-
fifths compromise by which the slave states had been in-
duced to come into the Union originally.[21]

The closer the elections came, the more shrilly did
Phillips bewail the laggardly course of legislation in Wash-
.ington. Serious race riots in New Orleans at the end of
July added fuel to his anger, and he repeatedly contrasted
the supposed boldness of public opinion with the timidity
of the political leaders. "Bring the masses face to face with
this problem, and they would in sixty days have exterminated every white man in the South before they would have
perilled peace and welcomed dishonor by betraying the
negro." In another editorial in the *Standard*, entitled
"The President's Riot in New Orleans," he wrote "The
whites of the South are our enemies . . . the only true
principle is to reconstruct on such a theory as will keep all
power exclusively in the hands of those who for the last five
years have lived and been ready to die for the Union."
Sniffing a possible revolution in the air, Phillips declared
that the radicals in 1866 stood where the Long Parliament
stood in 1649. "Though the block and axe in front of the
palace" might not be fitting now, he warned, the radicals

would have to find some way to get rid of the "usurping traitor" in the White House.[22]

Phillips stayed in the headlines not only because of his violent attacks on Johnson but also because a rumor began to spread that he would be a candidate for office himself. Radical papers like the *Independent* welcomed the news, while a moderate paper like the *New York Times*, reconciled apparently to having to put up with Phillips' influence in some form, wrote that, if somebody had to play Cromwell and lead the nation to another bloodbath, it might as well be Phillips. He could accomplish his ideal of racial equality, said the *Times*, by uniting the "carnage of the French Revolution" with the "horrors of St. Domingo," thus overwhelming all races in common ruin.[23]

In September a workingmen's convention nominated Phillips for representative of the Third Congressional District. He was grateful for the honor, he said, but declined to run because if elected he would "incur responsibility to a far greater extent than I should gain power." [24] It was a wise decision, not only for the reason that Wendell gave but because there would never have been room in Washington for both him and Thad Stevens.

The emphatic victory which the radicals scored at the polls in November filled Phillips with fresh enthusiasm. The clear verdict of the people, he said, was that the South must be rooted up and made over by the North and the President "deposed." Again it was Cromwell talking, contemptuously shrugging off constitutional restraints and arguing that in an emergency the people had the right to make their own laws and set their own precedents. "I say, therefore, impeach the President; and while he is in trial sequester him. What is the advantage? Then *we* run the machine." [25]

Phillips' speeches at this time exhibit a curious blending of irresponsibility and shrewd criticism. Although his remarks about the President were wildly demagogic, he refused to find anything very worthwhile in the Republi-

can party, or in a "swindling Congress" which was trying
to palm off the Fourteenth Amendment on a gullible people. Moreover, if it showed no great courage to insult
Andrew Johnson in November 1866, Phillips was also willing to jeopardize his influence by attacking an authentic
public hero like General Grant. Phillips believed that
Grant was being groomed for the Presidency, and he was
distinctly unhappy at the prospect. He had admired Grant
as a general but was unimpressed by his course since the
war. For one thing, Grant had made a tour of the South
for Johnson and had written a report which implied that
the Southern people were essentially loyal and ready to
come back into the Union. For another, he was Chief of
Staff and thus partly responsible for the fact that the
Negroes were not getting proper protection in the South.
Grant was probably the most popular man in the North,
but Phillips paid no attention to that, nor to the hisses
that followed when he said that Grant occupied "the most
humiliating position of any man on the continent." He
also spoke bluntly about the general as a potential President. Grant, he predicted, would be "content to be the
unassuming tool of men about him." A do-nothing Chief
of Staff, he would make a do-nothing President, and this
should surprise nobody, because "The routine soldier like
the routine sailor is generally unfit for anything else." [26]
    Despite his training in the law, Phillips had always
been out of patience with legalities, and this prejudice
became even more important after the war. The only law
that really mattered was the Higher Law. The abolitionists
had become used to thinking in terms of the Higher Law
during the fugitive slave crisis, and Phillips carried the
habit over to reconstruction days. When the Supreme
Court declared it unconstitutional for Congress to require
attorneys to take an oath testifying that they had never
borne arms against the United States, he was furious. The
law always seemed to be standing in the way of justice.
The Fugitive Slave Law, the Dred Scott decision, the mass
of legal technicalities which made it so hard to remove the

President—all these obstructions should be swept away. "It will need but little effort," he said after the test oath cases, "to show the people the true course to be taken in this emergency. *The nation must be saved,* no matter what or how venerable the foe whose existence goes down before that necessity. . . . The instincts of the masses, the consensus of just men, the spirit of the age, and God's law, all demand that the inspiration and corner-stone of this government shall be justice—the wind of the blow that demolished slavery were enough to scatter this obstacle from our party." [27]

What Phillips wanted was something like Rousseau's General Will. He wanted the government to do what the nation would demand if it were in a state of virtue. He and the little band of abolitionists he represented, like Robespierre and the Jacobins, believed that their will was the General Will. When Congress began to dream up a plan for reconstruction which would divide the South into military districts and place it under close federal supervision, Phillips thought that the public virtue was beginning to assert itself. He had gone beyond the point of looking to Negro suffrage as a panacea for the Southern problem, and he now believed that the Negro would have to be protected and rehabilitated under the strong arm of federal authority.

Wendell Phillips had become a national institution by 1867. Whenever he brought a new address to the platform, it was recorded stenographically and reprinted so widely that the citizens of Manhattan, Kansas, as well at those in Boston and New York, were able to read it in their local paper. His trip through the Western states in 1867, the first he had taken since the end of the war, was also one of his most successful. As usual, the people who had never seen Phillips before and expected to find a fierce, fire-breathing fanatic were surprised at his genteel appearance. "Gray-haired, benignant-featured, mild" was the way a correspondent in Keokuk described Phillips. "This placid countenance, benevolent, quietly-speaking old gentleman,

who has a cordial shake of the hand and a hearty greeting
for even the youngest boys—this can scarcely be the terrible
Abolitionist and fierce Radical who has been the best-
abused and most all-abused man in the country." [28]

Everywhere he went, Phillips' name and his oratorical
prowess worked their magic and lyceum treasuries grew fat.
The gospel he preached was the same radical gospel he had
been preaching in the East, adjusted from time to time to
keep pace with events in Washington. His audiences were
sympathetic, and the Chicago *Tribune* reported that his
speech was the best political address Chicago had heard
since the war. Not even his digs at Grant or his fierce
attack against anti-Negro laws in Ohio and Michigan
aroused the kind of heated reaction he had experienced
in the past. It was a personal triumph, but it was also a
triumph for abolitionists generally, and, whenever they
could, the old crusaders rallied around Phillips. In one
town in Illinois, Wendell was deeply touched when a
seventy-three-year-old man who had labored with Theodore Weld at Lane Seminary came up to the platform and
kissed him on the cheek, a form of greeting which the
earliest recruits to the cause had borrowed from the early
Christians. Another veteran abolitionist traveled fifty
miles on horseback through Indiana mud to hear Phillips
in Fort Wayne and talk over old times.[29]

On April 14, Wendell made a pilgrimage to Alton,
Illinois. He walked past the plain stone store which Lovejoy had occupied when his first press had been taken away
and thrown into a creek. He went up to the hill over-
looking the river, and there in the city cemetery found a
simple, oblong stone with the inscription, "Here lies Lovejoy, spare him, now, in his grave." The testimonial had
been made brief and mild deliberately in order to keep the
people of Alton from destroying it. Someday, Phillips
predicted, a monument would be built on the spot over-
looking the Mississippi River, so that all who saw it would
be reminded of Elijah Lovejoy, the man "who consecrated
this grand valley to liberty."

From Alton, Phillips went on to St. Louis where the

cream of society turned out, along with one of the largest audiences in the city's history, to welcome him. It would have done Lovejoy's heart good to see the man whose anti-slavery career he had launched received so warmly in Missouri. The hostile St. Louis *Dispatch* described Phillips as "the man who as a private citizen, has exercised a greater influence upon the destinies of this country than any public man or men of his age." Perhaps Lovejoy would have considered this the only monument he needed.[30]

On returning to Boston in May, Phillips fell into a furious controversy with Horace Greeley over the release of Jefferson Davis. The former president of the Con-federacy, held in military custody for the last two years, had been released in bail pending his trial in federal court. Greeley had been among those helping to raise the money for bail. While the war was still in progress, Phillips had repeatedly gone on record as opposing blood vengeance against the Confederate leaders. "I want no gallows," he said; "I want no punishments; not one jot or tittle of it. The nation is strong enough to crush her rebels and not punish them." [31] Now he responded to the news of Davis' release with an editorial in the *Standard* entitled "TREASON MADE EASY AND RESPECTABLE." Davis, he wrote, was the "wretch" who had tried to crush the government and pre-serve slavery, "The man who turned a happy land into a field of blood, and made the name of America hideous with the murders of Andersonville." What decent man, Phillips asked, dared to stand up and clasp hands "with the bloodiest, most heartless and selfish villain of the century?" The answer was that Greeley did, and this proved that the famous editor was "generally obtuse in his moral sense." [32]

The roots of the long, tiresome debate that followed went much deeper than the Jefferson Davis case. Phillips and Greeley had been sniping at each other for years. To the extent that Greeley was a reformer and a courageous journalist, Phillips respected him; to the extent that he was a leading Republican, Phillips suspected him, and to the extent that he wielded great influence as a moulder of public opinion, Phillips distrusted him. Greeley, on the other hand, looked on Phillips as a silver-tongued fanatic who might occasionally make telling points against the enemy but who could almost always be counted on to embarrass the efforts of men trying to work for constructive ends in practical affairs. Greeley respected Phillips' influence and knew that the full reports which the *Tribune* carried of his speeches helped to sell papers, but he felt that Wendell, who, he said, had "winning ways to make people hate him," pandered too often to the passions of the mob.[33]

Greeley, of course, had no difficulty in showing that Phillips' present position on the punishment of Davis was wildly inconsistent with his earlier speeches. Wendell replied by saying he had not pushed for Davis' punishment in 1865 and 1866 because he had known it could not be accomplished with Johnson in the White House and Greeley at the helm of the *Tribune*. His position, therefore, was "submission to the inevitable," while Greeley's was "fellowship with the disgraceful."[34] A more plausible explanation is that as the war ended Phillips was simply more concerned in agitating for Negro suffrage than in worrying about how the Confederate leaders would be punished. Later, when Davis' release became a matter of broad public concern and Phillips feared that a soft attitude toward Davis might influence the people's willingness to sustain stern reconstruction policies, he lashed out against it. His shift on the Davis matter is another in a growing list of examples showing that Phillips could put expediency above consistency whenever the occasion demanded it.

By the summer of 1867 it had become clear that the radicals were in the saddle in Washington. Overriding Johnson's veto, Congress had passed a Reconstruction Act that divided the South into five military districts, sent 20,000 Federal troops back into the Southern states and required the states to ratify the Fourteenth Amendment and provide for Negro suffrage before they could be admitted to the Union. In addition, the Congress, which had earlier curbed the President's power over Supreme Court appointments, now shackled him even further by weaken-

ing his control over the army with the Command of the
Army Act and by passing the Tenure of Office Act, which
made it illegal for him to remove certain of his own appointments in the Executive Department without Senate
approval. Radical legislation like this was exactly what
Phillips had been hoping for, and his only quarrel with
the Congress now was that it chose to adjourn instead of
staying on the job and pulling the noose even tighter
around Johnson's neck.

In August the President suspended his Secretary of
War, Edwin M. Stanton, in defiance of the Tenure of
Office Act. Phillips was vacationing at the time, but he
immediately wrote an editorial for the *Standard* urging
impeachment. When Grant was appointed to Stanton's
post, Phillips described him as "the staff which holds up
the traitor President." If Congress refused to impeach, it
would be only because they were more interested in Presi-
dent-making than in justice and feared that impeachment
might hurt Grant.[35] Because everything that Phillips said
was newsworthy, the New York *Herald* sent a man up to
the little village of Sterling, Massachusetts, where Wendell
and Ann were summering, to get an interview on the national situation as Phillips saw it in September, 1867. The
Herald printed the full interview under the headline "MR.
PHILLIPS DOES NOT DESPOND." It must have been a rare
experience for Wendell to see the paper which before the
war had tried to incite riots against him now going out of
its way to get a report of his opinion for *Herald* readers.
The opinions themselves were as extreme as ever, and the
reason why Mr. Phillips did not despond was that it was
not the people but the politicians who were retarding "the
just growth of revolution." [36]

During the autumn all of Wendell's old suspicions of
the Republican party and the Congress returned. The continued refusal of the Republicans to concern themselves
with Negro rights in the North was one irritation; another
was the failure of Congress to impeach the President. He
began to lecture on "the Dawdling Congress" and the "Surrender of Congress" and to write in the *Standard* about the

"DOUBLE-FACED" Republican party. The Republicans, he said, were more interested in votes than Negro rights and would willingly admit ten Southern states tomorrow if they thought they would vote Republican. At the same time, he continued to snipe away at Ulysses Grant, the Republicans' most valuable political property.[37]

When the House of Representatives finally impeached Johnson on February 24, 1868, Phillips was on tour in the West. He had hoped that the President would be suspended while being tried, but even without this he felt that the people had "at last made their way and carried out their purpose." The stage was set for the dramatization of great principles, and Phillips wanted the indictment drawn up in universal terms as Jefferson had arraigned George III in the Declaration of Independence. Thomas Jeffersons, however, were hard to find in Washington in 1868, and Phillips knew in his heart that the Republicans were out to get rid of Johnson for reasons that had little to do with "absolute justice." Nevertheless, the event alone was enough to make him optimistic. "In such an emergency," he wrote for the *Standard,* "we see our advantage. No matter for the motive; all hail the result." [38] When Johnson was acquitted, Wendell quoted his favorite slogan ("Liberty knows nothing but victories") and expressed the belief that, despite the result, the trial had played an important role in the moral education of the nation. Refusing to believe that anyone could have voted for acquittal out of conscience, he blamed it on the weakness of Chief Justice Chase, who presided, and the political cowardice of some senators who feared the President's patronage power. "Women, whiskey, cowardice, greenbacks, Free Masonry, Negro-hate, offices for one's sixteen Pine-tree cousins, a diseased Chief Justice, spite, dyspepsia and noodleism" had combined to save Johnson's skin.[39]

A few days after Johnson's acquittal, the Republican National Convention met in Chicago and on the first ballot nominated Ulysses S. Grant for the presidency. Phillips followed the campaign with mixed feelings. His unflattering estimate of Grant was well known, and he had admitted

several times that Republicans as a party were much less
interested in the moral rehabilitation of the South than in
a kind of political reconstruction most favorable to themselves. He was aware of the corruption that the reconstruction program stimulated and that an "era of traders and
place-hunters, of blacklegs, charlatans and gulls" had begun. As late as August 15, Phillips was saying that the Republican party had "proved its utter incompetency to
govern." When Thaddeus Stevens died, Phillips felt that
the Republican plight was truly desperate. He had held
no public man except Sumner in such high esteem, and
with Stevens' passing the Republicans lost one of the very
few among them characterized by "utter disinterestedness;
entire loyalty to justice." [40] That Phillips could be so
extravagant in praising Stevens, who had openly avowed
that Republican supremacy was the chief objective of his
reconstruction policies, shows once again that Phillips'
primary concern was with a man's actions, not with his
motives.

Despite his misgivings, Phillips had no alternative but
to endorse the Republicans. He called them "shuffling,
evasive, unprincipled, corrupt, cowardly and mean—mad
for office, cankered with gold, poisoned with spite, cowards
from the first," but could not escape the realization that
victory for them meant "the loyal North in the saddle."
The fact that the Ku Klux Klan had begun to ride in the
South helped to force his hand. The Republicans stood
for the nation and the use of federal power. In 1864 the
hour had demanded a third party; in 1868 it demanded
unity. "We must accept the hour, not force it. *Grant's*
election means progress." [41]

When the results of the election were disclosed in
November, Phillips wrote an editorial for the *Standard*.
"The loyal party has triumphed," he announced. "We
hold this to be reason for deep gratitude." He still professed no great expectations for Grant, but he apparently
hoped that Grant would be restricted to the role of figurehead by a truly radical Congress. "The tendency of all
free states is to depress the Executive and enlarge the

authority of the Legislative element," he wrote in the
Standard. "Progress in that direction seems almost synony-
mous with liberty." [42] Phillips had a way of discovering
fundamental principles of government whenever the occasion demanded. He was apparently oblivious to the difficulties involved in reconciling this assertion that the
legislature should control the executive with his earlier
criticism of Grant as a man who would not be a leader.

During the winter of 1868 and 1869, Phillips continued his agitation for a constitutional amendment which
would guarantee the ballot to the Negro. If anything, his
prestige was higher than it had been two years earlier when
he had begun to cry for Johnson's scalp. It was not that
the nation had fallen in love with the Negro. It was rather
that he himself had become institutionalized, and audiences had come to respect his independence and his complete freedom from political affiliation. Phillips' idealism
would soon sound like a voice from the past, but it had
not yet begun to grate on the ears of those whose memories
of the war were still hot.

When Congress actually began to draw up the kind of
amendment that Phillips wanted, he found himself in the
curious position of urging them to proceed more cau-
tiously. The proposal which passed the House decreed
that no state could deprive any citizen of the vote because
of race. The Senate, largely through Sumner's influence,
attempted to make the amendment more comprehensive by
prohibiting discrimination for nationality, education and
property, as well as for race. When the proposal was returned from the Senate with these additions, the House
refused to confirm it. Phillips looked on unbelievingly.
The Senate was actually asking for more than the public
could bear. Amazed at such a "total forgetfulness of the
commonest political prudence," he wrote an editorial in
the *Standard* (which was regularly sent to every member
of Congress) asking the radicals in the Senate not to
jeopardize the whole amendment by being too radical.
"For the first time in our lives we beseech them to be a
little more *politicians*—and a little less reformers." [43] A

few days later Congress rejected the Senate's additions and passed the amendment in its original form. George S. Boutwell, one of the advocates of the amendment in the House, wrote Phillips that the editorial in the *Standard* had helped to break the impasse. "Its influence was immediate and potential. Men thought that if you, the extremest radical, could accept the House proposition, they might safely do the same." Reflecting on the matter, Boutwell felt that Phillips' voice "saved the Fifteenth Amendment." Wendell welcomed this tribute to his influence without realizing, apparently, how ironic it was that he should have made an immediate and practical impression on Congress in his first attempt as a counselor of moderation.[44]

With the Fifteenth Amendment now before the nation, Phillips began to agitate for ratification. He knew that the votes of some Southern states would be necessary, and if they balked he wanted the Federal government to secure ratification by carving new states out of the loyal areas in the South. He also advocated a radical plan for social and economic reconstruction, according to which Negroes would be given farms, and the New England village, including the New England common school system, would be introduced in the South. "The education of all classes and conditions of children *together*," he said, was "at the root of our Republican Institutions" and as important for Alabama as for Massachusetts. Phillips was always hazy about the details of his scheme, but he seemed to believe that rebuilding the South along these lines would solve the South's economic problems by bringing in Northern capital and forcing the Southern states to bid for the Negro's labor. In this situation the Negro, able to bargain for his labor, equipped with a basic education and the power of the ballot, would make his own way. He estimated that it would cost about one billion dollars to satisfy the Negro's just claim ("forty acres of land, one year's support, a furnished cottage, a mule and farm tools, and free schools for life"), but he argued that the nation had extorted twenty times that out of the slave.[45]

If anything approaching Phillips' plan was actually to be put into effect, it would require a period of dictatorial control by the North over the South, high-handed methods like those employed by Peter the Great to civilize Russia 150 years before. Phillips recognized this and was frustrated because President Grant did not. As reports of the intimidation of Negroes and loyal whites continued to come to his attention, he grew restive, and in the summer of 1869, after a period of several months during which he had made no serious attack on the President, Phillips began to call Grant to account. Contending that existing policy was too much concerned with the rights of rebels and not enough with those of Negroes, Phillips said he would no more waste civil rights on the rebels of Texas and Georgia than he would "try adders by a jury." Groping for presidential leadership, the nation found nothing in Washington but air. "Mr. President, if you cannot draw your sword, at least show your hand!" What was happening, Phillips told the readers of the *Standard*, could have been predicted when the nation "trusted an empty soldier" to settle the profound problems left by the war.[46]

Despite the lack of leadership in Washington which Phillips decried, the Fifteenth Amendment was finally proclaimed on March 30, 1870. Wendell was in Leroy, New York, when he heard the news, and he immediately sent off a note to his friend John Sargent. "Our long work is sealed at last," he wrote. "The nation proclaims Equal Liberty. Today is its real 'Birthday.' " [47] A few days later he joined the members of the American Anti-Slavery Society at a final meeting called to disband the organization. In some ways the occasion represented a personal triumph for Phillips. He had staked everything on the campaign for Negro suffrage and won; with political power in his hands for the first time, the Negro could begin to fight his own battles. Moreover, Phillips felt that the events of the last few years had vindicated him in refusing to let the abolitionists disperse at the end of the war and turn the Negro question over to the politicians. Still he felt no jubilance. The amendment was a necessary, practical measure, a great stride forward, but it could not establish justice and morality where injustice and immorality had so long prevailed. To be jubilant would be to attribute to the nation an integrity it did not possess. Thirty years of agitation had made him so conscious of the gap between the American ideal and the American reality that he had come to identify national pride with idolatry. In his final speech to the abolitionists he said:

> I am no longer proud, as I once was, of the flag, or the name of an American. I am no longer proud of the Declaration of Independence. My only joy today is that I can look into the face of the world and read the first line of the Declaration of Independence without a blush. Still I do not read it with any national pride. I do not read it feeling that we had lifted ourselves up to the sublime level where we had a right to use those words."

Phillips knew that his years in antislavery harness had doomed him always to be an outsider. He would not be honored like Garrison. He could not retire to aristocratic leisure like Quincy or go into politics like Frederick Douglass. Phillips had been permanently disenchanted, and society would always be out of joint for him. Nevertheless, he was not a bitter, nor even a melancholy, man, for, in refusing the fellowship of a hypocritical nation, he had found his faith renewed in fellowship with other outsiders. Looking into the faces of people like Lucretia Mott and Abby Foster, Charles Burleigh, Henry Wright and Stephen Foster, faces that were now wrinkled and weary but still vibrant with the same stubborn devotion to a common cause, Phillips confessed that the great privilege of being an abolitionist for him had been that it had brought him to know "the noblest men and women" of his day and elevated his conception of human nature. "When I read a sublime fact in Plutarch, of an unselfish deed in a line of poetry, or thrill beneath some heroic legend, it is no longer fairy land. I have seen it matched by the sublime devotion of a human being whose hot blood I felt in his or her hand clasped in mine. That is what I owe to the cause." [48]

18

The Moral Legacy of the War
1870–1880

Although the abolitionists had formally disbanded, Phillips continued to think of himself as an antislavery reformer, and a large share of his importance to our history during the 1870s derives from his unflagging interest in the Negro citizen. The great majority of Americans were tired of the problems created by the war, and the idealistic challenges it had posed were fast giving way to the challenges of the Gilded Age. The people who in preserving their nationality had destroyed slavery now threw their energies into subduing a vast continent and tying it together with iron rails, into exploiting undreamed of natural resources, into building blast furnaces, oil refineries and factories—above all, into making money. The critical years of the 1860s had offered a golden opportunity for the antislavery reformer; the 1870s were made to order for the entrepreneur and speculator, the man who lived by his wits and not by his conscience. During this period, Wendell Phillips was one of the few men of influence who continued to think of the legacy of the war in purely moral terms.

As we have already seen, Phillips felt that the key to the whole reconstruction problem could be found in Negro suffrage. Although race prejudice remained powerful and conspired to keep the freedman in an inferior position, he would now have the power to redress the balance. "Our colored friends have the remedy in their own hands," Phillips announced. If they used the ballot "pitilessly,"

never forgetting or forgiving any politician who pandered
to prejudice, the unjust social system in the South could
be overturned in a single generation.[1]

How could Phillips be so confident that the immediate
enfranchisement of four million illiterate ex-slaves would
produce happy results? His confidence was partly the expression of his faith in the egalitarian philosophy of the
Declaration of Independence. Like the Jeffersonians
whom his father had so much despised, Wendell believed
that all men were "created free and equal," not only in
principle but in fact, and that the unshackled slave had
as much right to a voice in the government of his country
as a Harvard professor. This conviction was influenced
also by his experience with Negroes, an experience which
included not the ordinary plantation hand but educated
Negro abolitionists and enterprising fugitive slaves.

According to the Southerners, radical reconstruction
was a return to the Dark Ages. According to Phillips, it
was the triumph of civilization over barbarism. Indeed, as
he surveyed the scene in 1870, much of the reconstruction
program seemed to have been drawn up to his own specifi-
cations. Believing, as he did, that "two-thirds of the adult
population in the South" should never be given political
rights, he welcomed the disenfranchisement of Southern
whites and the re-establishment of state governments by
Negro votes. Federal troops were still assigned to preserve
order, and the government, through the comprehensive
activities of the Freedman's Bureau, had undertaken to
rehabilitate the Negro and provide him with educational
opportunities. In one important area Phillips had been
disappointed. Recognizing the relationship between politics and economic power, he had wanted the government
to break up the plantations and distribute land to the
freedman, thereby breaking the economic, as well as the
legal, bond between master and slave. To this extent the
reconstruction program was not truly radical, but Phillips
was apparently willing to overlook one omission in order
to applaud the rest of the program.

While Southerners shrank in horror from the spectacle of Negro lawmakers dominating the legislature where Calhoun had launched his career, and the even more astounding sight of a Negro sitting in Jefferson Davis' old place in the Senate, Phillips embraced the events as symbols of the new age. To support his contention that Negroes were capable of handling the responsibilities of citizenship, he could point to the new state constitutions, the most progressive in the history of the South. To those who warned that Negro rule would lead to anarchy and pillage, he could point to the five Negroes serving respectably in Congress and to the generally magnanimous attitude of the Negroes in the state legislatures toward the disenfranchised whites.[2]

Nothing did more to reinforce Phillips's belief in the perversity of the South than the activities of organizations like the Ku Klux Klan and the Knights of the White Camellia. Relying on the effects of lynchings and threats of violence to intimidate Negroes and carpetbaggers into surrendering their political influence, the Southern underground aimed at returning political control to the Democrats and re-establishing white supremacy. By 1871 this counterrevolution, together with the gradual re-enfranchisement of ex-Confederates, was beginning to produce results. The border states began going over to the Democrats. North Carolina and Virginia threatened to slip out of Republican control, and the morale of the Negro voter and officeholder was shattered by the knowledge that his continued political activity might result in his being tortured or murdered. Because the activities of the Klansmen met with the tacit approval of large numbers of people in the South, local attempts to enforce laws against them were unsuccessful. In April 1871, Congress authorized the President to suspend the writ of *habeas corpus* and deal with the Klan as the agency of armed rebellion. The law gave Grant extraordinary powers, but Phillips wanted something even more drastic. "I want him to go down to arrest some ex-general, who counts his acres by thousands, numbers his wealth by millions, and who stands enshrined in the loving admiration of half the South. I want to track him to his lair in this nest of assassins, and then arrest him at midnight, try him by sunrise, and shoot him before the sun is an hour high—and when it is done Georgia and South Carolina will learn unmistakably that they have a master." The South was still in a state of war, said Phillips, and must be put down with the war power; if she were not, she would seize political control of the nation and the Civil War would be fought all over again. Considering the alternatives, Phillips thought that his solution was an easy one. "It does not need an army, it does not need a hundred men. You do not need five lives taken; but they must be lives of the topmost line; lives that stand out like the peaks of the Alps above society." [3]

Phillips intended his speech to have a sensational effect, and he was not disappointed. Some of the old abolitionists in his audience were shocked by the bloodthirsty language, and the nation was notified of his plan through the critical columns of the New York *Tribune*. Once again Phillips found himself in a duel with his old adversary, Horace Greeley. The New York editor had good material to work with in this speech, and he made the most of it. Accusing Phillips of trying to solve every problem with an epigram, Greeley announced that the merit of this plan lay in its simplicity. "Many of the most prominent men down there have never been hung," he wrote, "and it isn't possible that they would object if it was put to them in the right light. It is to be a peaceable proceeding. . . . Hang five of the first men in the South in this quiet, unostentatious, winning manner, and no more will want to be hung. We don't need any army or any courts; nothing, in fact, but a rope, and perhaps a cheerful epigram as they swing off." [4]

Although Phillips was probably more interested in whipping up popular opinion to do something about the Klan than in hanging generals, this latest brush with Greeley foreshadowed things to come. Greeley was one of a growing number of Republicans joining hands in an attempt to defeat Grant in 1872. The motives which drew men into the liberal Republican movement were various. Some, like Charles Francis Adams, were idealists who feared the effects of the continued centralization of government power. Some, like Greeley, had become disenchanted with radical reconstruction and felt that the Negro must forgo full equality and the South be returned to white leadership if peace and prosperity were ever to prevail. All were distressed by the scandals uncovered in the Grant administration, and some, like Charles Sumner and his friends, were profoundly antagonistic to the President himself.

In order to properly appreciate Phillips' role with respect to the liberal movement, it is necessary to know something of Sumner's fall from grace in the Republican party. In March 1870 the Massachusetts senator collided with the Grant administration by blocking the President's pet scheme for the annexation of Santo Domingo. When Sumner, in the lofty moral tone which so infuriated other politicians, said the administration wanted to commit the nation to "a dance of blood" and likened its course to proslavery imperialism of earlier Democratic administrations, Grant decided that Sumner would have to be disciplined. The first step was to recall the senator's (and Wendell's) personal friend, Lothrop Motley, from his post as ambassador to England. The second step, not culminated for almost a year, was to have Sumner removed as chairman of the Committee on Foreign Relations. If Phillips had ever allowed personal considerations to influence his position in public affairs, Motley's removal and the rebuke to Sumner would have placed him in a difficult position. As it was, he never wavered. Motley had been recalled shortly before the election of 1870. Phillips condemned the action at the same time that he was making speeches denouncing the Republican party in Massachusetts. Almost in the same breath he endorsed Grant's leadership in domestic affairs. The peculiarity of his position was quickly picked up by the press. The Boston *Post* implied that Phillips was soliciting favors from Grant, and the *Herald* reported that Wendell had actually been offered the English ambassadorship himself.[5]

Although a good many people believed that Phillips had finally succumbed to the lure of a ripe political plum, there is no evidence to support this. That he supported Grant for other than personal reasons is clearly suggested when we examine his attitude toward Sumner. Wendell's admiration for Sumner was genuine and intense. "It is useless for me ever to try to say to you what I would of my affections," he wrote in one of his letters, and, when the two men were seen together socially, observers marveled at Phillips' eagerness in flattering his friend. In the midst of his squabble with Grant, Sumner fell ill, and Wendell went to Washington to see him. He was impressed again with the man's statesmanship and his indispensability to the Senate, and he agreed with the estimate of the Russian ambassador, who said, "No man in Washington can fill his place." [6] Two weeks after Phillips left Washington, Sumner was deposed from the chairmanship which he had held for ten years. Phillips immediately came to his friend's support in the columns of the *Standard* and accused the Republicans of junking Sumner for fear of incurring Grant's displeasure in matters of patronage. Arraigning the President for his high-handedness, Phillips declared ominously that Grant had "entered on the course where Andrew Johnson perished." [7]

Now that Sumner was hopelessly at odds with the administration, it was natural for him to shift allegiance to the liberal Republicans, and many of his friends shifted with him. Phillips, however, was not persuaded. On April 11, 1872, a few weeks before the liberals held their convention in Cincinnati, he wrote Sumner that he still felt Grant to be a better man than anyone the liberals were considering. The nomination of Horace Greeley served only to strengthen this conviction. When Sumner delivered a fierce, three-hour attack on Grant early in June, Phillips sent him a gentle letter telling him that they would find each other in different camps during the next few months.

Perhaps Wendell sensed the pathos in Sumner's present role. Aging before his time, ill and disappointed, Sumner was trying to stir up the coals that had fired his great diatribe in 1856, only then it had been the "crime against Kansas," whereas now, try as he would to paint Grant as one of the archvillains in all history, it was really the crime against Sumner he was protesting. Wendell tried to let his friend down easily. "I have been saying that your speech was all true," he wrote, "only it was not all the truth. You omit Grant's claims; some he can fairly make. Come home and change the air before you follow Greeley's lead. You know no one is more tender of your good fame than I, almost tempted sometimes to sacrifice principle as I see it in defence of what you do." [8]

Phillips would not sacrifice principle, not even for Charles Sumner. As always, the principle involved the Negro. One of the reasons for Phillips's denunciation of Grant after Sumner's removal had been his fear that such summary treatment for the most celebrated radical in the Senate presaged a soft attitude toward the South, but Grant's prompt and vigorous enforcement of the Ku Klux Klan Act had put this fear to rest. As for Greeley, Phillips was simply in complete disagreement with his position on reconstruction. In 1865, Greeley had sounded like a good radical and insisted on complete equality for the Negro. Gradually he had become more conservative. His part in the release of Jefferson Davis had been intended as a gesture of reconciliation toward the South, and by 1872 he had become convinced of the power of racial prejudice and was saying that segregation would have to be accepted as a fact and the South returned to its white leadership.[9]

Phillips was as set against conciliation as ever. "Who can respect a power that offers pardon," he said, "before it has shown that it can subdue?" [10] Consequently, he had bitterly opposed the Amnesty Act, which Congress passed in May, removing the political disability on all but a handful of ex-Confederates. Conciliation was only a euphemism for surrender, for giving the South everything she had had before the war, including arbitrary power over the Negro. The rebels were still trying for victory, and Phillips quoted Greeley's own words to prove it. "They propose to renew the fight, but not with gun and sabre," Greeley had written during his Southern tour the year before. "They expect to regain as democrats, through elections, the power they lost in the war." If the rebels were successful, Phillips warned, and rode back into power before the Negro was rehabilitated, before the last vestiges of the caste system had been extirpated, the fruits of victory would all turn rotten on the vine. In working to avoid this eventuality, Phillips spared no words in attacking Horace Greeley. He compared him to Andrew Jackson, called him "a secession candidate" and hinted darkly about a deal "by Mr. Greeley's friends with Jeff Davis and his staff as to office and patronage." [11]

Many people thought it strange that Phillips, who had lambasted Grant so freely in the past, should now be found endorsing him for re-election. In 1868, Phillips had been vociferously opposed to Grant's nomination. The general had been just another soldier then, a man who had done reasonably well in his military assignments without displaying any talent to qualify him for political office. Phillips had even gone so far as to help circulate the reckless rumor about the general's "drunkenness in the streets of Washington." Greeley dug up Phillips' old speeches and tried to make what capital he could of his sudden change in sentiment.[12] Wendell had been through all this before, however, and he still made it a rule never to let what he had said about a man yesterday disturb him in what he had to say today. He freely admitted that he had not wanted Grant in the beginning, and he would make no apology for the weaknesses in his administration. "The defects of his administration are no surprise to me. I may say, without boasting, that I prophesied those defects." Grant had been wrong about Santo Domingo, wrong in turning over so many offices to relatives and cronies, wrong in tolerating the activities of corrupt subordinates. Despite these weaknesses, Grant was still the better candidate, and, in a public letter addressed to the colored citizens of Boston Phillips made a case for him which included the President's "statesmanlike and Christian policy" toward the Indians, his patience in foreign relations, his contribution to the prosperity of the nation, his prompt action regarding the eight-hour law for government employees, his decisive action regarding the Klan, his endorsement of the Fifteenth Amendment. The seventh and last reason, that Grant had become "the symbol and representative of loyalty" in America, was undoubtedly the most important. Whatever his defects, Grant stood for a strong policy in the South, and Phillips was ready to put up with all the rest in order to hold on to this. "For a loyal administration to protect the Negro" and "awe the rebel," Grant's little finger was worth a dozen Greeleys.[13]

Grant won handily in 1872, but Phillips surveyed the result with misgivings. Greeley had carried only six states, but half of these had been in the South, showing that the political alliance between carpetbaggers and Negroes was no longer invincible. Moving into their second term, the President and his administration were losing steadily in popularity. This was due partly to the repercussions of the Credit Mobilier scandal, which had come to light shortly before the election, partly because of the depression which the nation plunged into in 1873 and partly the result of a growing revulsion to the seamy by-products of radical reconstruction.

Although Phillips was dismayed at the drift away from radicalism, he does not seem to have understood the connection between it and the abuses which accompanied reconstruction in practice. In this connection, it is hard to explain why he never visited the South after the war. As one of the most traveled lecturers in the country, he could boast that he knew "every locomotive, every conductor, and the exact depth of the mud in every road in the country," [14] yet Phillips apparently never ventured any farther south than Washington. The result was that all of his information about the postwar South came to him at second hand, and much of it was biased, coming from people who shared his own prejudices. It is not surprising, therefore, to find almost no mention in his speeches of the graft and corruption which make up such a notorious chapter in Reconstruction history. The fraudulent connivings of carpet-baggers and scalawags, the expenditure of public revenues for whiskey, wine, cigars and champagne for Negro legislators seem to have passed him by completely. If pressed on the issue, he would undoubtedly have replied that these scandals were no necessary result of Negro suffrage and, in any event, were as nothing compared with the machinations of gifted thieves like Boss Tweed and the schemers behind Credit Mobilier. Despite the merits in this argument, it is still true that on this count, at least, Phillips was very nearly the doctrinaire theorist his critics accused him of being. With no practical experience of the Southern problem, he was like a physician who proposes a remedy before he has studied his patient.

One of the sorriest pages in Reconstruction history was being written in Louisiana, and it was over Louisiana that Phillips fought one of his last great battles for radicalism. In compliance with the terms of the Congressional Reconstruction Act, Louisiana had been readmitted to the Union in 1868 with a liberal constitution (containing the first bill of rights in the state's history), a carpetbag governor and a legislature divided about equally between whites and Negroes. As in other Southern states, the cost of Republican government in Louisiana was expensive, and the state debt grew from six million to fifty million dollars in two years. Part of the expenditures went for railroad and school construction and levee control along the Mississippi, but much of it went into the pockets of politicians. Governor Warmoth later testified that his income during his first year in office was $100,000, more than twelve times his official salary.

By 1872 the Republicans in Louisiana had split. One faction, under Warmoth, joined the Democrats in supporting Greeley for President and a conservative candidate named McEnery for governor. The regular Republicans,

led by Collector of Customs James Casey, who was also
Grant's brother-in-law, ran William Kellog for governor.
The election was a travesty, with each side claiming victory
and sending a certified set of returns to Congress. When
Congress refused to act, Grant supported his brother-in-law
and kept the regular Republican organization in power
with the occasional help of Federal troops.

There had been a history of violence in Louisiana ever
since 1866, when thirty-four Negroes were killed in a riot
in New Orleans. In the present circumstances, efforts to
break Republican control of the state through violent resistance were intensified. In April 1873 more than a hundred Negroes were killed in the bloody Colfax riots. As
the election of 1874 approached, White Leagues were organized in many of the parishes of the state for the purpose
of putting down Governor Kellog and destroying the political alliance between Negroes and Republicans. The
worst flare-up came in Red River Parish, where between
August 26 and August 31 four Negroes and six white office-
holders were shot to death by mobs. A fifth Negro leader
was tortured and burned to death.

In this atmosphere the election of 1874 took place,
and the fraudulent and chaotic results of 1872 were practically duplicated. When the two opposing factions tried to
organize a government in January 1875, New Orleans was
on the verge of revolution, and Grant ordered General
Sheridan to use Federal troops to maintain order and support the Republican administration. Sheridan managed to
keep peace in Louisiana, but his presence there was widely
denounced by a North which had registered its increasing
conservatism by voting Democratic in the recent election.
Grant was accused of using the army to suppress the will
of the people, and protest meetings were called in the
larger cties. On January 15 such a meeting was held in
Faneuil Hall.[15]

Phillips was not invited to participate, but he went
anyway and picked a seat in the corner of the gallery near
the platform, where he would be in full view of the audience. The Democrats were in charge, determined to pass

a series of resolutions condemning Grant for having violated the fundamental principles of American government.
By the time John Quincy Adams of Quincy, a perennial
Democratic candidate for governor, had finished his speech,
some of the men on the floor, having caught sight of
Phillips, began to call his name. Everyone in the hall knew
where Phillips stood on the issue, because he had already
addressed a public letter to the Secretary of War congratulating him for the prompt action of the army and suggesting that he permit Sheridan to have his way and dis-
pose of the rioters in military courts. The chairman was
understandably reluctant to surrender a platform acquired
by the Democrats for their own purposes to the silver
tongue of the most famous radical in the country. He
ignored the clamor as long as he could but was finally
forced to give in and invite Phillips to state his position.

Not since the early days of the war had Wendell participated in such a stormy scene in Faneuil Hall. This
time, however, the heckling and hisses which so frequently
interrupted him were less threatening and more designed
to add spice to the occasion. Wendell Phillips in Faneuil
Hall had long since become a legend, and men did not pass
up the opportunity of hearing him, even when they expected him to speak nonsense. In this case the nonsense
began with Wendell berating the organizers for having
called a Boston meeting and then filling their platform
with men from Quincy, Walpole, Salem and Plymouth.
Having justified his own presence, Phillips proceeded to
state the case for Grant. The President was legally and
morally justified in his action, legally because Congress
had refused to act, morally because he was acting to preserve order and protect human life. For the nation not to
act would be tantamount to murder. The Negro, emancipated not out of any philanthropic reason but in order to
win a war, would be abandoned to his enemies. "What
more contemptible object than a nation which, for its own
selfish purpose, summons four millions of Negroes to such
a position of peril and then leaves them defenceless? What
more pitiable object than the President of such a nation,

vested with full power to protect these hunted men (and you will not let him protect them), if he yield to this contemptible clamor, and leave them defenceless?"

In the Boston papers the next morning there was general agreement that the city had not seen the likes of the Faneuil Hall meeting since early in the war. Wendell himself had not faced such an antagonistic audience for fifteen years, but in the press accounts he came off as the star performer. It was natural for those who could remember to compare his latest effort to Phillips' first great victory in Faneuil Hall. A shrewd observer, however, would have sensed the difference. When Phillips raised his youthful voice to defend Lovejoy, it was the voice of the future; when he stood up to defend Grant, he was an old man fighting a rear-guard action. Not only was he unable to prevent the passage of resolutions censuring the President, but it seemed as if most of the men in the hall, however fascinated by his eloquence, had been unable to take him seriously. "My anxiety is for the hunted, tortured, robbed, murdered," he had said, and someone had hooted "That's played out." [16]

The sad truth was that the harsh, brawling voice of the heckler was the voice of the future now. As evidence that the "nigger question" was played out and the nation tired of worrying about the freedman, Wendell had only to notice the disappearance of the abolitionists from Congress. Stevens was long since dead; George Julian, one of the few genuine idealists among the political radicals, had been out of Congress since 1870, and Sumner, ostracized by the Republicans after 1872 and censured by the party in his own state the following year, had died in March 1874. Ironically, Sumner had been censured for what was, perhaps, his only magnanimous gesture toward the South. His proposal that the names of Civil War battles not be continued on the army register or placed on the regimental colors of the United States had brought him violent abuse from Massachusetts politicians who were afraid of alienating the veteran vote. Phillips had stood by his friend then,[17] and with Sumner's death there passed the only man in the Senate whom Wendell had ever admired without serious qualification.

Sumner's death symbolized the end of an era. The old abolitionists who had played such an important role in fashioning the Republican party were now practically extinct. Phillips, who had so often goaded and insulted them, lashing them on to what he took to be a purer moral effort, now mourned their passing. "With all its shortcomings—and they were many—it was still the noblest political party this country ever saw and achieved grander results than any other party ever even attempted." This had been the Republican party of governors like John Andrew, representatives like Giddings and Julian, senators like Sumner, Wade and Stevens and (now Wendell would admit it) a President like Lincoln. In the postwar period these men had gradually disappeared, and their places were taken by politicians like Hayes, Blaine, Garfield, Sherman, Morton and Conkling. Phillips observed the ascendancy of this new generation of politicians, "the men whom the Republican party created," with loathing.[18]

Phillips's contempt for the new Republicans derived from more than one source, but it was motivated above all by the knowledge that, under their leadership, the social question in the South was being returned to local control and the noble experiment of radical reconstruction was sputtering to an end. One by one the Southern states had been slipping into the hands of conservatives until by the summer of 1876, eighteen months after Wendell had made his Louisiana speech, only Florida, Louisiana and South Carolina remained under radical control. The coup de grace was delivered in the election of 1876.

The sordid affairs of Grant's second administration, culminating in the impeachment of his Secretary of War, William Belknap, made honesty in government the paramount issue. Both Hayes and Tilden ran on reform platforms, and, although the Republicans, as usual, tried to get as much mileage as possible out of waving "the bloody shirt" and warning the electorate about the dangers of an unreconstructed South should the Democrats return to power, this appeal had begun to lose its magic. In addition to what appeared to be complete victory in the South, Tilden also carried the Northern states of New York, New Jersey, Connecticut and Indiana. When the Republicans refused to acknowledge Tilden's election on the ground that the returns in four states (Florida, Louisiana, South Carolina and Oregon) were in dispute, the election was thrown into doubt, and from November 1876 until the end of February 1877, the American people did not know who their next President would be.

No one observing the American political scene during these critical winter months was more frustrated than Wendell Phillips. Entirely without faith in the Republican party, he was at the same time unable to stomach the thought of a Democratic victory, which would surely mean the end of Reconstruction and the success of the Southern "plot." When Hayes was officially declared elected, Phillips found all of his blackest fears confirmed. The compromisers had won again. The Democrats had agreed to go along with the Electoral Commission's decision, provided that Hayes withdrew Federal troops from the South, placed a Southerner in his Cabinet and favored the South in the matter of internal improvements. Here was another covenant with death, and Wendell hastened to predict what would result if the terms were kept. If Hayes withdrew the troops, "starvation and blood" would rule the South; our next Congress and President would be Democratic, and "a 'sold south'—the slave power under a new name," would control the nation.[19]

Phillips' rhetoric was familiar, but to most of the people in the North it had lost its sting. The New York *Tribune* expressed the majority voice when it reprimanded the Republicans who wanted to continue bayonet rule in the South. Emphasizing that "sentimental considerations have no place in the stern business of politics," the *Tribune* was willing to leave the Negro, with his constitutional protections, to fight for his place in Southern society.[20] Disgusted with the climate of public opinion which would sustain such a compromise, Phillips was determined to make his voice heard. On March 26 he gave a speech in Philadelphia which received national publicity. His target was the newly appointed Hayes Cabinet. The President had endeavored to pick men whose ideas complemented his own approach toward reform in government and sectional reconciliation. William Evarts, a distinguished New York attorney who had fought the Tweed gang, was the new Secretary of State. John Sherman, moderate Republican Senator from Ohio, was appointed to the Treasury. G. W. McCrary, one of the younger generation who had served in Congress since the war and had been active on the committee investigating Credit Mobilier, was Secretary of War. R. W. Thompson, a machine Republican from Indiana, was appointed Secretary of the Navy. The postmaster-generalship went to David Key of Tennessee, who had fought under the Confederate flag at Vicksburg, and the attorney-generalship to Charles Devens, Justice of the Supreme Judicial Court in Massachusetts. Carl Schurz was to be Secretary of the Interior.

From a historian's point of view, Hayes' Cabinet was a good one. Purely political appointments had been kept to a minimum, and the appointees as a body were able men who probably represented the mood of the nation as well as any group could. When Phillips looked at them, however, all he could see was the complete absence of radicalism. Evarts had once made a speech supporting the Fugitive Slave Law and had later been the most active attorney for the defense of Andrew Johnson. Sherman and Thompson were old-line Whigs with no genuine antislavery record. McCrary, the Secretary of War, had been one of the men to engineer the compromise between Hayes and Tilden and was known to favor pulling Federal troops out of the South. David Key was a rebel, and Devens was the man who as United States marshal had loaded Thomas Sims onto a ship in Boston Harbor and sent him back to slavery in 1851.

The paragraph in Phillips's speech most widely quoted in the press was one in which he likened Hayes picking his Cabinet to an artist painting a picture. The canvas is full of drab figures until the introduction of Devens suddenly enlightens the whole.

There is Sherman who will leave a name linked to no measure or idea—his only record that he entered Congress poor and leaves it rich. Evarts reminds one of the Protestant riots in London, when men chalked on their closed shutters "No Popery" to conciliate the mob. . . . Amid this death grapple between Caste and the Declaration of Independence, Evarts writes on his flag "No Principle!" Then comes Schurz, the Swiss soldier, always to let. Hayes gazed at the colorless piece, which was hardly visible. Suddenly he remembers slave-hound Devens—the low monotony of whose life rose only once into noticeable infamy, when, with his own hands, he put chains on Thomas Sims and dragged him down State Street. Hayes flung that blood-red drop on the canvas, and behold! it flows immortal!—the slave-hound Cabinet! [21]

The speech was telegraphed to the press throughout the nation, and the response was immediate and violent. Back in Boston, the *Advertiser* ran an editorial entitled "Mr. Phillips Last Frenzy," while the *Post* called Wendell a "crazy rhetorical buffoon" and described his address as "a blue stream of hatred." The New York *Tribune* surveyed the reaction in the press and reported happily: "The magnificent blackguardism and splendid venom of Mr. Wendell Phillips' recent lecture have been everywhere received with expressions of loathing and disgust." The *Tribune* rightly saw that he was not really concerned about the personalities in the Cabinet, but was striking at the policy their appointments foreshadowed—"the new policy of confidence and kindness as the basis of unity and peace." The hiss of disapproval with which the people had received his effort was proof, the *Tribune* concluded, that "the mission of Mr. Phillips as the apostle of unforgiving and relentless hate was ended long ago." [22]

Once again Wendell Phillips' voice had made great excitement, but now it seemed to be entirely without influence. A few days after his Philadelphia speech the *Nation*, reporting that Hayes had definitely decided to recall Fed-

eral troops from the South, declared that their continued
use appeared to have "absolutely no defenders left." [23]

Wendell always advised others to develop their muscle
by battling against the current. He had followed the practice all his life, but now as he approached his seventieth
year the currents seemed swifter than ever and the other
battlers fewer. His old friend, Thomas Wentworth Higginson, the man whose hot enthusiasm for the Negro in
1854 had almost succeeded in freeing Anthony Burns, took
a trip through Virginia, South Carolina and Florida in
1878. On his return he wrote in the *Atlantic* that the
Southern states were "abreast of New England in granting
rights and privileges to the colored race." [24] Admitting the
past atrocities of the Ku Klux Klan in South Carolina,
Higginson advised his readers to remember that the provo-
cation had been great. Higginson, like so many of the
other old crusaders, had left his revolutionary zeal behind
with his lost youth and was now telling the people what
they wanted to hear—that the Negro was safe in the hands
of his old master.

Although Phillips' evaluation of the results of Reconstruction suffered from a basic inconsistency (he could not
understand that arbitrary power in the hands of carpet-
baggers and Negro legislators must eventually lead to oppression and corruption, just as it had in the case of the
master and his slave), his analysis of the situation was more
profound than that of most of his contemporaries. He
knew that all the constitutional amendments in the world
could not guarantee the rights of citizenship to the Negro
if the federal government was not willing to protect him.
Theoretically enfranchised, he would soon be practically
disenfranchised. White supremacy would rule in the
South, and caste society would again have a controlling
voice in national politics. Phillips was, perhaps, naive in
thinking that any politicians could have done the work of
saints after the war, but he had the vision to see through
the moral pretensions of the Republican party. For ten
years the Republicans had played politics with the Negro
without having any sincere interest in him as a person.

Not only had they not punished the Ku Klux Klan, Phillips decided, "but the only reason they hunted out these crimes and made catalogues of 'outrages' was a heartless and merciless calculation to use such records for party purposes at election times. They played with dying men as counters on the chess board the game of party success." [25]

Why had the nation acquiesced in this default in leadership? One of the reasons, Phillips thought, was that a new generation had grown up in the fifteen years since the war. The active young men in the country, the men who would be thirty in 1880, had been infants during the great fugitive slave excitement, barely in their teens when the war broke out. They did not have behind them the grand lessons from 1830 to 1860—"Sumner in the Senate chamber borne down by assassin blows, Garrison dragged through the streets." These memories had faded into the twilight; now young people would come up to Phillips after a lecture and ask, "Was there ever a mob in Boston, and what was it about?" [26] Phillips could understand a certain sad inevitability about this, but it did not prevent him from heaping his invective upon the heads of "wicked politicians." Nothing disgusted him more than the sight of Republican orators in election times trying to make capital by exploiting the moral issues of the war. "No party in our history," he said, "has ever fallen from such a height to such a depth of disgrace." [27]

As the decade of the seventies drew to a close, Wendell continued to take every opportunity to tell the people what they did not want to hear. In an essay addressed to the conservative readers of the *North American Review,* he painted a harrowing picture of what they might expect with the Democratic South back in the saddle. "That Confederate soldiers will soon receive the same pension as our veterans," he wrote, "seems a foregone conclusion." [28] He painted a grim picture; the national debt would be doubled and Northern capital taxed to pay the bill. He wanted his readers to squirm. They had made it clear that they felt no further responsibility for the Negro; now let them tremble for their pocketbooks!

When the northward migration of Southern Negroes was blocked by some of the Southern states in 1879, Phillips participated in a mass meeting in Tremont Temple. What was happening, he said, was a part of the nightmare which had accompanied the nation's premature decision to declare the "Southern question" solved. "Is the Mississippi a public highway," he asked, "or have the Southern planters a right to put a fence across it? Are the Negroes free? Was there ever a rebellion? Did Lee really drive Grant out of Virginia, and was it Jefferson Davis who pardoned Abraham Lincoln? What is the meaning of that pile of granite on the Common [the Soldiers' and Sailors' monument]? Did the folks it commemorates succeed in settling anything, or do their graves mark the half-way house between somewhere and nowhere?" [29]

The *Tribune* had said that Phillips was becoming an anachronism. He must have known in his heart that there was truth in this assertion, but he tried not to be bitter. Unlike many men who let themselves be soured by the disappointments of their last years, he had kept fighting in his sixties for the goals he had discovered in his twenties. At no time was he more eloquent in this pursuit than when he addressed the war veterans of Boston in the summer of 1879:

If I have any lesson for you, standing on the edge of life— perhaps half a dozen years will close my interest on this scene . . . it is better that you make that monument something better than a lie. You and I went down comrades, by the hundred, and all our kindred went down, to make that pile of granite which Webster consecrated at the rising sun to tell of liberty on Bunker Hill something better than a lie, and we made it. You wrote it out, as in lines of light with a pencil of iron on the surface of the continent, that it never again should be trodden by a slave. In the coming ten years you are to make this government so strong . . . that on the remotest plantation of Mississippi and Texas a Negro can draw himself up with serene consciousness and say "You smite an American citizen!" sure that if the grave closes over him America will smite his murderer remorselessly.[30]

19

Labor Reform   1870–1880

Standing in front of the railroad station in a town in central Pennsylvania sometime after the war, Phillips watched a procession of miners file by on their way to work. "First came a little boy in rags, grimy from head to foot so that there was nothing upon him to distinguish whether he were white or black—solely the flashing of his eyes could be seen. He was perhaps nine, possibly ten years of age. In his little ragged bit of a cap was sewed a lamp." The boy was followed by a dozen contemporaries, straggling off to begin an eleven-hour stint in the mines. The incident stuck in Phillips' mind. He had not witnessed such a scene since he left England thirty years ago, and it helped to confirm his opinion that a new kind of slavery in the North was coming to replace the old system of chattel slavery in the South.[1] As public enthusiasm for a radical solution of the Negro problem declined during the seventies, Phillips' enthusiasm for a radical solution of the economic and social problems in the industrial North increased. "While this delusion of peace without purity" lasts, he was saying at the end of the decade, "labor claims every ear and every hand." [2]

A Boston man, of course, did not have to go all the way to Pennsylvania to see the working classes exploited. He need only open his eyes and look around. Boston was no longer the rustic, uncluttered community of Phillips' childhood. Some of the changes were picturesque, like the new bronze fountain on the Frog Pond (now called Crystal Lake), which could send a jet of water ninety feet into the air, and the elaborate flower displays in the Public Garden,

planted on land reclaimed from the waters of the Back
Bay, where Wendell had splashed so happily as a child.
Other changes, the congestion in the city streets, for example, were more profound. In 1871 an expressman, going
from Charles Street to Union Square by way of the Mill-
dam, counted 1,300 teams en route.[3] The increase of traffic
was a function of the city's growth as an industrial center.
A vast reservoir of labor, supplied by the influx of Irish
immigrants in the forties and fifties, had made Boston
the fourth-largest manufacturing city in the nation. While
many neighboring towns were built almost exclusively
around the shoe or textile industry, the prosperity of Boston had become dependent on a diversified system of manufactures including ready-made clothing, iron works, sugar
refineries and piano factories.

Phillips didn't have to be an economist or a statistician
to see that relatively little of the wealth produced in Boston was ending up in the pockets of working people. A
master mason called in to patch the brickwork on his house
could tell him that the wages of a skilled mechanic would
barely stretch to cover the basic needs of a wife and two
children, and it was common knowledge that an Irishman,
with nothing to sell but his muscle power, could hardly
keep himself alive, let alone a family. The inflation
brought on by the war made matters even worse, with
prices rising almost twice as rapidly as wages. "We have
a common saying now in this country," wrote the members of an American union to the Iron Workers of Great
Britain in 1866, "that you go to market with the money in
a basket, and carry home the goods in your pocket." [4]

In the Boston of Phillips' boyhood, poverty and slums
had been almost unknown, but by mid-century the Hub
had developed a quarter at Fort Hill and in the North End
which, in misery and squalor, could rival anything that
London or Paris had to offer. The great mass of Boston's
Irish population, too poor to pay the cost of transportation
into and out of the city where they must sell their labor,
had huddled together here out of necessity. As the great

tide of impoverished immigrants swept over the peninsula, almost every square foot of space in the North End and Fort Hill areas had been transformed into some kind of improvised hovel. Ramshackle tenement houses, consisting of sunless, unventilated one-room apartments, were thrown up in narrow alleys. Families unable to afford these murky holes lived in cellars and sheds in conditions that a thrifty New England farmer would find intolerable for his animals. Some of them had no furniture and slept on heaps of dirty straw. Some had to pass by stopped-up privies and splash through pools of human filth to draw their drinking water. Many lived on the absolute edge of starvation. And, of course, they died—four times faster than their neighbors up on Beacon Hill.[5]

Phillips saw the connection between child labor in the Pennsylvania coal mines and misery on Stillman Street, and this intensified a concern over the labor problem which had begun almost as early as his interest in slavery. The desperate plight of the English working classes had made a forcible impression on him when he visited London in 1840, and when he returned to America he prepared a lecture on Chartism for which he memorized a set of statistics showing the relationship between crime, mortality and the price of wheat in England. Whenever the price of wheat went up, there were more crimes and more deaths, proof that the masses lived on the brink of starvation. When the first meeting of the New England Workingmen's Association convened in Boston in 1845, Wendell was a delegate and helped to draw up a resolution recommending that the workers query all political candidates on their willingness to support labor reform. He also subscribed to George Henry Evans' paper *Young America* and sympathized with the agrarian reformer's ideas on the distribution of public lands.[6]

During these early years, however, Phillips dismayed some of the more militant labor leaders by insisting that slavery take precedence over labor reform. He warned against being taken in by the specious argument that wage slavery in the North could be equated with Negro slavery. American laborers "as a class," he said, "were neither wronged nor oppressed," and, if they were oppressed, the workers, unlike slaves, possessed a remedy. "Does legislation bear hard upon them? Their votes can alter it. Does capital wrong them? Economy will make them capitalists. Does the crowded competition of cities reduce their wages? They have only to stay at home, devoted to other pursuits, and soon diminished supply will bring the remedy." Phillips wrote these words in 1847. He admitted that "the imperfections which still cling to our social and political arrangements bear hardest on the laborer." This situation might be alleviated by such measures as a better system of taxation and wiser use of public lands, but real improvement would come only with the "economy, self-denial, temperance, education, and moral and religious character" of the laboring class.[7]

As his experience in the antislavery movement ripened, however, Phillips came to see that the two problems could not be separated. The hand, representing the power of consolidated wealth, that kept the operative chained to his machine was also the hand that tried to gag the abolitionists. It had been the gentlemen of property who mobbed Garrison, and it was their lackeys in the churches and the press who continued to fight the abolitionists. Twenty-five years' struggling against the power of State Street changed Phillips' concept of American society so completely that on the eve of the Civil War he was making speeches that would have done justice to a convinced Marxist. "The pulpit can never be anything but a slave in a country like ours," he said on one occasion. "The pulpit is nothing but the outer shed of those colossal treasure-houses at Lowell. The overseer inside the mills, at a salary of three thousand dollars a year, takes care of the hands of the operatives for six days, the subordinate overseer, in the town church, on Sunday, takes care of their morals for twelve hundred a year. They are both hired by the same wealth, owned by the same stockholders, and preach to the same whirring of the shuttle that is heard six days in the week, and echoed on Sunday." [8]

There were two concepts basic to all of Phillips' thinking about the labor problem. The first was his vision of the ideal society, a vision strongly influenced by the New England of his childhood. "My ideal of a civilization is a very high one," he once told a group of working people, "but the approach to it is a New England town of some two thousand inhabitants, with no rich man and no poor man in it, all mingling in the same society, every child at the same school, no poorhouse, no beggar, opportunities equal, nobody too proud to stand aloof, nobody too humble to be shut out." [9] The Jeffersonian flavor here is obvious. Phillips was too much a believer in social change to expect to see the idyllic conditions of rural New England duplicated in the booming industrialized society of postwar America, but he did expect to see the old ideal of equality honored in the new society.

Phillips' second concept was that the labor reformers should pattern their activities after the abolitionists and work to educate a public opinion which would support legislation favorable to the workers. He conceived of the labor union as a means of organizing the workers for politics rather than as an economic force in competition with capital. The remedy for the exploited classes lay not in strikes and picket lines but in the ballot. "When a laborer in Massachusetts wants his rights recognized, he disdains to strike. That is not American. It is getting down upon his knees and acknowledging that he has no remedy but to bully. He says, 'No, I am a man; the same as the capitalist; I can speak; I must be heard; I can vote; I must be attended to.' His remedy is the orderly operation of the focus of society." [10]

Armed with these two essential ideas, Phillips first came into prominence in the labor movement when he joined hands with the leaders of the National Labor Union and campaigned for the eight-hour day. The National Labor Union, a loose federation of trade unions and reform groups, had been organized primarily for political action and sought, above all, to enact the philosophy of a Boston machinist by the name of Ira Steward. Steward, perhaps the most creative thinker among the early American labor reformers, was a stocky, bald-headed man with a full, brown beard and the hot eyes of an enthusiast. The intensity of his convictions alone would have been enough to attract Phillips, who insisted that every reform effort be a "cause." In addition, Steward's eight-hour philosophy provided a panacea for all economic ills. Believing that wages were not governed by the ratio between the amount of capital and the size of the working population but by the customs and needs of the working population, Steward contended that increased leisure for the worker would diversify his interests and multiply his wants. The general increase in demand would stimulate greater production and therefore raise wages.

It is not hard to see why the eight-hour movement ran into such stiff resistance. In Massachusetts in 1865 the average skilled mechanic was working ten hours a day, the factory hand eleven to thirteen and bakers up to seventeen hours a day. When a special legislative commission conducted hearings on the feasibility of shortening the work day by law, employers came from all over the state to protest. "Men are injured by idleness more than by overwork," they said. "Ten die of 'nothing to do,' where one dies of doing too much. Men and women used to work twelve or fifteen hours a day without injury. It is only the drones who plead for a reduction. . . . More leisure would lead to more vice and crime." [11] There is no question but that the majority of middle-class Americans agreed with these sentiments. The gospel of hard work prevailed, and the sweat on the brow of an honest laborer was considered a badge of honor and a reproach to all idlers. In America everybody worked, and everybody who worked honestly and hard could improve his station in life. This, at least, was the American ideal.

What drew Phillips into the eight-hour movement was

an awareness that the facts did not fit the ideal—at least not in Fall River, where John Wild worked. Wild was a spinner in a mill. In 1866 he appeared before the Massachusetts Labor Commissioners to plead for a state law shortening hours of work. His testimony was as follows:

I don't know as I have any more to say, except that I have two little boys, one seven and the other about eight and a half. I am no scholar myself, because I have always been working in the mill, and I am sorry for it. I don't want my children to be brought up in the same way. I wish to get them to work a little less hours, so that I can send them to night school. I want, if it is possible, to get a law so that they can go to school, and know how to read and write their names.

Q. Do they work in the mill?

A. I have been forced to send them in. My earnings would not keep the door open. I had to send them in to help me earn a living. They are getting pretty big, and they want a deal of clothing, and I could not get it out of my earnings. I wish to get shorter hours. I am willing to lose the extra hours for the good of my children.

Q. Do they work by the day?

A. By the day.

Q. How old are the children?

A. Seven and eight.

Q. Have you a child of seven working in the mill?

A. Yes, I have.

Q. You have only two children working in the mill?

A. Only two.

Q. What wages do these children get?

A. $2.30 per week, the smallest one.

Q. Does the other get the same?

A. Yes sir.

Q. How long has the youngest worked in a mill?

A. About five or six months.

Q. Had he been kept in school up to that time?

A. Yes sir, but he didn't learn much—not so much as I'd like to have him.

Q. Does he get any schooling now?

A. When he gets done in the mill, he is ready to go to bed. He has to be in the mill ten minutes before we start up, to wind spindles. Then he starts upon his own work, and keeps on till dinner time. Then he goes home, starts again at one, and works till *seven*. When he's done, he is tired enough to go to bed. Some days he has to clean and help scour all dinner hour, but we stopped that some little time ago. It takes us till about half past twelve; some days, all the time. Some days he has to clean spindles. Saturday he's in all day.

Q. Is there any limit on the part of the employers as to the age when they take children?

A. They'll take them at any age when they can get them, if they are old enough to stand.

Q. How young are the youngest?

A. I guess the youngest is about seven. There are some that's younger, but very little.

Q. Do you know that your children are working contrary to law?

A. I didn't know there was any law.

Q. Did you know that if I should go to Fall River and prosecute their employer, he could be compelled to pay a fine for employing your children?

A. No, sir, being no scholar.[12]

When Phillips endorsed the eight-hour movement in Faneuil Hall, twenty-nine years to the month after his first speech there, he was thinking of men like John Wild. The long struggle over slavery, "the struggle for the ownership of labor," was nearing its end, and it now remained "to arrange the true relations of capital and labor." The problem was to find a way of redressing the balance between the capitalist's son and the laborer's son so that "every child born in America" would have an equal chance in life. Let a man give eight hours to work, eight hours to sleep and eight hours to himself. Every man had a right to do as he wanted with his leisure, but Phillips, good Puritan that he was, expected him to spend it earnestly in education and in the study and discussion of public questions. The liberated workman would thus become better equipped to secure his own advancement and, at the same time, become a more intelligent, better-informed citizen.

For thirty years Phillips had been predicting nothing but victory for the abolitionists. Now he began to predict victory for the labor reformers. Let them unite behind the eight-hour campaign, force every political candidate to take a stand on the issue, he said in 1865, and in two years, "instead of having an Ishmaelite like me to address you, you can take your pick out of all the politicians in the country." [13] Five years later the politicians were still looking the other way, and the workers were still relying on Ishmael, who was still predicting victory. Rather than compromise on the hour question, Phillips advised the workers to demand even more pay for eight hours than for the ten or twelve they were now working. Let the capitalist laugh if he wanted to; time was on the workers' side. "Born of the Yankee race, that never yet yielded to a difficulty," Phillips said, "I do not care for these temporary possessors of capital . . . all I know is, the world gropes its way onward to a better civilization, and this is one of the gropings. They may laugh at it, they may deride it, they may endeavor to smother it, but it is the tendency of the times, and it will certainly conquer." [14]

Even though Phillips' extravagant predictions were not fulfilled, the eight-hour agitation did yield some results. At the municipal level, especially in Massachusetts, the workers succeeded in electing friendly candidates, and in almost all the state legislatures in the North the eight-hour question was discussed. By 1867 eight-hour laws had been passed in six states but in such a way as to have no practical effect. Phillips was disappointed in Massachusetts. Partly because of his goading, the state had appointed a special commission to study the problem and would soon establish the first Bureau of Labor Statistics in the nation. Conservative thinking, however, was far too strong for the kind of labor legislation that Phillips sought. The labor commissioners in 1866, for example, readily acknowledged the plight of the working classes, but, although they were prepared to recommend more stringent supervision of a ten-hour law for children under twelve, they contended that the adult workers were beyond the reach of the law. Because the legislature could not give the laborer a larger share of the value he created without "subverting the right of individual property and establishing communism," it was up to the workers to elevate themselves "by temperate and industrious habits, by ambition in work and workmanship,"—in short, by becoming their own capitalists.[15]

Phillips agreed that the individual worker was still bound to try and improve himself, but he was distressed by the commissioners' unwillingness to recognize that the economic situation in postwar America had changed so drastically that many workers were afraid to exercise their freedom. Phillips knew something of this at first hand. On one occasion after the war, he had given a lecture on labor to a group of mill workers and found that, although they believed in what he had to say, not one worker would sit on the platform with him, for fear of being tagged as a troublemaker and losing his job.[16] The commissioners obviously believed that it was wrong for society to tinker with the natural economic forces governing prices, wages and working conditions. As a young man, with the lessons from Adam Smith and David Ricardo fresh in his mind, Wendell would have agreed;[17] as an old abolitionist, however, he had come to feel that it was just as immoral to let economic laws get in the way of social justice as it had been to quibble over the Constitution when the clear call of duty was to abolish slavery at any cost. The conservatism of the commissioners and the ruthlessness of the mill owners in New Bedford and Fall River in crushing the attempts of the spinners to get even a ten-hour day all seemed part of a conspiracy which was threatening the very existence of American democracy.

It was a conspiracy, first of all, to eliminate the differences between the laboring man in America and in the old world. What made the American worker unique,

Phillips thought, was his ability to lay something aside in savings every week after paying the grocer and landlord. This saving, however modest, was the springboard which made it possible for him to be an employer himself some-day. The capitalists who refused to recognize organized labor, who blacklisted union men and turned deaf ears to the plea for shorter hours, were trying to destroy the spring-board and create "a permanent laboring class, so that there is not one chance in ten, compared with what there was, that the children of these men shall lift themselves." [18]

What made Phillips' criticism of American society in the seventies so much more profound than that of the other "reformers" of the day was the fact that he could see the connection between the poverty of John Wild in Fall River and the gluttony of Boss Tweed in New York. A working population, denied adequate wages and leisure and massed together in cities, would naturally be exploited by thieves and demagogues. While so-called liberals held their noses at the stench and talked about the necessity for civil service and honest men in government, Phillips said "you cannot afford to cut up American population into these chunks of ignorance, and let one man's ambition, and another's selfishness and another's greed throw them into which scale he pleases." [19] The hundred-million-dollar swindle in New York City was a direct result of the fact that "the needy, ignorant, vicious, dangerous class . . . . cunningly handled by party leaders, elects the magistrates of our great cities." Phillips could remember as a very young man the dire predictions of the Federalists if too much democracy were put into effect. The Federalists had been proved wrong by the success of rural, small-town democracy before the war. The challenge to the postwar generation was to show the world that social justice and political honesty in New York and Boston were as much the natural outgrowth of American principles as "a just, peaceful, law-abiding New England town." [20]

When he was lecturing in the seventies, Phillips rarely missed an opportunity to relate the celebrated anecdote about Tom Scott in the Pennsylvania legislature. "Mr. Speaker," the famous lobbyist was reported to have said, "I move we adjourn unless the Pennsylvania Railroad has some more business for us to transact." People laughed at the remark as a joke, but Wendell pointed it up as an example of the arrogance of consolidated wealth in a day when state governments were rapidly becoming the property of corporations and millionaires. This was another example of the conspiracy against democracy, and Phillips lashed out against it. After a grisly railroad disaster in Massachusetts he rushed into print in the *Standard* with an editorial entitled "Railroad Murders." Contending that "the Railways run the Legislatures," Phillips was trying to whip up public opinion against the abuses of the great tycoons by employing the same techniques he had used against slaveholders. "The only way to accomplish our object is to shame greedy men into humanity," he wrote. "Poison their wealth with the tears and curses of widows and orphans. In speaking of them call things by their right names. Let men shrink from them as from slave-dealers and pirates." Millionaires who both robbed and killed the people deserved to be in jail, Phillips said, and he argued that life sentences for a score of railroad directors would soon teach the others that the roads should be run for public service and not for public plunder.[21]

The prudent men in State Street who had found Phillips' pronouncements so dangerous before the war found new reason to shudder now. The spectre of communism, which had been haunting Europe ever since Marx and Engels had published their famous manifesto in 1848, was very much on their minds when revolution broke out in Paris in 1871. Without knowing very much about the Paris Commune, Phillips saw in it a symbol of the growing protest against privilege, and he embraced it with his characteristic enthusiasm. "Such efforts never fail," he said. "Brutus, falling on his useless sword,—Hampden, riding out of the last battle, leaning death struck, on his saddle bow—Vane, Sydney and John Brown, from their scaffolds, call out to these, their last followers, 'Be of good cheer, *Brothers*, the seed your blood has planted shall not die.' " [22]

It was bad enough to praise revolution in Europe, but Phillips seemed to countenance it in America. After the terroristic activities of the Molly Maguires had been discovered in Pennsylvania, he refused to let the blame fall on the miners. "Pennsylvania, which breeds ignorance and then cheats it," he said, "which leaves boys all day in the bowels of the earth to grow up in ignorance into tools and voters, may expect to see her labor, like that of Europe, driven to the task at the point of the bayonet." [23] The labor violence in the seventies, especially the railroad strikes in 1877, made Phillips see that strikes and the threat of strikes were necessary weapons for labor. When the federal government, having refused troops to protect the Negro, employed them to subdue the railroad workers, he praised the militancy of the unions for their willingness to stand up against oppression.

As always, it is necessary to distinguish between the tone and essence of what Phillips had to say about the labor problem. In tone he was every inch the revolutionary, prophesying bloodshed. In essence, he was always careful to distinguish Europe from America. Communism might be a good thing for Europe, but it was too doctrinaire for America. The Communists believed that a just, classless society would be brought about only by class struggle and revolution. Phillips was doing everything he could to prevent the development of class struggle in America. His ideal was not a Utopia at history's end, but the relatively classless society that flourished in Jefferson's day. American society had been jolted out of joint by the Industrial Revolution, and only the concentrated effort of the whole people, exerted through the ballot, could bring about a cure. The disease lay too deep for any one medicine, and the people had an obligation to do whatever they thought might bring about a cure.

Without being a systematic socialist, Phillips did believe in government planning. "We have more than enough of the babble and chaff of 'supply and demand,' " he said. "That is a political economy which forgets God, abolishes hearts, stomachs and hot blood, and builds its world as children do, out of tin soldiers and blocks of wood. Here every man reads, votes and carries arms. The physical force, the voting majority, and a large share of the intellectual ability, are in the possession of the employed." In democratic society, public welfare was not at the mercy of impersonal forces but subject to political control. Governments were not "merely scavengers to keep the streets clean, or constables to watch the back door, or savings banks to guard what misers can snatch," but organizations "to secure culture and leisure, to help work out the social problems of the day." What Phillips wanted to achieve through legislation was very similar to the situation that obtains today: shorter hours, a graduated income tax, laws to prevent the abuse of power by big corporations and recognition that the worker had a right to help determine his own wages. "Corporations that employ a large number of workingmen," he said, "should appoint a committee to meet a committe of workingmen. Before such a committee should be laid open all the details of the business. After mutual consultation such committee should decide the amount of wages to be paid. If they cannot agree, an umpire should be chosen to make the final decision." Almost alone among the Americans of his generation, Phillips saw that the future lay in this direction. Seventy years from now, Phillips predicted in 1871, children growing up in America would listen to the story of Vanderbilt "with as much wonder as a modern audience hears Agassiz describe the habits of a mastodon." [24]

As a labor agitator Phillips was in a much lonelier position than he had been as an abolitionist. In the antislavery movement he had been surrounded by colleagues, some of whom came from a similar social background and many of whom were close personal friends. These reformers were generally out of sympathy with the labor movement, and Wendell's association with it tended to make more complete the estrangement which his split with Garrison had begun. Samuel May, Jr., spoke for many of Wendell's old friends when he described labor leaders as "a set of idle and noisy men and women" who did not deserve the suport of honest reformers.[25]

As an abolitionist, Phillips had to overcome the hostility of labor leaders who felt that antislavery reformers had always been more solicitous about black people far away than the plight of their own working classes. The "proud and haughty" reformers who had worked the mills during the war and harangued poor, consumptive operatives into giving twenty-five cents that their names might be upon "some trifling subscription list" had made a bad impression on many workers. Moreover, the mere fact that Phillips came from the aristocracy was enough to arouse resentment. When he seemed to be addressing the working people as members of a special class, he was lectured in the columns of the labor press. "The working people of this country do not regard themselves as a class," he was told, "and do not wish to be so considered. They are citizens—belonging to this and that church and political party, like other citizens; and never intending to remain what they are, but to rise to some better condition as soon as possible." On other occasions Wendell ran afoul of the very class consciousness which this writer denied. At a meeting in Framingham, for example, when he was advocating shorter hours and the establishment of night schools for working people, he said he had never met a worker who had read a book on finance. An outspoken delegate by the name of Jennie Collins, who did not like the tone of these remarks, denounced Phillips as "the representative of the men and women who lived upon interest without producing anything." Before she finished, the indignant lady had branded Wendell as a dilettante who lived in the midst of "imported" luxuries, had "never worked a whole week in his life," and was "nothing but a great baby" who had "never yet played the part of a man." [26]

The more astute labor leaders, however, recognized that Phillips was a valuable addition to their ranks. In 1866 they had supported a movement to draft him as a labor candidate for Congress. Preoccupied with reconstruction matters at this time, Phillips had refused to run. In 1869 the labor party in Massachusetts participated in the state elections and succeeded in sending twenty-seven representatives and four senators to the legislature as well as capturing 10 per cent of the total vote for governor. Encouraged by this success in their first attempt, the party leaders hoped for more substantial victories in the election of 1870, but they needed a candidate with a reputation. Wendell Phillips was their man, and at the Labor Reform convention on September 8 he was unanimously nominated for governor.

For the only time in his career, Phillips allowed himself to be drawn into political combat as a candidate for public office. "I have no wish to be Governor of Massachusetts," he said, "and flattering as is this confidence, I thoroughly dislike to have my name drawn into party politics, for I belong to no political party." Nevertheless, he was willing to lend his name to the cause of enlightening public opinion and organizing the ranks of labor. Believing that he was enlisting in an educational, rather than a political, campaign, he advised his supporters that, "though we work for a large vote, we should not be discouraged by a small one." [27]

In addition to his nomination by the Labor Reform party, Phillips was nominated for governor by the Prohibitionists' party. Although nobody seriously thought he could win, it was expected that he might pull as many as 50,000 votes. If he could bring enough votes into the Labor Reform and Prohibition camps to control the balance of power in the legislature, it was believed that Phillips would have a chance of unseating Henry Wilson in the Senate.

Working in Phillips' favor was the fact that public interest in the labor problem was unusually high in 1870 because of the "coolie problem." The coolie problem was a direct result of the friction between the shoe manufacturers in Massachusetts and the powerful shoemaker union, the Knights of St. Crispin. In July 1870 a manufacturer named Sampson, announcing that he would deal with the Knights no longer, imported seventy-five Chinese from San Francisco to man his factory in North Adams. Hired on a three-year contract, the Chinese workers were to receive transportation, fuel, quarters and twenty-three dollars a month. In addition, the Chinese custom of burial among one's ancestors was to be respected, "Sampson pledging to box up each corpse and send it to Kwong Chong Win Co. in San Francisco, who will take charge of the rest of it." Most of the papers in the state, strongly antilabor, greeted the arrival of the Chinese shoemakers as a deliverance. "They are with us!" exulted one enthusiastic writer, "the 'Celestials'—with almond eyes, pigtails, rare industry, quick adaptation, high morality, and all—seventy-five of them—hard at work in the town of North Adams, making shoes." The general sentiment was behind Sampson for his initiative in freeing himself from "the cramping tyranny" of an arrogant union.[28]

The labor press, of course, was not so happy. Disregarding the fact that the Chinese were skilled workers, the *American Workman* emphasized that they were willing to work for about a third of a Crispin's pay—coolies working for coolie wages! The *Workman* devoted its entire first page to the drawing of a coolie with a pigtail reaching to the ground. Over his shoulder he carried a stick from which five dried rats were hung by the tail—coolie food. On another occasion the *Workman* published a drawing which featured Simon Legree, standing, whip in hand, in a barracks crammed with four-tiered bunks, a pigtail dangling over the end of each bunk—"COOLIE SLAVERY IN MASSACHUSETTS." [29]

Phillips wrote a long editorial on this problem for the

Standard. He was opposed to any harsh restrictions on immigration. The Chinese, he said, were an "industrious, thrifty, inventive, self-respectful" people and would make good citizens. To counteract the importation of cheap coolie labor for purposes of destroying American unions, Phillips suggested that a tariff be placed on products manufactured by such labor and that immigration be made gradual, so that Chinese workers could be absorbed without lowering the American worker's standard of living. The editorial was reprinted and distributed in pamphlet form during the campaign. A more clever politician might have exploited the coolie issue more skillfully; Phillips' discussion of it was intelligent and consistent with his convictions against all kinds of discrimination.[30]

Because the platform was his natural element, it was impossible for Phillips to let anyone else do his campaigning for him. Toward the end of October he went on a two-week tour of the state. His campaign oratory was unique in that he was more interested in lecturing his audiences than in appealing for votes. Having spent a large part of his adult life in lambasting politicians of every variety, Wendell was obviously concerned lest people mistake him for one now. There was a time, he told his audiences, when he had been ambitious, but thirty bitter years of "isolation and contempt" in the antislavery cause had "ground that weakness" out of him. Now "success" and "reputation" were empty words, and his only concern was "to educate the people of Massachusetts and to plant the seeds of a new purpose in the effete ranks of the Republican party." Phillips never seemed to tire of lashing the Republicans for not embracing the great question of the hour. "The Republican party is dead," he announced. "It has nothing in the world to do but rot; that is the duty it owes to society." In matters concerning national politics, Phillips was always leery of doing anything that might help the Democrats, but he was free from these inhibitions now. "I don't care a chip which party places its nominee in the gubernatorial chair," he said. "My only purpose this year is to inform the Republican party what the people of Massachusetts want. And if I can sting them into sobriety and attention by letting a Democrat sit in the gubernatorial chair, then I hope he will sit there. I am out as schoolmaster." [31]

Phillips received plenty of publicity during the campaign, and it was almost all bad. Despite the labor party platform, which was composed of such mild proposals as a ten-hour day for women and children and speedy payment of the national debt, Phillips was accused of being a socialist. The fact that he was known to favor a graduated income tax probably had something to do with this, as did the revolutionary flavor of his rhetoric. Even though he was frequently quoted as being opposed to class violence in America, the militancy of his speech on other occasions was sufficient to conjure up in the minds of wealthy Bostonians an image of gutted mansions and millionaires hanging from the lampposts on Beacon Street.

Because Phillips had developed a habit of relying increasingly on the first person singular, his speeches sounded more pontifical now than ever. The papers were quick to point this out and charge him with being an egomaniac. He said he intended the word "I" to stand for the people and the principles he represented, but there was more to it than that. Phillips was more alone than he had ever been. Except for the *Standard* and the American *Workman,* he was scourged almost daily in the press. No matter where he looked he could find no one in a position of influence standing up for the ideas he believed in. E. L. Godkin, who fancied that his *Nation* was a successor to the *Liberator,* was a good example of what might be expected from the "liberals." One of Phillips' sternest critics, the *Nation* went out of its way to dissociate itself from the labor movement, saying "anybody who seeks to persuade the workingmen that there is any other way to better their condition really than becoming capitalists themselves" was "either a false prophet or a charlatan." [32] At the same time, many of the people whom Phillips had counted among his close personal friends a few years before were now saying harsh things about him in private. "His egotism increases every day," Fanny Garrison Villard wrote to her husband, "and now he talks as if he alone abolished slavery." [33] Wendell's old colleague and confidante, Edmund Quincy, said in a letter: "W. P. went into the caucus with all his talents and more than his usual disregard of truth. He does not seem to know a lie when he sees it and to invent his facts as he goes along as he needs them." [34] To combat these powerful, hostile forces, Phillips could rely only on a skimpy, loosely organized personal following, and the strength of his own convictions. If he sometimes felt that he alone had been singled out for a vision of the future and was called to trumpet out the message until the wilderness rang with the sound of truth, it was understandable. It was a bad decade for prophets, however, and to many ears the silver tongue was beginning to sound like a cracked horn.

When the results of the election were tallied in November, Phillips was found to have polled 22,000 votes, about 12 per cent of the total. The Labor Reform party made no appreciable gain in the legislature. The reasons for this disappointing outcome are fairly obvious. Not only was the press solidly against him, but in some towns postmasters refused to distribute his campaign literature, just as they had refused to distribute antislavery tracts thirty years earlier. In addition, he had to buck the traditional reluctance of the voters to "throw away" their votes on a third-party candidate. Moreover, large numbers of people still associated labor unions with lawlessness and were probably influenced by such reports as that published in the Boston *Advertizer* on the eve of the election of strikers beating up a new hand in a Worcester wire factory. The workers themselves had at least two good reasons for not supporting Phillips. In the first place, many of the mill operatives were intimidated by their employers and voted Republican to hold their jobs. Others, who would ordinarily have been expected to vote the Labor Reform

ticket, were scared off by Phillips' Prohibitionist supporters. Wendell had accepted the Prohibitionists' nomination
because he believed that temperance was one of the great
issues of the day and intimately connected with the problems of graft and corruption in big city government. He
was convinced that cheap rum made it possible for Boss
Tweed to control the masses and make democracy a joke.
This reasoning, however, was too sophisticated for the
average workingman, who looked on the temperance agitation as a conspiracy to take away his glass of beer without
threatening the wine cellars of the wealthy. As a temperance candidate, therefore, Phillips was regarded with
suspicion by many workers who took the safe way out and
voted for the Democrats.[35]

"I am happy to tell you that Wendell Phillips has been
handsomely snubbed at the election of last week," Quincy
wrote to an English friend. "If he had acted with ordinary
common sense and good temper when slavery was abolished
and had gone into politics, it is very likely he might have
been the next Senator, and he certainly would have been
one of the Boston M.C.s. But he is 'played out' as we say,
and will be merely a popular lecturer and a small demagogue for the rest of his life." [36] A lot of people agreed
with Quincy that Phillips had been repudiated, but
Wendell refused to accept the notion. Since he had not
been trying to get elected, he would not admit the sting of
defeat. He had accomplished what he intended, to dramatize the great economic and social problems of the day,
and he was confident that the future would move in the
direction which he had pointed.

Although he never again allowed himself to become a
candidate for office, Phillips retained a lively interest in
Massachusetts politics throughout the decade. The immediate goal of the Labor Reform party, he thought, was
to remain an independent force until it succeeded in raising the labor problem to a level of public interest high
enough to attract one of the major parties. The regular
party politicians, however, still seemed unwilling to recog-

nize that there was a labor problem. When a ten-hour bill for women and children came before the legislature in 1871, Frank Bird, perhaps the most influential Republican in the state, opposed it because it would inhibit the laws of supply and demand and contradict the Biblical admonition that a person should labor from sunrise to sunset. A Mr. Goodman, from Berkshire County, opposed the law on the ground that children were better off in the factories than outside. The work was easier than "study in the Boston Latin School." A Mr. Pierce of Middlesex was against the bill because it would increase crime and "fill up reform and penal institutions." [37]

The ten-hour law lost by a large margin, and in the same issue of a paper reporting the debate there was a short article about the International Workingmen's Association and Karl Marx, "author of an important work in German entitled *Das Kapital.*" There is no clear evidence that Phillips ever read Marx, but he did claim to see the connection between the European crisis and what was happening in America. The American labor party was "the right wing of the broad labor movement throughout the world"; the masses were organizing "in terrible earnest," and only prompt political action could avert the possibility of class violence.[38] If the existing parties were not willing to absorb the great social and economic issues of the day, they would be challenged and replaced by a new party. In 1872 the national platform of the Republican party contained a labor plank closely patterned after a resolution drafted by Phillips. As we have seen, however, the support that he gave the Republicans in this election was dictated more by his desire to defeat Greeley than anything else. The revolt of the liberal Republicans, occurring simultaneously with the development of an independent labor party, suggested to him that a new party alignment was about to take place. "Whether Grant or Greeley, or whoever else is elected," he predicted in May 1872, "this is the last time the Republican and Democratic parties, as such, will take part in a Presidential canvass." [39]

In attempting to encourage the development of the party of the future, Phillips found himself more and more in the camp of Ben Butler and the Greenbackers, and this did as much as anything to keep him in a storm of controversy during his later years. Butler had emerged from the war as a political maverick of great power in Massachusetts politics. A former Democrat who did not like party discipline, he was always suspect by the Republican leadership, but he was also feared for his large personal following and the control of patronage which came from his close association with Grant. As a politician Butler was remarkably resourceful and resilient. His name was associated with a long list of scandals, but he survived them all and never apologized for anything. A poor boy who had made a fortune in practicing law, Butler was the most feared and hated man in the state among the wealthy and wellborn. In 1868 they had sponsored Richard Henry Dana in an attempt to wrest Butler's seat from him in the Fifth Congressional District. It was like feeding raw meat to a lion. Butler was at his best in the brawling political meetings which were customary in the shoe towns, and the gentlemanly Dana came out of the campaign so chewed up that he never ran for office again.[40]

Why did Phillips support Butler, a politician who adjusted his principles to get the most from every passing breeze? Although it does not appear that the two were ever personal friends, Wendell apparently saw certain similarities between Butler's position and his own. In the first place, Phillips admired the general's outspoken defense of the Negro. In 1866, for example, Butler had addressed a political rally in New York. Prevented from speaking by an anti-Negro mob, the general calmly stood his ground. When he was hit by an apple, he took out his knife, pared the apple, ate it and then denounced the mobsters. "I have hung your betters, and if you do not behave I shall get the chance to do the same to you," he said. "Do you suppose I shall flinch from onion-stinking breaths? A man who has smelt gunpowder can stand

garlic. You, the rooters here, think you are the equal of
the negro, Oh! no! The negro is as much, as immeasurably
your superior, as heaven is above the hell where you are
going." [41] Butler needed all the courage he could get, because the established institutions of the state—press, party
and property—were all ranged against him. A large part of
his support came from working people, and, like Wendell,
he was always carrying on a running battle with the newspapers and making sensational charges from the platform.
Still, Phillips confided to a close friend, he was not in the
least taken in by Butler. Sometimes one had to fight fire
with fire; sometimes entrenched rascality could be dis-
lodged only by employing another rascal.[42]

When Butler made an intense drive to capture the
Republican nomination for governor in 1871, Phillips
supported him in the hope that if he won the Republicans
would be more friendly to the labor cause. He attributed
the general's near success to the interest in the labor agitation. "The Commonwealth of Massachusetts had been
living on a set of potato Governors for a long time," he
said, "and they wanted some roast beef." Now, with Butler
defeated, there was not enough vigor left in the Republican
party to allow it "to digest its meals." [43]

As Phillips' interest in Butler increased, his faith in
the future of the Labor Reform party declined. He had
badly overestimated the political potential of organized
labor, and, when the National Labor Union collapsed in
1872 and union membership suffered a drastic reduction in
memberships during the depression years that followed,
Wendell was encouraged to take up a broader program of
reform. This flexibility brought him into dispute with
many of the Massachusetts labor leaders. In 1866 he had
been all for the eight-hour day and had advised the workers
to forget all other issues and concentrate on that. By 1872,
however, he was saying little about eight-hours and a great
deal about money reform. This led to a break with Ira
Steward, and Phillips began to appear at the labor conventions less often. When a friend tried to prevail on

him to come back, he said he had "worked 40 years, served
in 20 movements and been kicked out of all of them" and
had come to like paddling his own canoe. During the next
several years he spent considerable time and energy trying
to steer that canoe through the treacherous waters stirred
up by the great American currency debate.[44]

To understand Phillips' position on the currency question it is necessary to say something more about his basic
approach to economic problems. As we have seen, this approach was moralistic and uncomplicated. The best brief
introduction into Phillips' economic thinking can be found
in an editorial he wrote for the *Standard* in 1871. The
thesis is found in the title, "Labor the Creator of Wealth
Is Entitled to All It Creates." To illustrate his case Phillips used clam diggers. The simple laborer digs clams
with his hands and is entitled to whatever he gets. The
capitalist laborer, who makes a hoe one day and digs with
it the next, is also entitled to whatever he gets. On the next
level is the capitalist, who makes a hoe and lets it out for
a price. "Such a system has no inherent, essential injustice
in it," Phillips wrote, and, "if it can be properly arranged
and guarded, serves civilization. The difficulty is to keep
it from degenerating into despotism and fraud." Beyond
this, Phillips distinguishes two other classes. One is occupied by the "drone," the man who somehow gets possession of thousands of hoes, sits with idle hands "and arranges
a cunning network of laws, and Corporations, Banks and
Currency, Interest and 'Corners' to get seven out of every
ten clams that are dug." The last and most detestable class
is inhabited by "the man who sits in Wall Street and, by
means of Bank credit, buys up all this year's clams to raise
the price—who, taking fifty thousand honestly earned dollars, makes a 'Clam Digging Company'—bribes newspapers
to lie about it—creates ten banks and locks up gold, or
arranges a corner to depress its stock—then brings up every
share;—makes ten more Banks and floods the land with
paper and sells out;—returning, after a week of *such labor,*
with a fortune." According to Phillips, the drones, men

like Rockefeller and Vanderbilt and Tom Scott, and the thieves, men like Jay Gould, Jim Fisk and J. P. Morgan, were out to crush popular liberty in America. The best hope to thwart them, Phillips believed, lay in the Greenback movement.[45]

Greenbackism was a direct result of the inflationary tendencies of the war. Four hundred million dollars had been issued in greenbacks during the war. After the war, when an abortive attempt to retire the greenbacks was accompanied by lower prices and unemployment, the National Labor Union began to drive for currency reform by advocating an "American System of Finance." According to this system, adapted from ideas Edward Kellogg had developed before the war, money would be issued by the government in the form of legal tender paper, redeemable at the holder's option in "interconvertible bonds" bearing a low rate of interest. The supporters of the American system opposed the resumption of specie payments and the control of currency by banks. They believed that the unlimited issuance of legal tender by the government under the above conditions would ensure full employment, establish a lower rate of interest and "secure to labor its just reward." [46]

Phillips' ideas on finance were derived from the American System and developed naturally out of his participation in labor reform. With the abolition of slavery every laborer had been lifted to the level of wages. The slave problem made way for the labor problem, and in attempting to discover how labor could get a fair share of the joint product of labor and capital Phillips was struck with the importance of "the dollar in which labor was paid." He came to believe that it was "CURRENCY which, rightly arranged, opened a nation's well-springs, found work for willing hands, and filled them with a just return, while honest capital, daily larger and more secure, ministered to a glad prosperity; or it was CURRENCY, wickedly and selfishly juggled, that made merchants bankrupt, and stirred labor into discontent and slavery, while capital added house to house, and field to field, and gathered into its miserly hands all the wealth left in a ruined land." The tone of the quotation shows that Phillips approached the question of finance as a moralist and reformer rather than as an economist. The reformer must always be able to identify the villains in society and point the way to salvation. In this case the villains were the bankers and wealthy speculators who manipulated the currency, "the cannibals of Change Alley," Phillips called them, while the way to salvation was simply the unlimited issuance of paper money on government credit.[47]

During the last half of the decade, Phillips talked and wrote about Greenbackism at every opportunity. National finance was a far more technical subject than the other causes he had taken up, and Phillips could hardly qualify as an authority. When he tried to show that the free issuance of paper money would lower an excessively high rate of interest and thus encourage investment in industry, he was accused of identifying money with capital. When he attempted to show that England had thrived on a paper currency, he was accused of distorting history. Carl Schurz was quoted as saying that Phillips' ideas were "too childish to be discussed among serious men," and the *Nation* reported that he did not understand any system of currency and only read books on the subject "in order to give sham points or glitter to his paradoxes." [48] Wendell, on the other hand, objected to seeing the question put in anything but a moral light. His opponents were trying to confuse the issue with cunning technicalities. "They fool their dupes and instruct their agents to drag in the questions of paper money, inflation, bonds and a score of others in order to hide the real issue," which was simply whether the people or the "money-kings" should control the currency.[49] Employing the same highly charged rhetoric he had used in attacking slavery, Phillips was able to command a vast amount of newspaper space. Even the *Nation* had to admit that he was influential. Despite the imbecility of his ideas and the fact that he was no more amenable to argument than a phonograph, the *Nation* mourned that editors and politicians were constantly getting drawn into "solemn debate" with Phillips, thereby thus publicizing his ideas on currency and public credit.[50]

Quite apart from the economics and morality of Greenbackism, Phillips supported the movement because he believed there was a great political potential in it. He had lost faith in the two major parties. The Democrats were fastened like a leech to the South and white supremacy. The Republicans had defaulted on reconstruction and ignored the labor problem. None of the important reform movements of the day, women's rights, temperance, not even labor, when it was isolated from the question of finance, made a broad enough appeal, or offered enough discipline within its ranks, to provide a base for effective political action. In the matter of currency reform, however, Phillips believed that the nation was ripe. Because of the inflationary character of their program, the Greenbackers attracted support from the debtor classes everywhere. Although the movement had begun as a part of labor reform, by the mid-seventies it was receiving widespread agrarian support in the West and South. In 1875 the government announced its determination to resume specie payments, and this increased political interest in currency reform to such an extent that in 1876 the Greenbackers put their first presidential candidate into the field. Although the party polled few votes in 1876, the agricultural depression, railroad strikes and labor violence in the following year created a general feeling of discontent, much of which found expression in the Greenback movement, and the party polled more than a million votes in the congressional elections of 1878. Remarking this development with great satisfaction, Phillips fancied that he saw an analogy between the position of the Greenbackers and that of the Free Soilers in the forties. Just as the Free Soilers had matured into the Republican party and killed off the Whigs, so might the Greenbackers replace the Republicans as the party of the future. Phillips was particularly in-

terested in Greenback successes in the South, for he believed that the new issue would break the ranks of white
solidarity and re-enfranchise the Negro as competing
politicians bid for his vote.

Only by appreciating all of the considerations set
down above is it possible to understand the zeal with which
Wendell Phillips embraced the currency issue and the
Greenbackers. Just as the abolitionists had been raised up
by Providence to save the nation from slavery, so had
this movement been raised up to preserve American democracy. "This is no rotten party falling to pieces," he
said, "no discontented class clamoring in the dark: this is
a step in the ages, a revolution deeper than that which was
sealed at Appomatox. It began when Congress declared all
men equal; it will never end till it is settled that the people
are the source of all power, and safely to be trusted with its
exercise over every interest and in every direction." [51]

Now we are able to distinguish a final reason for Phillips' support of Butler: Butler was a Greenbacker. Phillips
was not supporting the man so much as the idea. Occasionally he would make a reference to the general's character. "In spite of all that is alleged against him," Phillips
said once, "I dare affirm that he is, in private life and in his
great offices, as upright and honorable as any political
servant of the state." [52] Considering Wendell's well publicized scorn for politicians, a man was free to take this any
way he wanted. The point to be made here is that, even if
Butler had been the "Beast" his enemies said he was, even
if he had stolen the silver spoons in New Orleans, Phillips
would have backed him for the role he was playing,
consciously or not, in "one of the last battles between
aristocracy and democracy."

In attempting to evaluate Phillips' career as a reformer after the war, one is struck, first of all, by the in-
accuracies in his predictions. He believed that the working
people could best help themselves through political action,
that the future would be devoted to labor parties rather
than to labor unions. History has proved him wrong.

Except for the abortive attempt in the seventies, with which Phillips was involved, American workers have, as a group, spurned politics and concentrated on achieving their goals through the economic power of highly organized unions. Phillips believed that the Greenbackers represented the voice of the future, that they would attract popular support among the masses in every section and sweep away the traditional two-party alignment. Again, history proved him wrong. The movement reached the high-water mark of its political fortune in the elections of 1878. The following year Ben Butler, running on a ticket backed by Greenbackers and splinter groups from both the Republicans and Democrats, narrowly missed being elected governor of Massachusetts. Phillips believed that his prediction was about to be fulfilled, but he was mistaken. By 1880, Greenbackism had begun to peter out, and when Butler finally did get elected in 1881 it was as the standard-bearer for the Democratic party. Phillips' hopes were frustrated partly because the nation had begun to pull out of the depression which had created popular sentiment for currency and other economic reforms and partly because he had overemphasized the dangers that he saw about him. He did not understand that, despite the injustice and inequality created by the Industrial Revolution in America, there still remained enough opportunity and equality among the masses and enough flexibility in the traditional political structure to avert a crisis.

What is it to make all these qualifications, however, except to say that Phillips, like most men, was more fallible than he realized? Surely, whatever errors in judgment and analysis he may have made, this chapter was one of the most honorable in his life. He could have chosen differently, as Edmund Quincy remarked, could have become a good Republican and probably have gone to the Senate.[53] Or he could, like Quincy, have retired to a life of quiet, gentlemanly leisure, remaining in the public eye occasionally as the nation's most popular lecturer but spending most of his time among his books and friends and memo-

ries. Or he could, like many other abolitionists, have
devoted the rest of his moral energy exclusively to refight-
ing the Civil War and waving the bloody flag. He chose
instead to remain a dissenter and be treated as a common
scold. The "Great Barbecue" had begun, but Phillips,
like a stern Puritan elder, would not sit down at the
boisterous table and celebrate. Vernon Parrington has
called Phillips ":a lone Puritan in a land of Yankees," and
the description is apt.[54] Custodian of both the American
dream and the New England conscience, Phillips did as
much as one man could do to point out the dangers of
American capitalism after the war. Nor did he allow disappointment and apparent failure to embitter him. An
old man, refusing to surrender the vision of his youth,
Phillips believed, and history was to bear him out, that the
nation would move toward greater economic and social
justice. Men accused him of looking at the world with
jaundiced eyes, of cherishing a morbid attraction for evil,
but it was not his fascination with evil that drove him on;
it was his faith in democracy.

I believe in the people, in universal suffrage as fitted to secure
the best results human nature leaves possible. If corruption seems
rolling over us like a floodmark, it is not the corruption of the
humbler classes. It is millionaires who steal, banks, mills and railways; it is defaulters who live in palaces, and make away with
millions, it is money kings who buy up Congress. . . . These are the
spots where corruption nestles and gangrenes the state. If humble
men are corrupted, these furnish the overwhelming temptation. It
is not the common people in the streets, but the money-changers who
have intruded into the temple, that we must sorely need some one
to scourge. If the hills will cease to send down rottenness, the
streams will run clean and clear on the plains.[55]

20

The Universal Reformer
1870–1880

Wendell Phillips and the Adamses did not get along very well. "The Adams family," Phillips said, "always means to stand just as far ahead as it is respectable and *useful* (to themselves) to stand." These words appeared in the *Standard* in an article denouncing Charles Francis Adams, Jr., for some remarks he had made deploring Chinese immigration. When Henry Adams heard the news he quickly sent a letter to his brother. "I congratulate you heartily on Wendell's attack," he wrote. "Besides being a perfect gentleman he is a good thermometer. One's value is fairly measured by his abuse. I confess always to a desire to do to him what we used to do to our dogs that misbehaved in the house—'rub his nose in it.' " [1]

Henry Adams' distaste for Phillips was shared by a good many of Wendell's more genteel critics. They objected to his self-righteous way of reprimanding well known people in public and to the way he seemed to stick his nose into every one else's business with the assurance that he was simply doing his duty as a reformer. Tactics that might have been excused at the height of the anti-slavery agitation became repugnant when they were employed on behalf of convicted murderers, marauding Indians or women in bloomers. Thus, many who, despite their disagreement with Phillips, still recognized him as a gentleman before the war came to look on him as a notoriety hound and name caller after the war.

The fact that he became deeply involved with the

labor movement does not, by itself, explain Phillips' unique position during the last fifteen years of his life. Phillips was the Cromwell of the Gilded Age, but, unlike Cromwell, he had lost his army. The old comrades had drifted away. Some had died. Others, like Frederick Douglass, had been swallowed up by the Republican party. Still others, like Edmund Quincy, had retired. When a friend asked Quincy to describe what his life was like in 1869, Edmund replied that he was living "in almost absolute solitude" at his estate in Dedham. The servants were so well trained he rarely had to speak to them, and he could spend his time dabbling over his books, taking an occasional drive to the family mansion in Quincy and, above all, enjoying "the sense of perfect leisure and absolute security from interruption in a pleasant country house." [2] It was almost superfluous for Quincy to add that he rarely saw Wendell Phillips. Garrison, meanwhile, was acting with all the benevolence of a prophet who has found honor in his own country. After the *Liberator* ceased publication, he began to write for the *Independent*, an influential religious weekly in New York, and, although he maintained his interest in the Negro, women's rights and temperance questions, the iron had gone out of his soul. He seemed to believe that the great reform of the nineteenth century had already taken place under his leadership and that any further radical reformation was out of place. When he attended a Women's Rights Convention in 1876, he recoiled from a resolution condemning corruption in public life, because, he felt, "we were purer in our public affairs than we ever had been." Clearly, the crusade was over for Garrison. [3]

Because reform was not an avocation or a profession but a way of life with him, Phillips found it impossible even to conceive of retirement. When the abolitionists had broken up after the war, the ostensible issue had been whether they had done their duty to the Negro. The more profound issue in Phillips' mind involved the immorality of leaving the field before total victory was won.

He wanted the abolitionists to go on and embrace all questions of reform, "to enlist *for the war,* as long as the struggle lasts, to remodel finance, Christianize law, enfranchise woman, protect and elevate the masses, break the bonds of superstitious observance, curb appetite, and make men fit for the freedom God intends for them." [4]

The importance of the religious impulse in Phillips' life has been mentioned before, but it needs to be reemphasized at this point. His withdrawal from the church some thirty years before had not cooled his zeal or impaired the orthodoxy of his religious beliefs. Wendell's friends were always amazed at the tenacity with which he defended the Calvinist position. Although he did not like theological discussions, he would occasionally turn up at his friend John T. Sargent's house to wrestle with the transcendentalists who made up the Radical Club. Emerson was sometimes there, as were T. W. Higginson, Cyrus Bartol, John Weiss, Longfellow, Louisa Alcott and others. Perhaps Wendell went because he had come to enjoy being in the minority. In any event, his customary contribution was to take issue with transcendentalist views of Nature and the World Spirit by defending the uniqueness of Revealed Christianity.[5] Invariably when he disputed with the transcendentalists, Phillips' mind would be drawn back to his dead friend Parker. The memory of Theodore Parker was still fresh in his mind, and, whenever someone from out of town would come to visit, Wendell would take him around to Parker's house on Exeter Place and ask Mrs. Parker to take them up to the third floor, where Theodore had kept his huge library and study.[6] It was, of course, not Parker the transcendentalist whom Phillips remembered but Parker the reformer, the preacher who insisted on applying his gospel to society. Applied Christianity, Phillips thought, should provide a common ground for all professing Christians, and Wendell, orthodox though he was, would have traded a hundred Bible-thumping Dwight L. Moodys for one Theodore Parker.

Although Phillips did not write or speak often on purely religious subjects, he deserves to be recognized as one of the forerunners of the Social Gospel. His address entitled "Christianity a Battle, Not a Dream," which he delivered in Boston in 1869, provides both a key to his thinking on this subject and the rationale for his varied reform activities after the war. The thesis of the address is that Christianity is not a contemplative, but an active. religion. "The great AGITATOR of the centuries is Jesus Christ of Jerusalem, who undertook to found his power on an idea, and at the same time to announce his faith and to teach his disciples, 'this idea shall remould the world.'" Christianity, Phillips said, was a militant faith. never at peace with society. Just as the soul was to be distinguished from the human body, so was Christianity. the soul of society, to be distinguished from every earthly institution, including the Church. These ideas were not new to Phillips in 1869. He had accepted them as the truth many years before when he left the church to join the abolitionists. He had believed then that the genuine religious impulse of the day was in the antislavery agitation, and he still believed that it was to be found in the fellowship of reformers rather than churchmen.[7]

In seeking to bring all of the postwar reformers together into a common congregation, Phillips was disappointed. In the spring of 1870 he did help to found an organization known as the Reform League. The report of its first annual meeting shows that most of the members were recruited from among the abolitionists who had stuck with Phillips to the end, zealous souls like Abby Foster, Lucretia Mott, John T. Sargent and George T. Downing. The *National Anti-Slavery Standard* (which came out in 1870 with a new format and was called The *National Standard*), was the journal for this organization and lent its support to a multiplicity of reforms including the Negro, Indian affairs, Chinese immigration, women's rights, labor, temperance, capital punishment and prison reform. As a practical matter, however, the Reform League was little more than a name. Phillips became a free-lance reformer after 1870, and the *Standard* was his personal sounding board.

Although Wendell had been brought up in a family which looked on wine as one of the good things in life, he appears to have espoused the temperance cause early in his career. In this he was undoubtedly influenced by other abolitionists ("you couldn't find one abolitionist out of a hundred who was not a temperance man," he said) and especially by Garrison, whose brother died of alcoholism. Phillips was not, like the famous orator and reformed drunkard John B. Gough, an evangelical temperance man who tried to convert drinkers into taking the "pledge." Although aware of the widespread personal tragedy which alcohol created, he was more interested in it as a social problem. Americans, especially during the first half of the nineteenth century, were a hard-drinking people. Rum, corn whiskey, hard cider and beer were abundant and cheap. The belief that strong drink made strong bodies encouraged heavy drinking among working men, and some idea of the level of popular indulgence is suggested by the fact that liquor was regularly used by preachers and freely dispensed at ordination services. It is estimated that in 1810, the year before Phillips was born, Americans were consuming approximately twenty-five million gallons of spirits a year at a cost greater than the total expenditure of the national government. Like other reformers, Phillips was struck by the relationship between intemperance and poverty and crime. Because of this connection, he insisted that the state had the power to control the liquor traffic, and his participation in the temperance movement was directed at influencing public opinion and gaining temperance legislation. He had been a vigorous advocate of the prohibitory law which was finally passed in Massachusetts in 1855, and when the law was ignored in Boston he had appeared before a special committee of the legislature to demand its strongest enforcement.[8]

Although Phillips was always quick to turn down his own wine glass, he was willing to tolerate moderate drinking among his friends. On one occasion, when he was writing his cousin Oliver Wendell Holmes about a place to stay when lecturing in New Haven, Wendell even went so far as to recommend the wine—a recommendation based on hearsay, of course.[9] As a temperance reformer before the public, however, Phillips was less lenient. "We are to bring to bear upon every man who indulges, the deliberate conviction of the sober part of the community that he is a criminal," he said in one speech, "that whoever can control his appetite is a sinner in the eyes of God if he does not." [10] When influential churchmen began to attack the temperance movement and cite scripture to show that Christian gentlemen could sip their wine with easy conscience, Phillips retaliated vigorously.[11] He would not tolerate aspersions on what he considered to be "one of the weightiest, broadest, most momentous" causes in America. He had often professed his faith in popular government, in the ability of the people to solve their own problems. Believing also that "a drunken people were never the safe depositories of the power of self-government," Phillips contended that the true significance of the temperance enterprise lay in its attempt to put democratic institutions into the hands of a sober people.[12]

Phillips was often quoted as saying in the 1870s that the three great questions of the day were labor, temperance and woman. Throughout the long years of antislavery agitation, he had kept up his interest in women's rights. He frequently spoke at women's rights conventions, and feminist leaders like Elizabeth Cady Stanton and Susan B. Anthony considered him one of their most powerful allies. Phillips, for his part, appreciated the vigorous leadership which these ladies and others, like Lucy Stone, gave to the abolitionist movement, and he was happy to lend his name to their effort to get equal rights for women. By the time the Civil War broke out, the advocates of women's rights were able to point to a significant list of achieve-

ments. Although female suffrage still seemed a distant
goal, married women in several states had won the right
to own property, to use their own earnings, to make con-
tracts and, in the case of separation or divorce, to be
awarded partial control of their children.

Although Phillips rejoiced in these gains and continued to participate in the agitation for woman's suffrage,
he was always a little uneasy in the company of the intrepid
ladies who led the movement. He would not soon forget
the time he had gone to a convention in New York before
the war and discovered that most of his colleagues were
wearing bloomers. Phillips had thought that women could
be emancipated without taking off their corsets, but Elizabeth Cady Stanton disagreed. "We have but little to
hope," she said, from a generation of women "whose vital
organs are forced to perform their revolutions in one half
the space required by nature." [13] Rather than spoil the
unity of the occasion, Wendell had swallowed his em-
barrassment, and while the ladies flounced around in their
baggy pants he sat on the lecture platform with them and
tried to ignore the heckling from the crowd.[14] He believed in women's rights, but nothing would ever convince
him that the right to wear bloomers was as important as
the right of the slave to his freedom.

Any man who became involved with the feminists
was apt to find his zeal questioned, and Phillips was no
exception. At one meeting, when he denied that the
whole plight of American womanhood was the result of an
organized conspiracy by husbands, he had a run-in with
Lucretia Mott. Wendell suggested that the ladies themselves were sometimes to blame, and he pointed out that
they were frequently as difficult to convert to feminism as
men. This was too equivocal for Lucretia. "Where there
is oppression, there is an oppressor," she said sharply, and
she would thank Mr. Phillips to be as unrelenting to those
who held their wives as chattel as he was to slaveholders.[15]

In the long run, however, Phillips had far less trouble
with the stern little Quaker Lucretia Mott than he did

with Elizabeth Cady Stanton. In the twenty years that Wendell had known her before the war, Elizabeth Cady had borne seven children, done yeoman work for the radical abolitionists and been a prime mover in the women's rights movement. A plump, handsome woman with great physical vitality, she combined a benevolent, grandmotherly appearance with the tenacity of a bulldog. Wendell admired her but was somewhat intimidated by her dominating personality. He had a habit of saluting her in letters as "Dear Empress," and he apparently thought of her in these terms so exclusively that he sometimes could not remember her first name.[16]

The periodic rifts which Phillips had with Elizabeth Cady Stanton and her partner, Susan B. Anthony, a lean, severe-looking spinster from upstate New York, were due primarily to the fact that he was, for once, less radical than the company he kept. He believed that the feminists should concentrate on changing public prejudices in order to get legislation guaranteeing women the ballot and full equality before the law.[17] He did not believe that marriage was a proper subject for debate.

To Elizabeth Cady Stanton and Susan B. Anthony, however, the woman question was all-embracing, and there were no taboos. They had served their apprenticeship under Garrison and Phillips, and much of their radicalism as feminists was patterned after the radicalism of the abolitionists. Accustomed to the vagaries in diet and dress that helped characterize Garrison's followers, the ladies had been prepared to accept the idea that women could be emancipated in bloomers. By 1860 both Elizabeth and Susan had let down their petticoats and skirts again, but a new difficulty was brewing. At the meeting of the tenth national Woman's Rights Convention in New York City, Phillips was astounded to hear Mrs. Stanton read a series of resolutions providing for more liberal divorce laws. In an instant Wendell was on his feet to oppose the resolutions. The convention was not called, he said, to discuss marriage but those laws that discriminated against women. The resolutions were out of order, and he would see them voted down and stricken from the journals of the convention. Susan B. Anthony leaped to her friend's defense. They had come together to discuss woman's inequality, she said, and no better example could be found than the institution of marriage. "By it man gains all; woman loses all; tyrant law and lust reign supreme with him; meek submission and ready obedience alone befit her." The delegates, however, found Phillips more persuasive, and the resolutions were defeated. Mrs. Stanton could not understand the vehemence of Phillips' position. She was trying to provoke free discussion on an important subject, and the abolitionists had always prided themselves on their devotion to free discussion. Now Phillips was trying to stifle it, and he made it very clear that he would never participate in a public meeting where the subject was to be taken up. The idea that the marriage bond was too sacred even to be mentioned, Elizabeth Cady thought, was just another device to keep woman in her inferior position. "With all his excellence and nobility," she decided sadly, "Wendell Phillips is a man." [18]

Although Phillips' friendship for these two militant ladies survived the controversy over divorce, the tension between them continued. According to Massachusetts law, if a woman were separated or divorced from her husband, she automatically lost control of her children, he being the legal guardian. Here, thought Susan Anthony, was an unjust law which should not be obeyed. Once when a fugitive from a tyrannical and unfaithful husband came to her for help, Susan did not hesitate to hide the mother and children. The husband turned out to be an important member of the Massachusetts legislature, and when Phillips and Garrison heard what had happened they were furious. Susan was bringing disrepute on the abolitionists by running an underground railroad for discontented wives. Didn't Susan know she was breaking the law? "Trust me," she replied sweetly, "that as I ignore all law to help the slave, so will I ignore it all to protect an enslaved woman." [19]

To Phillips' great relief, Susan and Elizabeth Cady gave the antislavery effort their top priority during the war. As radical as Wendell himself, they opposed Lincoln in 1864 and sided with Phillips against discontinuing the American Anti-Slavery Society in 1865. At the close of the war, however, the friction began again. The women wanted to run a combined campaign for Negro and female suffrage, but Phillips insisted on keeping the questions separate. It was a matter of policy, he explained, not of principle, and he predicted that mixing the questions "would lose for the Negro far more than we should gain for the woman." [20] This was too much for the embattled feminists. Phillips could put "Sambo, Hans, Patrick and Yung Fung" ahead of the ladies if he wanted to, but they would never agree to it. Elizabeth Cady accused him of assuming that the entire Negro race was masculine, and Susan Anthony, borrowing from Wendell's rhetoric, said she would rather cut off one of her hands than postpone her labors for female suffrage.[21]

Unable to get the assistance they wanted from Phillips, Susan and Elizabeth took their supporters wherever they found them. In 1867 they stumped Kansas with George Francis Train, agitating for the passage of a state constitutional amendment which would give the vote to women. Train was a wealthy adventurer with an eccentric's eye for unpopular causes and a hard-headed businessman's interest in developing the West for the Union Pacific Railroad. A flamboyant figure on the lecture platform, resplendent in brass-buttoned coat and lavender kid gloves, he was a popular speaker and drew big crowds. He disliked the abolitionists and made as much capital as he could out of their alleged desertion of his two companions. One of his favorite devices was to recite a jingle which began

> The Garrisons, Phillipses, Greeleys
> and Beechers
> False prophets, false guides, false teachers
> and preachers
> Left Mrs. Stanton, Miss Anthony, Brown
> and Stone
> To fight the Kansas battle alone.[22]

Phillips did not find Train very funny, and he felt that his friends were doing their own and the antislavery cause great harm by getting involved with him. This feeling was intensified after 1868 when the two women began to use the columns of the *Revolution,* a paper originally subsidized by Train, to snipe at the proposed Fifteenth Amendment. Elizabeth wrote Phillips that, although there was nothing personal about her attacks, she saw, "with a vividness and intensity no words can express," the deplorable consequences of an amendment which would degrade one half of America's citizens by giving suffrage only to men.[23] In vain did Phillips try to argue that the Negro and woman questions were "not equally ripe," that they should support the amendment for the good that was in it, rather than oppose it for what was omitted.[24] Susan and Elizabeth had sailed too often under the "no compromise" banner of the abolitionists to be influenced by expedient considerations now.

Because Phillips was pouring all of his hope and energy into the agitation for the Fifteenth Amendment, he was hurt by this attack from those whom he had counted as friends. At the height of the controversy, he is said to have met Elizabeth Cady Stanton in Boston and refused to shake hands with her, saying "Mrs. Stanton is no friend of mine." [25] When the woman's rights advocates split, the radicals going with Stanton and Anthony in New York while the more conservative followed the lead of a Boston group centering around Lucy Stone and Julia

Howe, Phillips lent his influence to the Boston organization. He did not, however, let the controversy discourage
him, and he continued to lecture and write on behalf of
woman's suffrage. As the decade progressed, his memory
of the sharp encounters with Elizabeth and Susan grew
more mellow. Even though he felt that woman's suffrage
would come through state action rather than through the
constitutional amendment for which they clamored, he
could not help but admire their intransigency. No one
knew better than he the value of a noisy, incessant agitation. Shortly before his death, Phillips was instrumental
in seeing that a bequest of fifty thousand dollars was
divided equally between Lucy Stone and Elizabeth Cady
Stanton.

Phillips had been an active opponent of capital
punishment before the war, and he continued to work for
its abolition after the war. Curiously enough, he based
his opposition on pragmatic, more than on moral, grounds.
He felt that society had a right to take life whenever this
could be shown necessary for its own preservation. He
was well read in the history of the subject and could cite
statistics to show that crime had diminished in proportion
to the abandonment of the death penalty. He rejected
the notion that capital punishment was sanctioned by
Christianity or that society had any right to revenge or
punishment. Punishment, he said, must be left to God,
who alone could fathom a man's motives; society could
only enact penalties for its own benefit. Seeing that the
course of history in the nineteenth century was away from
barbarous punishments and that the death penalty was
no longer being applied to petty misdemeanors, Phillips
believed that capital punishment should be abolished and
prisons should be transformed from punishment centers to
places of moral reformation. The most modern aspect of
Phillips' thinking about this subject was his realization
that both the condemned man and the gallows were
products of the same unjust social order. "Who are the
men that are hung?" he asked. "Are they the rich, the

educated, the men that are cared for by society? No, that is not the class that supplies the harvest for the gallows. The harvest of the gallows is reaped from the poor, the ignorant, the friendless. . . . They have been left on the highways, vicious, drunken, neglected. Society cast them off. She never extended over them a single gentle care; but the first time this crop of human passion, the growth of which she never checked, manifests itself,—the first time that ill-regulated being puts forth his hand to do an act of violence, society puts forth her hand to his throat, and strangles him!" [26]

When Phillips went up to Beacon Hill to plead with legislators to remove the death penalty, he was scholarly, urbane and legalistic. His most fully developed argument on the subject, written in 1855, is a very solid and impressive piece of work. When he entered the public forum to appeal to public opinion, however, he forswore this sober approach and relied on the same techniques that he used when he tried to free a fugitive slave. Invariably, when Phillips protested a hanging it was one of the outcasts of society he was trying to befriend. The case of Edward Green is one of many examples. When Green was sentenced to death for murdering a cashier in the summer of 1864, Phillips, busy as he was in beating the drums for Fremont in the coming elections, went before the Governor's Council on Green's behalf. Waiving the whole question of the legitimacy of capital punishment, Phillips asked the council to consider the special circumstances of the case: Green's father had kept a grog shop; his mother had been a drunkard; there was a long history of insanity in his family, and Green himself was feeble-minded. "If you must uphold the gallows," Phillips said, "let not the Commonwealth select its victim from among the diseased, the imbecile, the neglected, the failures of our social system." [27] When the council refused to act, Phillips turned to the governor himself, declaring him responsible for the man's life, and, when Green was finally hanged, Phillips branded Governor Claflin a murderer and publicly avowed that he would never speak to him again. Phillips resorted to these methods to dramatize an issue which, he felt, was closely connected with every other cause he believed in—the attempt to achieve a social arrangement in which every member might be awarded equal justice.

Phillips did not let his concern for the Negro's welfare blind him to the plight of other minority groups. He had always admired the American Indian. When Little Raven, Buffalo Good and Stone Calf came to Boston representing three Indian tribes from the Great Plains, Phillips appeared on the lecture platform with them. "I love the Indian" he said, "because there is something in the soil and climate that made him, that is fated in the thousand years that are coming, to mould us, and I hope we shall always produce heroes as persistent as Philip and Moketavato, the Philip Sidney of the prairies." [28] Along with a few other humanitarians in the East, Phillips was tormented by the outrages which he knew were being inflicted on the Indians during the settlement of the West. He knew how they had been mercilessly exterminated by the forty-niners in California, how, under the pretence of making the country safe for civilization, frontiersmen had deceived them and slaughtered their women and children, how they had lost their lands to scheming government agents and were now being shunted off to cramped reservations. When the Indians fought back, his sympathy was naturally with them. "All Hail and Farewell to the Pacific Railroad," he wrote, when the operation of the line was threatened by Indian attacks. "The telegraph tells us that the Indians have begun to tear up the rails, to shoot passengers and conductors on this road. We see great good in this. At last the poor victim has found the vulnerable spot in his tyrant." [29] Whenever he could, Phillips lectured or wrote to agitate for a more civilized Indian policy. Shortly after the annihilation of Custer's army at Little Big Horn in the summer of 1876, when rumor had it that the army favored launching an attack to exterminate the last of the Indians not on reservations, Phillips addressed an open letter to General Sherman, reminding him "that the worst brutality which prurient malice ever falsely charged the Indian with is but weak imitation of what the white man has often inflicted on Indian men, women and children." [30]

Sometime in March 1881, the governor of Massachusetts received an anonymous letter protesting Phillips' activities on behalf of the Irish. "I think it is time that some one stopped him from agitating the Irish in this country," the writer said. "The Americans do not know the Irish yet they say if they fail in Ireland they will try to get this country for themselves. There are enough of them to conker the D——d—— Yankees. They say they will try for it so look out govinor thay are trecherous." [31]

That Phillips could champion the cause of the Irish is a tribute to his sincerity and consistency as a reformer. No group had been more violently opposed to the "Niggerology" of the abolitionists or to the utopian goals of the other New England reform movements.[32] Phillips had probably had more insults and rotten eggs thrown at him by Irishmen than by anyone else. Nevertheless, when the American Anti-Slavery Society was about to dissolve, Phillips told his colleagues that one of the jobs still ahead for them was to overcome the "intense prejudice" which existed against the Irish.[33]

Phillips sympathized with the Irish on several counts. As a minority group, held down socially and economically by popular prejudice, they appealed to his humanitarianism. As a people related by blood to a nation which sought to free itself from England's arbitrary rule, they appealed to his love of liberty. Finally, one of their great heroes, Daniel O'Connell, was also his hero. On the hundredth anniversary of the birth of O'Connell a great celebration was held in the Music Hall in Boston, and Phillips gave the principal address. In this oration, which was frequently repeated, Phillips praised O'Connell, not only for his patriotism and eloquence, but above all for his ability as an "agitator." He had not been a demagogue, a man who merely rode the storm of public opinion for selfish ends. He was, rather, an agitator, a creator of public opinion, a man who was not afraid to use his eloquence in harsh ways for noble ends. In eulogizing O'Connell, Phillips was also writing a tribute for himself, and he was able to champion the cause of the Irish out of the same independence of spirit that thirty-five years before had led Daniel O'Connell to refuse a gift for Ireland because it came from a slaveholder.[34]

Believing that the reforms he championed in America were part of a world movement toward freedom and equality, Phillips took an active interest in the revolutionary struggles going on elsewhere in the world. "Wherever a man rises for his natural rights," he said, "we have a right to sympathize with and aid him." [35] Consequently, he sided with Ireland against England, was quick to join Samuel Gridley Howe and raise funds for the Cretans struggling to break away from Turkey and rejoiced at the unification of Italy and the liberation of Rome. This was "the people's hour," he thought, "when all classes are equal, and all nations, all races, are brothers." The future lay with freedom, and all the petty tyrants of Europe and America were destined to topple from their thrones as the new day dawned.[36]

Despite his hatred of conservatism and his mocking criticism of opponents for wanting to ape the ways of their fathers, Phillips knew the value of traditional symbols for a new nation. Once in Chicago he had seen, dwarfed among great warehouses, the log cabin where the first settler had lived. He had wanted to cover it with glass and let it stand forever, "the cradle of the great city of the lakes." Others had not shared his sentiment and the ancestral cabin of Chicago had disappeared. Another time he had taken a man from the Arkansas frontier, a man who had never seen a building more than twenty-five years old, to see John Hancock's house on Beacon Street. His guest had been overcome with emotion as he sensed, for the first

time, the meaning of the American past. Phillips would
never forgive Boston for tearing down the Hancock house,
and in 1876, when the Old South Meeting House was in
danger of being replaced by a modern business establishment, he did everything he could to help raise the money
needed to save it. "You spend half a million for a schoolhouse," he said in an oration designed to rally support for
preserving the famous hall. "What school so eloquent to
educate citizens as these walls? Napoleon turned his
Simplon road aside to save a tree Caesar had once mentioned. Won't you turn a street or spare a quarter of an
acre to remind boys what sort of men their fathers were?
Think twice before you touch these walls. We are only
the world's trustees. The Old South no more belongs to
us than Luther's or Hampden's or Brutus's name does to
Germany, England or Rome. Each and all are held in trust
as torchlight guides and inspiration for any man struggling
for justice, and ready to die for the truth." [37]

It was natural that Phillips' earnest application to
such a multiplicity of causes should have created a tiresome
image in the minds of many people. Men like Lowell, who
had long ago decided that "eyes were given us to look
about us with sometimes and not to be always looking
forward," [38] or pessimists like Henry Adams, were bound
to find Phillips tedious. His overwhelming confidence in
the truth of his opinions on almost every subject could
easily be used against him. "When I argue the temperance
question," he said once, "I do not go down to the drunkard and ask, 'Do you want a prohibitory law?' I know what
is good for him a great deal better than he does." [39] Such
paternalistic moralizing was hard to take and helped to
create an image of Phillips as a self-righteous and self-appointed censor, determined to impose his own dogmatic
morality upon the rest of the world.

Those who knew Phillips more intimately would
never be able to recognize this image. They knew him as
a man whose solemn denunciations from the platform were
balanced by a serene and genial disposition, as a man

whose delightful private conversation made him one of
the most charming dinner guests. They knew him as a
man who could, on occasion, even smile at his own earnestness. "I only wish I were to be there with you," he wrote
to a friend about to visit Congress, "and we could growl
over their wickedness together." [40] Although Phillips was
celebrated for his wrathful assaults on people in high
places, his friends remembered him for his compassion
toward people in low places. They remembered his cooperating with and befriending a Boston labor leader who
was a confirmed alcoholic.[41] They knew that, despite his
reputation and busy schedule, Phillips was as accessible as
any man in the city, willing to listen and give help to anyone who called. His correspondence is proof of the fact
that he was constantly trying to help individual people.
A colored sculptress who wanted an introduction to New
York, a deserving lady who sought a place in the public
library, an old abolitionist looking for a consulship in
Italy—they all came to Essex Street for help.

Perhaps the best example to show that Phillips was
not a cold-hearted idealist in love with abstractions can be
found in something he did in 1867. In August of that year
Abby Folsom died. Of all the eccentrics who used to appear at the famous reform conventions in the 1840s, Abby
had been the most spectacular and the most troublesome.
Phillips could remember that her refusal to stop talking
had made a shambles of more than one meeting he had
attended. She had given the reform movement much un-
favorable publicity and had been the butt of a good deal
of ridicule among the reformers themselves. What most
people did not know was that Abby, for all her queer ways,
had been an angel of mercy. A poor working woman, she
took drunkards into her house and nursed them back to
health. On one occasion she found an insane pauper
woman whom the town was keeping in a half-open shed
filled with straw. Abby took the woman home, fed her,
massaged her stiffened limbs and cared for her as a human
being and not an animal. Abby's death went practically

unnoticed, but Phillips, then at the height of his campaign against Andrew Johnson, took time to eulogize her in the *Standard*. Abby Folsom, he said, "had virtues enough to atone a thousand times for all her faults and defects" and was "one of the most generous, unselfish and devoted women" he had ever known. It is significant that Phillips could stop hurling thunderbolts at famous men long enough to say a few sweet words over the grave of this obscure and cranky lady, who, in her own way, with all the infirmities that life had placed upon her, was trying to hearken to the admonition "Bear ye one another's burdens." [42]

21

Conclusion   1880–1884

In September 1880, four years before his own death, Phillips wrote to a friend regarding the disposition of Henry C. Wright's papers. Wright had intended to give his manuscripts to the Boston Public Library, and Phillips thought that his wishes should be followed with regard to diaries and other personal papers but not with correspondence. Wright was not justified, Phillips said, in exposing his correspondents' letters, because future readers would "inevitably *light* on some private matter (the only thing objectionable in the mass) and display it—so letters I think should be burned." [1] These remarks, which make a biographer despair, explain not only the numerous gaps in the record of his own correspondence but also his preoccupation, during his last years, with preserving the reputation of the antislavery reformers.

When Wendell said in a letter to Theodore Weld in 1876 that "most of us are dead—the circle is narrow," he was simply stating what was on the minds of most of the surviving abolitionists. [2] Beginning about 1870, every year had witnessed the passing of at least one good friend. Charles Sumner, Henry Wright, Samuel May, Charles Burleigh, George Thompson, Stephen Foster, Sarah Grimké, Edmund Quincy, William Nell, Charles Remond —one by one the old crusaders were toppling into their graves. Some of them, like Sumner, were men of towering fame; others were obscure, but, so far as he could, Phillips tried to make himself custodian for them all.

Sumner had died in March 1874, and Phillips had visited him in Washington only a few days before. His

friend clung to him, as if he knew there would not be
another meeting. It had been time for Sumner to take his
foot bath, but he insisted that Wendell stay with him
through the process, and this was how they spent their
last conversation.[3] We can only surmise what was said, but
surely the two aging idealists would have reminisced about
their common efforts against slavery, the victories they had
won and the struggle that Sumner was now waging to push
a civil rights bill through the Senate. When Sumner died
a few days later and was brought back to Boston for burial,
the whole Commonwealth paid him homage. He had become such a symbol for northern righteousness that few of
his old enemies dared raise their voices against him.
Wendell was gratified to observe how the memory of his
friend was honored, and at a memorial service he called
Sumner "The greatest man & the purest, that Massachusetts has lent to the National Councils during this generation or the last." [4]

One of the things that helped to mend the breach
between Phillips and Garrison was their being brought together so often at the graves of old friends. When Henry
Wright died in Rhode Island, they were asked to speak at
the itinerant reformer's funeral and to decide where he
should be buried. Despite the sadness of the occasion, it
must have amused Wendell to learn that Garrison solved
the problem by visiting two mediums and conversing directly with Wright's departed spirit.[5] When Garrison's
wife, Helen, died in 1876, and he was too bereaved even to
attend the funeral, Wendell came and delivered a simple,
eloquent tribute: "She is not dead—she has gone before;
but she has not gone away. She has not left us, she has
rejoined them. She has joined the old band that worked
life-long for the true and the good." [6]

The bond of common associations in moments such
as these, and the awareness that they were both approaching the end of life, caused the two old reformers to reconcile their differences. To be sure, they were no longer colleagues, and Garrison remained aloof and almost hostile

to Wendell's efforts as a labor reformer.[7] In the light of their common antislavery heritage, however, such disagreement seemed relatively unimportant. Receiving a copy of the memoir Garrison wrote in honor of his wife, Wendell found himself almost overcome with nostalgia. "It takes me back so many years," he wrote, "& brings freshly to memory so many dear names—the morning of our toilsome, triumphant days. As I sit reading it, Cambridgeport, Pine St. & that somewhat bleak South End house come back to me, where so many happy & well freighted hours passed—the plans—the hopes—the hurry—the crowds—the eagerness—the sorrows—the oddities mixed with the saints. Then our sleigh rides to near towns, Stoneham, Lynn, Neponset—to hold Sunday meetings, & the cold drive home cheered by Helen's laugh and unflagging spirits. Once, I think, I mistook a railway for the road & locked the runners fast into the rails—how she laughed at my blunder. Your recollections go straight to one's heart." [8]

More and more, Phillips came to believe that he and Garrison had a responsibility to set the historical record straight. He kept agitating to get a collection of his friend's editorials and speeches published, began to place files of the *Liberator* in libraries where they would be available to future generations, tried to get Weld to do a life of Garrison and apparently even thought of writing one himself. At the same time, he continued to participate whenever an occasion presented itself for bringing together the dwindling survivors of the old band. On October 21, 1878, he met with Garrison, Bronson Alcott and a few other friends to celebrate the forty-third anniversary of the Boston mob. In their last meeting of this kind together, Wendell had the satisfaction of hearing Garrison say he would willingly be mobbed again if it would help to bring a powerful ally like Phillips into the cause.[9]

When Garrison died in May 1879, Phillips was asked to deliver the principal funeral oration, and it was only natural that he should have attempted to do for his friend's

reputation what they both had been doing for the other
abolitionists for the past several years. "We do not come
here to weep," he said, "but to remember the grand lesson
of that career." There is no doubt that he felt that history
would show Garrison to have been one of the greatest men
of his age. "What American," he asked, "ever held his
hand so long and so powerfully on the helm of social, intellectual, and moral America?" His greatness, Phillips
believed, lay not only in his own nobility of character but
in his having launched a movement which had only three
parallels in history—"The age of Vane and Cromwell,
Luther's Reformation, and the establishment of Christianity." [10]

It is ironic that, in his zeal for justifying their dead
father, Wendell should have alienated Garrison's children.
In his address he emphasized that when Garrison founded
the *Liberator* every institution, and the hand of almost
every man in Boston, was against him. In making this
point, he did not even spare the First Church in Roxbury, where the funeral services were being held. "The
very pulpit where I stand," Phillips said, "saw this apostle
of liberty and justice sore beset, always in great need, and
often in deadly peril; yet it never gave him one word of
approval or sympathy." The younger Garrisons, who were
on friendly terms with the minister of the church, thought
that Phillips had gone too far. "It was mean and unnecessary," wrote William Lloyd Garrison, Jr., "a violation of
good taste that Father never would have approved." When
one of the sons asked Phillips to cut the offensive remarks
from the published version of his speech, he indignantly
refused. The Garrisons grudgingly gave in. "No one but
himself will suffer from his bad taste and manners," wrote
one of them. "I am none the less indignant at the spirit
of our father's eulogist. . . ." [11]

How old it must have made Wendell feel to hear himself criticized for having shown in his eulogy the same
militant partisanship which had characterized Garrison's
whole antislavery career. The younger generation had

never seemed so alien. The truth, he must have realized, was that the conservatism which had afflicted Garrison in his respectable old age had become endemic in his children. The man who had wanted to be "as harsh as truth and as uncompromising as justice," who had not wanted "to speak or write with moderation," was leaving his name to a generation that wanted to enjoy the benefits of his reputation but was more interested in propriety than truth. Small wonder that their father's old colleague had become an acute source of embarrassment.

As for himself, Wendell cared no more for the little etiquette of society now than he ever had. One of his favorite lecture subjects at this time was Sir Henry Vane, "The noblest human being who ever walked the streets" of Boston. A born aristocrat with wealth and privilege laid out before him, this great seventeenth-century Englishman had renounced the sensual ways of his youth when he was converted to Puritanism. As governor of the infant Massachusetts Bay Colony, Vane had defended Ann Hutchinson and, on his return to England, had served with Cromwell. After the Restoration, Vane was convicted of treason and dragged to the block on Tower Hill, where, with the serenity of a saint, he submitted to the headsman's axe. It is easy to see why Phillips was fascinated by Henry Vane. He, too, had been born a cavalier, had been converted, had defended a famous dissenter, served in a great revolution, been accused of treason and was regularly beheaded in the national press. Like Vane, who in his dying speech had insisted on justifying the cause for which he suffered and was three times interrupted by the blaring of trumpets and the beating of drums to keep him from being heard by the people massed around the scaffold, Phillips was pledged to champion the cause he believed in with his final breath.

Harry Vane, a gentleman and scholar willing to sacrifice himself for righteousness in politics, was very much on Phillips' mind when he made his famous invasion of Harvard Yard in the spring of 1881. For years he had been complaining that Harvard was the handmaiden to Boston conservatism. Every year, he said, the college was "taken up bodily, and put away on the vaults of the State Street banks" to be taken out again in the fall like a fresh gold piece, "glittering and exceedingly cold." He found it a source of great weakness in American education that the academic was so rarely found in the company of reformers, and he spoke of "that Alpine height of intellectual indifference, where Lowell and Agassiz sit." Despite Phillips' misgivings about his alma mater, he could not resist the lure of his fiftieth class reunion. He endorsed a copy of the invitation, which had come through the mail, and sent it along to Tom Appleton, urging him to join in "one more meeting for auld lang syne." There was another reason for Wendell's enthusiasm; Harvard, having studiously refused to acknowledge her celebrated graduate for half a century, had finally paid tribute to his eloquence by inviting Phillips to give the Phi Beta Kappa oration.[12]

To prepare himself, Wendell simply brushed up a speech he had been giving off and on for thirty years, entitled "The Scholar in a Republic." The substance of the oration was an apology for Phillips' whole career, the thesis being that the duty of the scholar in a republic was to lead in the agitation of the great social issues of the day. He defined an agitator as a man who stands "outside of organizations, with no bread to earn, no candidate to elect, no party to save, no object but truth—to tear a question open and riddle it with light." The agitator, recognizing that we live not under a government of law but "under a government of men and newspapers," tries to shape public opinion and is willing to trust the people. "Trust the people—the wise and the ignorant, the good and the bad —with the gravest questions, and in the end you educate the race. At the same time you secure, not perfect institutions, not necessarily good ones, but the best institutions possible while human nature is the basis and the only material to build with." In a country like America, where the people have the power, the agitator must work through peaceful means, but in other situations, when it is the only alternative to slavery, violence may be necessary. Phillips was revolted at the horrified reaction of Americans to the activities of the Russian terrorists. "Of all the cants that are canted in this canting world, though the cant of piety may be the worst, the cant of Americans bewailing Russian Nihilism is the most disgusting." The young Harvard graduate, then, enthusiastically claiming kinship with the anarchists of Europe, was to pick up his cudgel and follow after the likes of Harry Vane, Theodore Parker and Wendell Phillips.[13]

As usual, Phillips captivated his audience even though most of his listeners violently disagreed with him. "Yes," Longfellow said as he was leaving the hall, "it was marvelous and delightful, but preposterous from beginning to end." [14] Charles Eliot Norton reacted like the elderly gentleman from Brattle Street who sat behind him, "applauding heartily and muttering at the same time 'the damned old fool, the damned old fool.'" [15] When the speech was reported in the press, ministers all over the country immediately began writing angry refutations. "Well may Phillips dread the lash of Christian invective," wrote one Episcopalian clergyman in Philadelphia, "for the utterance of such incendiary, diabolical and atheistic doctrine as this. In honoring Nihilism he dishonors God; in preaching revolt against the constituted authority of any land or nation he arrays himself against the plainest precepts of our religion, which teaches us not to revile but honor our rulers, and to submit ourselves to the powers that be as sent of God." [16] All told, Phillips must have thought it about as satisfactory a fiftieth anniversary as any man had a right to expect.

The Phi Beta Kappa oration was Phillips' final public triumph, the last three years of his life being spent in relative quiet and obscurity. In the spring of 1882, when the city of Boston decided to extend Harrison Avenue, he found that his house on Essex Street was condemned. The area had changed a great deal since Wendell and Ann moved there forty years earlier. For them, however, it was still home, and he protested the fate that made him give it up. The prospect of leaving the house which she had never left except for occasional pilgrimages to the country in the summer was so frightening to Ann that she took to her bed and for eight weeks was unable to "stand alone or turn her head or her pillow without help." Wendell had to threaten to ask the Supreme Court for an injunction to prevent the razing of a building next door, and he finally brought Ann away in an ambulance to their new house on Common Street.[17]

To see his home impersonally seized and reduced to rubble was a shock from which Phillips never fully recovered. Friends wondered why he had clung to the place as long as he had. The location, unfashionable to begin with, had become cluttered with leather and dry-goods shops, so that the Phillips home was one of the few residences in the neighborhood. Still, Wendell and Ann had lived here for nearly half a century; it was their oasis, their escape from a world too often hostile to their dreams. There was a certain irony in the fact that the apostle of progress should be displaced by an expanding business community. A younger man might have been able to smile at such a fate, but Phillips had passed his seventieth year. He was weary; most of his friends were already in their graves, and he could not understand why the city he loved, for whose honor he had so often battled, could not be patient enough to let him die in his own house.

The razing of 26 Essex Street dramatized the extent to which Phillips found himself out of step with America on the threshold of the 1880s. The man who had given voice to the national conscience during the critical years surrounding the war had outlived his colleagues only to see the great causes grind slowly to a stop. Phillips had risked everything, including his friendship with Garrison, to secure the ballot for Negroes with the Fifteenth Amendment. Now, as the Democrats returned to power in the South, the political power of the Negroes was steadily declining. White supremacy was a stronger rallying cry than loyalty to the Constitution, and the Southern states were inaugurating the experiments in subterfuge, intimidation and violence which have successfully disenfranchised the Negro to this day. Realizing that constitutional amendments would be worthless unless the federal government was willing to support them, Phillips had agitated also for a vigorous reconstruction policy and for effective civil rights legislation. Now the troops were gone, and the Supreme Court would soon invalidate Sumner's final work, the Civil Rights Act of 1875. The freedman, bowed once again under the lash of his white master, would no longer be able to look to Washington for help. What was more, Phillips found the spectacle in the North equally as dismal. The reformers who attracted the most attention ignored the labor problem and the gross inequalities in the existing class structure and squandered their energy on peripheral problems like the tariff and civil service. Meanwhile, the professional politicians, who a decade earlier had been bidding for abolitionist support, now felt safe in deriding any kind of reformer as a harmless but unwholesome aberration.

In addition to his anxieties over the state of the nation, Phillips was finding that for the first time in his life he had to worry about money. When Sanborn wrote soliciting contributions for a monument to John Brown, Wendell was forced to refuse. "I have done so much within the last ten years for the associates of J.B., that I have no more left to do with." [18] It is impossible to know just how much money Phillips gave away. After his death a memorandum book was found with a partial listing of his gifts to casual petitioners and needy friends. These donations alone totalled about sixty-five thousand dollars, to which must be added the many thousands of dollars he contributed to antislavery and other charitable organizations.[19] This drain on his fortune, together with losses from unfortunate investments, left Phillips a relatively poor man by 1880. Few realized it, but the lecture trips which he continued to take were more a matter of necessity than a labor of love, and the generous fees (between two and three hundred dollars a lecture) which had formerly been used to subsidize reform causes were now used to defray household expenses. That he was financially self-sufficient had always been a strong point in Wendell's career as a reformer, and he was humiliated to be reduced in his old age to having to lecture for money. "I am not well enough to lecture," he complained to a friend, "and it is not right that I should." [20]

With the move to Common Street the last phase of Phillips' life began. Remarking to a friend that he had begun to act as his own executor, Phillips appeared less frequently on the lecture platform. He filled a suite of hotel rooms with his books and papers and, with the help of two assistants, assembled some twenty-five hundred volumes of antislavery literature, most of which he gave to the Library of Congress and the Boston Public Library.

Throughout his married life, humanitarianism and the welfare of his invalid wife had competed for Phillips' energy and devotion. In the semiretirement that marked his life after 1882, he found himself devoting more and more time to Ann. For months after they left their house, Ann was unable to leave her bed without help, and Wendell did little else than take care of her. Sometimes he would be so engrossed in attending to her that he would not leave the house for weeks at a time.

Wendell had outlived all his brothers and sisters, and, conscious of the fact that he was the sole survivor of a whole generation of Phillipses, he clung to the ancestral past. Always proud of his lineage, he had begun to take an almost antiquarian interest in relics and mementoes, like the silver seal which one of his mother's ancestors had brought from England in the seventeenth century and the "Wendell Glass" that had been part of the wedding furnishing for his grandmother Margaret Wendell in 1760. Once he sent his cousin Oliver Wendell Holmes, Sr., two tiles which he had taken years before "from the old Wendell House which stood where now stands the Parker

House." [21] On another occasion he gave a panel from the old Walley House to his nephew John C. Phillips, who lived in a mansion at Marlborough and Berkeley streets. Because John Phillips did not share his uncle's zeal for ancestral relics, the panel ended up in his kitchen, where it could be seen only by servants and delivery boys. The discovery of this slight to the family tradition prompted Wendell to send a sharp note. "When I offered you that fragment of your great grandfather's home I thought I was giving you something of special value to anyone who shared his blood—something such a one would be glad to see near him and now & then yield himself to the old time suggestions it could not but call up. It is more than a hundred years old—it saw my mother & father married—looked down on the faces of the dead & witnessed the joys and sorrows of two generations very dear to us. I treasured it very carefully for more than twenty-five years. Your house is superb. It is surrounded by the dwellings of rich men, full of rare things. No one of those roofs covers anything capable of stirring deeper thoughts or wakening more profound emotion than that ancient fragment of dead wood. Proud men there would give a thousand for such an inheritance—and thoughtful men would enshrine it. . . . I ask therefore that you will return it to me. Tell me where I can send for it, and I will not put you to any further trouble about it." [22]

Childlessness adds cruelly to the loneliness of old age. Wendell and Ann were fortunate in their last two years together to be able to lavish the affection, which ordinarily would have been directed at their grandchildren, on their grandnephew Wendell Phillips Blagden, born in 1882. Wendell was touched to know that his name would persist in one branch of the family. "You'll both have to be seventy years old," he wrote to his niece and nephew, "before you'll know how grateful such an affectionate remembrance is." [23] Although the Blagdens made their home in New York City, Wendell and Ann avidly followed the baby's progress with the help of letters and photographs. Phillips reported that he had not seen his wife "so charmed & thoroughly delighted for years" as when she first saw a picture of "her baby." "I thank you most sincerely for many happy hours in that weary room where she lies in patient helplessness. She never parts with the picture, keeps it near her & expatiates to everybody. I can't say that I blame her very much (!) or that she has not good cause. He *is* a noble fellow in spite of his name and I don't believe that even that will keep him down." [24] Less than two months before Phillips' death, the Blagdens brought his little namesake to Boston on a visit. This was a special event, and Wendell's only regret was that he could not do justice to the occasion. "If I were only Govr. (as I ought to be)," he wrote, "I'd order a 100 guns fired when W.P.B. lands at the station & have him met by my staff in blue & gold." [25]

No amount of fascination with his infant namesake could keep Phillips from realizing that his own life was running out. He had once thought of death as "a fearful change," he said, but now "all my world—all with a dozen exceptions is over there—I sometimes feel impatient to see the good and great again." [26] For the first time in his life, people noticed a melancholy side to Phillips' personality. Now that his energy was spent, the prospect of continued suffering tended to depress him and sap his trust in Providence. His Calvinism was more a fighting than a submissive faith. Not that these moments of doubt and bitterness ever became characteristic of him. He could still be defiant when the occasion demanded, as, for example, during the election of 1883 when the Boston *Herald,* despite Phillips' denials, continued to write that he had come out against Butler. On being asked about the discrepancy, Phillips drew himself up and said "When· it comes to a question of who lies, the Boston *Herald* or Wendell Phillips, I am content to leave it to the people of Boston without another word." [27]

On December 26, 1883, Phillips made his last public appearance at the unveiling of Harriet Martineau's statue in the Old South Meeting House. Endorsing this memorial to the English reformer as an illustration of how "in moral questions there are no nations," Phillips based his tribute on her ability always to see truth "one generation ahead." [28] A few weeks later Phillips met Lucy Stone walking down Winter Street in Boston and spoke to her about women's rights with his usual vigor. "Never lose courage," he counseled, "this question will surely triumph in the end." [29] Yet, at the same time, his preoccupation was with something else. When he was asked to participate in a suffragist meeting, he refused on the ground that he must be in constant attendance to his wife. Her condition was such that he could allow himself "but twenty minutes leisure during the day." This had become the last great cause. "I have lived to have every hope and desire merge itself and be lost," he confided to Susan B. Anthony, "in the one wish that I may outlive Ann." [30] A week later Wendell Phillips was dead. One of his last letters was written to help an acquaintance falsely imprisoned, so he thought, in a Worcester jail. His last words were "Poor Ann."

  • Wendell Phillips' funeral was a national event, but not everyone wore mourning. The remark of a well known Concord squire, that, while he wouldn't attend the funeral, he still "approved of it," may be taken as an example of the attitude of those who could not forgive Phillips' repeated attacks on personalities and property.[31] Even Garrison's sons were a little embarrassed to find themselves in charge of the arrangements. "I cannot look back upon my relations with Mr. Phillips with any satisfaction since my residence in N.Y. . . . The breach with Father, the attack on the *Nation,* his wild talk on economic problems, his political affiliations, destroyed every vestige of intellectual and moral sympathy between us." [32] Wendell Phillips Garrison spoke for a younger generation that had no taste for radicalism. The old reformers, however, mourned the passing of their leader. The sight of so many old antislavery faces at the funeral was like a resurrection. George

Burleigh, Frederick Douglass, Samuel Sewall, Theodore
Weld, H. I. Bowditch, Susan B. Anthony and others all
knew that the likes of Wendell Phillips could not soon be
seen again.

After the service in the Hollis Street church, the body
was taken to Faneuil Hall, where it lay in state as thousands of people, white and black, Irish and Yankee, young
and old, rich and poor, filed by to get one last look at the
man whose name had become identified with that historic
hall. From there, escorted by a military guard of Negro
soldiers, Wendell Phillips was conducted to the Old Granary Burial Yard, where he was buried in the family plot
near the graves of James Otis and Sam Adams.

In most of the obituaries and eulogies a sharp line
was drawn between Phillips' career before and after the
Civil War. "To be at war with society was his normal
state for half a century," wrote the *Tribune,* "and at the
end of the anti-slavery agitation he was hardly less hostile
to the established order than he had been when the 'broadcloth mob' was dragging Garrison through the streets with
a rope around his body." Attributing the eccentricity of
Phillips' later career to his being an apostle of "one great
idea" and to his having "a very imperfect comprehension
of matters outside his special line of thought," the *Tribune*
was willing to excuse his "wild agitation" on behalf of
labor and currency reform. "He has kept very queer company of late years and sustained very bad causes; but
nobody has ever doubted the purity of his intentions. His
errors will soon be forgotten; his thirty years' war for freedom will keep his memory green." [33] The editorial tells
us more about the *Tribune* and the rest of the North than
it does about Phillips. In praising him in this way the
paper was simply praising its own righteousness for opposing slavery before the war and defending the established
order after the war.

A generation later, President Theodore Roosevelt,

speaking both as historian and politician, tried to sum up what he thought about Wendell Phillips. Roosevelt, who liked to think of himself as a Lincoln figure, repeatedly put the radicals of his own time with the "wild-eyed fanatics" like Phillips who had harassed Lincoln. "These men," Roosevelt said, "have in them the spirit of which martyrs, and under certain circumstances heroic leaders of forlorn hopes are made." [34]

Our nation has traditionally been divided into those who believe that the literal translation of American ideals into practice is a forlorn hope and those who feel compelled to strive for the immediate achievement of these ideals. The former have always been in the saddle. The latter, the true American radicals, have always been in the minority, and they have usually been too individualistic to work together. At their worst they have been simple cranks and dangerous fanatics. At their best they have forced a conservative majority to hearken to the voice of the American conscience.

Wendell Phillips represented the spirit of American radicalism at its best. Nevertheless, history has not been kind to his reputation. Except for the early Northern writers who exulted over Phillips' abolitionism and forgot about the rest of his career, most American historians have believed, with Theodore Roosevelt, that his radicalism went too far. Everyone has agreed that Phillips was one of the most eloquent men of his time, but, as Roosevelt observed, that only made his sins "more heinous."

It is clear, however, that Phillips exerted profound influence on other members of the younger generation. Eugene Debs was a twenty-two-year-old grocery clerk when he first heard Phillips lecture before the lyceum in Terre Haute, but he never forgot the great orator's withering attacks on monopoly power and unjust labor practices. He said later that Phillips was "the most perfect aristocrat in the true sense" that he had ever seen, and, when he became the nation's top socialist and labor agitator, Debs often returned to Phillips' speeches for inspiration.[35] Out in Chicago, a brilliant young journalist by the name of Henry Demarest Lloyd pored over Phillips' speeches. "A silent conspiracy endeavors to hush up his last and greatest utterances," Lloyd wrote to a friend, "and I should like to see it defeated. Of all the anti-slavery leaders he alone saw that its work built but the vestibule of the real temple. I thought of him always as the greatest orator of his day, but his discovery of the continuity of the abolition movement and the labor movement mark him as the greatest social thinker." [36] In 1894, Lloyd published *Wealth Against Commonwealth,* the most powerful and influential attack on monopolistic power ever written in America.

As long as some men are willing to fight and sacrifice themselves to attain freedom and equality for all men, there will always be friends to honor the memory of Wendell Phillips.

Notes

BIBLIOGRAPHICAL NOTE

There is no collection of Phillips papers which even approaches completeness. The bulk of his letters are in the Boston Public Library, the Houghton Library, the Massachusetts Historical Society and the Library of Congress. The rest are scattered in libraries and historical societies throughout the country. Almost all of Phillips' letters refer to his career as a reformer. I have been able to find very few letters between him and the immediate members of his family and relatively few letters of any kind to him. The presumption is that most letters of this kind were destroyed by him or by his wife. A valuable collection of material relating to Phillips' personal life in his youth and old age was collected by Oswald Garrison Villard, and I have had the advantage of using this material.

I have used the following abbreviations in referring to manuscript sources:

O.G.V. MSS. Oswald Garrison Villard Manuscripts; G.P. William Lloyd Garrison Papers; B.P.L. Boston Public Library; H.L. Houghton Library, Harvard; M.H.S. Massachusetts Historical Society, Boston, Mass.; M.W.A. American Antiquarian Society, Worcester, Mass.; L.O.C. Library of Congress.

CHAPTER I

1. Bostonian Society Publications, vol. 8, 1911, pp. 123–136.
2. This early recollection, one of the very few that Phillips ever committed to paper, may be found in a footnote to Justin Winsor's *Memorial History of Boston* (Boston, 1881), vol. 3, p. 225.
3. Information about Phillips' early life is extremely scanty. In attempting to transmit the flavor of his boyhood I have relied heavily on the recollections of his chum and neighbor, Thomas Gold Appleton. The preceding three paragraphs are based on

descriptions in Appleton's essay "Old Boston" in *A Sheaf of Papers* (Boston, 1875), pp. 333–351.

4. *Ibid.*
5. John T. Prince, "Boston's Lanes and Alleys," *The Bostonian Society Publications*, vol. 7, 1910, pp. 9–33.
6. Appleton, "Old Boston," p. 343.
7. An excellent description of Election Day festivities can be found in Oliver Wendell Holmes, *The Writings of Oliver Wendell Holmes* (The Riverside Press, 1891), vol. 8, pp. 158–160.
8. The details of John Phillips' life can be found in *New England Historical and Geneological Register* (October 1866), pp. 297–299, "Memoir of John Phillips," *Boston Monthly Magazine* (November 1825), pp. 281–292, and James S. Loring, *The Hundred Boston Orators* (Boston, 1852), pp. 248–252.
9. Justin Winsor, *Memorial History of Boston*, vol. 3, p. 224.
10. Samuel Eliot Morison, *Harrison Gray Otis 1765–1848* (Boston, 1913), vol. 1, pp. 229–233.
11. Oliver Wendell Holmes, *Dr. Holmes' Boston*, Caroline Ticknor, ed. (Boston, 1915), p. 45.
12. Samuel Eliot Morison, *Harrison Gray Otis 1765–1848*, vol. 1, p. 233.
13. Carlos Martyn, *Wendell Phillips: The Agitator* (New York, 1890), p. 27.
14. James S. Loring, *The Hundred Boston Orators*, p. 249.
15. This letter is printed as an appendix to the "Memoir of John Phillips," *Boston Monthly Magazine* (November 1825), pp. 281–292.
16. Carlos Martyn, *Wendell Phillips: The Agitator*, p. 27.
17. *Ibid.*, p. 41.
18. John C. Winthrop, *Addresses and Speeches on Various Occasions* (Boston, 1879), pp. 491–492.
19. This letter is included in a bound volume of Phillips Latin School and Harvard exercises, O.G.V. MSS.
20. Phillips Theme Book, O.G.V. MSS.
21. *Ibid.*
22. *Ibid.*
23. Carlos Martyn, *Wendell Phillips: The Agitator*, p. 35.
24. Phillips' Theme Book, O.G.V. MSS.
25. For a vivid personal account of this celebrated incident see M. A. De Wolfe Howe, *The Articulate Sisters* (Harvard University Press, 1946), p. 73.
26. Caleb Snow, *History of Boston* (Boston, 1825), p. 380.
27. Carlos Martyn, *Wendell Phillips: The Agitator*, p. 37.
28. George Austin, *The Life and Times of Wendell Phillips* (Boston, 1884), p. 29.

CHAPTER II

1. Edgar Buckingham MS., Harvard Archives. Buckingham was secretary of the class of 1831.
2. This is stipulated in a little booklet entitled *Abstract of Laws and Regulations of the University in Cambridge for the Information of Parents and Guardians of Students accepted on Examination.*
3. Frederick Holland MS. Diary. Harvard Archives.
4. In drawing this description of the college routine I have relied on S. F. Smith, "Recollections By the Author of America," *Harvard Graduates Magazine,* vol. 2 (December 1893), pp. 161–170; Jacob Motte, *Charleston Goes to Harvard: The Diary of a Harvard Student of 1831* (Harvard University Press, 1941), and Andrew P. Peabody, *Harvard Reminiscences* (Boston, 1888), in addition to the sources already cited.
5. Andrew P. Peabody, *Harvard Reminiscences,* p. 200.
6. Frederick Holland MS.
7. Roscoe Conkling Bruce, "The College Career of Wendell Phillips," *Harvard Illustrated Magazine* (April 1901), p. 184.
8. Carlos Martyn, *Wendell Phillips: The Agitator* (New York, 1890), p. 28.
9. Thomas Hopkinson, *Autobiography and Letters* (privately printed, 1922), p. 13.
10. George Austin, *The Life and Times of Wendell Phillips* (Boston, 1884), p. 39. See also the entries for December 19, 1830, and March 13, 1831, in R. A. Coker's Manuscript Journal, Harvard Archives.
11. This is the testimony of James Freeman Clarke, *Autobiography, Diary and Correspondence* (Boston, 1891), p. 37. Phillips later recalled having spent an entire semester in Spanish class doing nothing but listening to the reminiscences of the instructor, "an old European Revolutionist." Lillie Buffum Chace Wyman, *American Chivalry* (Boston, 1913), p. 3.
12. George Austin, *The Life and Times of Wendell Phillips,* p. 35. The library records are in the Harvard Archives.
13. O.G.V. MSS.
14. *Ibid.*
15. *Ibid.*
16. *Ibid.*
17. MS. Harvard Archives.
18. Edgar Buckingham MS.
19. *Ibid.*
20. The MS. of Phillips' response to the question, "Will the Present

Proposed Parliamentary Reform endanger the Monarchical and Aristocratical Portion of the British Constitution?" is in The Harvard Archives.

21. John H. Morison to T. D. Weld n.d., Clements Library, Ann Arbor, Michigan.

CHAPTER III

1. *The Centennial History of the Harvard Law School 1817–1917* (Harvard Law School Association, 1918), p. 12.
2. Josiah Quincy, *Figures of the Past* (Boston, 1926), p. 159.
3. Edward L. Pierce, *Memoirs and Letters of Charles Sumner* (Boston, 1877), Vol. 1, p. 92.
4. M. A. De Wolfe Howe, *The Articulate Sisters* (Harvard University Press, 1946), p. 228.
5. *Boston Herald,* October 29, 1883.
6. Phillips Commonplace Book MS., p. 613, O.G.V. MSS.
7. *Ibid,* p. 601.
8. MS. Harvard Archives.
9. Thomas Hopkinson, *Autobiography and Letters* (privately printed, 1922), p. 49.
10. *Ibid.,* p. 60.
11. W. P. to John Farmer, April 2, 1836, New Hampshire Historical Society.
12. Phillips Commonplace Book MS., p. 603.
13. George Austin, *The Life and Times of Wendell Phillips* (Boston, 1884), p. 44.
14. Carlos Martyn, *Wendell Phillips: The Agitator* (New York, 1890), p. 78.
15. W. P. and F. J. Garrison, *William Lloyd Garrison, 1805–1879* (New York, 1885–9) vol. 1 and vol. 2 through p. 72.
16. Carlos Martyn, *Wendell Phillips: The Agitator,* p. 56.
17. *Liberator,* August 1, 1851.
18. W. P. and F. J. Garrison, *op. cit.,* vol. 2, p. 15.
19. *Report of the Boston Female Antislavery Society* (Boston, 1836), p. 50.
20. W. P. and F. J. Garrison, *op. cit.,* vol. 1, p. 225.
21. *National Antislavery Standard* (New York), May 25, 1867.
22. Deborah Weston to Anne Weston, January 22, 1836, Weston Papers, B.P.L.
23. Anne Weston to Deborah Weston, November 19, 1836, Weston Papers B.P.L.

24. Anne Weston to Deborah Weston, December 15, 1836, Weston Papers, B.P.L.
25. Lucia Weston to Deborah Weston, December 18, 1836, Weston Papers, B.P.L.
26. C. H. Parker to Amos Lawrence, December 14, 1836, Amos Lawrence Papers, M.H.S.
27. Anne Weston to Deborah Weston, October 17, 1837, Weston Papers, B.P.L.

CHAPTER IV

1. An elderly gentleman, the very flower of the New England aristocracy, wishing to rebuke his young nephew who had spoken admiringly of Garrison, "replied with perfect gentleness, sipping his wine, 'It may be as you say. I never saw him, but I always supposed him to be a man who ought to be hung." Thomas Wentworth Higginson, *Cheerful Yesterdays* (Boston, 1898), p. 125. A more famous example of the way the Boston aristocracy responded to anyone tainted with abolitionism is found in the snubbing which William Ellery Channing, one of the most renowned ministers in America, received from his own congregation after he spoke out against slavery. David P. Edgell, *William Ellery Channing: An Intellectual Portrait* (Boston, 1955), p. 41.
2. Phillips Commonplace Book MS., p. 471, O.G.V. MSS.
3. *Liberator*, January 28, 1837.
4. Oliver Johnson, *William Lloyd Garrison and His Times* (Boston, 1885), p. 218.
5. *Liberator*, Feb. 4, 1837.
6. The recollections of the Grimké sisters and the advertisements for escaped slaves together with a wealth of other documentary evidence of the barbarism of slavery would soon be available to Phillips in Theodore Dwight Weld's *Slavery As It Is: Testimony of a Thousand Witnesses* (New York, 1839).
7. *Liberator*, February 4, 1837.
8. Anne Weston to Deborah Weston, January 30, 1837, Weston Papers, B.P.L.
9. Phillips, *Speeches, Lectures and Letters*, second series (Boston, 1900), p. 5.
10. The most reliable treatment of Lovejoy is John Gill's *Tide Without Turning: Elijah P. Lovejoy and Freedom of the Press* (Boston, 1958).
11. Bliss Perry, *The Heart of Emerson's Journals* (Boston, 1926), p. 119.

12. *Boston Courier,* December 8, 1837.
13. The published materials regarding Phillips' role in this meeting are considerable. Both the Austin and Martyn biographies of Phillips cover the incident in detail. It is exhaustively reported in the *Liberator* for December 15, and is mentioned in greater or less detail in the other Boston papers. For a collection of reminiscences by people who were in the hall that day see W. P. Phillips, *The Freedom Speech of Wendell Phillips* (Boston, 1890).
14. *Liberator,* December 15, 1837.
15. *Ibid.*
16. Phillips, *Speeches, Lectures and Letters* (Boston, 1892), p. 3.
17. *Ibid.,* p. 9.
18. *Ibid.,* p. 10.
19. *Liberator,* December 15, 1837.
20. *National Anti-Slavery Standard* (New York), May 25, 1867.
21. W.P. to Elizabeth Davis, February 23, 1839, G.P. B.P.L.
22. *Liberator,* February 22, 1839.
23. Anne Weston to Deborah Weston, March 11, 1839, Weston Papers, B.P.L.
24. Oliver Johnson, *William Lloyd Garrison and His Times,* p. 23.
25. Hazel Catherine Wolf, *On Freedom's Altar: The Martyr Complex in the Abolition Movement* (Madison, Wisconsin, 1952), p. 53.
26. MS. dated August 26, 1867, May Papers B.P.L.
27. Henry C. Wright MS Diary, H.L.
28. Hazel Catherine Wolf, *On Freedoms Altar,* pp. 3, 25.
29. *Liberator,* April 19, 1839.
30. *Liberator,* June 21, 1839.
31. *Ibid.*

CHAPTER V

1. Anne Weston to Mary Weston, July 9, 1838, Weston Papers, B.P.L.
2. *Liberator,* June 14, 1839.
3. Quoted in Russel B. Nye, *William Lloyd Garrison and the Humanitarian Reformers* (Boston, 1955), p. 80.
4. George Thompson, *A Voice to the United States from the Metropolis of Scotland* (Edinburgh, 1836).
5. Louisa May Alcott, *Life, Letters, and Journals* (Boston, 1890), p. 28.
6. Phillips, "Letter to George Thompson," *Speeches, Lectures and Letters,* 2d series (Boston, 1900), pp. 13–19.

7. Ann Phillips to Maria Weston Chapman, July 30, 1839, Weston Papers, B.P.L.

8. Carlos Martyn, *Wendell Phillips: The Agitator* (New York, 1890), p. 127.

9. The early abolition movement has been written in such a way as to give all the credit to Garrison in Oliver Johnson's *William Lloyd Garrison and His Times* and in the ponderous four volume biography by Garrison's son: *William Lloyd Garrison* (New York, 1885–1889). The importance of the western movement is emphasized in William Birney's *James G. Birney and His Times* (New York, 1890), and in an important modern monograph by Gilbert Hobbs Barnes: *The Antislavery Impulse* (New York, 1933). The split between the two factions can be best traced in Barnes' essay, in Benjamin P. Thomas, *Theodore Weld, Crusader for Freedom* (Rutgers University Press, 1950), and in Russel B. Nye, *William Lloyd Garrison and the Humanitarian Reformers*, pp. 89–126.

10. William Birney, *James G. Birney*, p. 274.

11. Gilbert Hobbs Barnes, *The Antislavery Impulse*, p. 93.

12. Russel B. Nye, *William Lloyd Garrison and the Humanitarian Reformers*, p. 126.

13. *Liberator*, September 28, 1838.

14. *Liberator*, January 11, 1839.

15. *Liberator*, February 15, 1839.

16. *Liberator*, February 22, 1839.

17. Alma Lutz, *Created Equal: A Biography of Elizabeth Cady Stanton* (New York, 1940), p. 26.

18. *Ibid.*, p. 24.

19. *Ibid.*, p. 22.

20. Anna Davis Hallowell, *James and Lucretia Mott: Life and Letters* (Boston, 1884).

21. Frederick B. Tolles, *Slavery and the Woman Question: Lucretia Mott's Diary of Her Visit to Great Britain to attend the World's Antislavery Convention of 1840* (Friends Historical Society, 1952), p. 30.

22 Carlos Martyn, *Wendell Phillips: The Agitator*, p. 131.

23. Alma Lutz, *Created Equal: A Biography of Elizabeth Cady Stanton*, pp. 28, 29.

24. *Ibid.*, p. 28.

25. Frederick B. Tolles, *op. cit.*, pp. 19–43.

26. Benjamin R. Haydon, *Autobiography and Memoirs of Benjamin Robert Haydon*. 1786–1846 (New York, 1926), vol. 2, p. 685.

27. *Ibid.*, Vol. 1, p. VII.

28. Frederick B. Tolles, *op. cit.*, p. 42.

29. Benjamin R. Haydon, *op. cit.*, vol. 2, p. 684.

30. Michael Macdonogh, *The Life of Daniel O'Connell* (London, 1903), pp. VI, 136.
31. Phillips, *Speeches, Lectures and Letters,* second series (Boston, 1900), p. 408.
32. W.P. to Elizabeth Pease, November 19, 1840, G.P. B.P.L.
33. W.P. to William Lloyd Garrison, April 12, 1841, G.P. B.P.L.
34. *Ibid.*

CHAPTER VI

1. Ann Phillips to Richard Webb, July 27, 1841, G.P. B.P.L.
2. Ann Phillips to Elizabeth Pease, September 17, 1841, G.P. B.P.L.
3. *Ibid.*
4. *Ibid.*
5. W.P. to Elizabeth Pease, August 26, 1841, G.P. B.P.L.
6. Thomas Wentworth Higginson, *Wendell Phillips* (Boston, 1884), p. VIII. This essay was reprinted from the *Nation.*
7. Ann Phillips to Elizabeth Pease, July 3, 1841, G.P. B.P.L.
8. Ann Phillips to Elizabeth Pease, September 17, 1841, G.P. B.P.L.
9. Note by Ann Phillips attached to W.P.'s letter to Elizabeth Pease, April, 1844, G.P. B.P.L.
10. Note by Ann Phillips attached to W.P.'s letter to Elizabeth Pease, February 24, 1845, G.P. B.P.L.
11. Ann Phillips to Elizabeth Pease, January 31, 1846, G.P. B.P.L.
12. Ann Phillips to Helen Garrison, September 8, 1846, M.H.S.
13. *Ibid.*
14. W.P. to Elizabeth Pease, October, 1844, G.P. B.P.L.
15. Francis J. Garrison, *Ann Phillips, Wife of Wendell Phillips: A Memorial Sketch* (Boston, 1886), p. 17.
16. Edmund Quincy to Richard Webb, July 14, 1846, Quincy-Webb Correspondence, B.P.L.
17. Carlos Martyn, *Wendell Phillips: The Agitator* (New York, 1890), p. 86.
18. Walter C. Alvarez, *The Neuroses* (Philadelphia, 1951), p. 218.
19. Note by Ann Phillips attached to W.P.'s letter to Elizabeth Pease, February 24, 1845, G.P. B.P.L.
20. Edmund Quincy to Richard Webb, March 9, 1848 and January 13, 1853, Quincy Webb Correspondence, B.P.L.
21. W.P. to Elizabeth Pease, November 25, 1841, G.P. B.P.L.
22. Mary Caroline Crawford, *Romantic Days in Old Boston* (Boston, 1922), p. 175.
23. Lillie Buffum Chace Wyman, *American Chivalry* (Boston, 1913), p. 3.

24. Edmund Quincy to Richard Webb, March 26, 1843, Quincy Webb Correspondence, B.P.L.

25. W.P. to Edmund Quincy, September 11, 1841, Edmund Quincy Papers, M.H.S.

26. This information is found in the MS. of the minutes of The Executive Committee of The American Anti-Slavery Society, O.G.V. MSS.

27. *Liberator,* May 12, 1858.

28. Henry Wilson, *History of the Rise and Fall of the Slave Power in America* (Boston 1874–1877), vol. 1, p. 489.

29. *Ibid.,* p. 491.

30. *Liberator,* February 23, 1844.

31. Samuel J. May, *Some Recollections of Our Anti-Slavery Conflict* (Boston, 1869), pp. 62–66.

32. Vincent Yardley Bowditch, *The Life and Correspondence of Henry Ingersoll Bowditch* (Boston, 1902), Vol. 1, p. 138.

33. *Liberator,* January 13, 1843.

34. W.P. to Elizabeth Pease, October 1844, G.P. B.P.L.

35. Edmund Quincy to Richard Webb, March 9, 1848, Quincy-Webb Correspondence, B.P.L.

36. W.P. to Elizabeth Pease, February 24, 1845, G.P. B.P.L.

37. *Liberator,* August 13, 1841.

38. *Liberator,* July 9, 1841.

39. *Liberator,* February 18, 1842.

40. *Liberator,* March 4, 1842.

41. *Report to the Primary School Committee on the Abolition of Schools for Colored Children* (Boston, 1846), p. 7.

42. *Liberator,* August 28, 1846.

43. *Liberator,* September 11, 1846.

44. *Liberator,* December 24, 1847.

45. *Liberator,* February 11, 1848.

46. W.P. to Elizabeth Pease, December 30, 1842, O.G.V. MSS.

47. Newspaper clipping, Harvard Archives.

48. Phillips, *Speeches, Lectures and Letters,* second series (Boston, 1900), p. 20.

49. W.P. to Richard Allen, March 30, 1842, G.P. B.P.L.

50. W.P. to Richard Webb, June 29, 1842, G.P. B.P.L.

51. *Liberator,* November 24, 1843.

52. *Liberator,* August 24, 1849.

53. W.P. to Elizabeth Pease, July 29, 1849, G.P. B.P.L.

54. Quoted in the *Liberator,* August 31, 1849.

55. W.P. to Richard Webb, July 27, 1841, G.P. B.P.L.

56. William Birney, *James G. Birney and His Times* (New York, 1890), p. 275.

57. Samuel J. May, *Some Recollections of Our Anti-Slavery Conflict,* p. 329.

58. Oliver Johnson, *William Lloyd Garrison and His Times* (Boston, 1881), p. 72.
59. Edmund Quincy to Richard Webb, September 22, 1844, Quincy-Webb Correspondence, B.P.L.
60. Samuel J. May, *op. cit.,* pp. 335–345.
61. Stephen S. Foster, *The Brotherhood of Thieves or A True Picture of the American Church and Clergy* (New London, 1843).
62. *National Anti-Slavery Standard* (New York), May 25, 1867.
63. *Liberator,* May 16, 1845.
64. *National Anti-Slavery Standard,* May 25, 1867.
65. Charles A. Stoddard, *A Discourse Commemorative of the Reverend George Washington Blagden* (Boston, 1885).
66. George W. Blagden, *Remarks and a Discourse on Slavery* (Boston, 1854), p. 12.
67. *Liberator,* July 30, 1841.
68. In 1859 Phillips said in a speech, "They put the Atlantic betwixt them and a corrupt Church; they came three thousand miles away. The man who came over in the *Arbella,* whose name I bear, said, *'If you think me a minister by the calling they gave me in England, I will throw off the robe; for a corrupt church cannot make a true minister.'* " *Liberator,* May 27, 1859.

CHAPTER VII

1. *Liberator,* November 26, 1841, and June 7, 1844, Anne Weston to Caroline Weston, May 30, 1844, Weston Papers B.P.L.
2. *The Diary of John Quincy Adams* 1794–1845, Allan Nevins. ed. (New York, 1951), p. 511.
3. Quoted in the *Liberator,* November 5, 1841.
4. William Birney, *James G. Birney and His Times* (New York, 1890), p. 257.
5. *Liberator,* August 13, 1841.
6. Anne Weston to Deborah Weston (probably 1841), Weston Papers, Vol. 4, p. 28, B.P.L.
7. A. B. Hart, editor, *Commonwealth History of Massachusetts* (New York, 1927–1930), Vol. 4, p. 320.
8. Thomas Wentworth Higginson, *Contemporaries* (Boston, 1899), p. 271.
9. Edmund Quincy to Richard Webb, May 23, 1846, Quincy-Webb Correspondence, B.P.L.
10. W.P. and F. J. Garrison, *William Lloyd Garrison, 1805–1879* (New York, 1885–1889), Vol. 3, p. 22.
11. *Liberator,* January 1, 1847.
12. *Liberator,* January 16, 1847.

13. *Letters of James Russell Lowell* (New York, 1894), Vol. 1, p. 125.
14. W.P. to Elizabeth Pease, April 1, 1844, G.P. B.P.L.
15. W.P. to Mrs. Garrison, August 20, 1847, G.P. B.P.L.
16. W.P. to Elizabeth Pease, April 1, 1844, G.P. B.P.L.
17. W.P. to W. L. Garrison, January 6, 1846, G.P. B.P.L.
18. W.P. to Elizabeth Pease, October 22, 1849, G.P. B.P.L.
19. *Liberator,* June 30, 1848.
20. Walter M. Merrill, ed., *Behold Me Once More: The Confessions of James Holley Garrison* (Boston, 1954), p. 110.
21. Lillie Buffum Chace Wyman, "Reminiscences of Two Abolitionists," *New England Magazine* (January, 1903), pp. 536–550.
22. *Ibid.*
23. *Ibid.*
24. Quoted in the *Liberator,* June 27, 1845.
25. Thomas Wentworth Higginson, *Contemporaries* (Boston, 1899), p. 263.
26. W.P. to Elizabeth Pease, August 26, 1841, G.P. B.P.L.
27. W.P. to Richard Webb, May 25, 1845, G.P. B.P.L.
28. W.P. to Elizabeth Pease, June 29, 1842 and to Richard Webb, same date, G.P. B.P.L.
29. W.P. to Elizabeth Pease, April 1, 1844, G.P. B.P.L.
30. W.P. to Elizabeth Pease, August 29, 1847, G.P. B.P.L.
31. W.P. to Elizabeth Pease, March 21, 1845, G.P. B.P.L.
32. W.P. to Richard Webb, August 12, 1842, G.P. B.P.L.
33. W.P. to Richard Webb, June 29, 1842, G.P. B.P.L.
34. *Liberator,* April 13, 1847, April 13, 1849.
35. *Liberator,* April 29, 1847.
36. W.P. to Richard Webb, December 27, 1842, G.P. B.P.L.
37. *Liberator,* October 19, 1849.
38. W.P. to Richard Webb, May 30, 1845, G.P. B.P.L.
39. W.P. to Caroline Dall, May 3, 1849, M.H.S.
40. *Letters of James Russell Lowell,* op. cit., p. 158.
41. W.P. to Lowell, May 24, 1848, H.L.

CHAPTER VIII

1. W.P. MS. Harvard Archives.
2. W.P. to S.J. May, March 18, 1842, May Papers B.P.L.
3. *Liberator,* February 4, 1842.
4. *Liberator,* March 11, 1842.
5. *Liberator,* October 28 and November 18, 1842.
6. *Liberator,* November 11, 1842.

7. Quoted in the *Liberator*, November 4, 1842.
8. W.P. and F. J. Garrison, *William Lloyd Garrison, 1805–1879* (New York, 1885–1889), vol. 3, p. 88.
9. Ralph Volney Harlow, *Gerrit Smith, Philanthropist and Reformer* (New York, 1939), pp. 280–83.
10. Phillips, *The Constitution: A Pro-Slavery Document* (New York, 1844).
11. *Liberator*, June 14, 1844.
12. Wendell Phillips, *Can Abolitionists Vote or Take Office Under the United States Constitution* (New York, 1845), p. 26.
13. *Ibid.*, p. 24.
14. W.P. to Sumner, February 17, 1845, Sumner Papers B.P.L.
15. *Liberator*, May 19, 1843.
16. Lyceum Records MS., Concord Public Library.
17. *Liberator*, February 16, 1844.
18. Lyceum Records MS.
19. *Letters from Ralph Waldo Emerson to a Friend*, Charles E. Norton, ed. (Boston, 1899), p. 60.
20. *Liberator*, March 28, 1845.
21. W.P. to Sumner, February 17, 1845, Sumner Papers, H.L.
22. *Liberator*, December 31, 1841.
23. *Liberator*, January 7, 1842.
24. *Liberator*, June 9 and 23, 1843.
25. *Liberator*, July 7, 1843.
26. W.P. to Elizabeth Pease, April 1, 1844, G.P. B.P.L.
27. W.P. to Elizabeth Pease, October 1844, G.P. B.P.L.
28. *Liberator*, August 16, 1844.
29. W.P. to Elizabeth Pease, October 1844, G.P. B.P.L.
30. *Liberator*, May 16, 1845.
31. W.P. to Sumner, August 17, 1845, Sumner Papers B.P.L.
32. W.P. to Elizabeth Pease, January 25, 1846, G.P. B.P.L.
33. W.P. to Elizabeth Pease, January 31, 1846, G.P. B.P.L.
34. Edmund Quincy to Richard Webb, December 13, 1845, Quincy-Webb Correspondence, B.P.L., Forbes and Greene, *The Rich Men in Massachusetts* (Boston, 1851).
35. *Liberator*, June 5, 1846.
36. *Liberator*, December 4, 1846.
37. *Liberator*, January 8, 1847.
38. *Liberator*, February 4, 1848.
39. *Liberator*, January 14, 1848.
40. Samuel May to J. B. Estlin, September 5, 1848, and to Richard Webb, September 19, 1848, May Papers, B.P.L., *Liberator*, September 22 and October 6, 1848.
41. *Liberator*, February 2, 1849.
42. *Liberator*, May 30, 1849.

43. Robert C. Winthrop Jr., *A Memoir of Robert C. Winthrop*
    (Boston, 1897), p. 92.
44. *Liberator,* June 8, 1849.

CHAPTER IX

1. *Liberator,* June 9, 1848.
2. *Ibid.*
3. *Liberator,* May 16, 1845.
4. *Liberator,* June 4, 1847 and June 9, 1848.
5. In the description of the circumstances surrounding Webster's
   speech, I have relied chiefly on Allan Nevins, *Ordeal of the
   Union* (New York, 1947), vol. 1.
6. Bliss Perry, *The Heart of Emerson's Journals* (Boston, 1926), pp.
   45, 252–4. Ralph L. Rusk, *The Life of Ralph Waldo Emerson*
   (New York, 1949), p. 367.
7. *Liberator,* March 22, 1850.
8. *Liberator,* March 29, 1850.
9. Quoted in *Liberator,* May 17, 1850.
10. For a detailed description of the Rynders' riot see the eyewit-
    ness account of W. H. Furness, *Discourse on the Fiftieth Anni-
    versary of His Ordination* (Philadelphia, 1875), and *Liberator,*
    May 17, 30, 1850.
11. *Liberator,* May 24, August 23, 1850.
12. Quoted in Abel and Klingberg, *A Sidelight on Anglo American
    Relations 1839–1858* (Association for the Study of Negro Life
    and History, 1927), p. 244.
13. *Liberator,* July 26, 1850.
14. *Letters of James Russell Lowell* (New York, 1894), vol. 1, p. 151.
15. Wilbur H. Siebert, *The Underground Railroad in Massachusetts*
    (Worcester, 1936).
16. The *Liberator* for October 11, 1850 asked its readers to send
    bundles of clothes clearly marked "For Fugitives" to the news-
    paper office.
17. *Liberator,* October 18, 1850.
18. MS. Records of the Vigilance Committee, B.P.L.
19. Parker's role in freeing the Crafts is described in John Weiss,
    Life and Correspondence of Theodore Parker (New York, 1864),
    vol. 2, pp. 91–124.
20. *Liberator,* November 22, 1850.
21. Phillips, *Speeches, Lectures and Letters,* second series (Boston,
    1900), p. 38.
22. Quoted in *Liberator,* December 20, 1850.

23. Garrison to W.P., January, 1851, G.P. B.P.L.
24. W.P. to Richard Webb, March 18, 1851, G.P. B.P.L.
25. *Liberator,* January 31, 1851.
26. Charles Francis Adams, *Richard Henry Dana* (Boston, 1891), vol. 1, p. 182.
27. Siebert, *op. cit.,* p. 15.
28. *Liberator,* February 21, 1851.
29. *Ibid.*
30. *Ibid.*
31. W.P. to Elizabeth Pease, March 9, 1851, G.P. B.P.L.
32. *Ibid.*
33. *Ibid.*
34. *Liberator,* April 11, 1851.
35. Deborah Weston to Anne Weston, April 15, 1851, Weston Papers, B.P.L.
36. Phillips, *Speeches, Lectures and Letters* (Boston, 1892), p. 76.
37. Deborah Weston to Anne Weston, April 15, 1851, Weston Papers, B.P.L.

CHAPTER X

1. *Liberator,* June 6, 1851.
2. Phillips, *Speeches, Lectures and Letters,* first series (Boston, 1891), pp. 35–55.
3. Phillips, *Speeches, Lectures and Letters,* second series (Boston, 1900), pp. 40–69.
4. Phillips, *Speeches,* first series, p. 48.
5. *Ibid.,* pp. 55–72.
6. *Liberator,* June 6, 1851.
7. Edward L. Pierce, *Memoir and Letters of Charles Sumner* (Boston, 1877–1893), vol. 3, p. 264.
8. W.P. to Sumner, April 27, 1852, Sumner Papers, B.P.L.
9. *Liberator,* July 9, 1852.
10. W.P. to Helen Garrison, July 19, 1852, G.P. B.P.L.
11. W.P. to Helen Garrison, August 24, 1852, G.P. B.P.L.
12. *Ibid.*
13. W.P. to Sumner, September 3, 1852, Sumner Papers, H.L.
14. Edmund Quincy to Richard Webb, January 13, 1853, G.P. B.P.L.
15. Edmund Quincy to George Talbot, October 27, 1852, M.H.S.
16. *Liberator,* December 24, 1852. For further discussion of the reasons for the abolitionists' bitter resentment of Webster see James Freeman Clarke, *Anti-Slavery Days* (New York, 1883), pp. 135–145.

17. W.P. to Elizabeth Pease, November 21, 1852, G.P. B.P.L.
18. Phillips, *Speeches, Lectures and Letters,* first series, pp. 98–154.
19. W.P. to Sumner, March 7, 1853, Sumner Papers, H.L.
20. *Liberator,* March 4, 18, April 8, 1853.
21. *Liberator,* March 25, 1853.
22. W.P. to Edmund Quincy, March 22, 1853, M.H.S.
23. W.P. to Edmund Quincy, June 1853, M.H.S.
24. Phillips spelled out these ideas in a speech published in the *Liberator,* June 24, 1853.
25. *Liberator,* January 20, 1854.
26. *Liberator,* March 10, 17, 1854.
27. Austin Bearse, *Reminiscences of Fugitive-Slave Law Days in Boston* (Boston, 1880), p. 33.
28. My source for most of the personal details of Phillips' role in the Burns affair is a letter of Anne Weston who was staying at the Phillips house during the excitement. Anne Weston to "Dear Folks," May 30, 1854, Weston Papers, B.P.L.
29. Ann Phillips to Anne and Deborah Weston, May, 1854, Weston Papers, B.P.L.
30. Phillips, *Speeches, Lectures and Letters,* first series, p. 87.
31. *Ibid.,* p. 192.
32. Charles Francis Adams, *Richard Henry Dana* (Boston, 1891), vol. 1, p. 265.
33. *Ibid.,* p. 129.
34. *Liberator,* June 2, 1854.
35. Charles Francis Adams, *op. cit.,* p. 273.
36. MS. B.P.L.
37. A full report of this meeting containing the reported text of Phillips' speech is in the *Liberator,* June 2, 1854.
38. In a letter to Samuel May, Higginson, who explained how the attack was supposed to have worked, made it clear that Phillips had not been privy to it. Higginson to Samuel May Jr., October 11, 1855, Anthony Burns Papers, B.P.L.
39. O.G.V. MSS.
40. *Liberator,* June 9, 1854.
41. MS. B.P.L.
42. *Liberator,* June 9, 1854.
43. W.P. to Elizabeth Pease, August 7, 1854, G.P. B.P.L.
44. John Weiss, *Life and Correspondence of Theodore Parker* (New York, 1864), vol. 2, p. 140.
45. W.P. to Higginson, June 14, 1854, Anthony Burns Papers, B.P.L.
46. Austin Bearse, *op. cit.,* p. 37.
47. M. W. Chapman to E. P. Nichols, January 5, 1855, G.P. B.P.L., *Liberator,* January 5, 1855.

48. Henry Steele Commager, *Theodore Parker* (Boston, 1936), pp. 244–247.
49. *Liberator*, February 2, 1855.
50. Phillips, *Speeches, Lectures and Letters,* first series, pp. 154–213.
51. Charles Francis Adams, *op. cit.,* p. 343.
52. *Liberator*, April 20, 1855.
53. W.P. to Elizabeth Pease, August 7, 1854, G.P. B.P.L.

CHAPTER XI

1. *Liberator*, October 19, 1855. *Anti-Slavery Bugle* (Salem, Ohio), February 24, 1855.
2. *Liberator*, June 15, 1855.
3. *Ibid.*
4. *Ibid.*
5. *Liberator*, August 10, 1855.
6. W.P. to Mr. Hudson, November 24, 185?, Smith College Library.
7. O.G.V. MSS.
8. Frank P. Stearns, *Sketches from Concord and Appledore* (New York, 1895), p. 198.
9. *Journals of Ralph Waldo Emerson* (Boston, 1911), vol. 9, p. 455.
10. Thomas Wentworth Higginson recalled how Phillips once dismissed the members of a certain Boston club which had censured him as "men of no family." *Contemporaries* (New York, 1899), p. 271.
11. *Ibid.,* p. 268.
12. *Journals of Ralph Waldo Emerson,* vol. 6, p. 542.
13. James Monroe, *Oberlin Thursday Lectures, Addresses and Essays* (Oberlin, Ohio, 1897), p. 41.
14. *Liberator*, February 11, 1859.
15. *Liberator*, May 18, 1860.
16. *Liberator*, July 8, 1859.
17. *The Journal of Henry D. Thoreau* (Boston, 1949), vol. 7, p. 211.
18. Forbes and Greene, *The Rich Men of Massachusetts* (Boston, 1851), p. 49.
19. Quoted from the *Yonkers Examiner* on the *Liberator*, February 20, 1857.
20. See the Biographical Sketch at the beginning of the 1892 edition of Phillips, *Speeches, Lectures and Letters,* first series, p. vi.
21. David Macrae, *The Americans at Home* (New York, 1952), p. 481ff.

22. Quoted in the *Liberator,* April 5, 1861.
23. Robert C. Winthrop, Jr., *A Memoir of Robert C. Winthrop* (Boston, 1897), p. 185.
24. *Liberator,* July 13, 1855.
25. *Liberator,* July 8, 1859.
26. *Liberator,* August 14, 1857.
27. *Ibid.*
28. *Liberator,* February 2, 1855.
29. *National Anti-Slavery Standard,* January 18, 1868.
30. Quoted in the *Liberator,* May 16, 1845.
31. Quoted in the *Liberator,* December 28, 1860.
32. In a speech before the Pilgrim Society in Plymouth, December 21, 1855, *Speeches,* 1st series, p. 230.
33. *Liberator,* January 4, February 15, 1856.
34. *Liberator,* August 10, 1855.
35. MS. A.A. Lawrence Papers M.H.S.
36. For the description of Sumner's speech and the circumstances surrounding it, I have relied on Edward L. Pierce, *Memoirs and Letters of Charles Sumner* (Boston, 1877–93), vol. 3, pp. 425–525 and Allan Nevins, *Ordeal of the Union* (New York, 1947), vol. 2, pp. 437–446.
37. *Liberator,* May 30, 1856.
38. W.P. to Sumner, July 12, 1856, Sumner Papers H.L.
39. W.P. to Sumner, August 13, 1856, Sumner Papers H.L.
40. *Liberator,* October 31, 1856.
41. *Liberator,* July 4, 1856.
42. "I know he has battled with nature," Phillips said, "with the frost and the snow, with starvation, with want—all of that; but when has he battled as the unflinching advocate of an unpopular idea?" *Liberator,* August 1, 1856.
43. *Liberator,* February 20, 1857.
44. *Liberator,* August 1, 1856.
45. William G. Bean, *Party Transformation in Massachusetts* (Dissertation Harvard 1922), p. 344.
46. Edward L. Pierce *op. cit.,* pp. 509–513.
47. W.P. to Elizabeth Pease, November 9, 1856. O.G.V. MSS.
48. *Liberator,* January 30, 1857.
49. *Liberator,* May 22, 1857.
50. For an excellent biography of Banks see Fred H. Harrington, *Fighting Politician, Major General N.P. Banks* (Philadelphia, 1948).
51. *Liberator,* July 10, 1857.
52. *Liberator,* August 1, 1857.
53. *Liberator,* May 27, 1854.
54. *Liberator,* July 16, 1858, February 25, 1859.

CHAPTER XII

1. There is an account of this meeting in W.P. and F. J. Garrison, *William Lloyd Garrison 1805–1879* (New York, 1885–1889), vol. 3, p. 487.
2. Phillips recalled the incident in his lecture, "Harpers Ferry," *Speeches, Lectures and Letters,* first series (Boston, 1892), p. 274.
3. Henry Thoreau, *Walden and Other Essays* (Modern Library), p. 686.
4. Emerson, *The Complete Essays and Other Writings of Ralph Waldo Emerson* (Modern Library), p. 879.
5. Oswald Garrison Villard, *John Brown* (Boston, 1911), p. 273.
6. Shortly before he died Phillips told a friend that he "did not know that [Brown] intended to attack Harpers Ferry, but I knew he was working in such ways. I had seen him. I knew he was down there in that vicinity doing something about slavery, I did not know exactly what." Lillie Buffum Chace Wyman, *American Chivalry* (Boston, 1913). The evidence that Phillips was invited to the final meeting of Brown's band in Canada is found in the photostat of a letter in the O.G.V. MSS. which reads as follows:

> Monday
> Dear Brown
>   Say please to my friends that I have every wish to serve them, and would do so if it were possible. But the state of my health is such that I have been obliged to cancel some thirty western engagements and I don't feel able to continue work at present. I must therefore be excused.
>
>   Yrs truly
>   WENDELL PHILLIPS

Although the letter is undated, a note on the back, presumably by Villard, states that it refers "to the meeting of Brown's band just prior to the Harper's Ferry raid."
7. W.P. to Lysander Spooner, July 16, 1858, Spooner Papers, B.P.L.
8. *Liberator,* October 28, 1859.
9. Franklin B. Sanborn, *Recollections of Seventy Years* (Boston, 1909), vol. 1, pp. 191–2.
10. Villard, *op. cit.,* p. 516.
11. *Liberator,* October 28, November 25, 1859.
12. Phillips, *Speeches,* first series, pp. 263–289.
13. *Liberator,* December 9, 1859.
14. An eyewitness account of the funeral procession is printed in the New York *Daily Tribune,* December 12, 1859.

15. Phillips, *Speeches,* first series, pp. 289–94.
16. *Liberator,* December 23, 1859.
17. Boston *Evening Transcript,* March 10, 1884.
18. *Liberator,* December 16, 1859.
19. Annie Brown to unknown correspondent, probably Higginson, December 9, 1859, John Brown Papers, B.P.L. Allan Nevins, *Ordeal of the Union* (New York, 1947), vol. 2, p. 6.
20. Villard, *op. cit.,* pp. 508–510.
21. Phillips, *Speeches,* first series, p. 278.
22. Nevins, *op. cit.,* p. 8.
23. *Liberator,* December 2, 1859.
24. Villard, *op. cit.,* pp. 148–189.
25. Phillips, *Speeches, Lectures and Letters,* second series (Boston, 1900), p. 305.
26. *Ibid.,* p. 308.

CHAPTER XIII

1. *Liberator,* May 18, 1860.
2. Frederick W. Seward, *William H. Seward* (New York, 1891), Vol. 2, p. 263.
3. W.P. to Mrs. Wright, April 8, 1860, Smith College Library.
4. *Liberator,* June 8, 1860.
5. *Ibid.*
6. James G. Randall, *Lincoln The President: Springfield to Gettysburg* (New York, 1945), vol. 1, p. 190.
7. *Liberator,* June 22, July 13, 27, Aug. 24, 1860.
8. W.P. to Samuel May, July 18, 1860, G.P. B.P.L.
9. *Liberator,* November 16, 1860.
10. *Ibid.*
11. Phillips, *Speeches, Lectures and Letters,* second series (Boston, 1900), p. 423.
12. W.P. to Samuel May, December 27, 1860, G.P. B.P.L.
13. Phillips, *Speeches, Lectures and Letters,* second series, pp. 252–276.
14. *Liberator,* December 7, 1860.
15. *Liberator,* December 14, 1860.
16. *Liberator,* December 21, 1860.
17. *Liberator,* December 14, 1860.
18. Phillips, *Speeches, Lectures and Letters,* first series (Boston, 1892), p. 325.
19. *Liberator,* December 21, 1860. George W. Smalley, *Anglo-American Memories* (London, 1911), p. 91.
20. *Boston Daily Advertizer,* January 3, 1861.

21. *Boston Daily Advertiser,* January 21, 1861.
22. Smalley, *op. cit.,* p. 99.
23. *Liberator,* January 25, 1861. The speech is included in Phillips' *Speeches,* first series, pp. 343–371.
24. Samuel Gridley Howe to Sumner, January 20, 1861, H.L.
25. *Liberator,* February 1, 1861.
26. Smalley, *op. cit.,* p. 102.
27. Quoted in *Liberator,* February 8, 1861.
28. Quoted in *Liberator,* January 4, 1861.
29. *Liberator,* March 22, 1861.
30. Phillips, *Speeches,* first series, p. 369.
31. *Liberator,* April 5, 1861.
32. *Boston Daily Advertizer,* April 17, 1861, *Boston Post,* April 22, 1861.
33. Smalley, *op. cit.,* p. 96.
34. Phillips, *Speeches,* first series, pp. 396–415.

CHAPTER XIV

1. *Liberator,* August 2, 1861.
2. MS. Minutes of The Executive Committee of the American Anti-Slavery Society, O.G.V. MSS.
3. *Liberator,* July 12, 1861.
4. A. G. Riddle, *The Life of Benjamin F. Wade* (Cleveland, 1886), pp. 245–7. Carl Sandburg, *Abraham Lincoln: the War Years* (New York, 1939), vol. 4, p. 572.
5. *Ibid.,* pp. 389, 396.
6. W.P. to Sumner, July 15, 1861, Sumner Papers, H.L.
7. W.P. to Sumner, March 16, 1861, Sumner Papers, H.L.
8. *Liberator,* July 12, 1861.
9. Sarah Forbes Hughes, *Letters and Recollections of John Murray Forbes* (Boston, 1899), vol. 1, p. 227.
10. *Liberator,* August 9, 1861.
11. *Liberator,* August 30, 1861.
12. Harry T. Williams, *Lincoln and the Radicals* (Madison, 1941), p. 41.
13. Phillips, *Speeches, Lectures and Letters,* first series (Boston, 1892), pp. 468–495.
14. *Ibid.,* p. 435.
15. W.P. to Sumner, December 26, 1861, Sumner Papers, H.L.
16. *Liberator,* January 17, 1862.
17. Russel B. Nye, *William Lloyd Garrison and the Humanitarian Reformers* (Boston, 1955), p. 176.

18. *Liberator,* March 21, 1862.
19. Ann Phillips to Garrison, March 24, 1862, G.P. B.P.L.
20. *Liberator,* January 17, 1862.
21. Carlos Martyn, *Wendell Phillips: The Agitator* (New York, 1890), p. 325. *Liberator,* April 25, 1862.
22. *Liberator,* May 9, 1862.
23. Quoted in *Liberator,* January 2, 1862.
24. *Liberator,* March 24, 1862.
25. *Liberator,* April 11, 25, 1862.
26. *Liberator,* April 25, 1862.
27. W.P. to Sumner, June 29, 1862, Sumner Papers, H.L.
28. W.P. to Sumner, April 29, August 19, 1862, Sumner Papers B.P.L.
29. *Liberator,* August 8, 1862.
30. Quoted in *Liberator,* August 15, 1862.
31. *Liberator,* November 28, 1862.
32. *Boston Courier,* January 1, 1863, *Liberator,* February 6, 1863.
33. *Boston Evening Transcript,* January 1, 1913.
34. *Liberator,* January 9, 1863.

CHAPTER XV

1. Carl Sandburg, *Abraham Lincoln: the War Years* (New York, 1939), vol. 1, p. 144.
2. A full report of Phillips' meeting with Lincoln and the circumstances surrounding it is to be found in Moncure Conway, *Autobiography* (London, 1914), vol. 1, p. 377ff.
3. *Liberator,* February 13, 1863.
4. William Starr Myers, *General George Burton McClellan* (New York, 1934), p. 421.
5. Bell Wiley, *The Life of Billy Yank* (Indianapolis, 1951), p. 109.
6. Charles Francis Adams, *Richard Henry Dana* (Boston, 1891), vol. 2, p. 264.
7. *Liberator,* June 5, 1863.
8. *Liberator,* May 29, 1863.
9. *Private and Official Correspondence of General Benjamin F. Butler* (privately printed, 1917), vol. 2, p. 580.
10. Robert S. Holzman, *Stormy Ben Butler* (New York, 1954).
11. *Liberator,* July 10, 1863.
12. *Liberator,* February 13, 1863.
13. Phillips, *Speeches, Lectures and Letters,* first series (Boston, 1892), p. 559.
14. Edward L. Pierce, *Memoirs and Letters of Charles Sumner* (Boston, 1877–1893), vol. 4, p. 126.

15. Phillips, *Speeches,* first series, p. 560.
16. *Liberator,* July 24, 1863.
17. *Atlantic,* December, 1863, p. 793.
18. *Liberator,* July 10, 1863.
19. Phillips, *Speeches,* first series, p. 552.
20. *Liberator,* July 17, 1863.
21. *The Collected Works of Abraham Lincoln* (Rutgers University Press, 1953), vol. 7, p. 81.
22. *Private and Official Correspondence of General Benjamin F. Butler,* vol. 3, p. 204.
23. *Ibid.,* p. 206.
24. *Liberator,* January 1, 1864.
25. Quoted in *Liberator,* January 8, 1864.
26. Lincoln, *Works,* vol. 7, p. 281.
27. W.P. to George Julian, March 27, 1864, L.O.C.
28. *Liberator,* May 13, 1864.
29. W.P. and F. J. Garrison, *William Lloyd Garrison 1805–1879* (New York, 1885–1889), vol. 4, p. 110.
30. *Liberator,* June 3, 1864.
31. The best biography of Fremont is Allan Nevins, *Fremont Pathfinder of the West* (New York, 1955).
32. *Liberator,* July 8, 1864.
33. *National Anti-Slavery Standard,* July 16, 1864.
34. W.P. to E. C. Stanton, July 20, 1864, Huntington Library.
35. W.P. to E. C. Stanton, August 22, 1864, L.O.C.
36. Samuel T. Pickard, *Life and Letters of John Greenleaf Whittier* (Boston, 1894), vol. 2, p. 487.
37. This is carefully studied in Nevins, *Fremont,* ch. 33.
38. Robert C. Winthrop, Jr., *A Memoir of Robert C. Winthrop* (Boston, 1897), p. 246.
39. W.P. to Samuel May, September 19, 1864, May Papers B.P.L.
40. W.P. to E. C. Stanton, November 20, 1864, L.O.C.
41. *Private and Official Correspondence of General Benjamin F. Butler,* vol. 5, p. 400.
42. W.P. to Sumner, March 1, 1865, Sumner Papers H.L.
43. W.P. to E. C. Stanton, April 23, 1865, Huntington Library.
44. Phillips, *Speeches, Lectures and Letters,* second series (Boston, 1900), pp. 446–454.

CHAPTER XVI

1. *Liberator,* May 26, 1865.
2. *Liberator,* February 4, 1859.

3. "Who is Charles Sumner," Foster asked, "that this society should espouse his quarrel with slaveholders. . . . He has been striking hands with villains and aiding them in their works of iniquity." A little later during this meeting Garrison announced that the latest dispatch from Washington said that Sumner was dying. "The probability is, therefore," he went on sarcastically, "that we shall soon be delivered from what we have been told is the greatest obstacle to our cause." Foster retaliated by objecting to the uncharitable spirit of Garrison's remark. *Liberator*, June 6, 1856.
4. Abby Foster to W.P., June 24, 1859, M.W.A.
5. W.P. to Abby Foster, June 30, 1859, M.W.A.
6. *Liberator*, January 15, 1864.
7. *Liberator*, February 5, 1864.
8. Henry C. Badger to Garrison, February 13, 1864, G.P. B.P.L.
9. *Liberator*, May 20, 1864.
10. W.P. and F. J. Garrison, *William Lloyd Garrison 1805–1879* (New York, 1885–1889), vol. 4, p. 109.
11. Quoted from the original in F. W. Garrison to Oswald Garrison Villard, March 15, 1949, Villard Papers H.L.
12. Oliver Johnson to W.P., June 22, 1864, G.P. B.P.L.
13. *Liberator*, July 1, 8, 1864.
14. W.P. to W.P. Garrison, July 12, 1864, O.G.V. MSS.
15. W.P. to Edmund Quincy, September 2, 1864, M.H.S.
16. W.P. to Samuel May, September 19, 1864, May Papers, B.P.L.
17. Samuel May to W.P., September 20, 1864, May Papers, B.P.L.
18. W.P. to Samuel May, September 22, 1864, May Papers, B.P.L.
19. *Liberator*, October 28, 1864.
20. Samuel May to Richard Webb, January 2, 1865, May Papers, B.P.L.
21. *Liberator*, February 3, 1865.
22. W.P. and F. J. Garrison, *William Lloyd Garrison 1805–1879*, vol. 1, p. 100.
23. *Liberator*, February 10, 1865.
24. *Liberator*, April 14, 1865.
25. *National Anti-Slavery Standard*, May 20, 1865.
26. *Liberator*, February 10, 17, 1865.
27. *Liberator*, May 12, 1865.
28. *Liberator*, May 26, June 2, 1865.
29. *National Anti-Slavery Standard*, May 20, 1865.
30. W.P. to W. P. Garrison, November 29, 1865, O.G.V. MSS.
31. Garrison to W.P., January 1, 1866, typewritten copy, O.G.V. MSS.
32. Lillie Buffum Chace Wyman, *American Chivalry* (Boston, 1913), p. 12.

33. *N.A.S. Standard,* February 3, 1866. Samuel May to Richard Webb, February 9, 1866, May Papers, B.P.L.

34. *N.A.S. Standard,* May 7, July 20, August 10, 24, 1867, March 14, 1868, March 13, 1869. Garrison to Anne Weston, January 23, 1868, O.G.V. MSS. Samuel May to "Dear Cousin Saml.," March 26, 1868, May Papers B.P.L. F. W. Garrison to Oswald Garrison Villard, March 14, 1949, Villard Papers, H.L.

35. Wyman, *op. cit.,* p. 13.

CHAPTER XVII

1. MS. L.O.C.

2. W.P. to Salmon P. Chase, July 23, 1865, Historical Society of Pennsylvania.

3. *National Anti-Slavery Standard,* May 27, 1865.

4. "The *AMERICAN NATION* is successor to the abolitionists!" announced Garrison. "It has confessed the essential justice of the principles, the predictions and the demands of the Anti-Slavery Societies." *Liberator,* November 24, 1865.

5. *N.A.S. Standard,* June 24, 1865.

6. *N.A.S. Standard,* June 17, 1865.

7. *N.A.S. Standard,* January 20, 1866.

8. *N.A.S. Standard,* June 3, 1865.

9. Walter L. Fleming, *Documentary History of Reconstruction* (New York, 1950), vol. 1, pp. 243–315.

10. W.P. to Sumner, May 5, 1865, Sumner Papers H.L.

11. *N.A.S. Standard,* June 3, 1865.

12. *N.A.S. Standard,* June 24, 1865.

13. *N.A.S. Standard,* October 28, 1865.

14. *Private and Official Correspondence of General Benjamin F. Butler* (privately printed, 1917) vol. 5, p. 675.

15. W.P. to Sumner, December 25, 1865, Sumner Papers, H.L.

16. *Diary of Gideon Welles* (Boston, 1911), vol. 2, p. 383.

17. Quoted in *N.A.S. Standard,* March 3, 1866.

18. W.P. to Sumner, March 24, 1866, Sumner Papers H.L.

19. James A. Woodburn, *The Life of Thaddeus Stevens* (Indianapolis, 1913), p. 397.

20. *N.A.S. Standard,* May 19, 1866.

21. *N.A.S. Standard,* July 16, 1866.

22. *N.A.S. Standard,* August 4, 18, 25, 1866.

23. Quoted in *N.A.S. Standard,* September 15, 1866.

24. *N.A.S. Standard,* September 29, 1866.

25. *N.A.S. Standard,* November 3, 1866.

26. *Ibid.*
27. *N.A.S. Standard,* January 19, 1867.
28. Quoted in *N.A.S. Standard,* April 27, 1867.
29. *N.A.S. Standard,* March 2, April 6, 27, 1867. Carlos Martyn, *Wendell Phillips: The Agitator* (New York, 1890), p. 444.
30. *N.A.S. Standard,* April 27, 1867.
31. *Liberator,* February 5, 1864.
32. *N.A.S. Standard,* May 25, 1867.
33. *New York Daily Tribune,* May 24, 31, June 8, 1867.
34. *N.A.S. Standard,* June 8, 1867.
35. *N.A.S. Standard,* August 17, 24, 1867.
36. Quoted in *N.A.S. Standard,* September 21, 1867.
37. *N.A.S. Standard,* November 16, December 14, 1867, January 4, 1868.
38. *N.A.S. Standard,* March 7, 14, April 4, 1868.
39. *N.A.S. Standard,* May 23, 30, June 6, 1868.
40. *N.A.S. Standard,* June 20, August 15, 22, 1868.
41. *N.A.S. Standard,* August 29, September 26, 1868.
42. *N.A.S. Standard,* November 14, December 26, 1868.
43. *N.A.S. Standard,* February 20, 1869.
44. George S. Boutwell, *Reminiscences of Sixty Years* (New York, 1902), vol. 2, pp. 43–52.
45. *N.A.S. Standard,* April 24, December 11, 1869, January 29, 1870.
46. *N.A.S. Standard,* July 3, 17, September 25, 1869.
47. Carlos Martyn, *op. cit.,* p. 370.
48. *N.A.S. Standard,* April 16, 1870.

CHAPTER XVIII

1. *National Anti-Slavery Standard,* October 15, 1870.
2. For a modern view of Reconstruction which emphasizes these positive aspects, see John Hope Franklin, *From Slavery to Freedom* (New York, 1947), ch. 17.
3. *N. A. Standard,* May 20, 1871.
4. *New York Daily Tribune,* May 15, 1871.
5. *Boston Post* and *Boston Herald,* November 2, 1870.
6. Edward L. Pierce, *Memoir and Letters of Charles Sumner* (Boston, 1877–1893), vol. 4, pp. 463, 560.
7. *N. A. Standard,* March 18, 1871.
8. Pierce, *op. cit.,* vol. 4, p. 528.
9. Glyndon Van Deusen, *Horace Greeley: Nineteenth Century Crusader* (Philadelphia, 1953), p. 381.
10. *N. A. Standard,* April 15, 1871.

11. *N. A. Standard,* July, September, 1872.
12. *Nation,* April 9, 1868, *New York Daily Tribune,* August 17, 23, 27, 30, 1872.
13. *N. A. Standard,* July, September 1872.
14. Carlos Martyn, *Wendell Phillips: The Agitator* (New York, 1890), p. 369.
15. For my discussion of the crisis in Louisiana I have relied on: William B. Hesseltine, *Ulysses S. Grant, Politician* (New York, 1935), pp. 341–358; G. W. McGinty, *A History of Louisiana* (New York, 1949), pp. 210–224; H. Oscar Lestage, Jr., "The White League in Louisiana and its Participation in Reconstruction Riots," *Louisiana History Quarterly* (July, 1935), pp. 617–696.
16. Phillips' speech and the circumstances surrounding it are reported in full in Jesse H. Jones, *His Last Battle and One of His Greatest Victories Being The Speech of Wendell Phillips in Faneuil Hall on the Louisiana Difficulties, January 15, 1875* (Boston, 1897).
17. Pierce, *op. cit.,* vol. 4, p. 554.
18. W.P. to Salmon Chase, *Boston Herald,* August 13, 1879.
19. *Boston Herald,* August 13, 1879.
20. *New York Daily Tribune,* March 31, 1877.
21. Quoted in the *New York Herald Tribune,* March 28, 1877.
22. *Boston Post,* March 28, 1877, *Boston Daily Advertizer,* March 29, 1877, *New York Daily Tribune,* April 3, 1877.
23. *Nation,* April 5, 1877, p. 203.
24. T. W. Higginson, *Army Life in a Black Regiment* (Boston, 1900), p. 377.
25. *Boston Herald,* August 13, 1879.
26. Phillips, "The Outlook," *North American Review* (July, 1878), p. 97.
27. *Boston Herald,* August 13, 1879.
28. Phillips, "The Outlook," *North American Review* (July, 1878), p. 98.
29. *New York Daily Tribune,* June 25, 1879.
30. *The Commonwealth* (Boston), June 14, 1879.

CHAPTER XIX

1. *National Standard,* May 20, 1871.
2. Phillips, "The Outlook," *North American Review* (July, 1878), p. 115.
3. *Weekly American Workman* (Boston), February 11, 1871.

4. J. R. Commons, *Documentary History of American Industrial Society* (Cleveland, 1910), Vol. 9, p. 71.

5. Oscar Handlin, *Boston's Immigrants* (Cambridge, 1941), pp. 93–98, 120.

6. *Liberator,* February 2, 1844, September 4, 1846, *W. A. Workman,* June 11, 1870, J. R. Commons, *op. cit.,* vol. 8, p. 111.

7. Commons, *op. cit.,* vol. 7, pp. 219–22.

8. *Liberator,* June 8, 1860.

9. Phillips, *Speeches, Lectures and Letters,* Second Series (Boston, 1900), p. 163.

10. *National Anti-Slavery Standard,* May 19, 1866.

11. Massachusetts House Documents, 1866, Number 98.

12. *Ibid.*

13. Phillips, *Speeches,* second series, pp. 139–145.

14. *N. Standard,* November 5, 1870.

15. Massachusetts House Documents, 1866, Number 98.

16. Oscar Sherwin, *Prophet of Liberty: The Life and Times of Wendell Phillips* (New York, 1958), p. 602.

17. Entries in Phillips' Commonplace Book probably written sometime in the early 1840's make it clear that he had read the classical economists and agreed with them that legislative interference and strikes were "useless" as a means of improving the workers' economic conditions. MS. O.G.V. MSS., p. 205.

18. *W. A. Workman,* April 22, 1871.

19. *W. A. Workman,* April 15, 1871.

20. *N. Standard,* August 5, 1871.

21. *N. Standard,* September 9, 1871.

22. *N. Standard,* July 8, 1871.

23. Phillips, "The Outlook," *op. cit.,* p. 111.

24. *Ibid., N. Standard,* December 3, 1870.

25. Samuel May to Richard Webb, August 24, 1872, May Papers, B.P.L.

26. *W. A. Workman,* June 19, 1872, July 24, 1869.

27. *N. Standard,* September 17, 1870.

28. Commons, *op. cit.,* vol. 9, pp. 84–86.

29. *W. A. Workman,* July 2, 23, 1870.

30. Phillips, *Speeches,* First Series, pp. 145–152.

31. *N. Standard,* October 29, November 3, 1870.

32. *Nation,* August 25, 1870, p. 115.

33. Fanny G. Villard to Henry Villard, October 28, 1870, Villard Papers, H.L.

34. Edmund Quincy to Richard Webb, November 13, 1870, Quincy-Webb Correspondence, B.P.L.

35. *W. A. Workman,* November 19, December 3, 24, 1870, *Boston Daily Advertiser,* November 7, 1870, *N. Standard,* August, 1872.

36. Edmund Quincy to Richard Webb, November 13, 1870, Quincy-Webb Correspondence, B.P.L.
37. *W. A. Workman,* May 27, 1871.
38. *N. Standard,* October 14, 1871.
39. *W. A. Workman,* June 22, 1872, *Standard,* June 1872.
40. Benjamin F. Butler, *Butler's Book* (Boston, 1892), pp. 921–2.
41. Quoted in Robert S. Holzman, *Stormy Ben Butler* (New York, 1954), p. 177.
42. Lillie Buffum Chace Wyman, *American Chivalry* (Boston, 1913), p. 24. Writing about Butler in the *N. Standard,* Phillips said, with respect to the pronounced anti-temperance views of the General, "We must concentrate, and if we cannot get saints, just put up with sinners who will do our bidding." October 7, 1871.
43. *N. Standard,* November 4, 1871.
44. *The Word* (Princeton, Massachusetts), February 1884.
45. *N. Standard,* October 21, 1871.
46. Solon J. Buck, *The Agrarian Crusade* (Yale University Press, 1920).
47. Phillips, *Who Shall Rule Us? Money or The People?* (Boston, 1878).
48. Scrapbook of Clippings Relating to Phillips, pp. 75–85, H.L. *Nation,* October 14, 1875.
49. Phillips, *Who Shall Rule Us?*
50. *Nation,* October 3, 1878.
51. Phillips, *Who Shall Rule Us?*
52. *Ibid.*
53. Edmund Quincy to Richard Webb, November 13, 1870, Quincy-Webb Correspondence, B.P.L.
54. Vernon Parrington, *Main Currents in American Thought* (New York, 1927), vol. 3, p. 147.
55. Phillips, *Who Shall Rule Us?*

CHAPTER XX

1. *Letters of Henry Adams, 1858–1891,* W. C. Ford, editor, p. 162.
2. Edmund Quincy to Richard Webb, September 13, 1869, Quincy-Webb correspondence, B.P.L.
3. *New York Daily Tribune,* June 1, 1826.
4. *National Anti-Slavery Standard,* November 27, 1869.
5. For a general discussion of these sessions see Mary E. Sargent, *Sketches and Reminiscences of the Radical Club of Chestnut Street, Boston* (Boston, 1880).

6. E. L. Taylor, *Wendell Phillips* (Columbus, 1909), p. 15.
7. Phillips, *Speeches, Lectures and Letters,* second series (Boston, 1900), pp. 276–294.
8. "The Maine Liquor Law," *ibid.,* pp. 178–194.
9. W.P. to O. W. Holmes, December 18, 1878(?), Oliver Wendell Holmes Papers, L.O.C.
10. *Proceedings of the Massachusetts State Temperance Convention* (Boston, 1866), p. 5.
11. In 1880 he crossed swords with Cyrus Bartol, one of Boston's most prominent Unitarian ministers, over this issue, *Boston Evening Transcript,* May 13, 1880. The next year he reprimanded the Chancellor of New York University, "Review of Dr. Crosby's 'Calm View of Temperance,'" *Speeches,* second series, pp. 195–219.
12. *Speeches,* second series, p. 180.
13. *Liberator,* November 7, 1851.
14. *Liberator,* September 16, 1853.
15. *New York Daily Tribune,* October 25, 1860.
16. The latent tension between Phillips and Mrs. Stanton is suggested in several undated letters from Phillips in the Elizabeth Cady Stanton Papers, L.O.C.
17. *Speeches,* second series, pp. 110–139.
18. Alma Lutz, *Elizabeth Cady Stanton 1815–1902* (New York, 1940), Chapter 11.
19. Alma Lutz, *Susan B. Anthony, Rebel, Crusader, Humanitarian* •(Boston, 1959), p. 90.
20. Alma Lutz, *Elizabeth Cady Stanton,* p. 132.
21. *Ibid.,* p. 167.
22. *Ibid.,* p. 134.
23. E. C. Stanton to W.P., June 20, 1869, L.O.C.
24. *N. Standard,* July 3, 1869.
25. Lutz, *op. cit.,* p. 179.
26. *Speeches,* second series, p. 97.
27. *Liberator,* July 8, 1864.
28. *N. Standard,* June 17, 1871.
29. *N. Standard,* June 12, 1869.
30. Clipping dated July 17, 1876, Scrapbook, H.L.
31. MS. dated March 8, 1881, M.H.S.
32. Oscar Handlin, *Boston's Immigrants* (Cambridge, 1941), pp. 131–136.
33. *N. Standard,* May 22, 1869.
34. *Speeches,* second series, pp. 384–421.
35. *N. Standard,* May 8, 1869.
36. W.P. to Gerrit Smith, January 9, 1867, Syracuse University Library. *N. Standard,* November 12, 1870.

37. *Speeches*, Second Series, pp. 231–244.
38. *Letters of James Russell Lowell* (New York, 1894), Vol. 1, p. 173.
39. *Speeches*, second series, p. 121.
40. W.P. to George W. Sterling, December, 1868, H.L.
41. *The Index* (Boston), February 21, 1844.
42. *National Anti-Slavery Standard*, August 31, 1867.

CHAPTER XXI

1. W.P. to F. J. Garrison, September 15, 1880, L.O.C.
2. W.P. to T. D. Weld, August 1876, L.O.C.
3. Edward L. Pierce, *Memoir and Letters of Charles Sumner* (Boston, 1877–1893), p. 591.
4. O.G.V. MSS.
5. W.P. and F. J. Garrison, *William Lloyd Garrison 1805–1879* (New York, 1885–1889), vol. 4, p. 253.
6. Phillips, *Speeches, Lectures and Letters,* second series (Boston, 1900), p. 457.
7. When Phillips sent Garrison a "tract on the money question," Garrison replied by saying that he considered the whole issue to be "a very subordinate question." He also was in vigorous disagreement with Phillips over Butler. Garrison to W.P., October 30, 1878, G.P. B.P.L.
8. W.P. to Garrison, May 6, 1876, O.G.V. MSS.
9. F. J. Garrison to Fanny G. Villard, October 27, 1878, copy in O.G.V. MSS.
10. *Speeches*, Second Series, pp. 459–473.
11. R. F. Walcutt to Samuel May, June 4, 1879, May Papers B.P.L. W. L. Garrison, Jr. to W. P. Garrison, June 2, 5, 1879, copies in O.G.V. MSS.
12. *Liberator*, August 14, 1857. *National Standard*, April 22, 1871. MS. Harvard Archives.
13. *Speeches*, second series, pp. 330–365.
14. *Letters of Charles Eliot Norton* (Boston, 1913), vol. 2, p. 126.
15. Walter P. Eaton to Oswald Garrison Villard, March 8, 1947, O.G.V. MSS.
16. *New York Daily Tribune,* August 31, 1881.
17. W.P. to Abby Foster, June 7, 1882, M.W.A.
18. W.P. to F. Sanborn, September 24, 1872(?), Concord Library.
19. Carlos Martyn, *Wendell Phillips: The Agitator* (New York, 1890), p. 510.
20. Lillie Buffum Chace Wyman, *American Chivalry* (Boston, 1913). After his death Phillips' estate was appraised at a little more

than $8,ooo, half in real and half in personal property. His losses from bad investments were apparently very large, for after his death he was found to have paid $90 a share for 1,000 shares of Safety Switch stock which later dropped to $10 a share. F. J. Garrison to Fanny G. Villard, March 30, 1885, copy in O.G.V. MSS.

21. W.P. to O. W. Holmes, December 25, 1878(?), L.O.C.
22. W.P. to John Phillips, April 3, 1879, Original in possession of William C. Phillips.
23. W.P. to Sam Blagden, September 24, 1882, O.G.V. MSS.
24. W.P. to Julia Blagden, January, 1883, O.G.V. MSS.
25. W.P. to Sam Blagden, November, 1883, O.G.V. MSS.
26. W.P. to Miss Thayer, November 29, 1880, L.O.C.
27. *Daily Evening Traveller* (Boston), February 4, 1884.
28. *Speeches,* second series, pp. 473–6.
29. Phillips' Scrapbook, B.P.L.
30. Wyman, *op. cit.*
31. Moncure Company, *Autobiography* (London, 1914), Vol. 1, p. 145.
32. W. P. Garrison to Fanny G. Villard, February 3, 1884, copy in O.G.V. MSS.
33. *New York Daily Tribune,* February 4, 1884.
34. Theodore Roosevelt, *Letters,* Elting Morison, ed. (Harvard, 1951–1954), vol. 7, p. 785.
35. Eugene Debs, *Writing and Speeches,* Introduction by A. Schlesinger, Jr. (New York, 1948), p. vi.
36. Carl Lloyd, *Henry Demarest Lloyd* (New York, 1912), vol. 1, p. 121.

Index

Adams, Charles Francis, 133, 148, 320
Adams, Charles Francis, Jr., 367
Adams, Henry, 367, 383
Adams, John, 1, 15
Adams, John Quincy, 8, 45, 46, 50, 100, 132, 327
Adams, Samuel, 15, 16, 50, 142, 179, 399
Alcott, Bronson, 112, 288, 388
Alcott, Louisa May, 61, 369
American Anti-Slavery Society, 63, 65, 68, 82–83, 111, 113, 143, 240–241, 276, 278, 279, 281, 282, 287–290, 293, 301, 314, 376, 381
American Revolution, 1, 14, 15, 22, 50, 52, 66, 182, 197, 234, 252
"American System of Finance," 361
American Workman, 352, 354
Amnesty Act, 322
Andrew, John, 211, 213, 223, 231, 233, 236, 329
Anthony, Susan B., 372, 374–378, 398, 399
Anti-Slavery Standard, see National Anti-Slavery Standard
Appleton, Nathan, 229–230
Appleton, Thomas, 8, 11, 20, 391, 402
Austin, James, 48–49, 50, 51

Banks, Nathaniel, 187, 205–206, 261, 284
Bartol, Cyrus, 369, 430
Bastardy Act, 84
Bearse, Austin, 171–172, 184
Beecher, Henry Ward, 146, 192, 206, 212
Beecher, Lyman, 11, 21, 55
Belknap, William, 329
Bell, John, 221, 226, 230, 233
Benton, Thomas Hart, 161
Birney, James G., 67, 68, 101
"Black Laws," 295–296
Blagden, Rev. George Washington, 76, 97–98, 180
Blagden, Miriam Phillips, 97
Blagden, Wendell Phillips, 396–397

Blaine, James G., 329
Boston *Courier*, 2, 47, 199, 255
Boston *Daily Advertizer*, 89, 252, 332, 355
Boston Female Anti-Slavery Society, 33, 34
Boston *Herald*, 397
Boston *Pilot*, 93
Boston *Post*, 53, 110, 236, 320, 332
Boston Public Latin School, 11–13, 14, 15, 17, 20, 27, 357
Boston School Committee, 87–88
Boston *Traveller*, 233
Boutwell, George S., 162, 313
Bowditch, Henry I., 85, 88, 117, 176, 399
Bradburn, George, 68, 70, 129
Bradford, William, 56
Breckinridge, John C., 221, 233
Brooks, Preston A., 201
Brown, Irael, How, 147
Brown, John, 108, 208–218, 219, 223, 226, 228, 229, 233, 234, 248, 255, 347, 394, 419
Brown, Mrs. John, 213, 214, 215
Buchanan, James, 202, 204, 206–207
Bunker Hill, 14, 15, 38, 66, 127, 128, 204, 212, 335
Burke, Edmund, 24, 91, 121
Burleigh, Charles, 101, 108, 115, 129, 145, 315, 386, 398–399
Burns, Anthony, 172–184, 189, 211, 218, 333
Butler, Andrew P., 200–201
Butler, Benjamin F., 260–262, 265, 266, 269, 274, 297–298, 358–359, 364, 365, 397

Cady, Elizabeth, *see* Stanton, Elizabeth Cady
Calhoun, John C., 139–140, 166, 318.
Calvinism, 10, 13, 58, 95, 100, 105, 121, 122, 125, 218, 224, 244, 369, 397
Capital Punishment, 2, 111, 114, 262, 367, 370, 378–380
Chandler, Zachariah, 242, 247, 273

Channing, William Ellery, 10, 47, 48, 224
Channing, W. H., 244
Chapman, Maria Weston, 33, 35, 36, 39, 40, 48, 60, 62, 77, 82, 83, 85, 94, 102, 128, 230, 277, 287
Chapman, Henry, 33, 36, 39, 40, 82
Chase, Salmon P., 190–191, 271, 310
Child, Lydia Maria, 127
Chinese immigration, 352–353, 367, 370
Choate, Rufus, 161
Choate, Rufus, Jr., 228
Civil Rights Act of 1875, 387, 394
Clay, Henry, 97, 139, 140, 141, 151, 153, 166, 273
Colver, Rev. Nathaniel, 111–112
Committee of Fifteen, 298, 300
Committee on Foreign Relations, 320, 321
Communism, 347, 348
Compromise of 1850, 147, 242, 266
Confederacy, 229, 238, 245, 269, 274, 307
Congress, 45, 61, 120, 130, 136, 137, 138, 139, 168, 171, 297–298, 299, 300, 301, 302, 304, 305, 308, 309, 310, 311, 312, 313, 318, 322, 326, 327, 328, 330, 332, 351, 364, 366
Constitution, 2, 58, 114, 116, 117, 118, 119, 120, 126, 132, 133, 134, 136, 149, 168, 169, 170, 188, 205, 207, 209, 222, 232, 240, 255, 266, 267, 271, 277, 278, 295, 345, 394
Constitutional-Union Party, 221, 226, 227, 232, 258
Conway, Moncure, 256
Crandall, Prudence, 42, 44, 55–56
Credit Mobilier, 324, 325, 331
Currency Reform, 360–364, 365, 369, 399
Curtis, George T., 155, 157
Cushing, Caleb, 215

Dana, Richard Henry, 152, 174–175, 181, 182, 186, 259, 358
Davis, Jefferson, 252, 254, 261, 307, 318, 322, 323, 335
Debs, Eugene, 400
Declaration of Independence, 1, 119, 222, 310, 315, 317, 332
Democrats, 31, 148, 153, 161, 167, 189, 194, 202, 203, 205, 214, 215, 219, 221, 226, 230, 241, 242, 258, 259, 261, 267, 271, 272, 273, 298, 300, 318, 320, 325, 326–327, 330,

331, 334, 353, 354, 356, 357, 358, 363, 365, 393
Devens, Charles, 331, 332
Discrimination against Negroes in North, 83–84, 86–91, 294, 306
Disunion, 2, 46, 58, 66, 115–116, 117–119, 131, 143, 149, 189, 199, 200, 202, 204, 212, 217, 229, 230, 232, 234–235, 237, 238, 269
Douglas, Stephen, 170, 200–201, 220, 221, 233
Douglass, Frederick, 43, 83, 85, 91, 102, 144, 145, 148, 198, 210, 211, 284–285, 315, 368, 399
Downing, George T., 288, 370
Draft Riots, 264–265
Dred Scott Case, 205, 218, 266, 304
Dresser, Amos, 42, 44, 46, 52

Eight-hour Day, 340–344, 359
Election: of 1842, 128; of 1848, 134–135; of 1852, 167, 189; of 1854, 189; of 1856, 202–203; of 1857, 205; of 1860, 219–223; of 1862, 271; of 1864, 269–274, 279, 282–284; of 1866, 302–303; of 1868, 310–311; of 1870, 320, 351–356; of 1872, 319, 321, 324, 325–326, 357; of 1874, 326; of 1876, 329–330, 363; of 1878, 363, 365; of 1883, 397
Emancipation, 245, 246, 247, 249, 250, 251, 252, 253, 254, 255, 267, 270
Emancipation Proclamation, 254–255, 256, 257, 258, 260, 263, 266, 278, 287
Emerson, Ralph Waldo, 23, 47, 100, 110, 112, 125, 126, 142, 192, 193, 209, 213, 217, 232, 369
Evans, George Henry, 338
Evarts, William, 331, 332
Everett, Edward, 1, 193, 195, 221, 226, 230, 258

Faneuil Hall, 3, 15, 31, 47, 48, 49, 50, 51, 91, 92, 115, 117, 118, 132, 133, 134, 137, 138, 140, 142, 148, 150, 151, 161, 173, 176, 177, 179, 184, 185, 213, 215, 236, 286, 326, 327, 328, 343, 399
Father Mathew, 91, 92–93
Father Snowden, 94, 156
Fay, Richard, 228
Federalists, 7, 23, 24, 346
Fifteenth Amendment, 312–313, 314, 315, 324, 377, 393

Fillmore, Millard, 153, 159
Finney, Charles G., 55, 63
Fisk, Jim, 2, 361
Folsom, Abby, 99–100, 101, 109, 150–151, 384–385
Fort Sumter, 235, 237, 238, 241, 276, 287
Foster, Abby, see Kelly, Abby
Foster, Stephen Symonds, 96, 99, 102, 106–108, 109, 111, 115, 147, 182, 198, 277, 287, 290, 315, 386
Fourteenth Amendment, 300, 302, 304, 308
Franklin, Benjamin, 14, 85, 286
Free-Soil Party, 135, 136, 161, 162, 163, 175, 189, 203, 207, 211, 363
Freedman's Bureau, 260, 317
Freedman's Union, 291, 292
Freeman, Watson, 174, 175, 176, 179–180, 182–183
Fremont, John C., 202–203, 206, 245, 252, 256–257, 269–273, 279, 281, 282, 379
French, Jonas, 228
Fugitive Slave Law, 125, 138, 146, 147–149, 151, 159, 161, 165, 166, 169, 170, 171, 174, 184, 185, 189, 220, 252, 304, 331

Gardner, Henry J., 187, 190, 197, 203, 204, 205, 228
Garnaut, Phoebe, 138, 167, 176, 178, 180
Garrison, Fanny, 290–291, 355
Garrison, Helen, 78–79, 82, 104, 163, 164, 280, 387, 388
Garrison, Wendell Phillips, 104, 105, 151–152, 280, 281, 282, 290, 398
Garrison, William Lloyd, 34–42, 44, 46, 48, 51, 52, 54, 55, 56, 57, 60, 61, 62–63, 64–66, 67, 69, 70, 71, 73, 79, 82, 85, 91, 93, 94, 95, 100, 112, 116, 118, 119, 120, 126, 127, 128, 129, 133, 134, 135, 136, 139, 143, 144, 145, 150, 151–152, 153, 159, 163, 164, 169, 170, 188, 198, 199, 202, 203, 208, 211, 212, 223, 224, 226, 228, 232, 233, 241, 248, 276, 277, 278, 279–292, 294, 315, 334, 339, 350, 368, 371, 374, 375, 377, 387–390, 393, 399
Garrison, William Lloyd, Jr., 280, 389
Gettysburg, 264, 299
Giddings, Joshua, 168, 190, 222, 329
Godkin, E. L., 354

Grant, Ulysses S., 264, 271, 272, 274, 304, 306, 309, 310, 311, 312, 314, 318, 319, 320, 321, 322, 323, 324, 325, 326, 327, 328, 329, 335, 357, 358
Greeley, Horace, 124, 222, 234, 254, 307–308, 319, 320, 321, 322, 323, 324, 325, 357, 377
Green, Edward, 379
Greenback Party, 358, 361–365
Greene, Ann Terry, see Phillips, Ann Greene
Greene, Benjamin, 33, 40, 77
Grimké, Angelina, 44, 56, 65, 106
Grimké, Sarah, 44, 65, 106, 386

Halleck, Henry W., 245, 262
Hallet, Benjamin, 48, 182, 183, 184, 185
Hamlin, Hannibal, 248, 249
Hancock, John, 5, 6, 8, 14, 15, 50, 142, 177, 229
Harpers Ferry, 210, 211, 213, 214, 215, 217, 218, 219
Harvard College, 7, 10, 11, 14, 17–25, 27, 32, 37, 54, 102, 104, 114, 115, 140, 165, 173, 230, 240, 280, 317, 390–392
Harvard Law School, 26–30
Haydon, Benjamin, 70–71
Hayes, Rutherford B., 329–332
Hayne, Robert Y., 34, 142
Higginson, Thomas Wentworth, 77, 108, 178–179, 180, 184, 185, 210, 211, 215, 240, 333, 369
Holland, Frederick, 18
Holmes, Oliver Wendell, 20, 372, 395
Holmes, Oliver Wendell, Jr., 230
Hooker, Joe, 264
Hopkinson, Thomas, 20–21, 30–31, 32
Howe, Julia, 377–378
Howe, Samuel Gridley, 132, 133, 156, 176, 184, 210, 211, 231, 256, 382

Impeachment, 303, 304–305, 309, 310
Independent, 271, 303, 368
Indian Rights, 2, 324, 367, 370, 380–381
Industrial Revolution, 348, 365
International Workingmen's Association, 357
Irish, 2, 91–93, 337, 381–382

Jackson, Andrew, 31, 61, 323
Jackson, Francis, 56, 82, 102, 144, 291
Jefferson, Thomas, 1, 7, 15, 310, 317, 340, 348
Johnson, Andrew, 296–297, 298, 299, 300, 301, 302, 303, 304, 305, 308, 309, 310, 321, 331, 385
Johnson, Oliver, 54–55, 62, 281, 289, 290
Joint Committee on the Conduct of the War, 242, 247
Julian, George, 241, 247, 268, 328, 329

Kansas, 199–201, 207, 210, 216, 242, 322
Kansas-Nebraska Act, 170–171, 176, 189, 221
Kellog, William, 326
Kelly, Abby, 65, 106, 108, 115, 198, 277–278, 279, 285, 315, 370
Kemble, Fanny, 28–29
Key, David, 331
Knights of St. Crispin, 352
Knights of the White Camellia, 318
Know-Nothings, 189–190, 202, 203, 206
Kossuth, Louis, 159–160, 162–163, 164, 212
Ku Klux Klan, 311, 318, 319, 322, 324, 333, 334

Labor Reform, 2, 336–366, 368, 370, 372, 388, 399, 401
Labor Reform Party, 351, 355, 356, 359
Lafayette, Marquis de, 15, 61
Lane, Lunsford, 83
Latimer Committee, 117
Latimer, George, 116–118
Lawrence, Abbott, 83
Lawrence, Amos A., 39, 209
Lee, Robert E., 252, 254, 335
Liberator, 34, 37, 45, 63, 64, 66, 81, 85, 88–89, 90, 103, 104, 106, 111, 116, 117, 119, 124, 125, 128, 142, 147, 148, 152, 153, 163, 168, 202, 203, 211, 222, 226, 279, 280, 281, 282, 283, 285, 287, 354, 368, 388, 389
Liberty Party, 126–127, 128–129, 130, 273
Lincoln, Abraham, 1, 46, 220–223, 224, 225, 234, 235, 238, 241, 245, 246, 247, 248, 249, 250, 251, 252, 253, 254, 255, 256–258, 259, 260,

265, 266, 267, 268, 269, 270, 271, 272, 273, 274, 275, 276, 279, 280, 282, 283, 284, 288, 296, 297, 300, 329, 335, 376, 400, 422
Lloyd, Henry Demarest, 401
London Anti-Slavery Society, 60
Longfellow, Henry Wadsworth, 369, 392
Loring, Edward G., 173–174, 181, 182, 186–187, 190
Loring, Ellis Gray, 45–46, 82, 102
Louisiana, 284, 302, 325–326, 329
L'Ouverture, Toussaint, 86, 246, 248
Lovejoy, Elijah, 46–52, 53, 102, 119, 158, 159, 179, 217, 228, 242, 306, 307, 328
Lovejoy, Owen, 241
Lowell, James Russell, 102, 104, 113, 147, 383, 391

McClellan, George B., 245, 252, 254, 258–259, 262, 272, 273
McGrary, G. W., 331
Macrae, David, 195
Mann, Horace, 89–90, 93, 168–169
Marshall, John, 26, 27
Martineau, Harriet, 36, 397–398
Marx, Karl, 347, 357
Massachusetts Anti-Slavery Society, 42, 45, 57, 59, 60, 77, 118, 134, 136, 152, 231, 287, 291
May, Samuel, 55–56, 77, 82, 94, 95, 135, 145, 282, 284, 287, 289, 386
May, Samuel, Jr., 277, 350
Meade, George, 264
Mexican War, 131–132, 134, 136, 139
Missouri Compromise, 170
Molly Maguires, 348
Moody, Dwight L., 369
Morgan, J. P., 361
Morris, Robert, 176–177
Motley, Lothrop, 8, 11, 20, 240, 320
Mott, James, 68, 70
Mott, Lucretia, 67, 68, 69, 70, 315, 370, 373

Nation, 332, 354, 363, 398
National Anti-Slavery Standard, 81, 83, 113, 127, 281, 282, 290, 291–292, 293, 294, 297, 299, 302, 307, 309, 310, 311, 312, 313, 314, 321, 353, 354, 360, 367, 370, 371, 385
National Labor Union, 340, 359, 361
National Standard, see National Anti-Slavery Standard
Neal, John, 123

Negro Suffrage, 2, 284–285, 293, 294, 299, 300, 302, 305, 308, 312, 313, 314, 316, 317, 318, 325, 333, 363, 393
Nell, William, 386
New England Anti-Slavery Society, 54, 63, 65, 94, 120, 127, 146, 181
New England Workingmen's Association, 338
New York *Globe*, 143–144
New York *Herald*, 254, 255, 267, 309
New York *Observer*, 108
New York *Times*, 267, 303
New York *Tribune*, 234, 254, 267, 308, 319, 330, 332, 335, 399
North American Review, 334
Norton, Charles Eliot, 392

O'Connell, Daniel, 71–72, 91, 92, 381–382
Otis, Harrison Gray, 7, 8, 34, 286
Otis, James, 15, 16, 50, 51, 177, 229, 399

Pacifism, 64, 66, 104, 105, 108
Parker, Theodore, 82, 85, 132, 149–150, 155, 156, 165, 169, 177, 178, 180, 184, 185, 200, 208, 210, 224–225, 226, 228, 289, 369, 392
Pease, Elizabeth, 60, 62, 71, 72, 75, 76, 77, 78, 79, 80, 86, 90, 105, 110, 128, 131, 154, 204
Perkins, Thomas, 228
Personal Liberty Law, 147, 186
Phi Beta Kappa Oration, 391–392
Phillips, Ann Greene, 1, 33–34, 35–36, 38, 39–40, 41, 45, 46, 54, 59–62, 66, 67, 68, 69, 71, 72, 73, 74, 75–81, 83, 102, 104, 108, 111, 131, 138, 147, 156–157, 163–164, 165, 167, 170, 171, 173, 176, 178, 180, 181, 223, 230, 248, 280, 309, 392, 393, 395, 396–397, 398
Phillips, Rev. George, 6, 9, 98
Phillips, George William, 26, 76
Phillips, Grenville, 32, 82
Phillips, John, 3, 4, 7, 8, 9, 10, 11, 16, 18, 23, 24, 32, 41, 54, 192, 317
Phillips, John C., 396
Phillips, John Charles, 26
Phillips, Margaret Wendell, 9, 30, 395
Phillips, Samuel, 32
Phillips, Sarah Walley, 9-10, 24, 32, 39–40, 41, 59, 73, 75–77, 131
Phillips, Thomas, 26, 76, 180

Pierce, Franklin, 167, 180, 189, 215
Pillsbury, Parker, 108, 109, 115, 198, 277, 278, 290, 294
Pitts, Coffin, 172, 173, 175
Prison Reform, 111, 370
Proclamation of Amnesty and Reconstruction, 265
Prohibition Party, 351, 356

Quincy, Anna, 27–28, 33
Quincy, Edmund, 79–80, 81, 82, 95, 102, 103, 111, 118, 131, 135, 144, 165, 166, 169, 178, 277, 289, 292, 315, 356, 365, 368, 386
Quincy, Josiah, 6, 7, 102

Radical Club, 369
Reconstruction, 265, 268, 269, 272, 274, 276, 284, 293–314, 316–320, 322, 324, 325, 326, 329, 330, 333, 363, 394, 426
Reconstruction Act, 308
Reform League, 370
Remond, Charles, 86, 91, 136, 386
Republicans, 2, 129, 167, 189, 190, 191, 202, 203, 205, 206, 211, 214, 217, 219, 220, 221, 222, 223, 224, 234, 236, 241, 242, 243, 246, 257, 258, 259, 260, 267, 269, 271, 272, 274, 277, 278, 281, 288, 297, 300, 301, 302, 303–304, 307, 309–310, 311, 318, 319, 320, 321, 325, 326, 328, 329, 330, 333–334, 353, 354, 355, 357, 358, 359, 363, 365, 368
Reynolds, Dr. Edward, 180
Robinson, John, 289
Rogers, Nathaniel, 103, 109, 277
Roosevelt, Theodore, 1, 399–400
Ruggles, David, 77, 86–87
Rynders, Isaiah, 144, 145, 171, 414

St. Louis *Dispatch*, 307
Sanborn, Frank, 210, 211, 394
Sargent, John, 314, 369, 370
Schurz, Carl, 331, 332, 362
Scott, Tom, 347, 361
Scott, Winfield, 245
Secession, 225, 229, 234, 235, 236, 238
Sewall, Samuel, 102, 229, 399
Seward, William, 195, 219–220, 223–224, 230, 256
Shaw, Lemuel, 116, 155
Sheridan, Philip H., 326, 327
Sherman, John, 331, 332
Sherman, William T., 273, 274, 380

Sims, Thomas, 155–157, 158, 161, 162, 163, 171, 175, 177, 331, 332
Smalley, George, 233, 237
Smith, Gerrit, 119, 210, 211
Socialism, 348, 354
Spooner, Lysander, 210, 212
Standard, see National Anti-Slavery Standard
Stanton, Edwin M., 251, 253, 256, 287, 309
Stanton, Elizabeth Cady, 67, 272, 275, 372–378
Stanton, Henry B., 67, 70
Stearns, Charles, 199–200
Stearns, George, 210, 211, 255, 256
Stevens, Thaddeus, 242–243, 298, 299, 300, 303, 311, 328, 329
Stevenson, T. G., 262, 263
Steward, Ira, 341
Stone, Lucy, 372, 377, 378, 398
Story, Joseph, 26–27, 89, 114, 193
Stowe, Harriet Beecher, 43, 85, 188, 191
Sumner, Charles, 11, 27, 31, 33, 122, 130, 132, 133, 136, 161–163, 165, 167–168, 189, 190, 200–202, 203–204, 205, 218, 220, 231, 241, 242, 243, 246, 247, 248, 252, 253, 257, 262–263, 274, 277, 295, 296, 297, 298, 299, 300, 311, 312, 320–322, 328–329, 334, 386–387, 394
Supreme Court, 26, 27, 205, 265, 266, 304,•308, 393, 394
Suttle, Charles F., 172, 174, 177, 181, 182

Tammany Hall, 1, 144
Taney, Roger, 266
Tappan, Arthur, 63–65, 68, 101
Tappan, Lewis, 63–65, 68, 101, 146
Taylor, Zachary, 105–106, 113, 135, 144
Temperance, 8, 64, 93, 111, 356, 363, 368, 370–372, 383
Thirteenth Amendment, 268, 274, 286, 287, 288, 289, 295
Thompson, George, 34–35, 60–62, 68, 150, 153, 160, 386
Thompson, R. W., 331
Thoreau, Henry D., 125, 126, 188, 194, 209, 217
Tilden, Samuel, 329–330, 331
Train, George Francis, 376–377
Transcendentalists, 95, 100, 110, 125–126, 209, 217, 369
Tukey, Marshal, 155, 157
Turner, Nat, 34

Tweed Gang, 325, 331, 346, 356
Tyler, John, 127, 297

Underground Railroad, 147–148, 171–172, 184–185, 242
Unitarians, 94, 95, 100, 149, 224, 226
Utopianism, 104, 109–110, 122, 348

Vane, Sir Henry, 347, 389, 390, 392
Vigilance Committee, 148–149, 152, 154, 155, 157, 171, 172–173, 176, 177, 179, 183, 212
Villard, Fanny Garrison, see Garrison, Fanny

Wade, Ben, 242, 246, 329
Wade-Davis Bill, 272
Washington, George, 15, 128
Wealth and Commonwealth, 401
Webb, Richard, 71, 75, 92, 93, 109, 112, 128, 165
Webster, Daniel, 31, 39, 97, 126, 127, 137, 139, 140–143, 150, 151, 159, 161, 162, 165–167, 192, 193, 195, 197, 217–218, 236, 242, 266, 335
Weld, Theodore Dwight, 56, 63–64, 68, 306, 386, 388, 399
Weld, Angelina, see Grimké, Angelina
Welles, Gideon, 299
Weston, Anne, 39, 40, 53, 77, 102, 156, 176, 178, 181, 277
Weston, Deborah, 39, 40, 77, 102, 156–157, 277
Whigs, 31, 130, 133, 135, 139, 140, 148, 150, 151, 153, 161, 163, 167, 170, 189, 221, 228, 262, 272, 273, 281, 331, 363
Whittier, John Greenleaf, 61, 70, 102, 141–142, 273
Wild, John, 342–343, 346
Wilmot Proviso, 142
Wilson, Henry, 189, 190, 351
Winthrop, Robert C., 1, 2, 134, 195, 196, 273
Woman's Abolition Society, 60
Women's Rights, 2, 62, 65, 66, 67–69, 71, 81, 111, 114, 363, 367, 368, 369, 370, 372–378, 398
Women's Rights Convention, 368, 374
World Anti-Slavery Convention, 67–71, 78
Wright, Henry C., 56, 101, 103, 105, 108, 113, 265, 315, 386, 387